VIRTUE *and* POLITICS

PAUL BLACKLEDGE AND KELVIN KNIGHT

EDITORS

VIRTUE *and* POLITICS

ALASDAIR MACINTYRE'S
REVOLUTIONARY ARISTOTELIANISM

UNIVERSITY OF NOTRE DAME PRESS

NOTRE DAME, INDIANA

Published in the United States of America

Library of Congress Cataloging-in-Publication Data

Virtue and politics : Alasdair MacIntyre's revolutionary Aristotelianism /
edited by Paul Blackledge and Kelvin Knight.
p.   cm.
Includes bibliographical references and index.
ISBN-13: 978-0-268-02225-9 (pbk. : alk. paper)
ISBN-10: 0-268-02225-9 (pbk. : alk. paper)
1. MacIntyre, Alasdair C.   2. Marxism.   3. Liberalism.
I. Blackledge, Paul, 1967–   II. Knight, Kelvin.
JC257.M23V57   2011
321.9'2—dc22

2010052715

In memoriam

Chris Harman, 1942–2009

Émile Perreau-Saussine, 1972–2010

Contents

Contributors

Paul Blackledge is Reader in Political Theory at Leeds Metropolitan University. He is the author of *Freedom, Desire and Revolution: Marxism and Ethics* (State University of New York Press, 2011), *Reflections on the Marxist Theory of History* (Manchester University Press, 2006), and *Perry Anderson, Marxism and the New Left* (Merlin Press, 2004). He is co-editor, with Neil Davidson, of *Alasdair MacIntyre's Engagement with Marxism* (Brill, 2008); of *Revolutionary Aristotelianism*, with Kelvin Knight (Lucius & Lucius, 2008); and of *Historical Materialism and Social Evolution*, with Graeme Kirkpatrick (Palgrave, 2002). He is on the editorial boards of the journals *Historical Materialism* and *International Socialism.*

Andrius Bielskis is Professor of Political Theory at Mykolas Romeris University and a leading public intellectual in Lithuania. He is a visiting research fellow at the Centre for Contemporary Aristotelian Studies in Ethics and Politics at London Metropolitan University. He has taught political and moral philosophy at several British and European universities and is the author of numerous scholarly works, including *Towards a Post-Modern Understanding of the Political* (Palgrave, 2005) and *Demokratija be darbo judejimo?* (Democracy without Labour Movement?) (Kaunas, 2009). A founding member both of the progressive intellectual and political movement New Left 95 and of the DEMOS Institute of Critical Thought, he also writes political commentaries for the Lithuanian daily *Delfi.lt.* His research focuses on the utilization of virtue ethics in constructing an alternative political, economic, and institutional order in our postmodern world. He is also interested in the impact of the visual arts on our perception of ourselves and the world, and is currently working on structures of meaning.

Tony Burns is Co-Director of the Centre for the Study of Social and Global Justice (CSSGJ) in the School of Politics and International Relations at the University of Nottingham, UK. He is the author of *Political Theory, Science Fiction and Utopian Literature: Ursula K. Le Guin and The Dispossessed* (Lexington, 2008) and *Natural Law and Political Ideology in the Philosophy of Hegel* (Ashgate, 1996). He is co-editor, with James Connelly, of *The Legacy of Leo Strauss* (Imprint Academic, 2010), and, with Ian Fraser, of *The Hegel-Marx Connection* (St. Martin's Press, 2000). He contributed the chapter on Aristotle to *Political Thinkers: From Socrates to the Present,* edited by David Boucher and Paul Kelly, 2d ed. (Oxford University Press, 2009); the entry on 'Aristotelianism' to the *Sage Encyclopaedia of Political Theory,* edited by Mark Bevir (Sage Books, 2010); and is currently working on a book entitled *Aristotle and Natural Law* (Continuum Books, forthcoming 2011). He is Chair of the recently created Contemporary Aristotelian Studies Specialist Group of the Political Studies Association of Great Britain (PSA).

Alex Callinicos is Professor of European Studies at King's College London. He taught politics for many years at the University of York. His most recent books are *The Resources of Critique* (Polity Press, 2006), *Imperialism and Global Political Economy* (Polity Press, 2009), and *Bonfire of Illusions* (Polity Press, 2010).

Neil Davidson is a senior research fellow in the School of Applied Social Science at the University of Strathclyde. He is the author of *The Origins of Scottish Nationhood* (Pluto Press, 2000) and the Deutscher Prize-winning *Discovering the Scottish Revolution* (Pluto Press, 2003). He has co-edited, with Paul Blackledge, and contributed to *Alasdair MacIntyre's Engagement with Marxism* (Brill, 2008); and, with Patricia McCafferty and David Miller, *Neoliberal Scotland* (Cambridge Scholars, 2010).

Kelvin Knight is Director of CASEP, the Centre for Contemporary Aristotelian Studies in Ethics and Politics at London Metropolitan University.

He is also General Secretary of the International Society for MacIntyrean Enquiry, Secretary of the new Contemporary Aristotelian Studies specialist group of the UK Political Studies Association, editor of *The MacIntyre Reader* (University of Notre Dame Press, 1998), and author of *Aristotelian Philosophy: Ethics and Politics from Aristotle to MacIntyre* (Polity Press, 2007).

Anton Leist is a German philosopher and Professor of Philosophy at the Ethics-Center of the University of Zurich. His books include *Eine Frage des Lebens* (A Question of Life) (Campus, 1990), *Die gute Handlung* (Good Action) (Akademie Verlag, 2000), *Ethik der Beziehungen* (Ethics of Social Relationships) (Akademie Verlag, 2005), and, as editor, *Action in Context* (De Gruyter, 2007). He is coeditor, with Peter Singer, of *J. M. Coetzee and Ethics* (Columbia University Press, 2010). His interests are in ethics, political philosophy, and pragmatism.

Alasdair MacIntyre is Senior Research Fellow at the Centre for Contemporary Aristotelian Studies in Ethics and Politics at London Metropolitan University. Among his many publications are *Whose Justice? Which Rationality?* (University of Notre Dame Press, 1988), *Three Rival Versions of Moral Enquiry* (University of Notre Dame Press, 1990), *Marxism and Christianity* (Duckworth, 2d ed., 1995), *A Short History of Ethics: A History of Moral Philosophy from the Homeric Age to the Twentieth Century* (University of Notre Dame Press, 2d ed., 1998), *Dependent Rational Animals: Why Human Beings Need the Virtues* (Open Court, 1999), *Edith Stein: A Philosophical Prologue, 1913–22* (Rowman & Littlefield, 2006), two volumes of *Selected Essays* (Cambridge University Press, 2006), *After Virtue: A Study in Moral Theory* (University of Notre Dame Press, 3d ed., 2007), and *God, Philosophy, Universities: A Selective History of the Catholic Philosophical Tradition* (Rowman & Littlefield, 2009).

Sante Maletta was educated at the universities of Milan and Rome and at the New School for Social Research in New York. His publications include *L'etica tra storia e teorie: esperienze etiche anglosassoni contemporanee e rilevanza filosofica della letteratura* (Rome, 1999), *Hannah Arendt e Martin Heidegger: l'esistenza in giudizio* (Milan, 2001), *Il legame segreto: La libertà in Hannah Arendt* (Soveria Mannelli, 2005), and *Biografia della ragione: Saggio sulla filosofia politica di Alasdair MacIntyre*

(Soveria Mannelli, 2007). He has translated into Italian and edited *What Is Existenz-Philosophy?* by H. Arendt. He teaches political philosophy at the University of Calabria (Italy) and at the Institute for the International Education of Students (IES) in Milan.

Peter McMylor is Senior Lecturer in Sociology at the University of Manchester. He is the author of *Alasdair MacIntyre: Critic of Modernity* (Routledge, 1994) and works on the relationship between morality, ethics, and religion to social and political theory, and on the sociology of intellectuals as bearers of ethical resources and identities.

Niko Noponen taught ethics and political philosophy at the University of Helsinki from 1999 to 2003 and has since worked as a high school teacher. He has published in Finnish articles on virtues, practices, emotions, and moral psychology, and a translation of MacIntyre's *After Virtue* (*Hyveiden jäljillä*, Gaudeamus, 2004).

Emile Perreau-Saussine (1972–2010) was a Newton Trust Lecturer at the University of Cambridge. He was previously a Bradley Fellow at the University of Chicago. He held visiting research positions at Paris II and the École des Hautes Études en Sciences Sociales (2010) and was a visiting professor at Sciences Po (2008, 2009). He was the author of *Alasdair MacIntyre: une biographie intellectuelle. Introduction aux critiques contemporaines du libéralisme* (Presses Universitaires de France, collection Léviathan, 2005), for which he was awarded the Prix Philippe Habert, a prize for the best writing on political science in 2005 by a young researcher.

Sean Sayers is Professor of Philosophy at the University of Kent, Canterbury. He has written extensively on topics of Hegelian and Marxist philosophy. His books include *Plato's Republic: An Introduction* (Edinburgh University Press, 1999), *Marxism and Human Nature* (Routledge, 1998; 2007), *Reality and Reason* (Blackwell, 1985), and, with Richard Norman, *Hegel, Marx and Dialectic: A Debate* (Humanities Press, 1980). He was one of the founders of *Radical Philosophy* (1972) and of The Marx and Philosophy Society (2003). He is the founder and editor of the online *Marx and Philosophy Review of Books* (2010). He is currently working on a book on theories of alienation and self-realisation in Marx.

Introduction

Towards a Virtuous Politics

PAUL BLACKLEDGE & KELVIN KNIGHT

Alasdair MacIntyre's *After Virtue* ended with a seemingly insoluble dilemma: although he believed that we must stand up against the new 'dark ages' that have engulfed us, his analysis of modernity pointed to the *near* impossibility of so doing (MacIntyre 1985a, 263). Such was the overwhelming pessimism of this argument, coupled with his powerful critique of liberalism, that the mature thought of this ex-revolutionary socialist has often been misconceived as a conservative or communitarian response to liberal modernity (e.g., Mulhall & Swift 1996, ch. 2; Kymlicka 2002, 209). Accusations of conservatism have typically been underpinned by clumsy inferences from his Thomism or by a superficial reading of his relationship to the hermeneutic tradition. Claims that because he borrowed aspects of his conception of tradition from Gadamer, MacIntyre embraced the cultural and political conservatism that followed from Gadamer's Heideggerian standpoint, are doubly wrong. Whereas Gadamer imagined the concept of tradition in the singular, MacIntyre conceives traditions as plural and conflicting. Moreover, MacIntyre insists not only that virtue is predicated upon the existence of social practices

1

through which people are able to make sense of their lives within particular traditions, but also that capitalist and state institutions undermine these practices, thus preventing us from actualising our potential as social and rational animals. His critique of capitalism is as strong today as it was in his Marxist youth, and it continues to be informed by Marx's insights into the conflict inherent within the capitalist mode of production. For this reason, MacIntyre's turn to Aristotle since his break with the Marxist left in the 1960s is best understood not as conservative rejection of modernity but as an attempt to deepen insights inherited from Marx's critique of capitalism. This reinterpretation of MacIntyre's thought, and the re-characterisation of his mature thought as a form of 'revolutionary Aristotelianism', focusing upon practices as 'the schools of virtues', is now over a decade old (Knight 1996; 2007; MacIntyre 1998g, 235), and this book is intended as a collective culmination of that corrective process.

Nevertheless, there is a problem associated with the use of the word 'revolutionary' to describe MacIntyre's mature thought. In a comment on MacIntyre's claim that the energy he once invested in overthrowing the capitalist system was 'misdirected and wrongheaded', and that 'what we have to do is withdraw from it and not get involved in its disasters' (MacIntyre 1994c, 42), Paul Blackledge suggests that 'it is idiosyncratic to say the least to label as a revolutionary someone who dismisses any attempt to overthrow the existing order' (Blackledge 2009, 869). Indeed, MacIntyre has written that 'not only have I never offered remedies for the condition of liberal modernity, it has been part of my case that there are no remedies. The problem is not to reform the dominant order, but to find ways for local communities to survive by sustaining a life of the common good against the disintegrating forces of the nation-state and the market' (MacIntyre 1998g, 235; 1995b, 35). Although claims such as this have led many on the left to dismiss MacIntyre as an extreme pessimist, it is also the case that they point towards a model of virtuous anticapitalist and anti-statist politics that has something in common with the young Marx's comments on the virtues of working-class socialism (see Blackledge's essay in this volume, and Marx 1975a, 365).

Against the backdrop of the tension between MacIntyre's revolutionary opposition to capitalism and his political pessimism, this collection of essays aims to open a dialogue about the possibility of developing a virtuous political practice in the modern world; that is, of exploring the possibilities of struggling for, to abuse a phrase of Adorno's, the possibilities of leading a good life in and against a bad world.

The obstacles confronting any project of developing a virtuous politics in the modern world are obvious enough. Writing in 1995, MacIntyre commented that whereas Aristotle had understood *pleonexia,* the drive to have more and more, as the vice that was the counterpart of the virtue of justice, in bourgeois society it is portrayed as a virtue. MacIntyre comments that it is this inversion of virtue and vice that 'provides systematic incentives to develop a type of character that has a propensity to injustice' (MacIntyre 1995d, ix–xiv; 1985a, 137; 2006i, 39). MacIntyre has extended this critique of capitalism in a number of other places. For instance, in 'Some Enlightenment Projects Reconsidered', he argues that the 'free market economy' should be numbered among those modern institutions that are corrosive of the virtues, and that, like modern states, free markets act to frustrate the formation of a community of autonomous individuals who might otherwise be able to deliberate collectively on the good life (MacIntyre 2006m, 173). Similarly, in 'Politics, Philosophy and the Common Good', he suggests that the phrase 'free market' is a misnomer because in the modern world markets tend to be 'ruthlessly impose[d]', and once imposed they 'forcibly deprive many workers of productive work', condemning them to 'irredeemable economic deprivation' (MacIntyre 1998g, 249). Again, in 'Toleration and the Goods of Conflict', he claims that 'the values of state and market are not only different from, but on many types of occasion incompatible with, the values of' those kinds of local communities within which virtues might flourish. In the former, 'decision-making is arrived at by a summing of preferences and by a series of trade-offs', which depend upon 'the political and economic bargaining power of the representatives of contending interests'. By contrast, it is a characteristic of those local communities to which he refers that within them a shared conception of the common good 'provides a standard independent of preferences' (MacIntyre 2006o, 213). Concretely, MacIntyre argues that 'for there to be an identifiable common good there must be identifiable structures of community, so that one can understand how the parts which different individuals contribute are contributing to a common goal' (MacIntyre 1994c, 35). He concludes that only in small-scale communities is politics able to escape from the compartmentalisation that is endemic in the modern world and 'inimical to the flourishing of local communities' (MacIntyre 1998g, 248).

If this orientation towards local communities informs the widespread belief that MacIntyre is a communitarian thinker, the flaws in this interpretation of his ideas are apparent once we recognise that he is just as critical of state power as he is of modern 'free' markets. He points out that those who aim at conquering state power are themselves conquered by it, and through it 'become in time the instruments of one of the several versions of modern capitalism' (MacIntyre 1995d, xv). And in a more specific comment on communitarianism, he argues that, far from being an alternative to liberalism, this ideology has become part of the 'ragbag of assorted values' through which modern liberal states attempt to justify themselves (MacIntyre 1998g, 245).

So, against conservatives and liberals alike, MacIntyre argues that 'what is most urgently needed is a politics of self-defence for all those local societies that aspire to achieve some relatively self-sufficient and independent form of participatory practice-based community and that therefore need to protect themselves from the corrosive effects of capitalism and the depredations of the state' (MacIntyre 1995d, xxvi). This is not to suggest that he is unaware of the faults of local participatory communities. Rather, against liberalism's elitism and communitarianism's confusion of the politics of the state with politics practiced in such communities, he espouses a politics which recognises that while life within such communities is 'imperfect', such communities can at their best engender forms of life which might act as the utopian standards by which one ought to live one's life (MacIntyre 1995d, xxi). Moreover, he argues that the charge typically made by so-called pragmatic politicians against their radical opponents, to the effect that the political perspectives of the latter are utopian, is best understood as a damning critique not of radicalism but of the standpoint from which that charge is made (MacIntyre 1990a, 234–35). Specifically, he believes that it is only in some local communities that 'cooperation as a common good' can emerge spontaneously as an alternative to the individualism that is both generated by capitalism and taken to be axiomatic by liberals (MacIntyre 1999a, 114, 130). In his mature work, therefore, MacIntyre proselytises an anti-statist and anti-capitalist politics that is best understood as a development of the ideas of Marx, as well as those of Aristotle and Aquinas, and which MacIntyre understands to be rooted in the forms of practice that are found in some local communities (MacIntyre 2006n, 193).

The overlap between MacIntyre's mature thought and Marxism has a practical as well as a theoretical aspect. For instance, in 1994, long before the recent financial crash, he suggested that Michael Milken (the corrupt Wall Street banker who inspired the character played by Michael Douglas in Oliver Stone's 1987 *Wall Street*) was in the right against his 'moralist' critics when he claimed to have only been 'doing his job', but that he was wrong to believe that this should have kept him out of jail; on the contrary, 'it probably means that many other financial managers should be [in prison] too'. Commenting on politics at the other side of the barricades, in 2006 MacIntyre signaled his support for those struggles

> engaged in by members of some rank and file trade union movements, of some tenants' associations, of the disability movement, of a variety of farming, fishing, and trading cooperatives, and by some feminist groups, and on the other by those who work within schools, hospitals, a variety of industrial and financial workplaces, laboratories, theatres, and universities in order to make of these, so far as possible, scenes of resistance to the dominant ideology and the dominant social order. (MacIntyre 2006o)

Whereas MacIntyre's mature disdain for Wall Street and his support for some rank-and-file trade unionists—including the resistance they 'offer to attacks on their members' wages and working conditions' (MacIntyre 2007b)—displays an obvious affinity with his youthful Marxism, his contemporary distance from Marxism is best exemplified, as we noted above, by his argument that the energy he once invested in overthrowing the capitalist system was 'misdirected and wrongheaded'.

Nevertheless, as he argues in the essay which opens this collection, while the compartmentalisation characteristic of life in the modern world mediates against us asking such Aristotelian questions as 'What would it be for my life *as a whole* to be a flourishing life?' and 'What is my good *qua* human being and not just *qua* role-player in this or that type of situation?', by which we might begin to move from general ethical concerns about human flourishing to more specific political means which could foster such human flourishing, modern social relations do not completely foreclose discussion of such issues. Concretely, he suggests that when communities come together to build schools, for instance, general questions such as these can and do emerge spontaneously. Moreover, by answering such questions in an Aristotelian manner, many members of such communities will tend to challenge existing utilitarian modes of education, and in so doing will be met by representatives of the state and of capitalism who will inform them that their alternative proposals are 'unrealistic'. In such situations, MacIntyre argues, it is important for those communities to stand their ground and to insist on the possibility of the impossible. While this position appears to be 'utopian' from the standpoint of civil society, because it is a practical response to practical problems, MacIntyre labels it 'a Utopianism of the present, not a Utopianism of the future'.

This stress on the practical virtues associated with those community-based forms of opposition to capitalism and the state is a useful rider to what otherwise might easily appear as the one-sided political conclusion of *After Virtue*; for while MacIntyre's politics of resistance is apparent in this text, it is almost completely lost against the background of the book's dominant pessimism. This theme of the politics of virtuous resistance, when read in the context of the reinterpretation of MacIntyre's mature thought as a form of revolutionary Aristotelianism, is the departure point for the other essays in this volume. To varying degrees, the editors and contributors to this volume believe that MacIntyre's focus on ethical forms of resistance to capitalism and the state has created a space for a dialogue about the relevance of his thought to contemporary progressive politics. To this end, this book brings together a series of explorations of the strengths and tensions of MacIntyre's mature thought, with a view to developing their potential to inform virtuous political practice in the modern world.

After MacIntyre's opening essay, we republish Knight's virtually unobtainable 1996 essay 'Revolutionary Aristotelianism'. This essay first challenged earlier conservative appropriations of MacIntyre's critique of liberalism by reinterpreting his Aristotelianism through the lens of his earlier engagement with Marx. If this reading of MacIntyre's thought sets the scene for the arguments of the rest of the essays in this collection, it is nonetheless subjected to an important critique by Tony Burns in his contribution. He challenges not only the claim that MacIntyre's thought can be understood as a form of revolutionary Aristotelianism but also the argument that there is a strong affinity between MacIntyre's thought and Marxism. Nevertheless, he concludes that MacIntyre's thought might profitably be used to supplement gaps within classical Marxism. For Alex Callinicos, the divergence between MacIntyre and Marx is greater than this, and much to Marx's benefit. Callinicos defends Marx as the most important successor of the Enlightenment tradition, from which he inherited and radicalised the concept of equality as a basis for a thoroughgoing immanent critique of capitalism. In particular, Callinicos defends not only a dialectical analysis of both the oppressive and the liberating aspects of capitalism against what he considers to be MacIntyre's one-sided criticisms of modernity, but also the transhistorical normative needs principle, which he claims is implicit to Marx's critique of capitalism. While Sean Sayers would reject the idea that Marx embraced any transhistorical norms, like Callinicos, he criticises what he conceives as MacIntyre's 'one-sidedly' negative critique of modernity. Through a critical engagement with bureaucratic idiocies of Britain's pseudo-market in academic ranking, Sayers deploys Marx's dialectical critique of capitalism to argue that alongside the negative consequences of compartmentalisation and fragmentation, modern capitalism has underpinned the emergence of important values such as liberty, equality, individuality, and tolerance. Sayers points out that although MacIntyre's relentlessly pessimistic account of modern social relations can explain the negative side of the modern academic experience, for example, it is less able to recognise the positive side of liberalism's 'agreement to disagree' in a tacit critique of any attempt to impose a stultifying orthodoxy on thought. This vision of tolerance is an important inheritance from the Enlightenment, which reflects the contribution of liberalism to modern progressive politics. Sayers points to the continuities between liberalism and Marxism. Niko Noponen, in contrast, explores the commonalities between MacIntyre's critique of the consequences of liberal modernity and

Marx's theory of alienation, a concept which he claims underpins not only Marx's but also MacIntyre's critique of liberalism and capitalism. For his part, Paul Blackledge explores MacIntyre's concrete criticisms of the practice of Marxist revolutionaries through the lens of his deployment of Marx's third thesis on Feuerbach. He argues that although MacIntyre has made use of this argument to develop a powerful critique of managerialism and Stalinism, it is far from an immanent critique of all forms of socialist leadership, as the mature MacIntyre suggests. Blackledge follows the younger MacIntyre to argue that Marx's *Theses on Feuerbach* actually point towards something like Lenin's politics (but most certainly not to the mythical 'Leninism' that was invented by Stalin and embraced as an authentic representation of Lenin's politics by Stalin's liberal critics). By contrast with Blackledge's defence of the contemporary relevance of anti-Stalinist Marxism, Émile Perreau-Saussine argues that MacIntyre points towards an ethical alternative not only to liberalism but also to Marxism, and that far from there being an important slippage between MacIntyre's early Marxist criticisms of Stalinism and his later rejection of Marxist politics *tout court*, the latter position was the logical conclusion of the former. Marxism, he claims, has been found wanting by the tribunal of history, and MacIntyre's work points to Marx's failure to escape the limits of bourgeois ethical theory.

Neil Davidson addresses the question of MacIntyre's Marxism by exploring his relationship to the thought of Stalin's greatest critic, Leon Trotsky. To those readers of *After Virtue* who are unaware of MacIntyre's past, the concluding portrayal of Trotsky alongside St. Benedict tends to come as something of a surprise. Davidson contextualises these comments with reference to debates within postwar Trostskyism, and in so doing, highlights not only the way that MacIntyre's critique of Marxism in *After Virtue* involved an over-hasty deployment of some comments by Trotsky, but also the fact that in the 1960s MacIntyre embraced an importantly different interpretation of Trotsky and Trotskyism, which can act as a Marxist point of departure for a critique of the pessimistic conclusions of *After Virtue*. In his contribution to the collection, Sante Maletta explores a different but related aspect of MacIntyre's critique of liberalism. He explicates and defends MacIntyre's deployment of the concept of natural law as a powerful and subversive critique of liberalism, and, in an argument that complements Noponen's thesis, he points to the complementarities between MacIntyre's deployment of the natural law tradition and his reference to themes taken from Marx's theory of alienation. From a very different perspective, Anton Leist challenges what he conceives as MacIntyre's absolutist criticisms of liberalism, and defends from these criticisms those elements of liberalism that he considers to be a lasting contribution to progressive politics. Peter McMylor explores the sociological underpinnings of MacIntyre's critique of modern ethical theory as a consequence of the debilitating effects of the compartmentalisation of modern life through an analysis of his comments on the work of Erving Goffman. He considers the importance both of MacIntyre's contribution to an adequate sociology of modernity, and of the possibilities inherent within his model of modernity for an ethical alternative to that compartmentalised world. The second of Kelvin Knight's essays in this volume is an exercise in the history of ideas. The identification of communitarianism in the 1980s and '90s coincided with a revival of classical republicanism. MacIntyre's work was widely identified with both. In this essay, Knight opposes MacIntyre's work to that of J. G. A. Pocock and Quentin Skinner. Despite the sympathy MacIntyre once expressed for republicanism, Knight argues that its compartmentalisation of society into public and private spheres laid conceptual and practical bases for liberal modernity. Knight also opposes MacIntyre to the classical liberalism of F. A. Hayek and to Hayek's politically influential account of capitalism as a free and spontaneous order. In the wake of the state-led bailout of the recent financial crisis, the superiority of MacIntyre's account of modern political and economic order to that of Hayek should be clear. In the penultimate essay, Andrius Bielskis attempts to move the debate towards a more concrete register through an analysis of MacIntyre's influence on Lithuania's new left. He suggests that MacIntyre's conception of ethical anti-capitalism has informed the creation of a left that has attempted to move beyond the limits of earlier debates between reform and revolution. Finally, MacIntyre replies to his critics in a survey that adds to our understanding of the relationship between his Aristotelianism and Marxism, while simultaneously suggesting some concrete aspects of Aristotelian political practice. As he concludes, there is far more to be said. We hope that this book will contribute to opening that debate.

Two powerful contributors to the conferences at which this book was conceived suffered untimely deaths before its publication. Chris Harman, whose thought was influenced by MacIntyre's early Marxist writings, was one of the most important Marxists of his generation. Émile Perreau-Saussine was a gifted young academic and author of an important study of MacIntyre's oeuvre, *Alasdair MacIntyre, une biographie intellectuell*. Their deaths came as shocks to all who knew them, and this collection is dedicated to their memories.

1

How Aristotelianism Can Become Revolutionary

Ethics, Resistance, and Utopia

ALASDAIR MACINTYRE

If we listen to much contemporary discussion of ethics, we might conclude that ethics is principally or only a matter of arguments. Yet Aristotle says that rational argument in the areas of politics and morals will be ineffective with those who lack adequate character formation. And, if this is true, as it is, we need to know more about what adequate character formation would be for us here now. Aristotle also remarked that it is impossible to teach ethics and politics to the young, not only because their passions are insufficiently controlled, but also because they have not yet had sufficient practical experience. Yet we know that it is often true of adults too that they lack the kinds of experience from which they are able to learn. And so the question that I need to address is 'What is the relationship between character formation, being able to learn from experience, and being open to political and moral argument?' Aquinas says that we only learn adequately when we are on the way to becoming self-teachers. So we can reformulate our question as: 'What kinds of experience might those be as a result of which we can become self-teachers about politics and morals? What kinds of experience might those be that enable us to achieve the character formation necessary for this?'

In *After Virtue* and elsewhere I focused attention on the relationships between practices and institutions, on the types of practice in which a kind of learning goes on that enables us to identify and pursue individual and common goods, and on the ways in which institutions that provide the social framework for practices may sustain and reinforce that learning, but may also undermine, subvert, and corrupt it. It is clear that in our present culture learning how to ask Aristotelian questions at the level of practice, let alone formulating Aristotelian answers, is difficult precisely because of the institutional structures within which most contemporary practices are carried on. Consider four characteristics of such structures. In our everyday lives we recurrently find our activities compartmentalised. Our lives are divided between different spheres, each with its own roles and its own set of norms. So in the course of a single day someone may move from their role in the home as, say, parent or sibling to their role in some particular kind of workplace, and later on to dealing in quite another capacity with some government or private agency, with, say lawyers or social workers, and later still return to their role in the home. As they enter each different sphere of activity they find themselves cast in some different role that requires that they satisfy some different set of expectations. So day after day our lives are compartmentalised into distinct areas to the norms of each of which we are expected to adapt, so that adaptability itself, social malleability, has become an important social characteristic. The problem, however, with this kind of compartmentalisation is that the point of such Aristotelian questions as 'What would it be for my life *as a whole* to be a flourishing life?' and 'What is my good *qua* human being and not just *qua* role-player in this or that type of situation?' disappears from view, so that such questions no longer get asked or become very difficult to ask.

The questions substituted for them are 'What do I feel about my life?' and 'Am I happy or unhappy?', questions about psychological states. And one consequence of this is that we now have in academic life a growing happiness industry. Recent research concerning happiness is problematic in more than one way. Some of its findings need unusually careful scrutiny. So, for example, the discovery that most Danes take themselves to be happy with their lives looks very different when it is discovered that most Danes have very low expectations. More importantly, what matters is not so much whether people do or do not feel happy about their lives as whether they do or do not have good reason to feel happy about them. And most importantly of all, this focus on psychological states once again gets in the way of asking the Aristotelian questions.

A second feature of our institutionalised cultural life that is inimical to asking Aristotelian questions concerns our habits of character formation from childhood onwards. Part of what we need to learn as children and adolescents is how to distinguish between those of our desires that are desires for genuine goods from those that are not. Failures in making this distinction both distort our character formation and lead to the frustration of those desires that are most important for our human flourishing. But we inhabit a social order in which a will to satisfy those desires that will enable the economy to work as effectively as possible has become central to our way of life, a way of life for which it is crucial that human beings desire what the economy needs them to desire. What the economy needs is that people should become responsive to its needs rather than to their own, and so it presents to them as overridingly desirable those goals of consumption and goals of ambition, pursuit of which will serve the economy's purposes. Desires to achieve these goals, when they become central to our lives and to our self-evaluations, prevent us from becoming self-critical about our desires and so prevent the asking of Aristotelian questions about character and desire.

A third example is closely related to the first two. It is not just that our lives are compartmentalised, and it is not just that we are continually seduced and solicited by desires that are corrupting, it is also that we live under conditions of gross inequality—inequality of money, inequality of power, inequality of regard—and it is an undeniable fact that even the most successful examples of growth in the present globalising economy generate further inequalities. Aristotle pointed out long ago that a rational polity is one that cannot tolerate too great inequalities, because where there are such, citizens cannot deliberate together rationally. They are too divided by their sectional interests, so that they lose sight of their common good. The poor are driven to defend themselves, in order to meet even their basic needs, and cannot learn how to rule.

The rich are concerned with accumulation and self-advancement and cannot learn how to be ruled. Therefore a precondition for a rational polity is a radical reduction of inequality. And, so long as that is not achieved, the questions that Aristotle poses about what it is to have a rational polity remain questions for which it is difficult to get a hearing, let alone answer.

For a fourth example I go to Aquinas's development of Aristotle's thought. It is not just that our lives are compartmentalised, that we are continually having our desires solicited and distorted, and that we suffer from the effects of gross inequalities, it is also the case that the nature of the rule of law, something necessary for adequate human relationships in any society, in ours is systematically misunderstood and misrepresented. There was an important moment in our past history when the protagonists of the modern state first claimed for it an unqualified autonomy in respect of law, that is, claimed that the state should have the last word on what law is. By so doing, the modern state and its protagonists set themselves against Aristotle's and Aquinas's conception of natural justice and of the natural law as having an authority prior to and independent of the authority of any state. What we need to have learned from Aristotle and Aquinas is that it is only insofar as our social relationships are structured by the precepts of the natural law, only insofar as we acknowledge the authority of the natural law, that we are able to engage together in rational deliberation aimed at the common good. For only conformity to those precepts enables us to trust each other and to listen to each other as rational agents, rather than as agents of money or of power. It is those precepts that enable us to act on the basis of compelling arguments, rather than as a result of being threatened or seduced or charmed. But when the modern state was born, the rule of law was taken to be the rule of positive rather than natural law, and positive law was taken to be whatever the modern state takes it to be. And nowadays, since the modern state has become so well integrated with the market, it is in fact the state-and-the-market that is our lawmaker. So the formulation of Aristotelian questions about our present social order involves a critique not only of compartmentalisation, desire, and inequality, but also of law. What kind of critique?

No theoretical critique by itself will provide what we need, no matter how insightful, right-minded, or scholarly. And this for a reason that we have already noticed, that argument by itself, even sound argument, is ineffective upon those who have not had the kind of experiences from which they can learn. So what kind of experiences are needed in our social order, if we are to be able to learn what we need to learn about ethics and politics, in order to transform that order? Everything turns on the kind of projects in which plain people may get involved. Here I can give only one example, but there are of course many others. From time to time it becomes possible in some local community either to bring into being a new school or to remake some existing school, so that it can provide an education for the children of that community. When such an opportunity arises, it is sometimes possible for parents, teachers, and other interested members of the community to become involved and to participate in discussion and decision-making. By so doing they become unable to avoid such questions as 'What kind of school do we want to construct for our children?' and 'What do we want our children to learn?' This latter question, however, cannot be answered unless we also ask not only 'What do we take the goods of childhood to be?' and 'How through achieving the goods of childhood can our children be prepared to achieve later on the goods of adult life?' but also 'What are the virtues of teachers, children, and parents?'

All of these are recognisably Aristotelian questions, practical questions that will be well answered only if we answer them in the light of what we have learned from Aristotle and Aquinas, but also in the light of things that we now know, that Aristotle and Aquinas perhaps did not know, about how children have to be taught if their needs are to be met. One of the things that we now know is that children become unteachable if they are too hungry. So the question 'How do you make sure that the children in your school are not going to be too hungry?' becomes an educational question. We also know that children are generally unable to learn well in school unless they enjoy a stable family life. And therefore the question 'How can we produce effective schooling?' is also the question 'How can we provide the bases for an effective family life, by providing for the kind of stability in employment and the kind of income that will enable parents and teachers to bring up their and our children well?' We cannot therefore set ourselves to create an adequate school, let alone a good one, unless we also set ourselves to make and sustain a society in which jobs are not abolished in the name of growth, in which income is perennially uncertain, or in which both parents have to work so hard in order to achieve an adequate minimum income that they are unable to give the time that they need to their children. In other words, once you begin to map out what is involved in the project of bringing this kind of school into being, you are will have to raise at the level of everyday practice a much wider range of political and moral questions about human goods.

When you do so—and we can observe this happening in many places in the world—and when you try to secure the resources that you need in order to educate children, you find almost immediately that you encounter the systematic resistance of the representatives of the larger social and economic structures. The word 'resistance' in my title may have been taken to refer to the resistance that, for example, trade unions offer to attacks on their members' wages and working conditions. And that resistance is certainly not irrelevant to my thesis. But the resistance with which I am primarily concerned is the resistance of the established order, of the representatives of the established patterns of power, to any attempt to ask and answer Aristotelian questions at the level of practice. As you and I encounter the resistance elicited by any systematic attempt to achieve central human goods, we learn how to define what we are politically. It is this kind of project and this kind of encounter that provide the experience and the character formation that enable us to learn, to learn at the level of everyday practice, what our good consists in, in concrete and particular terms. We also become able to learn why, when we try to achieve the human good, there is going to be entrenched resistance to it.

What you will be told by those who represent established power is that the kind of institutions that you are trying to create and sustain are simply not possible, that you are unrealistic, a Utopian. And it is important to respond by saying 'Yes, that is exactly what we are'. This Utopianism of those who force Aristotelian questions upon the social order is a Utopianism of the present, not a Utopianism of the future. Utopianisms of the future have been and are misleading and corrupting, because they are always apt to and almost invariably do result in a sacrifice of the present to some imaginary glorious future, one to be brought about by the sacrifice of the present. But the present is what we are and have, and a refusal to sacrifice it has to be accompanied by an insistence that the range of present possibilities is always far greater than the established order is able to allow for. We need therefore to acquire a transformative political imagination, one that opens up opportunities for people to do kinds of things that they hitherto had not believed that they were capable of doing. And this can happen when someone becomes involved for the first time in community organisations and actions, when parents become involved in some community that sustains their children's school in the inner city, or when unorganised workers struggle to create a union, or when immigrants find themselves involved in forms of communal enterprise that enable them to resist attempts to treat them as no more than a disposable labour force. It is in these contexts of everyday conflict that the accusation of Utopianism becomes important, since it is in such contexts that the achievement of human goods often takes new and unpredicted forms, for which the existing social order hitherto afforded no space. But such new forms of practice and new relationships between institutions and practices often desperately need to be able to draw on what we have learned from past forms of community.

It is here that the importance of empirical studies of past and present relationships between institutions and practices in particular contexts becomes evident, studies such as Ron Beadle's recent admirable study of the circus both as practice and as institution. What matters is that such empirical studies should provide occasions for further learning, so that what is learned can be put to use in the kind of projects that I have been describing. So we badly need good empirical studies of both success and failure in creating forms of schooling that enable children, their parents, and their teachers to achieve forms of good not otherwise achievable, just as we need good empirical studies of many other kinds of experience that illuminate the relationships of practices and institutions to each other and to the human good.

Instructive examples can be found in the history of the practices and institutions of fishing crews and fishing communities in various parts of the world. I think particularly about the history that I know best, that of fishing crews in the northeastern United States, but much the same story can be told of other places. Almost everywhere fishing crews are now suffering badly, as a result of overfishing, as a result of forces that make it difficult to survive, unless you participate in large-scale factory fisheries, that is, in the kind of capitalist fishing that has no place for the traditional fishing crew. Yet we also need to remember that capitalist prosperity could be bad for fishing crews too.

Fishing has always been hard and dangerous work, and those who take on this work often do so initially for purely economic reasons. They need the wages and they have no other way to get them. But they soon discover that their lives and their livelihood now depend on other people, in whom they have to put their trust, and that those other people depend on them not only to do their work well—often boring, fatiguing work—but also expect them to be prepared to risk their lives on occasion to save other crew members. Moreover, although fishing boats are always competing with each other, everyone knows that if another boat is in danger, you have to go to its aid, if at all possible. So in the life of a fishing crew common goods—of the crew, of the fishing fleet, of the fishing community—are achieved only through the exercise of virtues, both cardinal virtues, such as the courage of endurance and risk-taking, and virtues of acknowledged dependence. And over long periods of varying prosperity a way of life, a tradition of the virtues, has been developed in many fishing communities. But then, not too long ago in New England, modern technology brought about a dramatic change. It became possible to fly tuna from New England to Japan, so that it arrived in prime condition. And the price of tuna in Japan was such that a quite new kind of prosperity—riches by the standards of the past—became possible. And of course it was good that this was so. But with the prospect of becoming rich, competitiveness intensified, the costs of going to the aid of others were weighed against the benefits of successful competition, and the solidarities of fishing crews and fishing communities were threatened and sometimes weakened. In fact, the norms and values of the community were upheld, and virtues that had sustained individuals and communities in New England through bad economic times also sustained them through their prosperity, but the lesson for the rest of us is clear.

The practice of the virtues, conceived as Aristotle and Aquinas conceived them, is difficult to reconcile with functioning well in the present economic order, whether it is a time of hardship or a time of prosperity. It is of this kind of episode that we need good empirical studies, histories of past success and failure in the life of the virtues, histories of those experiences from which, as we engage in our present projects, we need to learn. That learning develops still further as the projects that challenge the limitations of the existing order move forward. And such projects are important, not only because and insofar as they are informed by a desire to achieve the human good, both individual goods and common goods, but also because they bring into being types of community through which we are liberated from compartmentalisation, from distorted desires, from inequalities, and from the lawlessness of the present order.

They are important too because within them we discover the indispensability of the virtue of hope, a virtue that directs us beyond the facts of our present situation, whatever it is. Lenin urged us not to bow down before the tyranny of the established fact, before established conventional opinions about what is possible and what is not. And St. Paul and St. Thomas Aquinas tell us how there is always more to be hoped for in any and every situation than the empirical facts seem to show. It is insofar as we are able to find through the virtues a mode of social life in which practical rationality is informed by shared hope that we will know that we have begun to learn what we need to learn.

2

Revolutionary Aristotelianism

KELVIN KNIGHT

E. P. Thompson once expressed a 'wish that MacIntyre could complete his own thought' about 'emergent socialist consciousness within capitalist society', a consciousness that Thompson perceived in the 'ways in which men and women seem to be more "realised" as rational or moral agents, when acting collectively in conscious rebellion (or resistance) against capitalist process' (Thompson 1974, 58–59).[1] More recently, however, it has been claimed that Alasdair MacIntyre 'locates himself in the Aristotelian tradition, and can be read as a conservative' and, more particularly, that his 'central' concept of a practice is apolitical in that it does not involve an account of 'the exercise of power which calls for justification or critical scrutiny' (Frazer and Lacey 1993, 103, 19; 1994, 267, 271).

I shall argue that it is profoundly mistaken to 'read' MacIntyre as a conservative and that the political conclusions he draws from the Aristotelian tradition are, on the contrary, revolutionary. More particularly, I shall argue that his theory of practices most certainly does involve sub-

---

1. This essay is a slight revision of that first published as Knight 1996.

jecting the exercise of power to critical scrutiny, and that it provides sound reasons for opposing the prevailing justifications and forms of power in contemporary society. MacIntyre has, therefore, continued to develop his ideas about conscious resistance to capitalism, as Thompson hoped he would. These ideas constitute MacIntyre's politics, his view of how philosophy should inform collective action.

Practices

The concept of practice is basic to MacIntyre's entire project. 'The concept of a virtue ... always requires for its application the acceptance [of] some prior account of certain features of social and moral life in terms of which it has to be defined and explained'. The primary feature in MacIntyre's novel account is that of a practice (MacIntyre 1985a, 186–87).

This linking of practice to virtue immediately distinguishes MacIntyre's theory from that of most other theorists of social practice who, whether advocates or antagonists of conventional practices, identify morality with their subject in considering morality to comprise individuals' subordination to conventional rules of behaviour. MacIntyre, in contrast, does not reduce morality to convention or rule-following. Instead, he adopts the Aristotelian approach of identifying morality with virtues, or good dispositional qualities, that may be cultivated by persons. Social practices are not constitutive of morality, but they are the schools of the virtues. Such cardinal virtues as justice, courage, and truthfulness are cultivated through participation in practices, as practitioners come to find outside of themselves things that may be valued for their own sake and to devote themselves to pursuit of those goods.

What is also immediately distinctive about MacIntyre's conception of social practice is the way that it involves rationality. Every practice has a particular form of reasoning internal to it, enabling practitioners to pursue 'internal goods' that can 'be had *only* by engaging in some particular kind of practice' (MacIntyre 1985a, 188, MacIntyre's emphasis). This idea of practical rationality differentiates MacIntyre's concept of practice from both conservative conceptions, of practices as subrational, and Foucauldian conceptions, of practices as discourses of power. His basing of reason in practices also, of course, differentiates MacIntyre from what he calls 'the Enlightenment project' of justifying morality with a universalising reason.

It is 'the concept of the best, of the perfected, [that] provides each of these forms of activity with the good toward which those who participate in it move', its internal good of excellence (MacIntyre 1988a, 31). As practitioners advance towards that concept, the concept is itself further advanced, if the practice is in good order, so that practitioners always have a goal ahead of them. Both practices and human lives should, then, be understood teleologically, the goals of human lives deriving from those of social practices.

In specifying what he means by a practice, MacIntyre differentiates it from a 'technique'. Practices include architecture ('but not bricklaying'), 'the game of football' (but not 'throwing a football with skill'), chess, farming, 'the enquiries of physics, chemistry and biology . . . the work of the historian . . . painting and music', as well as 'politics in the Aristotelian sense, [and] the making and sustaining of family life' (MacIntyre 1985a, 187–88; 273). He continues by discussing the politically trivial cases of chess and painting (MacIntyre 1985a, 188). When pressed, however, he has acknowledged that certain points that are vital to understanding his idea of practices 'may have been obscured by [his] lack of attention to productive crafts such as farming and fishing, architecture and building' (MacIntyre 1994b, 284).

As a vital aspect of practices is that pursuit of the good internal to a practice enables a person to give narrative order to her life, they might be thought of as vocations. Nevertheless, 'practice' should not be considered a synonym of 'job'. Bricklaying is not a distinct practice but a technique, a means to the good internal to building. One might also, of course, engage in practices other than that of which one's job is a part. For example, one might be a professional builder who plays chess. In this case, one is engaging in the same form of practical reasoning as does a professional chess grandmaster, but it is more likely that the grandmaster is the one who plays a significant part in advancing standards of excellence in chess. Conversely, it is master builders who establish and advance standards of excellence in building, and a chess grandmaster who dabbles by building an extension to his house will gain by learning from the techniques and maxims developed by professional builders.

In attempting to achieve a good internal to a practice, a practitioner has 'initially to learn as an apprentice learns' from the standards already established (MacIntyre 1985a, 258). However, 'the greatest achievements in each area at each stage always exhibit a freedom to violate the present established maxims' by those practitioners who have become expert through such learning (MacIntyre 1988a, 31). It is in this way that practices and practical rationalities advance. The goods internal to practices are properly regarded as prior to rules within those practices, the purpose of those rules being to subserve pursuit of the goals of the practice.

This, then, is, in part, how MacIntyre furnishes his virtue ethics with an account of social life in terms of which it may be elaborated. However, MacIntyre is not content to elaborate his own moral philosophy. He also argues for its superiority over rivals, and each of these rivals also 'presupposes a sociology' because it supposes that the concepts it employs to describe reasons and actions 'are embodied or at least can be in the real social world' (MacIntyre 1988a, 23). The most influential rival is that which he characterises as emotivism, which issued from the failure of the Enlightenment project and anticipates the challenge to that project from Nietzscheanism. Emotivism gains much of its influence from the plausibility of its Humean supposition that sociology must be value-free because 'no valid argument can move from entirely factual premises to any moral or evaluative conclusion'. MacIntyre counters this contention with the idea of 'functional concepts'; 'from the premise "He is a sea-captain", the conclusion may be validly inferred that "He ought to do whatever a sea-captain ought to do"' (MacIntyre 1985a, 56–58). The reasoning internal to a practice enables practitioners to judge between right and wrong actions, while a more general form of practical reasoning enables people to judge between good and bad practices.

MacIntyre characterises the social embodiments of such general forms of practical reasoning and enquiry as traditions, and the tradition with which he identifies as that in which Aristotle and Aquinas are the seminal figures. 'It is rival conceptions of practical rationality . . . which are in contention' between Aristotelians and others, embodied in 'the life of particular communities which exemplify each specific conception' (MacIntyre 1990c, 355). 'What Aristotelian theory articulates are in fact the concepts embodied by such modes of practice' as those found 'in some relatively small-scale and local communities—examples range from some kinds of ancient city and some kinds of medieval commune to some kinds of modern farming and fishing enterprises—in which social relationships are informed by a shared allegiance to the goods internal to communal practices'. This contrasts with the mutually 'competing moral idioms' of contemporary liberal and conservative ideology, which have abstracted 'different aspects of the life of practice' from their particular contexts and transformed them into 'a set of rival theories' (MacIntyre 2006l, 155–56). Aristotelianism is, then, less a particular (syllogistic) conception of practical rationality than the general rationality of practices as such, in contrast with which all other rationalities may be described as ideologies.

It may be inferred from this that 'the life of practice', in the absence of ideological obfuscation, tends to generate a commonly intelligible morality that facilitates the cultivation of virtue. The Aristotelian tradition of philosophy is that which justifies the life of practice and characterises itself in terms of higher-level reflection upon the reasoning generated by traditional practices. This contrasts with both Enlightenment philosophy, which attempted to transcend practice and tradition, and Nietzscheanism, which shared the Enlightenment aim of liberating people from practice and tradition but denied epistemological certainty to any means of so doing. Aristotelianism is also, then, the philosophical tradition that maintains the rational validity of tradition and practice against other traditions that attempt to deny it (MacIntyre 1990a).

Since *After Virtue,* MacIntyre's primary concern has been with elaborating and justifying his claim that all of the claims of philosophy can only be properly understood within the context of the historical development of philosophy, that this history can only be properly understood within the wider context of the history of society as a whole, and that, thus understood, the proper way in which we should couch philosophical claims is that developed within the Aristotelian tradition. In attempting to persuade his philosophical opponents of the veracity of his case, MacIntyre has been drawn into arguments conducted on a level of theoretical abstraction that is inhospitable to the combination of theory with practice that he is arguing for. This was bound to produce 'a tension between [his] account of what it is to be rational and [his] account of the possibilities of understanding alien, rival traditions' (MacIntyre

1991b, 620). While he maintains that the Aristotelian tradition is incommensurable with other Western philosophical traditions and that Western culture is incommensurable with other cultures, he nonetheless recognises that other cultures have philosophical traditions concerned with articulating the practical wisdom of members of their own societies and, therefore, calls for more 'importance . . . to be accorded to the study of what . . . the philosophy and practice of [China,] Japan, India, Africa and elsewhere' have 'contributed to virtue ethics' (MacIntyre 1992, 1281). Aristotelianism is the tradition of the moral theory of practice that has developed in the West, but other civilisations have other such traditions. What is important everywhere is to guard both against the moral stultification of practices legitimated by ideological obfuscation, such as that which occurred in Polynesia with *taboo* (MacIntyre 1985a, 111–13) and in the West with the Enlightenment, and against the institutional concomitants of such stultification.

Practices versus Institutions

'Debate and conflict as to the best forms of practice have to be debate and conflict between rival institutions and not merely between rival theories' (MacIntyre 1990c, 360). A concept of institutions is, therefore, vital to MacIntyre's social theory of practices. Whereas other such theories may be vulnerable to the criticism that they cannot explain how such a thing as a practice can be reproduced through the behaviour of different individuals (e.g., Turner 1994; Turner does not acknowledge MacIntyre's idea of institutions), MacIntyre explains such transmission as largely conducted through formal organisations and their rules, which are, therefore, necessary to the sustenance of practices.

> Practices must not be confused with institutions. Chess, physics and medicine are practices; chess clubs, laboratories, universities and hospitals are institutions. Institutions . . . are involved in acquiring money and other material goods; they are structured in terms of power and status, and they distribute money, power and status as rewards. Nor could they do otherwise if they are to sustain not only

themselves, but also the practices of which they are the bearers. . . . Indeed so intimate is the relationship of practices to institutions . . . that institutions and practices characteristically form a single causal order in which the ideals and the creativity of the practice are always vulnerable to the acquisitiveness of the institution, in which the cooperative care for the common goods of the practice is always vulnerable to the competitiveness of the institution. In this context the essential function of the virtues is clear. Without them, without justice, courage and truthfulness, practices could not resist the corrupting power of institutions. (MacIntyre 1985a, 194)

Money, power, and status are all what MacIntyre calls goods external to practices. Such goods are (to repeat) 'never to be had *only* by engaging in some particular kind of practice'. If our grandmaster were to give up chess for building because he calculated that he could earn more money as a cowboy contractor than as an excellent chess player, then he would be acting in pursuit of goods external to any practice. He thereby would be foregoing the opportunity of cultivating the virtues, because he would be pursuing no goal other than that of satisfying his egoistic desires. External goods also differ from those internal to practices in 'that when achieved they are always some individual's property. Moreover, characteristically they are such that the more someone has of them, the less there is for other people' (MacIntyre 1985a, 190).

Because external goods are necessary to institutions and institutions are necessary to practices, the tension between goods internal and external to practices is ineradicable. MacIntyre is no utopian. Indeed, he identifies the Athenian *polis* of Aristotle's day (towards which he has, misleadingly, been accused of longingly looking backward) as the place where the conflict between these two types of goods became explicit (MacIntyre 1988a, 42).

The relative importance that people attach to internal and external goods is profoundly affected by the dominant beliefs in their society. If practices are not to be corrupted by the goods pursued by institutions, those institutions must always be subordinated to the goods internal to practices, which constitute the ends to which institutions should be considered means. Institutions should be structured and run in accordance with the requirements of the particular practice of which they are the bearer. In the post-Enlightenment world, however, the reverse rationale has increasingly prevailed. Both capitalist corporations and states are structured in the same, bureaucratic way.

Managerial reasoning and action are, MacIntyre claims, an embodiment of emotivist moral philosophy, which 'entails the obliteration of any distinction between manipulative and non-manipulative social relations' by denying the reality of the latter (MacIntyre 1985a, 23). Managers are obliged to adopt a certain attitude to the world through their work, such that they may be described as 'typical characters' or 'moral representatives' of emotivism. Their power and status are justified by their claims to be cost-effective and impartial means to any given end. Their concern is with organisational 'effectiveness' and, therefore, with manipulating the behaviour of others, treating others as means rather than ends (MacIntyre 1985a, 25–31, 73–78).

The sociology presupposed by emotivism is that of Weber, who denied that disagreements about ends can be rationally resolved. Both liberals' 'belief in an irreducible plurality of values' and the way in which 'Marxists organise and move toward power' are, for MacIntyre, best accommodated within Weber's sort of political sociology, 'for in our culture we know of no organised movement towards power which is not bureaucratic and managerial in mode and we know of no justifications for authority which are not Weberian in form' (MacIntyre 1985a, 109). Contemporary authority is legitimated by reference to bureaucratic effectiveness, thereby reducing authority to 'successful power' (MacIntyre 1985a, 26).

Weber is right in explaining how the idea of their effectiveness 'is used to sustain and extend the power and authority of managers', and he elevates that idea into an entire theory of modernity. Nevertheless, he is wrong in claiming that social science gives managers veritably predictive knowledge, such that they really can exercise control over society. Instead, MacIntyre asks us to 'consider the following possibility: that what we are oppressed by is not power, but impotence', 'a masquerade of social control' (MacIntyre 1985a, 75; cf. 1970, 70–72). Bureaucratic institutions affect society, but their effects are less often intended than unintended. Institutions do manage to manipulate people's behaviour, but this does not enable them to achieve the sort of society that their plans envisage. Totalitarianism (MacIntyre himself predicted, in 1981) is, therefore, heading for defeat (MacIntyre 1985a, 106–7).

Weber's conception of the iron cage of bureaucratic rationality is, for MacIntyre, a 'moral fiction' (MacIntyre 1985a, 76–77). The dominance of bureaucratic rationality is possible only because of the prior discrediting of substantive rationality by the failure of the Enlightenment project. Management is a mere technique, not a practice with goods internal to itself, and therefore putting administrative technique and its goods of effectiveness before the goods of excellence internal to practices is a moral error.

What the intellectual and social dominance of instrumental rationality does achieve is the atomisation and demoralisation of society. As people come to think of themselves as without moral purpose and as manipulated 'means' to others' arbitrary ends (MacIntyre 1985a, 23–24), those people are likely to attempt to retain a sense of themselves as effective actors by becoming manipulative also. In this context, of a society demoralised by bureaucratic manipulation and the failure of the Enlightenment project, we face the alternatives of continued demoralisation and manipulation (emotivism, which is not a reasonable option), of substituting will for morality and asserting our will over others (the Nietzschean option), or of enacting our lives as the narrative of a quest for our true good through participation in social practices, thereby finding a teleological justification for morality (the Aristotelian option). The Nietzschean option is that which is effectively taken by those who wield institutional power, in attempting to impose their will over others and, also, upon an intractable, social reality.

'Government itself' is, for MacIntyre, 'a hierarchy of bureaucratic managers' (MacIntyre 1985a, 85). Therefore, although he is bound to agree with the familiar communitarian claim that the liberal state's claim to neutrality is fictitious, given that Weber's claim about the morally neutral instrumentality of bureaucratic rationality is fictitious, MacIntyre is also bound to agree with much of the liberal counter-critique of communitarianism. 'Where liberals have characteristically urged that it is in the activities of subordinate voluntary associations, such as those constituted by religious groups, that shared visions of the good should be articulated, communitarians have insisted that the nation itself through the institutions of the nation-state ought to be constituted to some significant degree as a community', an ideal against which MacIntyre sides with liberals in 'understanding how it generates totalitarian and other evils' and, therefore, in 'resisting' (MacIntyre 1994b, 302–3).

Just as, in *After Virtue,* MacIntyre cites the criticisms of different justifications of rule-constituted morality against each other as demonstrating that incoherence is the inevitable result of attempting to elaborate such a justification, so, since then, he has cited the criticisms of liberal and communitarian legitimations of the state against each other as demonstrating that incoherence is the inevitable result of attempting to elaborate any such legitimation. On the one hand, the state is justified as the guarantor of individuals' rights to pursue their own self-chosen goals. On the other hand, it is justified as the expression of a form of social life for which its subjects may, whenever necessary, be required to risk their lives. There cannot be a rational legitimation of the state that satisfies both of these criteria. As both criteria represent necessary aspects of the state, there cannot be any coherent solution to the modern problem of political obligation (MacIntyre 2006f, 163; 1998f, 226–27; 1995a, passim). Unfortunately, however, exposing incoherence is far from sufficient to achieve its transcendence.

In going beyond the exposure of rational inconsistency in legitimations of modernity, MacIntyre draws on Marx for a critique of its characteristic institutions. He indicts 'the institutional injustice of capitalism' for the alienation and exploitation of labour. 'It becomes impossible for workers to understand their work as a contribution to the common good of a society which at the economic level no longer has a common good, because of different and conflicting interests of different classes. The needs of capital formation impose upon capitalists and upon those who manage their enterprises a need to extract from the work of their employees a surplus which is at the future disposal of capital and not of labour', so that practitioners are considered dispensable means to the goal of profitability. MacIntyre's classes are, however, different from those of Marx. 'Small producers' are in a similarly unfortunate position to workers, since both are practitioners manipulated by others through 'market relationships'. Conversely, MacIntyre's remarks about capitalism's 'systematic incentives to develop a type of character that has a propensity to injustice', if conjoined with his critique of managers as characters, indicate that management rather than ownership constitutes the opposing interest (MacIntyre 2006l, 147–49).

Under capitalism, 'work tends to become separated from everything but the service of biological survival and . . . institutionalised acquisitiveness'. Work 'on a production line, for example', has 'been expelled from the realm of practices with goods internal to themselves', and '*pleonexia* [acquisitiveness], a vice in the Aristotelian scheme, is now the driving force of productive work' (MacIntyre 1985a, 227, 137). His critique of capitalism therefore shares something with R. H. Tawney's influential contrast of 'the acquisitive society' with the socialist or 'functional society', in which work is recognised as a duty to be undertaken for the common good (Tawney 1921). However, MacIntyre's teleological conception of work enables him to avoid the 'banal earnestness' for which he had earlier dismissed what we might call Tawney's anticipation of deontological communitarianism (MacIntyre 1971a, 39).

MacIntyre clearly departs from Marxism, also, in rejecting its form of revolutionary politics. He rejects the way that its adherents organise and move towards power, along with any other 'systematic political action of a conventional kind' aimed at achieving power or influence within the state (MacIntyre 1984a, 252). Marxists may seek to use state power to overthrow capitalism and effect a communist utopia, but all they thereby achieve is harsher imprisonment within the iron cage of instrumental rationality. 'Those who make the conquest of state power their aim are always in the end conquered by it', just as reformist trade unionism inevitably leads to 'the domestication and then the destruction of effective trade union power' (MacIntyre 2006l, 150, 153). Marx did not perceive the dangers in managerial rationality that Weber theorised and that the past century has made evident. Instead, he inherited from Hegel the belief that bureaucratic administration can be transparently rational and, therefore, that it represents the social liberation of humankind. Although he identified the proletariat as the revolutionary class that would put scientific socialism into practice, it remained the bureaucracy that would represent the universal interest in administering an ostensibly classless society.

If his rejection of Marxist politics is a clear change in MacIntyre's stance since the 1950s and '60s (when he moved from the Communist Party to the Socialist Labour League to the International Socialists), he has nevertheless been constant in his wholesale opposition both to dominant institutions and ideologies and to any kind of reformism. He also remains sympathetic to Marxism insofar as it is 'a body of theory designed to inform, direct and provide self-understanding in the practice of working-class and intellectual struggle against capitalism', although he considers that Marxists 'were the agents of our own defeats' in failing to think through the practical bases of reason, and, therefore, that what is to be done now is 'first to understand this and then to start out all over again' (MacIntyre 2006l, 157; 1998f, 234).

Politics

MacIntyre's notoriously pessimistic conclusion to *After Virtue* is that 'what matters at this stage is the construction of local forms of community within which civility and the intellectual and moral life can be sustained through the new dark ages which are already upon us', given that 'the barbarians . . . have already been governing us for quite some time' (MacIntyre 1985a, 85). He persists in his belief that 'the problem is not to reform the dominant order, but to find ways for local communities to survive by sustaining a life of the common good against the disintegrating forces of the nation-state and the market' (MacIntyre 1995b, 35). He suggests looking for such a way in 'a politics of self-defence for all those local societies that aspire to achieve some relatively self-sufficient and independent form of participatory practice-based community' (MacIntyre 2006l, 155). In illustration, he cites 'the account given by Edward Thompson in *The Making of the English Working Class* . . . of the communal life of the hand-loom weavers of Lancashire and Yorkshire' two hundred years ago. 'What the hand-loom weavers hoped to, but failed to, sustain "was a community of independent small producers"'. MacIntyre compares them and their later Chartism with 'the insurrection of the Silesian weavers of the Eulengebirge in 1844', adding that Marx 'seems not to have understood the form of life from which that militancy arose, and so later failed to understand that while proletarianisation makes it necessary for workers to resist, it also tends to deprive workers of those forms of practice through which they can discover conceptions of a good and of virtues adequate to the moral needs of resistance'. The practice of such weavers, in contrast, was 'entitled to be called "revolutionary"' because 'those engaged in it transform themselves and educate themselves through their own self-transformative activity, coming to understand their good as the good internal to that activity' (MacIntyre 1998f, 231–22).

Unfortunately, although workers were often able to collectively 'make' their own way of life in local communities during the formative stages of industrial capitalism, it does not follow that such a possibility still exists. Even those local communities embodying the 'Gaelic oral culture of farmers and fishermen' that engrossed MacIntyre's early imagination have now all but succumbed to the demands of state and market, as MacIntyre acknowledges (MacIntyre 1998i, 255). He also acknowledges 'that an adequate sense of tradition manifests itself in a grasp of those future possibilities which the past has made available to the present' (MacIntyre 1985a, 223). Such a sense should, then, manifest itself in identifying other available possibilities for resisting the dominant order, given that 'there are forms of institutionalised community in the modern world other than those of the state, and the preservation of and enhancement of certain at least of such forms of community may set tasks for a less barren politics' (MacIntyre 2006f, 171).

I suggest that the rationale of MacIntyre's social theory of practices is that the bases of these certain forms of community are to be found no longer in locality, but rather in particular practices. Accordingly, the tasks for a politics in the Aristotelian tradition are to defend the rationality, ideals, creativity, and cooperative care for common goods of practices against institutional corruption and managerial manipulation, and to uphold internal goods of excellence against external goods and claims of effectiveness. The present dominance of institutions over practices, and of bureaucratic technique and procedural rules over practical wisdom, is the embodiment of the dominance of abstract reason and will over tradition, of Kantianism and Nietzscheanism over Aristotelianism. It is, therefore, in collective defence of the goods and rationalities of practices against those of institutions that the bases for a politics in the Aristotelian tradition are now to be found.

MacIntyre indicates how the tasks of such a politics might be undertaken. 'When an institution—a university, say, or a farm, or a hospital—is the bearer of a tradition of practice or practices, its common life will be partly, but in a centrally important way, constituted by a continuous argument as to what a university is and ought to be' (MacIntyre 1985a, 222), affording scope for opposing the goods internal to a practice against those external to it. MacIntyre contends that the 'peculiar and [socially] essential function' of universities is, now, to be 'places where . . . the wider society [can] learn how to conduct its own debates . . . in a rationally defensible way' (MacIntyre 1990a, 222). Exposing the incoherence 'of the rhetoric of official academia' is, of course, far from sufficient to prevent the advance of managerialisation because such rhetoric is symptomatic 'of a much deeper disorder' (MacIntyre 1990a, 227), and the same is true regarding farms and hospitals. Nevertheless, given that the 'hierarchical division between managers and managed is . . . legitimated by the superior knowledge imputed to themselves' by managers (MacIntyre 1998f, 231), if that legitimacy is to be challenged it is necessary to theorise a general justification of the priority of practical over instrumental reason, and this is what MacIntyre does in opposing the abstraction of moral and organisational theories from personal virtue and social practice.

This challenge to the legitimacy of the modern age provides bases for a form of class politics. Those who have acquired money, power, and status have an interest in maintaining the institutions and ideologies of manipulation. Conversely, 'Aristotelian theory articulates the presuppositions of a range of practices a good deal wider than Aristotle himself was able to recognise', including those of many workers and small producers (MacIntyre 1994b, 301). Perhaps proletarianisation has alienated many from the ends of their activity as workers, rather than from their ends as paid employees. However, proletarianisation lacks the universalising logic that Marx imputed to it. 'A production line' already characterises work in industrialised countries less than it did when MacIntyre wrote *After Virtue,* and managers are having to find new ways of deskilling or otherwise marginalising workers. One way is casualisation. Another is through the second managerial revolution being carried out in the name of Total Quality Management, the culmination of which would be the total proceduralisation of work. That this is producing massive demoralisation and alienation throughout the economy is obvious, but that its victory is a foregone conclusion is no more obvious than was that of Soviet planning. Self-management of practitioners remains a future possibility. What Aristotelian theory may contribute to pursuit of the subordination of institutions to practices is legitimation and co-ordination, so that previously isolated struggles can be transformed into a new class war of attrition.

MacIntyre offers no blueprint for a society in which institutions are subordinated to practices. Nevertheless, since an Aristotelian practice of politics comprises 'the making and sustaining of forms of human community—and therefore of institutions' (MacIntyre 1985a, 194), this practice must involve some conception of excellence in the making of institutions. The institutions of an entire territorial polity must be 'concerned, as Aristotle says . . . with the whole of life, not with this or that good, but with man's good as such' (MacIntyre 1985a, 156). Such a polity must provide 'an ordering of goods . . . to be achieved by excellence within specific and systematic forms of activity, integrated into an overall rank-order by the political activity of [its] citizens' (MacIntyre 1988a, 133). All may share in the practice of politics if the polity comprises what might be called a community of communities or, even, a functional society.

No hierarchy of practices or of their internal goods is given by either nature, a priori reasoning, or history. MacIntyre rejects any such 'notion of an absolute standpoint, independent of the particularity of all traditions' (MacIntyre 1994b, 295). He is, instead, a radically political thinker.

He is also a politically radical thinker. His novel juxtaposition of practices to institutions prohibits any susceptibility to the 'deification of the state', 'institutionalism', and political conservatism with which Critical Theorists (Schnaedelbach 1987, 235) and Foucauldians typically charge Aristotelians. It also renders him innocent of 'extreme philosophical idealism' (Shapiro 1990, 150–51). Rather, his opposition to the Enlightenment's legitimation of capitalism is 'not only [to] a theoretical mistake. It is a mistake embodied in institutionalised social life. And it is therefore a mistake which cannot be corrected merely by better theoretical analysis' (MacIntyre 1998f, 229).

MacIntyre should, therefore, still be read along with Thompson and Marx, not with either conservatives or conventionally academic philosophers. The philosophers have only *interpreted* the world in rival ways; the point is to *change* it.

3

Revolutionary Aristotelianism?

The Political Thought of Aristotle, Marx, and MacIntyre

TONY BURNS

Some commentators, for example, Paul Blackledge and Neil Davidson, are interested in exploring the intellectual relationship between the views of Alasdair MacIntyre and those of Karl Marx (Blackledge and Davidson 2008; Blackledge 2005). Others are interested in exploring the relationship between the thought of MacIntyre and that of Aristotle. To be more specific, they develop the idea that MacIntyre can be associated with a form of 'revolutionary Aristotelianism'. Among these is Kelvin Knight, who published an essay on MacIntyre's political thought entitled 'Revolutionary Aristotelianism' in 1996 (Knight 1996, included in this volume; see also Knight 2007). Knight's essay is especially significant because MacIntyre is on record as endorsing its account of his own views; as he wrote after its publication, 'for an accurate and perceptive discussion of my political views see Kelvin Knight, "Revolutionary Aristotelianism"' (MacIntyre 1998g, 235).

At first sight, these appear to be quite separate issues. There is no obvious reason why those who are interested in MacIntyre's relationship to Marx and Marxism should necessarily be interested in his relationship to Aristotle and to Aristotelianism, and vice versa. On the other hand, there is also no obvious reason why one could *not* be interested in both of these issues at the same time. Indeed, one might take the view that they are necessarily connected. This depends, of course, on one's assessment of MacIntyre's understanding of Marx's relationship to Aristotle.

Aristotle, Marx, and MacIntyre

For those who are interested in linking MacIntyre with both 'revolutionary Aristotelianism' and with Marx, it is arguable that MacIntyre's intellectual development occurred in three stages. The first, 'Marx without Aristotle', refers to the 'early' MacIntyre's enthusiastic Marxism in the 1950s and '60s, in which he has relatively little to say about Aristotle. The second, 'Aristotle without Marx', refers to the middle decades of MacIntyre's life, when he was disillusioned with Marxism and became an Aristotelian. This phase runs from the mid-1960s to the mid-1990s and is associated with MacIntyre's best-known works, especially *After Virtue* (1981). The third and final phase, 'Marx and Aristotle', is one in which MacIntyre rekindles an interest in Marx and Marxism and considers the possibility of a rapprochement between the ideas of Marx and those of Aristotle. This is the phase of the 'late' MacIntyre, running from the mid-1990s to the present.

The Early MacIntyre: Marx *without* Aristotle

As Paul Blackledge has observed (Blackledge 2005, 695), commentators who have written about MacIntyre have often ignored the positive relationship which exists between his views and those of Marx, especially in the earlier years of his intellectual career. Indeed, one has the impression that they are not even aware of the fact that MacIntyre was once a Marxist (cf. Horton and Mendus 1994). As Blackledge points out, an important text in this connection is MacIntyre's 'Notes from the Moral Wilderness', which was published in 1958–59 (Blackledge 2005, 70–76).

In 'Notes from the Moral Wilderness', MacIntyre addresses the issue of Marxism and morality, and specifically the question whether there is such a thing as a Marxist ethic—a question which he answers in the affirmative. He briefly outlines the intellectual basis of such an ethic and talks about different ways in which one might 'revive the *moral* content within Marxism' (MacIntyre 1998a, 34). MacIntyre thinks that official Marxism has fallen away from an earlier Marxist ethical ideal, which he endorses. MacIntyre associates this with the 'young Marx's' *Economic and Philosophical Manuscripts of 1844* (MacIntyre 1953; 1968; McMylor 1994, 177).

The argument developed in the 'Notes' begins by contrasting two opposed positions. The first is that of 'Stalinism'. MacIntyre's account of this is somewhat idiosyncratic. Surprisingly, MacIntyre does *not* maintain that Marxists of this stamp claim that Marxism is a 'science' and that, as such, it rejects 'ethical arguments', just as it rejects 'utopian theorising'. Rather, he maintains that there *is* an ethic associated with Stalinism, but one which is completely immersed in 'history'. What is morally 'right', from this point of view, is determined by the 'laws of historical development'. The Stalinist 'identifies what is morally right with what is actually going to be the outcome of historical development'. Thus, 'the "ought" of principle is swallowed up', MacIntyre argues, 'in the "is" of history' (MacIntyre 1998a, 32).

MacIntyre contrasts the approach adopted by Stalinism with that of 'liberal morality'. Again somewhat idiosyncratically, he argues that for liberal morality there are no objective moral values which might be said to have an application to all human beings. All value judgments are individual, subjective, and arbitrary. Liberal morality takes the view that moral values and norms are created by a decision—an individual act of will. This way of thinking is based on the principle, usually associated with David Hume, that one cannot derive an 'ought' from an 'is'. According to MacIntyre, for liberal morality 'no "is" can entail an "ought"'' (MacIntyre 1998a, 41). 'Factual assertions cannot entail moral assertions' (MacIntyre 1998a, 33). And the 'isolation of the moral from the factual' associated with Hume's principle is 'presented as a necessary and ineluctable truth of logic' (MacIntyre 1998a, 41). Thus, for advocates of this doctrine, 'on ultimate questions of morality we cannot argue, we can only choose' (MacIntyre 1998a, 33). In MacIntyre's view, for this reason liberal morality 'seems somehow irrational and arbitrary'. For liberal moralists, moral principles are 'completely isolated from the facts of their existence and they simply accept one set of principles rather than another in an arbitrary fashion'. Hence we are justified in claiming that 'their morality has no basis' (MacIntyre 1998a, 34). According to MacIntyre, this 'isolation of the moral from the factual, the emphasis on choice, the arbitrariness introduced into moral matters, all these play into the hands of the defenders of the established order' (MacIntyre 1998a, 35).

In contrast to the Stalinist, then, MacIntyre argues that for the liberal moralist the laws of morality must be thought of as standing completely outside of history. This type of moral critic 'puts himself outside history as a spectator. He invokes his principles as valid independently of the course of historical events' (MacIntyre 1998a, 32). For the 'moral values encapsulated wholly in history' of the Stalinist he substitutes 'moral values wholly detached from history' (MacIntyre 1998a, 40). Thus, for the 'liberal moralist', 'the "ought" of principle is completely external to the "is" of history' (MacIntyre 1998a, 32).

Having contrasted Stalinism and liberal morality, MacIntyre goes on to ask 'whether there can be an alternative to the barren opposition' of these two approaches to questions of ethics (MacIntyre 1998a, 36). He suggests that there is a 'third moral position', which he associates with a 'rereading' of Marx. This can, MacIntyre suggests, provide us with a 'basis for our moral standards' (MacIntyre 1998a, 37). He claims that 'a contemporary rereading of Marxism' might 'suggest a new approach to moral issues' (MacIntyre 1998a, 31). However, this requires 'replacing a misconceived but prevalent view of what Marxism is', that is to say, Stalinism or orthodox Marxism, 'by a more correct view' (MacIntyre 1998a, 37).

Central to this rereading of Marx is the idea that it is possible to ground a Marxist ethic on the 'conception of human nature' which Marx outlines in the *Economic and Philosophical Manuscripts of 1844* (MacIntyre 1998a, 40). MacIntyre insists that 'the crucial concept for Marxists is their concept of human nature, a concept which has to be at the centre of any discussion of moral theory' (MacIntyre 1998a, 45). It is this view of human nature which 'binds together the Marxist view of history and Communist morality' (MacIntyre 1998a, 49). We saw earlier that, according to MacIntyre, 'one of the root mistakes of the liberal belief in the autonomy of morality' is that the liberal moralist 'attempts to treat his fundamental moral precepts as without any basis'. They are his simply and solely 'because he has chosen them' (MacIntyre 1998a, 41). In MacIntyre's opinion, Marx's view of human nature can provide such a 'basis'. It provides us with an 'is' from which it is possible for us to logically derive an 'ought'.

In the 'Notes', MacIntyre claims that for Marx this view of human nature is associated with a commitment to essentialism. He also claims that Marx 'inherits from *Hegel*,' and not from Aristotle, his conception of the 'human essence' (MacIntyre 1998a, 40). Aristotle's philosophy is conspicuous by its absence from MacIntyre's argument. It seems clear that MacIntyre had not yet developed an interest in Aristotle's 'virtue ethics' independently of Marx. Nor, at this stage in his intellectual development, did he associate Marx's approach to ethics with Aristotle's philosophy.

There is an affinity between Marxist ethics, as MacIntyre understands it in the 'Notes', and the outlook of 'Hegelian' or 'Western' Marxism, especially that of Herbert Marcuse and the 'critical theory' of the Frankfurt School. This is obvious in the case of MacIntyre's criticism of liberal morality's association with the principle of 'instrumental' or 'means-ends' rationality (MacIntyre 1998a, 36, 39).

To summarise, MacIntyre's 'Notes from the Moral Wilderness' is of interest for four reasons. The first is that here MacIntyre demonstrates a commitment to a certain kind of Marxism. The second is that MacIntyre is interested in the issue of Marxism and ethics. The third is that there is a striking affinity between MacIntyre's views on this subject and the Critical Theory of the Frankfurt School. And the fourth is that MacIntyre discusses this issue independently of any reference to the views of Aristotle and 'virtue ethics'. In short, MacIntyre's approach to ethics at this time is Marxist and not yet Aristotelian.

The Middle Period: Aristotle *without* Marx

In the 'middle period' of his intellectual life, starting perhaps with *A Short History of Ethics* (1966), but associated above all with *After Virtue* (1981) and *Whose Justice? Which Rationality?* (1988), MacIntyre became disillusioned with Marxism. He was either uninterested in Marx and his ideas, and therefore ignored them, or he rejected them.

Evidence that he was no longer interested in Marx can be found in both the *Short History of Ethics* and *After Virtue*. The former contains a very brief discussion of Marx in a short chapter on 'Hegel and Marx'. The chapter is sixteen pages long, and twelve of these are devoted to Hegel. Similarly, in the preface to the second edition of *After Virtue,* published in 1985, MacIntyre states that Marxism 'is only a marginal preoccupation' in that work (MacIntyre 1985a, x).

Evidence that during this period MacIntyre became hostile to Marxism can be found in a number of his writings. Perhaps the best example of this is MacIntyre's study of Herbert Marcuse, published in 1970. One of the ironies of this book is the fact that MacIntyre uses arguments usually associated with 'orthodox Marxism' to criticise, not just Marcuse, but also the theoretical project which he had himself defended in 'Notes from the Moral Wilderness'. Thus, for example, he criticises Marcuse for being 'endlessly willing to talk of "man" rather than of men, of what "man" desires or suffers' (MacIntyre 1970, 21). And he contrasts this with the views expressed by Marx in *The German Ideology,* where Marx attacks Feuerbach 'precisely because he says "man" instead of "real, historical men"', and 'for speaking of "the essence of man"'. Not surprisingly, MacIntyre's conclusion is that Marcuse was not a genuine Marxist at all. He was, rather, a 'pre-Marxist thinker' who had 'regressed' to 'that practice of "criticism"' which Marx himself had criticised (MacIntyre 1970, 22). The implications of this are clear. By 1970 MacIntyre had come to reject the very 'rereading of Marx' which he had proposed, and opposed to Stalinism, in 1958–59.

This abandonment of what in 'Notes' he had taken to be the standpoint of Marx and Marxism continued throughout the 1970s, while MacIntyre was working on *After Virtue*. It is probably best exemplified in *After Virtue* itself, where MacIntyre 'agrees' with the view that there is 'no tolerable alternative set of political and economic structures which could be brought into place to replace the structures of advanced capitalism'. Someone who holds such a 'pessimistic' view would, he concedes, 'in an important way cease to be a Marxist'. Nevertheless, MacIntyre goes on, 'this conclusion agrees' with 'my own'. For 'I too', he says, 'take it that

Marxism is exhausted as a *political* tradition' (MacIntyre 1985a, 262). This attitude can also be found in MacIntyre's writings published in the later 1980s and early 1990s. For example, in an essay published in 1984, MacIntyre described his 'increasing recognition of the gross inadequacies of Marxism' (MacIntyre 1998c, 69), and in an interview given in 1991 he maintained that 'Marxism is not just an inadequate, but a largely inept, instrument for social analysis' (MacIntyre 1998i, 258). Clearly, in this period MacIntyre thought that Marx provides no intellectual resources at all for the development of an adequate approach to ethics or for a critique of existing society. Presumably for this reason he turned to an alternative intellectual source as a potential basis for a *non-Marxist* approach to ethics and for a non-Marxist critique of existing society, namely, the philosophy of Aristotle.

Four things, in particular, must be noted in connection with MacIntyre's views in this middle period. The first is that he sought to develop an alternative approach to ethics which bypassed the ideas of Marx and Marxism altogether. The second is that MacIntyre associated this project with the philosophy of Aristotle. The third is that he evidently did not think that the ethical views of Marx and those of Aristotle were connected to one another. He did not think of Marx as being an Aristotelian thinker. And finally, if it is true that at this time he considered his own ethical position to be in any sense critical or even revolutionary, that is to say, some kind of 'revolutionary Aristotelianism', then this could not possibly have been because of any associations which it might have had with Marx and Marxism. For in MacIntyre's opinion, no such associations existed.

The Later MacIntyre: Aristotle *and* Marx

One of the interesting developments in Marx scholarship from the 1980s onwards has been an exploration of the intellectual relationship, not between Marx and Hegel, but rather between Marx and Aristotle, in respect of a number of issues, including philosophy (ontology and metaphysics) (Meikle 1985), economics (McCarthy 2003), sociology (Meikle 1997), psychology (T. Burns 2000), and above all, for present purposes, ethics (T. Burns 2005). So far as ethics is concerned, the general thrust of this work has been to suggest that there is an ethic which might be associated with Marx and Marxism, and that this ethic is in some sense Aristotelian. Commentators, however, have disagreed over the question of what exactly this involves (cf. T. Burns 2005).

It is interesting to consider MacIntyre's views on ethics in light of the above. Given that MacIntyre has, at different times, been enthusiastic about both Marx and Aristotle, one would expect him to be sympathetic to this project. In fact, however, throughout much of his intellectual career (from his early twenties to his mid-sixties) he had little contact with it. In his early career, when he was concerned with Marx and ethics, he said nothing about Aristotle in this connection. And in the later part of his career, when he developed his thinking about Aristotle and 'virtue ethics', he had stopped writing about Marx and Marxism. Between the early 1950s and the mid-1990s, in short, MacIntyre had little or no interest in exploring the relationship between the ethical thought of Marx and Aristotle.

This is not true, however, of Macintyre's work since the mid-1990s, in which he has returned to his Marxist roots by attempting to show that the Aristotelian ethics which he defends in *After Virtue* is compatible with a certain reading of Marx's views on ethics. Thus, for example, in 'The *Theses on Feuerbach*: A Road Not Taken' (1994), MacIntyre refers to 'the defeat of Marxism', which has, he maintains, been '*our* defeat' (MacIntyre 1998f, 234). 'Marxism', MacIntyre continues, 'was self-defeated and we too, Marxists and ex-Marxists and post-Marxists of various kinds, were the agents of our own defeats'. The point is, MacIntyre insists, 'first to understand this' and then 'to start out all over again' (MacIntyre 1998f, 234).

Similarly, in an essay entitled 'Philosophy, Politics and the Common Good' (1997), MacIntyre states that although his own views have 'drawn systematically on the conceptual and argumentative resources of Thomistic Aristotelianism', it should nevertheless be noted how much this account is 'at odds with Aristotle himself'. For often, MacIntyre claims, Aristotle 'needs to be corrected, on the basis of his own principles'. MacIntyre argues that 'some of the positions for which I have contended in this paper constitute just such a correction'. He concedes, however, that 'still more is needed by way of correction'. And he concludes by accepting that 'a philosopher who can provide much of what we need at this point is Marx, Marx himself, that is, rather than those Marxist systems that have been apt to obscure Marx' (MacIntyre 1998g, 250–51).

One might have expected, in the light of these remarks, that MacIntyre would have sought to develop a 'virtue ethics' reading, not just of Aristotle, but also of Marx. In fact, however, he has not made any *direct* effort to do this, although some of those who have explored the relationship between the ethical views of Marx and Aristotle *have* attempted to do so (Brenkert 1983, 17, 19–21, 89, 129; Blackledge 2008b). Rather, what MacIntyre himself has done is to explore the relationship between the Aristotelian notion of 'the common good' and the approach to politics which he associates with Marx and Marxism, on the one hand, and what he refers to as social 'practices', on the other (MacIntyre 1998g, 235–54; 1985a, 187–203).

In 'Philosophy, Politics and the Common Good', then, we find once again the idea of 'rereading' Marx which lies at the heart of MacIntyre's 'Notes from the Moral Wilderness', written over three decades earlier. On this occasion, though, it is not Hegel but *Aristotle* whom MacIntyre considers to be the source of inspiration for Marx. Thus, MacIntyre acknowledges his debt to Carol Gould's 'account of Marx's ontology' and especially 'its Aristotelian antecedents'. And he maintains that the 'contrast' between the type of activity associated with a 'practice' and that associated with 'civil society' 'is best expressed in Aristotelian rather than in Hegelian terms' (MacIntyre 1998f, 225), for 'Hegel's idiom is just not adequate to the task' (MacIntyre 1998f, 226).

Blackledge has noted that MacIntyre has moved away from the 'pessimism' of *After Virtue*. In so doing, he rightly suggests, MacIntyre 'has significantly reduced the theoretical space between himself and Marxism' and, therefore, has opened up 'the possibility of a renewed dialogue between his ideas and Marxism' (Blackledge 2005, 720). If MacIntyre's views in this latest phase of his intellectual development can be accurately characterised as a form of 'revolutionary Aristotelianism', as Knight has claimed (and, as noted above, MacIntyre has endorsed), then it might be thought that what makes it 'revolutionary' is precisely its renewed association with Marx and Marxism. In the next section I will consider whether or not this is the case.

Revolutionary Aristotelianism?

Is the Aristotelianism of the Late MacIntyre Revolutionary?

There is some evidence in favour of the contention that the late Mac-Intyre embraces a 'revolutionary Aristotelianism'; but there is also some evidence against it.

The Argument in Favor

Knight rejects the view, advanced by commentators who associate Mac-Intyre with communitarianism, that MacIntyre 'is a political conservative' (Knight 1998, 20). He maintains that it is 'profoundly mistaken to "read" MacIntyre as a conservative', and that 'the political conclusions he draws from the Aristotelian tradition are, on the contrary, revolutionary' (Knight 1996, 885). According to Knight, MacIntyre 'has always held that conflict rather than community must be the starting point for any Aristotelian politics within capitalism' (Knight 1998, 21). Similarly, MacIntyre himself has strongly objected to being associated with 'contemporary communitarianism', precisely because of its conservatism. For example, in 'Politics, Philosophy and the Common Good', he states that 'several commentators have mistakenly assimilated my views to those of contemporary communitarianism', a doctrine which 'tends to immunise institutionalised oppression from criticism' (MacIntyre 1998g, 235).

As Knight observes, the claim that MacIntyre's Aristotelianism has 'revolutionary' implications is associated with the idea of a social 'practice' and the distinction which MacIntyre makes between a 'practice' and an 'institution'. Setting aside, for the time being, the *difference* between 'practices' and 'institutions', we may state provisionally that for MacIntyre a 'practice' is a socially cooperative activity, based on a division of labour, that is oriented towards the production of some common or collective 'good', to which all the individuals involved are connected because they occupy the different social roles associated with the practice in question. So far, there seems to be no difference between a practice and a social institution. Indeed, if MacIntyre did not explicitly differentiate between them then, as Knight points out, one might erroneously conclude that MacIntyre's account of social practices is politically conservative—

an ideological defence of existing society and its institutions, along lines usually associated with the social theory of Hegel, with the sociology of Durkheim (T. Burns 2006), or with contemporary 'communitarianism'.

It is for this reason that MacIntyre *distinguishes* between practices and institutions. For example, in *After Virtue* he insists that practices 'must not be confused with institutions'. Although 'chess, physics and medicine are practices', it is 'chess clubs, laboratories, universities and hospitals' that are 'institutions' (MacIntyre 1985a, 194). In MacIntyre's thought, then, practices and institutions, although related, are not the same thing. For MacIntyre wishes to reserve the possibility of *criticising* existing social institutions, using the notion of a practice. Knight is right, therefore, to claim that MacIntyre's social theory does not provide a normative sanction for existing institutions.

What then, for MacIntyre, *is* the difference between a practice and an institution? MacIntyre explains this by making a distinction between 'internal goods' and 'external goods'. This is a complex distinction, which touches partly on the types of 'things' produced by those involved with practices and institutions, and partly on their motivation.

By internal goods, MacIntyre has in mind, in part, the 'goods' produced by the individual practitioners who are associated with a practice, for example, health in the case of the practice of medicine, or education in the case of the practice of education; and in part, those goods which accrue to practitioners in consequence of their involvement in the practice in question, especially those associated with the cultivation of the 'virtues'. According to MacIntyre, what motivates those involved in a practice, and what *ought* to motivate those involved in an institution, is not egotism or self-interest, but altruism or voluntary self-restraint from something like a sense of duty—that is, a concern not for one's own immediate good (perhaps erroneously conceived) but for the good of others, or for the common good, which is shared by all of the practitioners involved in that practice.

By external goods, which are associated with 'civil society' and with social institutions, MacIntyre has in mind such things as money, status, and power. As MacIntyre puts it, 'institutions are characteristically and *necessarily* concerned with what I have called external goods. They are involved in acquiring money and other material goods; they are structured in terms of power and status, and they distribute money, power and status as rewards' (MacIntyre 1985a, 194). Such goods and the self-interested motivation associated with them have no part at all to play in social practices, but, according to MacIntyre, they *do* have a significant part to play in social institutions.

One of MacIntyre's basic ideas is that, although the common good of a practice is shared by all of the individuals involved, nevertheless it is *not* reducible simply to 'the aggregate' of individual interests or 'goods' which 'are pursued in common' by those individuals. As MacIntyre puts it, the 'goods' or 'ends' of a practice are 'characterisable antecedently to and independently of any characterisation of the desires of the particular individuals who happen to engage in it' (MacIntyre 1998f, 225).

To summarise, for MacIntyre, practices and institutions are similar to one another in that they are based on a complex division of labour, with different social roles, in which the individuals who occupy those roles mutually cooperate in the production of some good. They differ from one another because of the specific nature of the relationship which exists between their members, especially in respect of their motivation. Those involved in a practice are oriented towards the internal goods of that practice and are motivated by altruism, concern for others, the sense of duty, and the common good. Those involved in an institution, or who think in institutional terms, are oriented towards external goods and are motivated by egotism, self-interest, greed, vanity, and ambition, in short, by their own individual or 'private' good (erroneously conceived). In the terminology of Ferdinand Tönnies, a practice is a *Gemeinschaft*, whereas a social institution is a *Gesellschaft*.

So far, we have considered practices and institutions as if they could be entirely separated from one another, and could exist independently of one another. One feature of MacIntyre's social theory, however, is his insistence that this is not the case. MacIntyre's views on this subject are not consistent, but the dominant position is that practices cannot exist on their own. Rather, they require institutional embodiment. Thus, a social institution is by definition an 'embodied practice', or a practice which has been brought into existence in a particular institutional form. Institutions, MacIntyre says, are the 'bearers' of social practices, and 'no practice can survive for any length of time', if indeed at all, 'unsustained by institutions'. An important implication of this is that practices are always 'vulnerable to the acquisitiveness' or to the 'corrupting power' of institutions (MacIntyre 1985a, 194). A vital question for MacIntyre (and Knight), then, is whether this corrupting power of institutions can be resisted.

As Knight observes in his essay 'Revolutionary Aristotelianism', MacIntyre's conclusion regarding this issue in *After Virtue* is 'notoriously pessimistic', namely, that 'what matters at this stage is the construction of local forms of community within which civility and the intellectual and moral life can be sustained through the new dark ages which are already upon us' (Knight 1996, 893; MacIntyre 1985a, 263). Knight's own conclusion is somewhat different. In his opinion, MacIntyre's discussion of practices and institutions can be appropriated by those who wish to develop a new form of institutional politics which is much more optimistic, indeed revolutionary, in its social implications.

According to Knight, in every social institution there is a conflict or tension between those individuals who identify with the underlying practice (the institution as perhaps it *ought* to be) and those individuals who identify with the institution as it is: a conflict which is paralleled by the different patterns of motivation, namely, duty and virtuous conduct on the part of the practitioners and self-interest (money, status, and power) on the part of the institution's 'managers'. Knight also maintains that 'if practices are not to be corrupted by the goods pursued by institutions then those institutions must always be subordinated to the goods internal to practices, which constitute the ends to which institutions should be considered means' (Knight 1996, 890). 'Institutions should be structured and run in accordance with the principles associated with the particular practice of which they are the bearer' (Knight 1996, 890).

In Knight's view, then, MacIntyre's social theory can be used to justify a form of politics which focuses on existing social institutions and on the abuse of power taking place within them. As Knight puts it, 'I suggest that the rationale of MacIntyre's social theory of practices is that the bases of these certain forms of community is not now to be found in *locality*, but, rather, in particular practices. Accordingly, the tasks for a politics in the Aristotelian tradition is to defend the rationality, ideals, creativity, and cooperative care for common goods of practices against institutional corruption and managerial manipulation, and to uphold internal goods of excellence against external goods and claims of effectiveness' (Knight 1996, 894, emphasis added).

Knight refers to such a politics as a politics of 'resistance' (Knight 1998, 23). It is, he says, a 'form of class politics', a 'new class war of attrition' between practitioners and managers, within which it is clear that 'those who have acquired money, power, and status' as the 'managers' of 'institutions' have 'an interest in maintaining the institutions and ideologies of manipulation' (Knight 1996, 895). Elsewhere, Knight argues that 'there is scope' for such resistance 'within factories, workshops, studios, laboratories, hospitals, schools and other institutions'. Indeed, in his view, 'it is now *only* in such discrete communities of practice, and in familial and bipartisan relations, rather than in more integrated communities of locality, that most people have the opportunity to cultivate virtue and practical reasoning', as MacIntyre understands them (Knight 1998, 23).

Knight and MacIntyre maintain that the ethical ideals which Aristotle associates with the life of the citizens of a *polis* can be thought of as applying today to social practices. But why do they consider such a politics 'revolutionary'? Because in Western advanced capitalist societies, most employed persons are tied to social institutions that do not conform to this Aristotelian ideal. Aristotle's political thought provides us, therefore, with a critical standard which we can use to evaluate existing institutions and find them wanting—perhaps even 'unjust' in one sense of that term. But, of course, to be entirely successful in our pursuit of a politics of this kind would require the destruction of all existing social institutions, and hence a radical transformation of the basic structure of existing society. Knight does not, however, discuss the practical issue of how this new form of class politics is to be carried out or how it might be organised.

The Argument Against

For the distinction between a practice and an institution to do its work as a part of a critical theory of society, given that MacIntyre maintains that all practices must take some institutional form, it has to be possible for us to differentiate between malign and benign forms of social institution—

the former being associated with a motivation on the part of the individuals involved towards the external goods of money, status, and power, and the latter being associated with a motivation informed by virtues such as justice, truthfulness, and courage. We cannot assume in advance that all social institutions are necessarily malign. Any such assumption would undermine completely the political project envisaged above. Knight, however, appears to assume that all institutions *are* necessarily malign, a view which he also attributes to MacIntyre, with some justification. For example, at one point MacIntyre maintains that 'institutions are characteristically and *necessarily* (emphasis added) concerned with what I have called external goods. They are involved in acquiring money and other material goods; they are structured in terms of power and status, and they distribute money, power and status as rewards' (MacIntyre 1985a, 194). In response to this, Knight argues that because for MacIntyre 'external goods are *necessary* to institutions' and because 'institutions are *necessary* to practices,' it follows that 'the tension between goods internal and external to practices is *ineradicable*' (Knight 1996, 890, emphasis added). From which, not surprisingly, Knight concludes that 'MacIntyre is no *utopian* thinker (Knight 1996, 890, emphasis added).

These remarks are both unequivocal and interesting. Knight explicitly states that for MacIntyre, there can be no practices without institutions; and there can be no institutions which are not associated with the external goods mentioned earlier. There can, therefore, be no benign institutions. *All* practices are inevitably tainted because in order to exist at all they must be given a particular institutional form, and because all institutions are necessarily associated with the pursuit of wealth, status, and power. The problem, however, is that on this view it is not possible for the practitioners associated with a practice which has been embodied in a particular institution ever to be victorious in the power struggle between themselves and their managers. For victory in this struggle would amount to getting rid of the managers, which would, in turn, amount to the destruction of the institution in question. At this point, however, the view advocated by Knight, and endorsed by MacIntyre, is caught on the horns of a dilemma. For either the institution in question must be replaced by another institution, also oriented towards the external goods of wealth, status, and power (which evidently would not solve the problem);

or, alternatively, it must be replaced by a pure, uncorrupted practice. However, this second solution to the problem fares no better than the first. For it presupposes that it is possible for a practice to exist independently of any particular institutional form—but this is something which MacIntyre's remarks about the relationship between practices and institutions rule out in advance. As we saw earlier, one of MacIntyre's assumptions is that practices must always exist in some institutional form or other. In other words, for MacIntyre a practice is an 'abstraction' in the Hegelian sense. As Knight concedes, this account 'offers no blueprint for a society in which institutions are subordinated to practices' (Knight 1996, 896), and it is for precisely this reason that MacIntyre cannot be considered to be a utopian thinker (Knight 1996, 890).

This analysis leads to a pessimistic conclusion regarding the possibility of radically transforming existing institutions. It implies that those practitioners who actively involve themselves in institutional politics of the kind envisaged by Knight, and endorsed by MacIntyre, must always be fighting a rearguard action. The ultimate aim of such a politics must be either the abolition or radical reform of existing institutions and their replacement either with new or benign institutions or with pure, unadulterated practices. But this is the one thing that MacIntyre's social theory appears to assume is impossible. We are left, therefore, with a political struggle *against* social institutions, which is also a political struggle *within* them. On MacIntyre's account, it appears that those who are involved in this struggle must take for granted the existence of the very institutions against which they are struggling. In order for this outcome to be averted, it would be necessary to significantly qualify or clarify some of the assertions which MacIntyre makes about the nature of social institutions, and about the relationship which exists between practices and institutions.

Are the Views of the Late MacIntyre Marxist?

We have seen that in his 'The *Theses on Feuerbach*: A Road Not Taken', MacIntyre drew attention to the similarities between his own Aristotelianism and the views of Marx, especially ones associated with their views of human nature and their emphases on the notion of 'the common good'. As Peter McMylor has noted, this suggests that an appropriate label with which to characterise McIntyre's most recent views would be that of 'Aristotelian Marxism' (McMylor 1994, 46–73). Such a characterisation is supported by MacIntyre's remarks about the connection between the type of institutional politics referred to above and contemporary capitalism. Thus, for example, MacIntyre states that there are 'types of practice' which have been 'socially marginalised by the self-aggrandising and self-protective attitudes and activities characteristic of developing capitalism, types of practice alien to' what MacIntyre refers to as 'the standpoint of civil society' (MacIntyre 1998f, 223). Statements like this have led commentators like McMylor to conclude that it seems 'unmistakably the case that MacIntyre believes that Aristotelianism is incompatible with capitalism' (McMylor 1994, 44).

But there are also significant differences between the views of the late MacIntyre and those of Marx. In my view, the existence of these differences casts doubt on the claim that the late MacIntyre's views are best thought of as a form of Aristotelian Marxism. One such reason is the fact that MacIntyre's discussion of the social practices and their relationship to institutions is presented in *After Virtue*, a work in which, as we have seen, the views of Marx have very little part to play. MacIntyre refers to Marx hardly at all in this text, and when he does, he is critical of him. The theoretical underpinnings for the type of institutional politics referred to by Knight are provided in this text, but they are provided independently of the views of Marx and Marxism. This indicates that the conceptual connection between the two is a weak rather than a strong one.

A second reason is the fact that MacIntyre's notion of external goods has strong associations with the sociology of Max Weber. The goods in question—wealth, status and power—are obviously Weberian, and play an important role in Weber's account of social stratification. Weber is also the sociologist par excellence of bureaucracy in relation to the transition to modernity and the rise of the modern state. It is obvious that there is a strong connection between this aspect of Weber's sociological thought and the views of MacIntyre. Indeed, if we associate MacIntyre's latest views with a form of revolutionary politics, then those views might be seen as a form of inverted Weberianism. MacIntyre accepts Weber's analysis, but hopes to avoid his pessimistic conclusions regarding the 'iron cage' of bureaucracy in modern society. Needless to say, there is very little discussion of the phenomenon of bureaucracy in the writings of Marx. In particular, there is no discussion of bureaucracy as a source of political power and as a form of political oppression in its own right in modern society. Nor is there any serious discussion in MacIntyre's writings of the origins of those social institutions, the power of which he thinks ought to be resisted, specifically in relationship to the development of capitalism.

Following Weber, MacIntyre hints at times that *bureaucracy* and not *capitalism* is the fundamental problem. This focus on bureaucracy and social institutions as independent sources of social and political power, and on a form of politics associated with this phenomenon, has an affinity with the concerns, not so much of Marxism, but of classical anarchism. Despite Knight's dismissal of contemporary poststructuralism (Knight 1998, 26), it also has an affinity with the social and political theory of Michel Foucault, which has been characterised by Todd May as a form of 'poststructuralist anarchism' (May 1994; 1989; Call 2002; Newman 2001). For one of Foucault's principal concerns, throughout his life, was to explore the various institutions of contemporary society as the *loci* of a particular form of power and associated political oppression. And the issue of whether it is possible for there to be such a thing as benign social institution lies at the heart of Foucault's view, developed just before he died, that we might formulate a new kind of ethics based on the notion of the 'care of the self' (Foucault 1994).

Are the Views of the Late MacIntyre Revolutionary Because They Are Marxist?

I have indicated that I would address three questions. First, are the views of the late MacIntyre revolutionary? Second, are they Marxist? And third, are they revolutionary because they are Marxist? So far as the first question is concerned, we have seen that there is some doubt about the claim that they constitute a form of *revolutionary* Aristotelianism. They are certainly Aristotelian, but it is less clear that they are revolutionary. We also saw that those views might be reformulated so that the application of this label has a more obvious justification. So far as the second question is concerned, I have argued that although there are affinities between the views of the late MacIntyre and those of Marx, which are highlighted by Mac-Intyre himself, nevertheless there are also significant differences. These lead me to conclude that the connection between MacIntyre's 'revolutionary Aristotelianism' and Marxism is much weaker than some commentators think. Finally, with respect to the third question, it is tempting to say that if the views of the late MacIntyre are indeed revolutionary, then this is not *because* but rather *despite* any associations which they might have with Marxism. However, this would not be fair. It would be more accurate to say that the type of critique of existing social institutions which is hinted at by MacIntyre, and more fully developed in the writings of Knight, can be seen as an important *supplement* to those of Marx and Marxism. They might be said to contribute towards filling a gap in the critique of existing society traditionally offered by Marxists. There is no reason for thinking that this kind of social analysis and the kind of institutional politics associated with it is incompatible with the traditional concerns of Marx and Marxism.

4

Two Cheers for Enlightenment Universalism

Or, Why It's Hard to Be an Aristotelian Revolutionary

ALEX CALLINICOS

Escaping Marxism

The relationship between Marxism and the philosophical project—or succession of projects—pursued by Alasdair MacIntyre has always been an intimate one. This was most obviously true during MacIntyre's own Marxist phase, roughly from the early 1950s to the late 1960s. But even after he parted company with Marxism, the relationship remained a close one. Is it, as his old comrades in the Communist Party and the Socialist Labour League might have asked, an accident that *After Virtue*'s famous conclusion summoning 'another—doubtless very different—St Benedict' to rescue us from our moral anarchy is preceded by a discussion of Marxism? MacIntyre argues that '[a] Marxist who took Trotsky's last writings with great seriousness . . . would now see no tolerable alternative set of political and economic structures which could be brought into place to replace the structures of advanced capitalism. This conclusion agrees of course with my own' (MacIntyre 1985a, 262–63).

Here MacIntyre reveals his deep acquaintance with the Trotskyist tradition. Trotsky's last major theoretical works, written in 1939–40 to deal with rebellious followers inside the Socialist Workers Party, where he predicts that the survival of the Soviet Union after the Second World War would amount to the checkmating of the entire Marxist project, are little known outside restricted Trotskyist circles (Trotsky 1973; cf. Haberkern and Lipow 1996; Callinicos 1990). It is highly unlikely that MacIntyre would have taken this line of attack in his concluding portrayal of our moral predicament had he not passed through such circles—the Socialist Labour League at the end of the 1950s and the International Socialists in the early to mid-1960s.

But MacIntyre's engagement with Marxism cannot be reduced to such biographical facts. It continues at two levels. The first is substantive. As various texts make clear—for example, MacIntyre's 1995 introduction to a new edition of *Marxism and Christianity*—he continues largely to endorse the Marxism critique of capitalism. More precisely, he puts forward 'a Christian critique of capitalism' that 'relies in key part, even if only in part, upon concepts and theses drawn from Marxist theory'. Indeed, he expresses a greater sympathy with the labour theory of value than he did when the book first appeared in 1953 (MacIntyre 2008q, 416). This does not sit very well with disparaging remarks such as the following: 'Marxism is not just an inadequate, but a largely inept, instrument for social analysis' (MacIntyre 1998i, 258). The apparent inconsistency between these two passages suggests a degree of ambivalence on MacIntyre's part about his relationship with Marxism, though I shall not consider the possible reasons for it here.

Secondly, and philosophically more important, MacIntyre sees an intellectual affinity between Marxism and the Catholicism where his intellectual journey has, at least for the time being, halted. To quote again from the 1995 introduction to *Marxism and Christianity*:

Marxism does not stand to Christianity in any relationship of straightforward antagonism, but rather, just because it is a transformation of Hegel's secularised version of Christian theology, has many of the characteristics of a Christian heresy rather than of non-Christian unbelief. Marxism is, in consequence, a doctrine with the same metaphysical and moral scope as Christianity and it is the only secular post-Enlightenment doctrine to have such a scope. It proposes a mode of understanding nature and human nature, an account of the direction and meaning of history and of the standards by which right action is to be judged, and an explanation of error and of evil, each of these integrated into an overall worldview, a worldview that can only be made fully intelligible by understanding it as a transformation of Christianity. (MacIntyre 2008q, 412)

The significance of Marxism goes even deeper than this. Not only are Marxism and Christianity, in certain respects, similar kinds of intellectual tradition; Marxism also advances a conception of philosophy—as the rendering intelligible of, and criticism of, the social practices through which our lives gain meaning—that, MacIntyre now believes, is required to vindicate Christianity. To quote from his 1995 introduction yet again: 'By 1953, I had acquired not only from my Marxist teachers, both in and outside the Communist Party, but also from the writings of R. G. Collingwood, a conception of philosophy as a form of social practice embedded in and reflective upon other forms of social practice' (MacIntyre 2008q, 417). MacIntyre refers to Marxist *Ideologiekritik* as an example of this way of doing philosophy. Indeed, what is striking about his distinctively Marxist writings is that they seek to articulate just such a conception of philosophy and, more broadly, of the relationship between theory and practice. This is particularly true of the three brilliant essays he wrote in 1958–60, 'Notes from the Moral Wilderness', 'Freedom and Revolution', and 'Breaking the Chains of Reason', where he expounds a broadly Hegelian conception of Marxism. It is a matter of great regret (as others have noted) that MacIntyre did not include these texts in the first collection of his essays, *Against the Self-Images of the Age* (1971). This omission has been remedied by Paul Blackledge and Neil Davidson in their collection of MacIntyre's Marxist writings, *Alasdair MacIntyre's Engagement with Marxism* (2008), which allows us to trace the development and waning of his engagement with Marxism.[1]

---

1. MacIntyre's 'Notes from the Moral Wilderness' was also republished in Knight 1998. Paul Blackledge has provided an excellent detailed account of MacIntyre's Marxist phase (Blackledge 2005).

It is remarkable that 'Notes from the Moral Wilderness', which seems to me the most philosophically important of the three essays, to a large extent foreshadows the diagnosis of the fragmentation of moral discourse in modernity that is the central theme of *After Virtue*. Thus, MacIntyre develops a critique of the autonomy of morality as affirmed by 'the ex-Communist turned moral critic of Communism' (MacIntyre 1998a, 31). This way of rejecting Stalinism remains complicit with it, for both presuppose the fundamental mistake of separating morality from desire:

> The believer in the autonomy of morality attempts to treat his fundamental moral principles as without any basis. They are his because he has chosen them. They can have no further vindication. And that is to say among other things that neither moral utterance nor moral action can be vindicated by reference to desires or needs. The 'ought' of morality is utterly divorced from the 'is' of desire'. (MacIntyre 1998a, 41)

Stalinism represents the other side of this divorce, an affirmation of the 'is' that amounts to a version of utilitarianism:

> The liberal critic accepts the autonomy of ethics; the Stalinist looks to a crude utilitarianism. The liberal accepts the divorce of morality and desire, but chooses morality; the Stalinist accepts the divorce and chooses desire, renaming it morality. But this desire that he chooses is not the desire to be fundamentally at one with mankind. It is desire as it is, random and anarchic, seeking power and immediate pleasure only too often. So one finds under Stalinism the moral belief in an ultimate justifying end, combined with immediate power-seeking. The two do not go as ill together as they seem to at first sight. Both the autonomy of ethics and utilitarianism are aspects of the consciousness of capitalism; both are forms of alienation rather than moral guides. (MacIntyre 1998a, 47)

The way out involves rediscovering the relationship between theory and practice.

The moral critic rejected Stalinism because it represented the historical process as automatic and as morally sovereign. And for moral values encapsulated wholly in history he substituted moral values wholly detached from history. To this he added a thorough distaste for general theorising. But if we bring out as central to Marxism the kind of points which I have suggested, may not this suggest a third alternative to the moral critic, a theory which treats what emerges in history as providing us with a basis for our standards, without making the historical process morally sovereign or its progress automatic? (MacIntyre 1998a, 40)

Developing such a theory requires us to overcome 'the rift between our conception of morality and our conception of desire'. For 'we make both individual deeds and social practices intelligible as human actions by showing how they connect with characteristically human desires, needs and the like. Where we cannot do this, we treat the unintelligible piece of behaviour as a symptom, a survival or superstition.' Reestablishing the connection requires an appeal to the Marxist conception of human nature,

> a concept which has to be at the centre of any discussion of moral theory. For it is in terms of this concept alone that morality and desire can come together once more. . . . For Marx the emergence of human nature is something to be comprehended only in terms of the history of class-struggle. Each age reveals a development of human potentiality which is specific to that form of social life and which is specifically limited by the class structure of that society. This development of possibility reaches a crisis under capitalism. For men have up to that age lived at their best in a way that allowed them glimpses of their own nature as something far richer than what they themselves lived out. Under capitalism the growth of production makes it possible for man to re-appropriate his own nature, for actual human beings to realise the richness of human possibility. But not only the growth of production is necessary. The experience of human equality and unity that is bred in industrial working-class life is equally a precondition of overcoming men's alienation from

this and from themselves. And only from the standpoint of that life and its possibilities can we see each previous stage of history as a particular form of approximation to a climax which it is now possible to approach directly. (MacIntyre 1998a, 45–46).

'Notes from the Moral Wilderness' allows us to measure at once the proximity and the distance between the Marxist and the post-Marxist MacIntyre. As for proximity, (1) by 1959 MacIntyre is already portraying late-capitalist moral culture as oscillating between a foundationless universalism and a utilitarianism that all too easily collapses into a tool of power; and (2) the philosophical basis for the critique of this culture requires a form of theoretical reflection in which the moral standards governing the critique are drawn out of our social practices rather than descending supposedly from nowhere. This second element plainly foreshadows the account of the virtues as dispositions to seek the goods internal to practices in *After Virtue* and the exploration of tradition in *Whose Justice? Which Rationality?*

But if the Marxist MacIntyre has already come up with the idea of socially embedded and historically situated reflection as the answer to our moral anarchy, his precise characterisation of that reflection is profoundly removed from the descriptions found in his later works. For that reflection took the form of Marxism, conceived as the theoretical articulation of the practice of the industrial working class whose 'experience of human equality and unity' is 'a precondition of overcoming men's alienation from this and from themselves'. But that the working class can play this kind of exemplary role and thereby, in overthrowing a capitalism doomed irretrievably to crisis, at once liberate themselves and humankind as a whole is something that MacIntyre progressively ceases to believe in the course of the 1960s.

Part of the interest of Blackledge's and Davidson's collection is that it allows us to trace the process through which MacIntyre abandoned this belief. A key step seems to be represented by 'Prediction and Politics', published in *International Socialism* in 1963, where he offers an early version of his argument in *After Virtue* that law-like generalisations are unobtainable in the social sciences because human beings can learn from their experience and invent new concepts that fall outside the scope of these generalisations. But this initial variant is framed as a kind of immanent critique of Marxism and in particular of its claim that tendencies towards crisis and revolution are inherent in the capitalist mode of production. Thus, MacIntyre observes, capitalists responded to the Great Depression of the 1930s by developing a much greater reliance on economic planning:

> Thus, economic and sociological self-consciousness did enter the system. If capitalists had behaved in the 1940s and 50s as they did in the 20s, the apparently mechanical laws of the economy would have issued in a slump. But there are no longer slumps for the same reason that the pig-cycle [i.e., fluctuations in supply and demand for pork] is no longer with us: the changed self-consciousness of the participants. More than this, however, the capitalist class have confronted a working class which has not moved in the least towards a revolutionary consciousness of the kind predicted by Marx and Engels. (MacIntyre 2008o, 258; cf. 1985a, 84–95 and 1971h)

In a very interesting, previously unpublished text delivered as a lecture to an IS Day School in 1962, MacIntyre elaborates on the last assertion quoted, by offering a detailed portrait of the British working class in the contemporary Age of Affluence—increasingly skilled, but also fragmented, privatised, and depoliticised. At the time, he sketched out a programme of demands that would lead to a re-politicisation of the working class, but it is hardly surprising that this diagnosis eventually led him away from Marxism altogether (MacIntyre 2008p).

There are fairly obvious responses that a Marxist could make to MacIntyre's substantive criticisms. Capitalism looks a lot less planned today, after the great financial crash of 2008, than it did during the Long Boom of the 1950s and 1960s. Moreover, the working class forged in that boom proved to be far more capable of generalised militancy in the late 1960s and early 1970s than MacIntyre's analysis implied, even though it was, alas, eventually crushed under the Reagan-Thatcher juggernaut. But, for all the critical intelligence and detailed grasp that MacIntyre's social analyses display, the pursuit of this kind of discussion—part, of course, of a much larger and apparently unending debate about Marxism as so-

cial theory and political practice—seems less interesting than considering the significance of MacIntyre's work as a moral philosopher for those
seeking to continue the Marxist tradition.

Meta-ethical Dilemmas

One way to approach this topic is to note that it is difficult for a Marxist to read *After Virtue* and MacIntyre's other later writings without a
strong sense of ambivalence (perhaps mirroring MacIntyre's own apparently conflicted attitude to Marxism). On the one hand, these works
remorselessly target the dominant forms of moral reflection in liberal
capitalist society and subject them to a form of critique that resonates
with Marxist *Ideologiekritik* for the very simple reason that MacIntyre,
as we have seen, continues to understand philosophy as 'a form of social
practice embedded in and reflective upon other forms of social practice'. On the other hand, MacIntyre now includes Marxism in this critique, not simply because of the kind of substantive claims cited above,
but because, morally, Marxism offers merely another version of the
reigning anarchy.

Another way of putting it is that, whereas in 'Notes from the Moral
Wilderness' MacIntyre thought that Marxism (or rather the anti-Stalinist
Marxism that he had embraced through his involvement in the Trotskyist movement) was exempt from and indeed offered a way out of the
oscillation between liberal universalism and Stalinist utilitarianism, in
After Virtue he regards it as simply a symptom of this oscillation. Thus
he writes, 'in all those crises in which Marxists have had to take explicit
moral stances . . . Marxists have always fallen back into relatively straightforward versions of Kantianism or utilitarianism' (MacIntyre 1985a,
261; cf. 2008p). I think that MacIntyre is almost right about this. He is
wrong, first of all, in omitting a third party, one who looms very large
in the development of his own thinking, namely, Aristotle. Secondly, I
think that the oscillation, whichever philosophical traditions it occurs
between, is less a sign of epistemic disintegration than a register of the
theoretical sources out of which a satisfactory moral philosophy has to
be constructed.

MacIntyre's reduction of Marxism to a symptom of moral anarchy is only one way in which morality presents itself as a theoretical problem for Marxists. Another, probably more influential because it emerged from arguments among practising Marxists (so to speak), was the debate active in the 1970s and 1980s on Marx and justice. I take the main positive finding of that debate to be, as Norman Geras put it in his definitive critical survey of the problem, that 'Marx did think capitalism was unjust but he did not think he thought so' (Geras 1985, 70). In other words, the most coherent and defensible version of what Marx says about capitalist exploitation implies a transhistorical principle of justice. The problem is not just that Marx lacked such a principle, but that he denied that such principles were possible, treating them as expressions of the dominant ideology in the prevailing mode of production. As Jon Elster put it, 'like M. Jourdain, he did not know how to describe correctly what he was doing; unlike him, he actually went out of his way to deny that the correct opinion was appropriate' (Elster 1985, 216; cf. Lukes 1985). So, if one accepts Marx's theory of capitalist exploitation, then one needs some kind of non-relativist meta-ethics that will allow us to live comfortably with transhistorical normative principles.

This is where the trouble starts. In Marx's time, as now, the two most influential meta-ethical theories are MacIntyre's main targets, Kantianism and utilitarianism. For reasons that resonate with the arguments of both the Marxist and the post-Marxist MacIntyre, Marx himself believed that both these theories are deeply implicated in distinctively bourgeois ways of thinking. The reasons why this belief is plausible are more obvious in the case of utilitarianism, where even the most sophisticated contemporary versions equate the good with the satisfaction of desire. This offers no scope for critical reflection on what kind of desires one should have—an exclusion that is, to say the least, congenial to late capitalist consumerism. Kant, by contrast, focuses on the right, which is what is implied by universal moral principles. But critics have long pointed out that the Kantian categorical imperative collapses into the dilemma that these principles are either without content or depend on smuggling in substantive assumptions. Georg Lukács argued in *History and Class Consciousness* that this type of scission between form and content, with which Hegel had already reproached Kant, is a distinctive figure of bourgeois ideology.

Many Marxists seeking to find a place for the ethical have therefore rebounded onto Aristotle. His equation of the good with well-being, which is conceived as dependent on the virtues—dispositions that, as MacIntyre brings out in *After Virtue,* both seek and help constitute it—seems to resonate strongly with Marx's evocations of human flourishing, from his *Economic and Philosophic Manuscripts of 1844* to his 'Critique of the Gotha Programme'. Terry Eagleton, who calls Marx 'a closet Aristotelian of sorts', is probably the most prominent contemporary theorist who has sought to draw on Aristotle in order to give Marxism the moral foundation that it requires but lacks (Eagleton 2003, chs. 5 and 6, quotation on p. 123; 2007).

A failure to register the Aristotelian resonances of certain passages in Marx's writings is symptomatic of a larger defect of the MacIntyrian critique of Marxism. Thus, in expounding MacIntyre, Kelvin Knight writes: 'What was wrong with Stalinism is that it substituted the coercive and regulatory power of the state for the self-activity of workers. What is wrong with orthodox Marxism is that it sustains no objection to such a substitution' (Knight 2007, 168). At one level this assertion is so demonstrably false as almost to obviate comment. If by 'orthodox Marxism' Knight means the classical Marxist tradition that the Trotskyist groups in which the young MacIntyre participated sought to continue, a central tenet of this tradition has been the reaffirmation of Marx's conception of socialism as the self-emancipation of the working class and of socialist revolution as a process directly *against* the modern bureaucratic state (cf. Callinicos 1983; Draper 1977–90). If the thought is that Marxism's failure to develop an adequate approach to ethics helped to lead it to collapse in practice into a reliance on this state, then the case is an arguable one, but it still fails to give proper weight to those Marxists who resisted this collapse. Trotsky's discussion of morality in *Their Morals and Ours* may be unsatisfactory, but he still died fighting Stalinism (cf. Callinicos 2007, 28–36). Part of the problem with homing in on such texts is the tendency to exaggerate their overall theoretical significance. Their manifest inadequacy is symptomatic of the failure of the classical Marxists, because of their acceptance of a relativist meta-ethics, to devote serious intellectual resources to philosophical reflection on moral thought. But this failure and the mistakes it involved coexist with substantive judgments that entail important ethical commitments. This is true of Marx's theory of exploitation, as I have suggested above, and similarly for the themes of fulfillment through labour and of proletarian self-emancipation, which can be interpreted as pulling in an Aristotelian direction (cf. Gilbert 1981a; Miller 1989).

But attractive though Aristotelian virtue-ethics undeniably is, and resonant as it is with themes in Marx, it suffers from serious defects. I mention three of these, in the form of questions:

- As MacIntyre himself asks in *After Virtue,* can Aristotle's conception of well-being be detached from his teleological biology (MacIntyre 1985a, 162)?[2]
- Can the notion of well-being also be rescued from the approved list of activities (generally those of a cultivated Athenian gentleman) with which Aristotle equates it (Griffin 1986, ch. 4)?
- Is the exclusion of women and slaves from the full practice of the virtues merely a scope-limitation that can be lifted without significant impact on the rest of Aristotle's ethics (MacIntyre 1967, ch. 7)?

MacIntyre is, of course, now committed to the claim that these limitations can be overcome and indeed that 'the fruitful correction of these inadequacies and mistakes' is 'best achieved by a better understanding of Aristotelian theory and practice' (MacIntyre 2006l, 156). Thus he seeks to rescue Aristotle from his treatment of women and slaves: 'the claim that in the best kind of *polis* the distribution of public offices and the honouring of achievement will be in accordance with excellence, that is, with virtues, is independent of any thesis about what kinds of persons are or are not capable of excellence' (MacIntyre 1988a, 105). I have always been deeply uncomfortable about this type of defence of Aristotle. Hence I am dubious about the very idea of 'revolutionary Aristotelianism' that Knight has used to characterise MacIntyre's project (Knight 2007, ch. 4).

---

2. The Thomism that MacIntyre embraced subsequent to *After Virtue* has led him to become more sympathetic to both teleology and the integration of an understanding of our biological constitution into moral thinking: see, respectively, MacIntyre 1998e; 1999a.

To deny certain categories of human being the ability fully to practise the virtues is not just an accidental limitation of a theory's scope, but reveals a profound moral flaw in that theory, which requires its drastic reconstruction. As a Christian, MacIntyre seems indifferent to the potential egalitarian significance of the doctrine of grace: arguably, John Rawls offers a secularised version of this doctrine when he argues that justice must be disjoined from moral desert.[3]

The Aristotelian approach, by contrast, seems to tie the moral claims that others make on us to the extent to which they have demonstrated their own capacity for excellence through the contributions they make to us and to the political community that they and we share.[4] It is interesting to see how MacIntyre in *Dependent Rational Animals* (a splendid book from which there is much to be learned) seeks to reframe his account of the virtues in a way that avoids the anti-egalitarian consequences of the Aristotelian approach. What we owe each other emerges from our place in 'networks of giving and receiving' that start in our infancy, when we are no more (but no less) than other animals. MacIntyre argues that '[t]he making and sustaining of those relationships is directed towards each becoming an independent practical reasoner. So the good of each cannot be pursued without also pursuing the good of all those who participate in those relationships.' This claim is already closer to the Marx of the *Manifesto* (for whom the free development of each is the condition of the free development of all) than it is to Aristotle. Similarly, when discussing our duty to strangers, MacIntyre draws on Aquinas's views on pity and charity. But the tensions produced by his attempt to widen Aristotelianism become evident when he discusses justice in a community:

---

3. Not that MacIntyre ignores grace altogether: thus, it figures in his account of Aquinas's transformation of Aristotle in *Whose Justice? Which Rationality?* The egalitarian significance of the Christian doctrine of grace is one of the main themes of Badiou 2003. Eagleton draws on another Christian concept, charity, in order to give Aristotelian virtue-ethics the universality it lacks (Eagleton 2003, 122, 167–71).

4. This formulation is heavily indebted to some very helpful comments on an earlier version of this essay by Russell Keat.

Between independent practical reasoners the norms will have to satisfy Marx's formula for justice in a socialist society, according to which what each receives is proportionate to what each contributes. Between those capable of giving and those who are most dependent—children, the old, the disabled—the norms will have to satisfy a revised version of Marx's formula for justice in a communist society, 'From each according to her or his ability, to each, as far as is possible, according to her or his needs'. (MacIntyre 1999a, 107, 129–30; see also 122–26 on our duties to strangers)

MacIntyre thus commends 'a way of life characterised both by effective appeals to desert and by effective appeals to justice, and so by justice to and for both the independent and the dependent' (MacIntyre 1999a, 130).

As a principled approach to justice, this is quite hopeless. Marx in his 'Critique of the Gotha Programme' introduces the needs principle in order to correct what he identifies as the 'defects' of the contribution principle. His two grounds for rejecting the latter as defective foreshadow the arguments of contemporary egalitarian philosophers, respectively, John Rawls and Amartya Sen. First, individuals' productive contributions reflect talents whose origins and exercise depend on aspects of their genetic constitution and social environment for which they cannot be held responsible: as Marx puts it, allocating goods to individuals according to their contribution to society treats 'the unequal individual endowments and thus productive capacity of workers as natural privileges'. Secondly, the contribution principle fails to take into account differences in individual needs—'one worker is married, another not; one has more children, another not, etc, etc.' (Marx 1989, 86–87). Another way of putting it is that, despite Macintyre's effort to highlight our dependence and vulnerability as centrally important moral facts about humans, he underestimates the extent to which independent practical reasoners are dependent in how they acquire and develop their capabilities and in the possession of needs that track the particularity of their circumstances. Certainly, his attempt to reconcile the contribution and needs principles illustrates the difficulties inherent in giving Aristotelianism an egalitarian spin. This is not to say that the concept of desert has no place in a conception of social justice—consider, for example, the efforts of contemporary egalitarian liberals to integrate the considerations cited by Marx with a proper notion of individual responsibility. These efforts, however, pull in a very different direction from that taken by MacIntyre (cf. Roemer 1996; Callinicos 2000, ch. 3; 2006, ch. 7).

Pursuing Universal Emancipation

One irreducible merit of the infamous Enlightenment project is its affirmation of our moral and political equality. There may be something distinctively bourgeois about Kant's categorical imperative, but it provides a philosophical articulation of the promise of universal emancipation made by the great bourgeois revolutions—at the English Putney Debates of 1647, for example, and in the American Declaration of Independence, the French Declaration of the Rights of Man and of the Citizen, and their like. Marxists have pointed to the tacit or explicit limitations of this promise, which have led, again and again, to its betrayal. But it does not follow that the promise of universal emancipation is reducible to these limitations, so that it is merely the ideological mask of capitalist domination. Indeed, especially in the *Manifesto* and the *Grundrisse,* Marx welcomes capitalism as a universalising force, which, through the destruction of established institutions and parochial barriers that it effects, has a powerful liberating potential. Consider, for example, the following passage from the *Grundrisse*:

> Thus the old view, in which the human being appears as the aim of production, regardless of his limited national, religious, political character, seems very lofty when contrasted to the modern world, where production appears as the aim of mankind and wealth as the aim of production. In fact, however, when the limited bourgeois form is stripped away, what is wealth other than the universality of individual needs, capacities, pleasures, productive forces etc., created through universal exchange? The full development of human mastery over the forces of nature, those of so-called nature as well as humanity's own nature? The absolute working-out of his creative potentialities, with no presupposition other than the previous historic development, which makes this totality of development, i.e. the development of all human powers as such the end in itself, not

as measured on a *predetermined* yardstick? Where he does not reproduce himself in one specificity, but produces his totality? Strives
not to remain something he has become, but is in the absolute movement of becoming? In bourgeois economics—and the epoch of production to which it corresponds—this complete working-out of the
human content appears as a complete emptying-out, this universal
objectification as total alienation, and the tearing-down of all limited, one-sided aims as sacrifice of the human end-in-itself to an
entirely external end. This is why the childish world of antiquity appears on one side as loftier. On the other side, it is loftier in all matters where closed shapes, forms and given limits are sought for. It
is satisfaction from a limited standpoint; while the modern gives
no satisfaction; or, where it appears satisfied with itself, it is *vulgar.*
(Marx 1973a, 487–88)

Earlier in the same manuscript Marx emphasizes that both vulgar modernity and childish antiquity are equally necessary—and, in themselves,
equally false—positions:

In earlier stages of development the single individual seems to have
developed more fully, because he has not yet worked out his relationships in their fullness, or erected them as independent social powers
and relations opposite himself. It is as ridiculous to yearn for a return to this original fullness as it is to believe that with this complete
emptiness history has come to a standstill. The bourgeois viewpoint
has never advanced beyond this antithesis between itself and the
romantic viewpoint, and therefore the latter will accompany it as legitimate antithesis up to its blessed end. (Marx 1973a, 162)

These passages show Marx at his most dialectical, in understanding
both the attractions of what we would now call the communitarian critique of capitalism, which rejects that system's 'total alienation' in the
name of 'closed shapes, forms and given limits', and the attractions of
capitalism, above all the immense expansion of human possibility that
it brings, while at the same time refusing to make either of these standpoints his own. As Fredric Jameson puts it, '[t]here is certainly an ethical
dimension to this analysis, but it takes the complex and dialectical form

of the evocation of capitalism in general in the *Manifesto,* where the latter's simultaneously destructive and progressive features are celebrated, and its simultaneous capacity for liberation as well as for wholesale violence is underscored' (Jameson 2009, 407).

In his Marxist days, MacIntyre occasionally registered the liberating aspect of capitalism:

> The paradox of bourgeois society is that it at one and the same time contains both the promise of greatly enlarged freedom and the denial of that freedom. In two directions, capitalism enlarges freedom by destroying bonds and limitations. It transforms nature and ensures an effective human domination of nature. More than that, it makes men assume that they are not bound down by nature. In pre-capitalist societies, one finds a sense of inevitability and fatality about natural catastrophes such as floods and famine. In capitalist societies, men learn that there is no inevitability here. Where they come to feel inevitability and fatality is not in nature, but in society. Yet even here there is a first promise of freedom. The 'Marseillaise' and 'John Brown's Body' are bourgeois hymns. The feudal ties of the serf and the ownership of the slave are destroyed by capitalism and in their place there stands the free labourer, free to sell his labour, if there is a buyer, or starve. (MacIntyre 2008g, 126)

But this theme is fairly muted in MacIntyre's Marxist writings and completely absent from his later work. Indeed, the latter focuses on 'closed shapes, forms and given limits'. Thus, he argues that 'what is most urgently needed is a politics of self-defence for all those local societies that aspire to achieve some relatively self-sufficient and independent form of participatory practice-based community and that therefore need to protect themselves from the corrosive effects of capitalism and the depredations of state power' (MacIntyre 2006l, 155). The importance of such local communities is that they offer the most favourable conditions for the kinds of practices that promote and are promoted by the virtues:

> The modes of social practice in some relatively small-scale and local communities—examples range from some kinds of ancient city and some kinds of medieval commune to some kinds of modern

co-operative farming and fishing enterprises—in which social relationships are informed by a shared allegiance to the goods internal to communal practices, so that the uses of power and wealth are
subordinated to the achievement of those goods, make possible a
form of life in which participants pursue their own goods rationally
and critically, rather than having continually to struggle, with greater
or lesser success, against being reduced to the status of instruments
of this or that type of capital formation. (MacIntyre 2006l, 156)

What is missing here is the universality that capitalism claims for itself and that Marx does not simply dismiss when pointing out that
the 'absolute working-out' of human 'creative potentialities' takes the
form, under capitalism, of 'a complete emptying-out'. Had MacIntyre
remained a Marxist, he might have come to reflect that this view of capitalism offers an opportunity to develop, as quoted above, 'a theory which
treats what emerges in history as providing us with a basis for our standards, without making the historical process morally sovereign or its
progress automatic'. He might have concluded that capitalism's universalising tendencies—its subversion of existing institutions and practices,
its construction of a world economy long before the term 'globalisation'
was coined, its mingling of peoples and cultures—are what creates the
context in which the advancing of universal political claims begins to
seem plausible.

Etienne Balibar has coined the term *égaliberté* to refer to the demand
for the maximal realisation of both liberty and equality, which, he argues, was raised by the great bourgeois revolutions (Balibar 1990). From
this perspective, the tacit or explicit exclusions present in initial versions
of this demand—of women, slaves, labourers, blacks, and others—can
be seen both as limitations revealing the class realities underlying the formulation of the demand, and as incitements to a process of permanent
revolution, as those who have been excluded constitute themselves as
political subjects and assert their claim to equality and liberty. Marxism
inserts itself into this process in affirming that *égaliberté* cannot be realised within the framework of capitalism. Socialist revolution might then
be defended as realising the promise of universal liberty and equality
that capitalism offers but cannot fulfill.

A historical illustration might help to bring out this idea. In an essay on Marx's *Theses on Feuerbach*, MacIntyre draws on Edward Thompson's *The Making of the English Working Class* to describe how the experience of industrialisation led groups of craft-workers to embrace 'physical force' Chartism. The point of this narrative for MacIntyre is to demonstrate that the defence of constitutively local practices is the source of authentic political action—which Marx was unable to grasp (MacIntyre 1998f). But Gareth Stedman Jones has offered an important reinterpretation of the Chartists, in particular arguing that they took over the political language of English democratic radicalism as it had developed since the seventeenth-century revolutions. 'The self-identity of radicalism', he maintains, 'was not that of any specific group, but of the "people" or the "nation" against the monopolisers of political representation and power *and hence* financial or political power'. Philosophically influenced by poststructuralism, he uses his study to refute what he calls the 'social interpretation' of Chartism as the expression of the rising industrial working class (Stedman Jones 1983, 104).

This interpretation, however, leaves out of account the explosive sociopolitical significance—well understood by the Chartists' contemporaries—of the adoption of a radical-democratic ideology by a movement composed overwhelmingly of factory workers (cf. Saville 1987). Furthermore, the case of Chartism illustrates Balibar's conception of *égaliberté*: however much they were prompted by the invasion and violation of their local practices by modern capitalist mass production, the workers who rallied to the Chartist cause were also embracing a political ideology and programme that demanded *universal* emancipation. Their central demand—male suffrage—captures precisely the radical change (giving the vote to propertyless labourers) and the limitation demanding further radicalisation (the exclusion of women) that Balibar regards as characteristic of the dynamics of *égaliberté*. As Stathis Kouvelakis has argued, Marx constituted his own distinctive politics through a growing recognition in the mid-1840s that the new working class being forged by industrial capitalism was the inheritor of the radical-democratic project that Kouvelakis identifies above all with the period 1789–94 in France, but which can be traced back to the English Revolution of the 1640s (Kouvelakis 2003).

Understanding the socialist project as at once a continuation of and a break with an initially bourgeois project of political emancipation allows Marxists to maintain the kind of dialectical stance that Marx exemplifies in the passages from the *Grundrisse* that I cited above: on the one hand, the failure of capitalism to fulfill its own promise is criticised; on the other hand, the promise itself provides this critique with its normative resources. But it would be a mistake to see this as simply an immanent critique of capitalism, because the critique only gains bite as a *normative* critique, rather than a mere demonstration of inconsistency, if the claim to universal equality and liberty is transhistorically valid. If it is not, why should it be a merit of socialist revolution that it realises the demand for *égaliberté* first raised in the epoch of the transition from feudalism to capitalism?

Here, as in the problem of how to give Marx's critique of capitalist exploitation moral foundations, we confront the difficulty of providing transhistorical normative principles with some sort of philosophical grounding. The constant intrusion of this difficulty underlines how hard it is to escape from Kant. For, however dubiously grounded in Kant's premises, the version of the categorical imperative that commands us to treat all humans as ends and not only as means provides a reasonably robust support for the more specific principles required to support a critique of capitalist exploitation.[5] Meta-ethically, we seem to be caught in a kind of infernal triangle constituted by Aristotle, Bentham, and Kant. The temptation to turn this into a square by invoking Hegel should be resisted. Hegel claimed to resolve just the kinds of tension between and within classical and modern thought that I have been exploring, but only by making them contributors to the developing self-consciousness of Absolute Spirit. This is too high a price to pay.

The fact that I include Bentham in the triangle may be surprising, since he is in many ways a much cruder thinker than Aristotle or Kant. But his claim that the satisfaction of desire is the benchmark of the good

---

5. G. A. Cohen has shown that Kant's principle does not support Robert Nozick's conception of self-ownership (designed, among other things, to banish any idea of capitalist exploitation) (Cohen 1995, ch. 10).

has the same kind of bourgeois ambivalence as Kant's categorical imperative. Undeniably, it refuses any purchase for a critical reflection on desires—what Charles Taylor has called 'strong evaluation'. But there is a leveling, anti-hierarchical element in the insistence that watching *American Idol* is as valuable as presenting an academic paper. MacIntyre tells us that 'although Aristotle's account of the hierarchal ordering of the best kind of *polis* rests on certain kinds of mistake, the best kind of *polis* will have a hierarchical order. This is because it has to school its citizens in the exercise of the virtues. The hierarchy of the best kind of *polis* is one of teaching and of learning, not of irrational domination' (MacIntyre 1988a, 105–6). To anyone less than enthusiastic about the prospect of such a 'hierarchical ordering', Bentham's insistence that there is a connection between the equality of desires and the equality of persons offers some kind of refuge, however unsatisfactory.

James Griffin, in his book *Well-Being*, suggests that what he calls 'a padded-out utilitarianism' may be the best way to rescue the concept of well-being from Aristotle's metaphysical elitism. Well-being, he argues, consists in the fulfillment of 'informed desires'—that is, 'desires that persons would have had if they appreciated the true nature of their objects' (Griffin 1986, 372, 11). Informed desire is *desire*—that is, it roots well-being in the lives of distinct persons and thereby breaks with the idea that the good consists in an approved list of activities. But, because it is *informed* desire, it transcends what Griffin calls the dualisms of subjective and objective, or of desire and understanding, by opening a space for reflection on the kind of desires we should have and—a closely associated idea—on the kind of persons we should be. This seems to me to be a fruitful direction in which to reopen the path that is indicated by MacIntyre, but ultimately not taken by him, of reconnecting morality and desire. But I have no illusions about the philosophical difficulties involved.

What about MacIntyre's alternative account of practical rationality? His argument seems to be that one reason why the Enlightenment project fails is that it advances a Utopian ideal of universal rationality defined in opposition to tradition. His conception of 'tradition-constituted enquiries', according to which 'the standards of rational justification themselves emerge from and are part of a history in which they are vindicated

by the way in which they transcend the limitations of and provide remedies for the defects of their predecessors within the history of that same
tradition', is intended to show how particular intellectual traditions can
achieve rational progress despite failing to conform to this Enlightenment ideal (MacIntyre 1988a, 7; cf. chs. 18, 19). In one sense, this conception is highly congenial to a Marxist, since a helpful way of thinking about
what being a Marxist entails is to think of it as carrying on a tradition.
But this example illustrates the problem with conceiving rational progress as strictly internal to a tradition (as seems entailed by MacIntyre's en-
dorsement of the doctrine of incommensurability). Granted that Marxism is only worth persisting with if it overcomes the problems it has
generated in terms consistent with its own constitutive principles and
criteria, such a reformulation (whatever it might involve) is unlikely to
command assent even among Marxists unless it involves addressing phenomena identified as counterexamples, not merely from its own standpoint but also from the perspective of rival traditions such as mainstream
liberalism and MacIntyre's Catholicism. Indeed, the list of phenomena
disputed both among Marxists and between them and their opponents is
familiar to all concerned (and indeed has already figured in this essay)—
among them, the persistence of capitalism, the character of contemporary class structures, and the Stalinist catastrophe. MacIntyre envisages
adherents to a tradition in 'epistemological crisis' switching to another
more successful tradition, but it is plausible to judge that such a move
is rationally justified, as he claims it can be, only if the failure of one tradition and the success of the other can be characterized at least partly in
terms common to both. The combination of internal and external criteria involved is nicely captured by Imre Lakatos, when he argues that a
new version of a scientific research programme constitutes progress over
its predecessors if (1) it is consistent with the heuristic defining the problems the programme addresses and the methods it uses; (2) it predicts
some novel facts; and (3) some of these predictions are corroborated
empirically (Lakatos 1978). Such an approach does not require that we
reject the idea that rationality must be understood (partly) relative to a
tradition; it is, however, inconsistent with the claim that traditions are
mutually incommensurable. But we should reject this claim anyway, for
reasons best given by Donald Davidson (Davidson 2001). The standards

of rational justification, like everything human, emerge and develop historically, but they could not perform their function if they were entirely specific to a tradition.

Resistance or Revolution?

The philosophical undertaking all too sketchily commended above seems to me worthwhile, in part for political reasons. Despite all the complications and deviations of MacIntyre's evolution over the past thirty years, the following affirmation from *After Virtue* still seems to sum up his position: 'that all morality is always to some degree tied to the socially local and particular and that the aspirations of the morality of modernity to a universality freed from all particularity is an illusion' (MacIntyre 1985a, 126–27). The version of Marxism I have been trying to defend in this essay would not simply reject the two-part claim made here. '[T]hat all morality is always to some degree tied to the socially local and particular' is implied by the conception of theory, as the rendering intelligible and the criticism of social practices, that is common to MacIntyre in his Marxist and post-Marxist phases. The key point of difference lies in the fact that Marxists do not find the dissolution of the local and particular that is effected by capitalism to be simply negative and destructive. For them, the expansion of human powers and the subversion of tradition it brings are potentially liberating.

As to the second part of the claim, what Marxism sees emerging from this process is not 'a universality freed of all particularity'. The whole point of the proletariat, according to both Marx and Lukács, is that its specific social location at the apex of capitalist exploitation and commodification allows it to become the agent of universal emancipation: it is the class particularity of the proletariat that makes it what Marx (after Hegel) called the universal class. This dialectic of universal and particular has been taken up in different ways by contemporary critical theorists, such as Alain Badiou, Pierre Bourdieu, and Slavoj Žižek (Callinicos 2006, §§2.1 and 3.3).

Of course, MacIntyre, with his Hegelian-Marxist formation, is perfectly familiar with these points. His problem with the conception of the proletariat as the universal class is that he finds it incredible, for the substantive reasons cited above. But even if one accepts (as I do not) that Marxism is exhausted as a social theory and a political project, the alternative of a 'politics of self-defence' of those 'local societies' where MacIntyrean practices might flourish seems unacceptably defeatist. Without simply repeating all the tedious clichés of globalisation, it is clear enough that the greater transnational economic integration and the neoliberal restructuring of societies over the past generation have significantly changed the political context in which projects of collective action are formulated and pursued.

It is also undeniable that neoliberal globalisation since the mid-1990s has provoked powerful, if unevenly distributed, movements of resistance. Some of these do take the form of a 'politics of self-defence of . . . local societies'. But this is not a satisfactory framework for approaching these movements. One important reason why this is so is that many of them seek to cooperate on a transnational or even transcontinental basis (for example, under the aegis of the World Social Forum). Such cooperation demands the framing of a political language in which shared grievances and, more ambitiously, common programmes and strategies can be formulated and assessed. It is hard to see how this language can avoid being one in which various kinds of universal claims are made, even if there are strong reasons (political, in the first instance) why they should be connected to particular collective experiences and social forms. The necessarily particularistic politics that MacIntyre's philosophy authorises certainly encompasses *resistance* to neoliberalism, but (contrary to the claims made for it by Knight, for example) it cannot even imagine *revolution,* since, by definition, that would involve a comprehensive social transformation—and how could *that* get underway without the constitution of a collective subject that conceives itself as the bearer of some kind of universal interest (Callinicos 2003, ch. 3)?

When I put this kind of criticism to MacIntyre at the conference for which this essay was originally written, he responded by conceding that he didn't know how to change the contemporary global economic order—adding that I didn't know, either. This was a splendid put-down, much enjoyed by all of us present. But it did not really address the questions that I had posed. First of all, the biggest problem is not *how* to change global capitalism but *what* to replace it with: the collapse of the Soviet Union seemed to remove from our horizons any alternative to the market economy. Secondly, I not only agree that I share MacIntyre's ignorance, but I embrace this condition. To claim to know in any detail what a future postcapitalist society would be like is both politically and morally dubious—an instance of the bureaucratic rationality that MacIntyre targets in *After Virtue* and that was implicated in so many twentieth-century disasters. That the pretension to such knowledge is dangerous—as Marx puts it in the *Theses on Feuerbach,* it divides society into two parts, one of which regards itself as superior to society—is a primary motive behind his rejection of Utopian socialism, over-stated though this is. Thirdly, if MacIntyre's thought is that we cannot say anything useful about the principles that might govern a desirable alternative to capitalism, then this is simply false. A growing body of literature seeks to outline how a democratically planned economy based on self-management by producers and consumers could replace the market as the principal form of economic coordination (Devine 1988; 2007; Albert 2003; Albert and Callinicos 2004; Callinicos 2003). But it seems clear that MacIntyre has lost interest in the search for a global alternative (literally and metaphorically) to capitalism. He may present this loss of interest as an empirical response to the failure of Marxism, but it seems to me that it goes deeper than that: one of the shaping drives of his philosophy is a principled preference for the local and particular. Thus, when outlining the conditions favourable to practice-based communities, he simply asserts without any supporting argument that 'the modern state cannot provide a political framework informed by just generosity necessary to achieve the common goods of networks of giving and receiving' (MacIntyre 1999a, 133). As much a claim about the scope of possible community as the implication of a justified critique of the modern bureaucratic state, this is less a falsifiable statement than a founding assumption.

It is, finally, hard to see how the political language needed to articulate and coordinate resistance to neoliberalism can develop without drawing on the normative resources of what MacIntyre disparages as the Enlightenment project. This is not simply because, as he and Marxists can agree, this project is ideologically dominant in the form of some variant or other of liberalism. Much more interesting is the tension inherent in it between promise and achievement—between *égaliberté* and actually existing capitalism. It seems both unnecessary and imprudent not to avail oneself of the critical leverage offered by this tension. Even if one thinks, mistakenly, that the Marxist project is cloud cuckoo-land, why give up on the demand that capitalism live up to its promise of universal liberty and equality? MacIntyre's own achievement lies in the philosophical acuity and historical intelligence with which he has exposed the constitutive failure of liberal capitalism. His limitation is that he has lost the feel for contradiction so fundamental to the greatness of his two old masters, Hegel and Marx.

5

MacIntyre and Modernity

SEAN SAYERS

At a time when many professional philosophers in the English-speaking world have all but given up the attempt to think critically and in large-scale terms about the modern world, MacIntyre's work is defiantly untimely; and it is greatly welcome for that. It is remarkably wide-ranging, comprehensive, and thought-provoking. MacIntyre has been described as a 'revolutionary Aristotelian', but that is only part of the picture (Knight 1996; MacIntyre 1998g, 235; Knight 2007, 102–221). His work draws on ideas not only from Marx and Aristotle, but also from analytical philosophy, philosophy of science, and Thomist sources; and it combines these all together to construct a critical response to the modern condition. This has generated important debates among thinkers in all these areas. It is a shame to spoil the party. Nevertheless, in this essay, I criticise MacIntyre's picture of modernity and argue that these different strands cannot satisfactorily be combined together: 'revolutionary Aristotelianism' is an unhappy mix.

I

MacIntyre's central philosophical work in ethics and social philosophy has been driven by an agenda that can be traced back to his contribution to the debates which created the New Left in the 1950s, in which Mac-Intyre was an important participant (Blackledge 2005; 2006b; 2007a; 2007b). The Communist movement in that period was dedicated to the Soviet cause and dominated by instrumentalist moral thinking of the sort portrayed by Arthur Koestler in *Darkness at Noon* (Koestler 1946). Whatever served the movement was justified by the argument that 'the ends justify the means'. Many on the left had ceased to believe that the communist cause could be justified in this way, and they had come to the conclusion that Soviet-style communism was morally and politically bankrupt. The most influential response among the New Left was to re-affirm the non-instrumental ethical ideals of Marxism. There was a flowering of Marxist humanist thinking, inspired by Kantian ideas (see Kolakowski 1978, vol. 3).

MacIntyre's response was different and distinctive (MacIntyre 1998a). He rejected both the instrumentalism of communist orthodoxy and the New Left Kantian humanist alternative. There is no basis on which the choice between them can be settled, he argued; they lead to an interminable series of moral disputes. This situation arises because both approaches separate values from facts, and ethics from social practice, and thereby cut away the ground of shared understandings that must exist if moral differences are to be resolvable. Instead, according to MacIntyre, we must start from the assumption 'that every morality including that of modern liberalism, however universal its claims, is the morality of some particular social group' (MacIntyre 1998i, 258).

In his subsequent work, MacIntyre has extended this picture. He has come to see the situation on the left as a microcosm of the wider predicament of morality in the modern world. For modernity creates conditions in which there are a number of different and conflicting, commonly held moral positions, and yet in which disputes between them have become unresolvable. MacIntyre's long-term project has been to describe and explain this moral condition as characteristic of modernity. He does so by contrasting it with the situation in premodern societies. This theme was first mapped out in his *Short History of Ethics,* it is developed more fully in *After Virtue,* and expanded still further in subsequent works (see MacIntyre 1988a).

The story starts with the premodern world of the ancient Greeks. They lived in relatively cohesive and united communities that revolved around shared understandings of social roles and responsibilities, and shared values in terms of which moral disputes could be adjudicated. MacIntyre develops the concept of a 'practice' to describe the character of such societies. Participants in a 'practice' share common values which are constitutive of it and which define goods that are internal to the practice itself. Moral values in such communities are embodied in the idea of the virtues, understood as excellences in the pursuit of such internal goods. To be virtuous is to fulfill one's social role well. In this way, values are related essentially to the social relations in which they are rooted.[1]

For MacIntyre, Aristotle is the greatest theorist of such practices. He defends the ideal of the ancient Greek polis as a rational political community in which moral differences can be resolved by rational discussion. The tradition of moral and political thinking which he founded continued, with changes and adaptations, to be central right through to the dawn of the modern era (MacIntyre 1994b, 288). In the modern world, however, fixed and given social roles and shared expectations have dissolved. Communities have been fragmented. These changes in the social order have gone together with a fundamental transformation of the role of morality in modern life. A set of shared understandings that can provide the basis on which to resolve moral differences no longer exists.

The Enlightenment involved the rejection of Aristotelianism, not only in the natural sciences but also in ethics and social thought. Enlightenment thinkers attempted to replace Aristotelian virtue ethics, based in practices involving shared understandings, with systems of thought in which values are to be justified through the use of universal reason alone. According to MacIntyre, this project has 'failed' (MacIntyre 2006m). The premodern social order has been destroyed, and with it the social basis that once existed for shared understandings and values. In the modern world we retain only the language and the idea of rational moral debate, but the social basis for it in the wider society has been lost: moral differences have become unresolvable.

In *After Virtue,* MacIntyre portrays modernity as the outcome of the fragmentation of earlier communities. The old social order has been

---

1. For the somewhat different conceptions of the virtues developed in the writings of Homer, Plato, and Aristotle, see MacIntyre 1967.

dissolved into a multitude of disconnected atomic individuals. In a number of works since then, however, he has developed a richer and more complex account of modern social relations. Even so, the view that there is no overall context of shared understandings or values, no overall community, remains a constant of his thought. Modern society is composed of a series of compartmentalised subgroups, each with its own roles and values. In different situations and in relation to different groups, the modern individual has different values and standards, detached from each other, without any essential relation or connection (MacIntyre 2006m).[2]

Few of these compartmentalised groups constitute 'practices' in MacIntyre's sense, or deserve the title of 'communities'. They lack any shared understandings of values, they do not have common conceptions of internal goods or of the virtues. They are governed rather by external ends, especially the end of money-making—the external end par excellence, in that it is a universal end, not specific to any particular practice (Plato 1987, Book 1; Hegel 1991). They are prey to the influence of the market and the overwhelming political power of the modern nation state. These have more and more become the ruling forces of modern life. Thus, in the modern world, genuine practices with shared commitments to internal goods are rare and embattled forms that can be preserved only in limited and isolated areas of activity. MacIntyre's favoured examples include small fishing crews, family farms, and academic communities of scholars (MacIntyre 2006l, 156; MacIntyre 1994b, 288, 302). But in most areas of life, money and power exercise a dominating influence, imposing a regime of external goods and instrumental values.

What is to be done? Though MacIntyre is profoundly critical of modernity, he is not at all optimistic about the possibility of change for the better in the future. However, he is not a conservative either, as is sometimes charged. Although his ideal of rational community is drawn from Aristotelian sources and is based on an idea of community derived from the ancient Greek polis, there is no suggestion in his work that he believes that we can or should return to that way of life. He thus gives a

---

2. For a thought-provoking defence of the compartmentalisation of modern life, see Fish 2007.

profoundly pessimistic account of our modern predicament (MacIntyre 1985a, ch. 18; 1984; Wartofsky 1984).

II

Although MacIntyre is a fundamental critic of modernity in this way, it is difficult to see how this brand of Aristotelianism can properly be described as in any sense 'revolutionary'. MacIntyre describes his philosophy as a form of 'utopianism'. Some see it as implying a 'prefigurative' form of politics. Given MacIntyre's pessimism, however, it is not clear how it can be utopian, or what politics it prefigures. Putting the issue of revolutionary credentials aside, what are we to make of MacIntyre's critique of the moral predicament of modernity? This is based on the premise that moral values are related to the social situation in which they are formed. This provides an illuminating and valuable method of approach for the critique of modernity and for an understanding of the modern liberal values. For these values too, he insists, emerge from the particular social relations of liberal modernity (MacIntyre 1998i, 258).

However, MacIntyre's specific account of liberal modernity and the modern moral predicament is more problematic. He portrays the development of modernity in what I shall argue is a one-sided way. He sees modernity as a purely negative phenomenon, as the outcome of the destruction of the earlier united form of community and the moral order based upon it. The communal practices on which the morality of the virtues was based are replaced by the purely external and instrumental ways of thinking of the market. In moral terms, as MacIntyre sees it, modernity is thus a purely negative and destructive phenomenon.

This picture is questionable. The impact of modernity has been more complex and contradictory than MacIntyre's analysis suggests. The destruction of the premodern community of shared understandings is, indeed, one aspect of the process. However, there is a positive side to these developments as well. The emergence of modernity has also involved the construction of a new social and moral order. It cannot be understood as a purely negative process of fragmentation and destruction. It also involves the creation of new forms of social relation and new—liberal—values connected with them: values of liberty, equality, individuality, and tolerance. It involves the development of a social order in which differences in many areas of life are relatively more tolerated and accepted, a world of greater individuality and liberty.

According to MacIntyre, the destruction and dissolution of traditional social relations creates the modern atomic individual separated from all communal relations and values. This is, indeed, the way things appear. As Marx observes, 'in this [modern] society of free competition, the individual appears detached from the natural bonds etc. which in earlier historical periods make him the accessory of a definite and limited human conglomerate' (Marx 1973a, 84). However, as Marx goes on to argue, these appearances need to be questioned. For modern society is, in reality, a highly developed and complex social order, and not, as MacIntyre suggests, the result of the mere fragmentation and dissolution of social relations.

> The more deeply we go back into history, the more does the individual . . . appear as dependent, as belonging to a greater whole. . . . Only in the eighteenth century, in 'civil society', do the various forms of social connectedness confront the individual as a mere means towards his private purposes, as external necessity. But the epoch which produces this standpoint, that of the isolated individual, is also precisely that of the hitherto most developed social . . . relations. The human being is in the most literal sense a *zoon politikon* [political animal], not merely a gregarious animal, but an animal which can individuate itself only in the midst of society. (Marx 1973a, 84–85)

The modern form of individuality and the liberal outlook associated with it are products of the world of liberal modernity, the world of the free market (i.e., capitalism) and the liberal state (Sayers 2007).

As MacIntyre rightly stresses, and as Marx of course also argues, these forces at the same time also restrict freedom and stifle the very forms of individuality that they create. However, my point is that their effects have not been entirely negative. And unless the contradictory character of their impact is grasped, it is impossible properly to understand or criticise them.

III

It will be said that MacIntyre acknowledges these points and does not, in fact, treat liberal modernity in purely negative terms as the mere absence of social relations and shared values, as I am charging. For example, MacIntyre has explicitly come to acknowledge that liberalism itself is a moral 'tradition' in which there is a measure of agreement and shared assumptions that, ideally at least, ought to be able to provide a framework for discussion and disagreement that can lead to the development of a shared tradition of values. Knight makes this point well in his account of MacIntyre's philosophy.

> Liberalism, having originally challenged the authority of tradition in the name of a universalising Reason, has now itself been transformed into a tradition. It is a tradition of reasoning that legitimates the institutions of state and capitalism and, in turn, is sustained by them. . . . We do not live after the fragmentation of tradition *per se* but after the displacement from dominance of one socially embodied tradition by another. (Knight 1998, 21)

However, what MacIntyre gives with one hand in this regard he tends to take back with the other. Even though he recognises that liberalism is a 'tradition', he treats it as an 'incoherent' tradition, as Knight goes on to add—a tradition in which shared values are lacking and in which moral disputes are interminable, and this is because it arises from a fragmented and compartmentalised social order.

MacIntyre describes liberal modernity as constituted by a series of 'agreements to disagree' (MacIntyre 1994b, 292). This is accurate enough, provided that both aspects of this description are properly acknowledged. However, MacIntyre's stress is typically placed on the disagreements and differences in modern life, rather than on the agreement also acknowledged in this description. The idea that modernity involves a set of 'agreements to disagree' implies a common structure of relations, in which individual freedom is tolerated and the resulting differences are accommodated. This is the positive side of what appears negatively as the fragmentation and compartmentalisation of liberal modernity (Hegel 1991, 220–39).

Even in the most liberal society, it should be added, the agreement to disagree operates within limits and applies only to particular issues. Moreover, such limits are not clear-cut or fixed; they are the subject of ongoing dispute. Debates about how these limits can be specified have been central to the liberal tradition of moral and political thought, as MacIntyre is aware: communitarians and liberals, supporters of capitalism and socialism, have been divided by their answers to these questions. Nevertheless, fragmentation and compartmentalisation of this sort—areas of liberty and privacy in which disagreement and an absence of shared understandings can prevail—are an essential feature of liberal modernity. And within the liberal tradition there has been broad agreement that liberty and tolerance of differences are of importance and value. That is to say, there has been broad agreement in the liberal tradition that the compartmentalisation that MacIntyre criticises should rather be cherished and protected (Mill 1962; Fish 2007).

This is what constitutes the value of tolerance, a value that has played a central role in liberal social thought. In a recent thought-provoking essay (MacIntyre 2006o), MacIntyre makes it clear that he, too, values tolerance and agrees with the common liberal view that some limits to tolerance are necessary. However, for MacIntyre, tolerance is a virtue primarily because it furthers rational discussion, its limits should be set accordingly. Tolerance, he maintains, should be subordinated to the end of fostering 'shared understandings' (MacIntyre 2006o, 223).

What MacIntyre envisages is suggested by his discussion of the university in *Three Rival Versions of Moral Enquiry*. Before reforms in the nineteenth century, university membership was subject to moral and religious tests, which excluded Catholics, Jews, agnostics, and others, and imposed a moral and religious consensus. 'The preliberal modern university was a university of enforced and constrained agreements' (MacIntyre 1990a, 230). Today, by contrast, there is no consensus, and the university has become a place with an 'institutional tolerance of limitless disagreement' (MacIntyre 1990a, 225). What MacIntyre advocates instead is the university as a forum where different traditions of enquiry would be *required* to argue with each other in an attempt to resolve their differences by rational debate. What he envisages is 'the university as a place of constrained disagreement, of imposed participation in conflict, in which a central responsibility of higher education would be to initiate students into conflict . . . in which the most fundamental type of moral and theological disagreement was accorded credit' (MacIntyre 1990a, 230–31).

The liberal notion is quite different. It advocates toleration so that there can be realms of *difference,* spheres of *non*-discussion, areas of *privacy,* 'compartments', if you like, where individuals and groups can hold their own views and pursue their own practices in their own ways, *without* having to justify them or conform to the values or understandings of others. For MacIntyre, this is a recipe for social fragmentation; whereas for the liberal, MacIntyre's insistence on 'shared understandings' and the rational resolution of differences can all too easily lead to intolerance. What from the one perspective is the fragmentation and compartmentalisation of modernity is from the other the toleration of differences. These are simply different sides of the same coin: different ways of seeing the same social phenomenon.

IV

I have been arguing that modern society is not the result of mere fragmentation. Rather, it has its own positive and distinctive structure. Similarly, the modern liberal individual is not a mere atom but rather the product of particular social conditions, and so too for liberal values.

The liberal philosophers of the Enlightenment, from Locke to Kant, thought that they were contributing to the creation of a form of society in which economic relations were founded on agreement and mutual contract, governed by a liberal democratic state whose authority was based on free consent. This state of affairs would lead to the realisation of the values of liberty and equality, and to a free and equal community in which moral disputes could be resolved by rational discussion and debate.

It is evident that these hopes have not been fulfilled in modern liberal societies. Modern societies are beset by conflicts and by real moral and political differences, which cannot be resolved in purely rational or philosophical terms (MacIntyre 1998g, 243). In this way, MacIntyre is right to say that the Enlightenment project has failed. The Enlightenment values of liberty, equality, and community have not been secured by the creation of modern liberal society. It seems evident that they cannot be realised by reason alone, as the philosophers of the Enlightenment hoped. The world created by their policies is not a world of reason, but rather the modern individualistic and compartmentalised sort of society described by MacIntyre and Marx. In such societies, as MacIntyre says, communities have been destroyed and life is increasingly dominated by money and political power. These are somewhat vague phrases, but what they refer to is clear enough. Marx describes it more specifically as capitalism (the dominance of the free market) and the form of political power that supports it: the bourgeois state.

For MacIntyre, the market and the state are purely coercive and negative forces which destroy the possibility of the sort of rational community in which alone a conception of the virtues can survive. As we have seen, he believes that such communities can now exist only in small embattled enclaves, walled off, insofar as is possible, from the forces that threaten to subvert and destroy them.

There is some truth in this account, but again, it is too one-sided: the picture is not as purely negative as MacIntyre suggests. The impact of modernity has been more complex and contradictory than MacIntyre allows (see Sayers 1998, 79–91). It may be the case that premodern communities involved the common values and shared understandings that MacIntyre celebrates. However, for the most part they were also aristocratic and hierarchical social orders. The advent of the market imposes an instrumental outlook, but it also brings liberation from the subordination and privilege of earlier societies. Relative to what it replaced, the market has an equalitarian impact. It introduces a system of social relations which allows for a degree of autonomy and individuality. Relative to the conditions in the premodern world, it constitutes, in some important respects, an advance.

However, this is not the end of the story. Although there are liberating and egalitarian aspects to modernity, particularly when judged in comparison with premodern conditions, it is also true that liberal society has failed to realise the promises that its Enlightenment architects held out for it. As the power of the market and the liberal state have increased, they have come, more and more, to restrict the very freedoms and negate the forms of equality that they created.

In this respect MacIntyre is right, the market and the dominant form of political power of liberal modernity have become increasingly malignant forces in the modern world, penetrating and perverting all areas of life, and threatening to corrupt and destroy communal practices and relations of trust and mutual understanding where they still exist. However, this does not necessarily mean that the hope of realising liberal values should be rejected, or that the Enlightenment project should be abandoned altogether as a failure. On the contrary, liberal modernity, which gave birth to the project of freedom and equality, has ultimately been unable to provide the conditions for its realisation. But these values and aspirations still remain. The Enlightenment project is unfinished. And the standpoint from which these judgments should be made is not that of a premodern Aristotelian idea of community, but rather of the possibilities for its realisation that are immanent in the present (Sayers 1998, 111–48).

V

To illustrate some of the points that I have so far been making in rather abstract and general terms, I will focus on a particular example: the academic community. For MacIntyre, this is a prime case of an area of life which can be and often is governed by shared understandings and by values that are internal to the practice of academic life itself. It seems to me that MacIntyre's picture of the academic world as a 'community of scholars' is rather idealised. It has not been much like that, at least within the span of my memory. In any case, there can be little doubt that in recent years the scholarly world has been increasingly threatened by instrumental values, by the external goods of money and power.

This threat is clear for all to see in the regime imposed on universities in Britain since 1992 by the Research Assessment Exercise (RAE), superseded in 2008 by the Research Excellence Framework (REF). Both are attempts to create artificial market conditions in the area of research funding. The research 'outputs' (i.e., publications), external research grants, and research activities of every participating department are graded by panels of 'experts' on a quantitative scale. The purpose of this massive operation is to provide criteria for allocating funds according to the standard of the work being produced.[3] As a result, the scholarly work of thinking and writing has been ruthlessly subordinated to the external ends of being rated well in the RAE or the REF, of obtaining external grants and other 'indicators of esteem', of gaining promotion, and so forth. MacIntyre's critique of the way in which money and power have come to tyrannise over modern life applies here perfectly. Nevertheless, one should step back and consider how far his philosophy actually provides a satisfactory basis for understanding and criticising the present situation in British universities.

As MacIntyre's approach suggests, the values associated with the RAE and REF need to be understood in the context of the social and economic conditions in which they have developed. The RAE and REF are primarily mechanisms for the distribution of university 'research' funding.[4] The research rating system was introduced in 1992 to replace the previous arrangement, in which government money was distributed to the universities via a small, unelected group of 'the great and the good' called the University Grants Committee (UGC). This committee operated in an opaque and unaccountable way. The system was based on 'trust'. It worked on the assumption of 'common values' and 'shared understandings'. This functioned reasonably well when the university sector was small and relatively homogeneous up to the late 1960s.

Until then, philosophy in British universities, to take one example, was a small and relatively united subject. It was also extraordinarily narrow and limited. It was entirely dominated by the analytical approach, with the focus mainly on epistemology, ethics, and logic. Continental philosophy, critical social thought, and areas such as political philosophy and aesthetics were marginalised and all but excluded. As long as

---

3. In principle, this may appear fair and reasonable, but it has not worked out like that in practice (see Sayers 1997).

4. The very idea of a separate element of funding for 'research' was a product of the mechanisms introduced with the RAE.

this situation remained unchallenged, there could be, and there was, a large measure of agreement about what was important in the subject and about how funds should be distributed, and there was a sufficient measure of trust that an unaccountable body like the UGC would do the job satisfactorily.

This system came under increasing strain with the rapid expansion of the university sector in the 1960s. Subjects such as philosophy grew and attracted a greater diversity of teachers, many of whom had been students in the radical years of the 1960s. The analytic orthodoxy began to be challenged. The subject started to fragment, as different ideas and approaches gained adherents and demanded recognition. The cosy little academic community of philosophy was broken up. Perhaps in some respects this was regrettable, but I do not think one should spend much time lamenting its demise. The stranglehold over British philosophy of a narrow and intolerant analytical orthodoxy had to be challenged if freedom to explore other ideas and approaches was to become possible.[5]

The period of rapid expansion and fragmentation of the university sector in the 1960s was soon followed by savage funding cuts in the 1970s. A means of allocating increasingly scarce resources was needed that would carry more authority and trust across the sector than did the establishment cosiness of the UGC. The RAE was devised to fulfill this role. It purported to give a quantified and 'objective' measure of research quality, and thus to provide a transparent and open basis for determining funding allocation. Individuals and departments in all institutions—elite and non-elite alike—were to be enabled to obtain research funding if their work was demonstrably of sufficient 'quality'.

The whole exercise is a sham. Judgments of the 'quality' of philosophical work cannot be 'objective' in this way, nor can they be reduced to a quantitative measure. As the subject has become more fragmented the assessment process has had to be made more complex, but at the same time it has become less credible. At the end of the day, the judgments on which research ratings rest are still made by the small and unelected

---

5. The journal *Radical Philosophy*, of which I was one of the founders in 1972, played a significant part in this change.

groups who constitute the various subject 'panels', groups that are still often unrepresentative of the subjects over which they preside. The outcome of this absurdly cumbersome and costly exercise is, however, entirely predictable: namely, to concentrate the available funding in a predetermined little group of privileged institutions. In other words, although the research rating system is marginally more transparent and more equalitarian than the old UGC, in effect it has simply re-created in a different guise mechanisms remarkably like those it was supposed to replace.

On top of that, the system has other, perhaps unintended, but far more harmful and distorting effects on intellectual life right across the academic community. It has encouraged an artificial and one-sided emphasis on so-called 'research' (i.e., publication and research funding), to the detriment of teaching. Research has been made into an instrumental activity aimed at inclusion in the REF, and teaching—the essential activity of universities—has been devalued and sidelined. Moreover, the whole regime has had a disastrously conservative impact, discouraging work on anything innovative, risky, critical, or regarded as 'marginal', for fear that it will not rate well in REF terms. These pressures mean that philosophical work in the academy, rather than being a 'practice' in MacIntyre's sense that embodies and expresses the internal goods of scholarly thought, has been made into an activity pursued largely for the external goods of REF ratings and research funding, all in the context of an artificially created market.[6]

MacIntyre's criticisms of modernity describe this situation all too well. His philosophy provides the basis for a powerful condemnation of the instrumentalism that has thus been brought into academic life. However, it is less helpful when it comes to understanding the complexities of the situation or identifying ways to change it for the better. MacIntyre's ideal of small, embattled groups of true scholars, pursuing the internal

---

6. Ironically, the real market in publications—the academic book trade, which is determined by considerations of what sells, rather than by the imprimatur of an elite panel—has proved considerably more open, progressive, and responsive to new developments in philosophy (Sayers 1997).

goods of intellectual life and preserving themselves against the forces of money and power, is not helpful. The academic community is not like that. It probably never has been. In any event, it has not been able to remain an enclave, immune from the pressures of the modern world.

In some important respects, moreover, that should not be something to regret. The pressures of modernity have not been entirely harmful. They have also created the conditions in which diversity can exist. This tolerance of different approaches has meant that the subject has become fragmented and compartmentalised; but it would be a mistake to look back wistfully to the old days. The research rating regime has been obliged to acknowledge the variety of philosophical work now going on in a way that the old 'shared understandings' of the UGC era simply did not.[7]

I certainly do not intend to suggest that the REF has been a good thing for intellectual life. Far from it. But I am trying to show that the impact of the forces that led to it has been more complex and contradictory than MacIntyre's philosophy suggests. The freedoms it has been obliged to allow to different approaches are at the same time seriously threatened by the pressures towards conformity that are also inherent in it. This situation is not adequately described by MacIntyre when he says that the modern university is a place of 'unconstrained and limitless absence of agreement' (MacIntyre 1990a, 225).

MacIntyre envisages that the university might become an arena of discussion and argument between rival traditions. Ideally, it should be possible to achieve this, and to have a unified intellectual community in which different approaches participate in a common debate. However, such a community of 'shared understandings' has proved very difficult to create, at least in philosophy. In its absence, diversity and freedom have been achieved only through the compartmentalisation of the subject, in which different traditions coexist in mutually hostile and noncommunicating isolation.

This outcome may not seem very different from MacIntyre's vision of small enclaves preserving themselves against the pressures of modernity.

---

7. I am grateful to Jan Derry and Andrew Chitty for help in thinking out this line of argument.

What I am arguing, however, is that MacIntyre's picture of modernity is fundamentally flawed. For it is the very forces of modernity that have created the conditions for the diversity of approaches and these enclaves in the first place.

VI

The practical implications of this are that the areas of freedom to pursue critical work that exist within the system need to be defended and, where possible, expanded—if necessary by creating and defending a compartmentalised space where it can be carried on. MacIntyre is far more pessimistic. He sees little prospect for this, nor any possibility of change for the better in the modern world. Any hopes of realising liberty, equality, or community now or in a future society are illusory. The ideals which inspire radical liberalism, socialism, and communism, have failed. The market and the state have come to dominate and to exercise their corrupting influence throughout modern life. Moral values can be preserved and defended only in small enclaves, protected from effects of market and state, where there can be shared understandings and rational deliberation about values (MacIntyre 1998g).

The critique of the impact of the market and the state that leads MacIntyre to these conclusions is usually associated with socialism, but it is widely shared by many liberals and other sorts of radicals. However, such critics have generally had a different response to the problems of liberal modernity. They are reluctant to give up the Enlightenment project and to reject liberal modernity altogether in the way that MacIntyre advocates. On the contrary, they remain committed to the central aspirations of the Enlightenment. Like MacIntyre, however, they believe that the market and the capitalist state have become the main forces standing in the way of their realisation. To preserve and extend the liberal values of the Enlightenment, they maintain, the market and the state must be curbed and brought under social control. For these values can now be realised only by an economic, social, and political transformation, which will take us beyond free market capitalism and beyond the bounds envisaged by traditional liberalism.

Although MacIntyre had some sympathy with these views in his early years, when he was active on the left, he no longer has any time for them. Now he is convinced that no change for the better is possible. With the failure of Soviet communism, all hope of socialism and with it of radical social change has been refuted and discredited: 'Marxist politics have failed' (MacIntyre 2006l, 153). His assumption seems to be that the Soviet system and the other forms of Marxism that vied with each other in the last century are the only possible forms of communist politics, and that Marxism is now finished as a political force. In this respect, he appears to agree with those who hold that with the collapse of Soviet-style communism, we are at the 'end of history'. This is what leads to the profound pessimism that pervades MacIntyre's thought. All we can do is resign ourselves to the present situation and defend moral values in small embattled enclaves, where possible.

At least in the academic world, I have argued, even this minimal defensive project is misconceived. It has not been possible to defend the old 'community of scholars' against the forces of the market and the state; it is questionable whether that is even desirable. The academic world has become fragmented and compartmentalised, but that is no reason for MacIntyre's pessimism. For this very compartmentalisation has created what spaces there are for critical and radical thought in the universities. And such spaces still remain, even in the world of research ratings. MacIntyre's work is itself a small proof of this. The opportunities for critical work, such as they are, need to be defended and expanded, not negated and denied.

Similarly, in the larger political world, there are grounds for thinking that MacIntyre is mistaken in taking the failure of the Soviet system and the collapse of the socialist movement elsewhere as the final proof that there is no way forward. The contemporary world is riven with conflicts and contradictions, it is volatile and unstable. There is no good reason to believe that history has come to an end with capitalism and liberal democracy. If humanity does not destroy itself first, change is not only possible but likely.

Although volatility and crisis may lead to change, they are not by themselves sufficient to bring about a better world. For this, human agents with the will and capability to construct a new and better order are also necessary. There are few signs of these yet appearing. The industrial proletariat of the advanced industrial societies, in whom Marx rested his hopes for a better future, are a diminishing group who do not seem destined to fulfill this role. In any case, capitalism is now a global system. The forces for radical change appear more likely to originate in the third world and to take a different form than classical Marxism envisaged. Some commentators, such as Michael Hardt and Antonio Negri, look to an amorphous 'multitude' of the dispossessed and downtrodden to fulfill the role of revolutionary agents (Hardt and Negri 2000; 2005). The seeds of such forces may exist among them, but they will need to become much more united, conscious, and better organised if they are to fulfill this role. There is little evidence of this happening to date. Nevertheless, people all over the world want a better way of living than global capitalism can provide, and that is surely possible. It seems reasonable to believe that these aspirations will lead, sooner or later, to the emergence of more effective forces of opposition: perhaps in the underdeveloped world, and perhaps also by the imperatives created by immanent environmental catastrophe. Along these lines, I believe, we can look for a perspective that is both more hopeful and better justified than MacIntyre's pessimism.

6

Alienation, Practices, and Human Nature

Marxist Critique in MacIntyre's Aristotelian Ethics

NIKO NOPONEN

In *After Virtue,* Alasdair MacIntyre argues that Nietzsche's philosophy of unmasking is the ultimate moral philosophy of modernity, the moral philosophy that exposes the true nature of modern moral discourse.[1] In short, the emotivist language of modern Western culture tends to conceal the manipulative modes of social relationships. Nietzsche saw clearly the perpetually conflicting but denied wills behind civilised bourgeois modes of life, the conflicts that are concealed by universalist moral language (MacIntyre 1985a, ch. 9). Along with Nietzsche, Marx was the other major modern student of conflict. Where Nietzsche worked etymologically and genealogically among the historically formed conflictual modes of

---

1. I thank professors Timo Airaksinen and Matti Sintonen for their comments on earlier versions of this essay. The discussions of the essay are developed further and related to questions concerning the role of empirical research in my Finnish paper "Vieraantuminen käytännöistä kapitalistisessa yhteiskunnassa" (Alienation from Practices in Capitalist Society), forthcoming in *Tiede & edistys.*

language that express conflicting individual wills, Marx worked sociologically and dialectically among the historically formed conflictual
modes of actual human relations. It was Marx who really put the Hegelian concept of ideology to work.[2]

It is not difficult to recognise a Marxist tone in MacIntyre's historical
approach, and between MacIntyre's studies of the nature and the history
of ethics and the Marxist criticism of modern society there is a significant congruence. In the preface to *After Virtue*, MacIntyre states firmly
that he continues to 'accept much of the substance of that criticism' of
'liberalism [in] which Marxism originated' (MacIntyre 1985a, ix).

Marx and the history of Marxism have a small role in *After Virtue*.
Marx is quoted emphatically a couple of times, and some misunder-
standings by 'Marxist' social scientists are referred to, but that is almost
all. Halfway through the book, after the extensive study of the malaise
of our modern culture and Nietzsche's critical contribution, MacIntyre
mentions that he has been talking about masks and concealments, even
if he has not used the concept of 'ideology'. Nevertheless, he states, 'of
course part of the conception of ideology of which Marx is the ances-
tral begetter . . . does indeed underlie my central thesis about morality'
(MacIntyre 1985a, 110).

Along with its inspiring but disputable sketch of the history of ethics,
After Virtue famously defends a modified Aristotelianism in which the
role of the virtues is tied to a kind of teleological conception of human
nature. Certain virtues and their objective claims concerning social life
are required for human beings to be able to work and develop in various
kinds of social practices. These practices, with the skills they demand
and their internal standards and goods, form the basis for meaningful
human living. Even if 'Marxism itself is only a marginal preoccupation'
(MacIntyre 1985a, x) in *After Virtue*, MacIntyre makes clear his debt to
Marx; and we should keep in mind the possibility that his earlier deal-
ings with Marxism form a part of the background of his Aristotelian

2. In the last lines of chapter 12 of *After Virtue*, 'Aristotle's Account of the
Virtues', MacIntyre criticises Aristotle for dismissing the importance of understanding conflict.

being. Man has created a world that is ruled by powers produced by himself and in which he is a stranger. MacIntyre comments that man thus 'sees himself as powerless, and with the power that is really his but that he has given over to external forces, he endows the being that seems to him to rule the world. In other words, he creates the gods' (MacIntyre 1995c, 49).

One of Marx's motives, of course, was to criticise the condition of contemporary factory workers, but his critique extended to all modern bourgeois culture. The products of the factories in rapidly industrialising northern Europe were undoubtedly external goods to their producers, both capitalists and workers. The aim of capitalists was to get as good a price as possible for their products, and at any time they might change their plants to produce goods that were cheaper to make or for which there was more demand, and which therefore would be more profitable. The aim of wage labourers was to be paid, and they would surely have changed to better-paid jobs given the opportunity.

Economists who enquire into only one aspect of human activity—the market—have dismissed a point that Marx considered highly important: 'Political economy conceals the estrangement in the nature of labour by ignoring the *direct* relationship between the *worker (labour) and production*' (Marx 1975a, 325). Marx characterises the nature of the process in the following terms:

> The *devaluation* of the human world grows in the direct proportion to the *increase in value* of the world of things. Labour not only produces commodities; it also produces itself and workers as a *commodity* and it does so in the same proportion in which it produces commodities in general. This fact simply means that the object that labour produces, its product, stands opposed to it as *something alien*, as a *power independent* of the producer. (Marx 1975a, 323–24).

A wage labourer's relationship to his own products is, to use MacIntyre's term, 'external', and he lives in conditions in which he tends to be alienated from himself, from other human beings, and from human nature generally. In *Marxism and Christianity,* MacIntyre emphasises Marx's essentialist concept of man and Marx's conviction that the alienation innate in wage labour and the antagonism between labourer and owner-employer, both essential characteristics of capitalism, are destructive to natural humanity. Marx was able to give 'historical form to a concrete view of what man in society ought to be, of what he is, and of how his estrangement from his own true being comes about' (MacIntyre 1995c, 56–57).

According to MacIntyre (MacIntyre 1953; 1995c), Marxism includes a crucial Christian theme of alienation and hope for its overcoming, which was passed on to the young Marx's philosophy through Hegel and Feuerbach. That common theme is encapsulated in Marx's account of the alienating power of bourgeois, capitalist culture. Even if it is less noticeable in the mature works of Marx, the implicit idea of the possibility of overcoming alienating modes and structures provided Marxist movements with hope, a virtue also central to Christianity. But even though MacIntyre in 1968 explicates Marx's essentialist tension about 'what man in society ought to be' and what man's 'own true being' is (MacIntyre 1995c, 56–57), he was not at all satisfied with Marx's formulations of human essence. Even if the young Marx succeeded in characterising the conditions and the process of alienation, his conception of active, self-realising human being, communal work and living, and human nature remained on an abstract level. We need to ask what kind of selfhood, communal living, and human nature it is, from which modern man tends to be alienated.

MacIntyre's Concept of a Practice

The concept of 'practice' lies at the core of MacIntyre's virtue ethics, as presented in *After Virtue* (MacIntyre 1985a, ch. 14). According to his definition, the essence of any practice is the internal relationship between its ends or products and the acting or practicing itself. The chess example is often referred to: one can play chess in order to gain money or fame, but these are external ends to the practice of chess, and they may be attained in many other ways. The internal ends of the practice of chess are realised only through playing chess, and it is impossible to understand or evaluate the ends from the outside. That can be done only by taking part in playing chess.

With the concept of a practice, MacIntyre explicates the Aristotelian conception of *praxis,* a form of activity that primarily aims at nothing but that activity itself. Participation in practices is the basis of meaningful human living; by participating in practices, human beings develop themselves by developing their skills and character. Recognition of one's own abilities and accountability requires response from others. Thus, one's personality develops by conceiving oneself with the help of recognition by others in cooperative activities. Cooperative activities with commonly recognised ends, mutual help and endeavour, and competition in excellence are thus the basis of an individual's self-knowledge and identity and of the happiness of humankind.[4]

MacIntyre stresses that any specific characterisation or definition of practices cannot be found in Aristotle, but that in the *Nicomachean Ethics*, Aristotle uses examples of certain human activities such as flute playing. By the distinction between *praxis* and *poiesis*, Aristotle points to *praxis* as a type of activity that lacks external ends (*Nicomachean Ethics* VI.2). This is the main feature of MacIntyre's characterisation, even if his definition of practices allows the possibility that a practice could have features of *poiesis* as well (cf. Knight 2007, pp. 16–25, 51–58; Nederman 2008). We might add that Aristotle's arguments against attempts to define *eudaimonia* in terms of wealth, fame, or pleasure (*Nicomachean Ethics* I.5) show that his conception of *eudaimonia* involves activity, and indeed, activity that primarily does not aim at anything outside itself.

In his concept of practices, the substantial and conceptual connection between Aristotelianism and Marxism in MacIntyre's moral and political philosophy is plain. With this kind of characterisation of cooperative human activity and its essential inseparability of means and ends, Marx would have been able to support and clarify his conception of alienation. Marx's analysis of man's alienation from his own work, and therefore from his own active human essence, was brilliant and fruitful, but the

---

4. The Wittgensteinian root of the concept of a practice is quite clear, as Knight (1998, 3) has noted (cf. MacIntyre 2006c). MacIntyre's practices are kinds of 'life forms' with their own internal standards and 'language games', which, of course, resemble those of similar practices. According to the testimony of Marjorie Grene (1986, 356), MacIntyre told her that he got the idea of practices from Hegel, but he has not explicated these Hegelian roots. I would say that his characterisation of practices by the famous chess example (MacIntyre 1985a, 188–89) is a kind of mundane but telling example of the Hegelian master-slave relationship.

question Marx could not clearly articulate is that of *from what is the estranged one alienated.*

MacIntyre's most explicit formulation of the connection between Marx's critical aims and the Aristotelian conception of practices and human nature can be found in 'The *Theses on Feuerbach*: A Road Not Taken'. He contends that 'if Marx had done the work of spelling out in detail the key distinctions which the argument of the *Theses on Feuerbach* needs, he would have been compelled to articulate it in something very like Aristotelian terms' (MacIntyre 1998f, 226). MacIntyre interprets Marx to mean by 'objective activity' essentially something similar to what he calls participation in a practice.

> Objective activity is activity in which the end or aim of the activity is such that by making that end their own individuals are able to achieve something of universal worth embodied in some particular form of practice through cooperation with other such individuals. The relationships required by this type of end are such that each individual's achievement is both of *the* end and of what has become her or his own end. Practices whose activity can be thus characterised stand in contrast to the practical life of civil society. It is a contrast which is best expressed in Aristotelian rather than in Hegelian terms. (MacIntyre 1998f, 225)[5]

The connection between practices and alienation becomes even more clear when MacIntyre's characterisations of external goods are taken into account, even if the examples of *After Virtue* usually involve fine arts and games.

> It is characteristic of what I have called external goods that when achieved they are always some individual's property and possession. Moreover characteristically they are such that the more someone

---

5. It should be noted that in the background of Hegel's concept of civil society is, importantly, Adam Smith's conception of market exchange and competition.

has of them, the less there is for other people. This is sometimes necessarily the case, as with power and fame, and sometimes the case by
reason of contingent circumstance as with money. External goods
are therefore characteristically objects of competition in which there
must be losers as well as winners. (MacIntyre 1985a, 190–91)

Granted that MacIntyre does not explicitly speak of alienation in *After
Virtue,* it is reasonable to conclude that the Hegelian-Marxist conceptions of alienation and ideology underlie his critique of modern society.
The other crucial reason why Marx's conception of alienation fits Mac-
Intyre's views well is that Marx's conception of man is essentialist and
thus implicitly compatible with the Aristotelian conception.[6] The modes
of alienation characterised by Marx can be interpreted via MacIntyre's
conception of practices as follows: If a person focuses or is forced to concentrate only on activities aiming at external goods, he or she is alienated from (1) forms of work that are good, meaningful, important, and
enjoyable as such; (2) common understandings, shared experiences, mutual recognition, and acting together with other people; (3) personal relationships with fellow human beings; and accordingly, (4) that which is
essential and constitutive to human beings generally, or human nature.

Virtues in Practices, Institutions, and Civil Society

To live a good human life, participation in some practices is essential.
To achieve the internal goods of some practice, one has to participate in
that practice, play by most of its rules, and subordinate oneself to most
of the particular standards and relationships of that practice. 'We have
to accept as necessary components of any practice with internal goods
and standards of excellence the virtues of justice, courage and honesty'.
These virtues partly constitute the practices, and the characterisation

---

6. See Gould 1978; R. Miller 1989; Meikle 1991. On the connection between MacIntyre's Marxism and Aristotelianism, see McMylor 1994; Knight
1996; 1998; 2000; 2007.

of particular practices implies them. Disregarding these virtues affects any practice by deforming, dissolving, and even destroying it (MacIntyre 1985a, 191–93).

MacIntyre stresses that practices should not be assimilated to institutions, although the latter are often necessary for providing the former with external social and material facilities. The institutions exist characteristically for sustaining practices in pursuing external and instrumental goals, such as money, power, and status, that enable the continuation of practices. But because institutions acquire, allocate, and direct external resources, there are always possibilities for corruption and the danger that the institutionalised aiming at external goals will displace the aiming at the internal goods of practices. 'In this context the essential function of the virtues is clear', MacIntyre maintains: 'Without them, without justice, courage and truthfulness, practices could not resist the corrupting power of institutions' (MacIntyre 1985a, 194). Like Aristotle (*Nicomachean Ethics* I.8–10), MacIntyre reminds us that external goods are truly good and necessary requirements for human living. But the achievement of internal goods requires the cultivation of the virtues.

> And in any society which recognised only external goods competitiveness would be the dominant and even exclusive feature.... We should therefore expect that, if in a particular society the pursuit of external goods were to become dominant, the concept of the virtues might suffer first attrition and then perhaps something near total effacement, although simulacra might abound. (MacIntyre 1985a, 196)

According to MacIntyre, the ancient vice of *pleonexia,* 'the wish to have more *simpliciter,* acquisitiveness as such', has in modern society come to be considered a central virtue (MacIntyre 1985a, 137, cf. 238). This wholehearted concentration on external goods is exactly the perspective of civil society. With MacIntyre's distinction in mind, we can say that Marx claims that the overcoming of alienation requires the supersession of the external-goods perspective and the appreciation of the internal-goods perspective in conceptualising human activity. When human beings do whatever has to be done to achieve the internal goods of their practices, they also transform themselves through what is at once a change in their desires and an acquisition of those intellectual and moral virtues and those intellectual, physical and imaginative skills necessary to achieve the goods of that particular practice. So, as Marx puts it in the third thesis, there comes about a 'coincidence of that changing of circumstances and of human activity of self-changing'. (MacIntyre 1998f, 226)

Further, '[h]uman beings who genuinely understand what they essentially are will have to understand themselves in terms of their actual and potential social relationships and embody that understanding in their actions as well as in their theories' (MacIntyre 1998f, 229). For this reason, MacIntyre's Aristotelian conception of practices is revolutionary in the modern world: it differs radically from the perspective of civil society and enables individuals to conceptualise participation in ongoing activities as their development towards the human *telos*. According to MacIntyre (MacIntyre 1998f, 231–32), Marx's philosophical incompleteness is evident in his inability to conceive the revolutionary nature of the life forms of, for example, Silesian artisan communities: 'Only in and through such practices can the standpoint of civil society be transcended' (MacIntyre 1998f, 234).

    According to MacIntyre,

> the important question is not so much why Marx rejected Hegel and Feuerbach as why, in rejecting them, he rejected philosophy, and moreover that, by rejecting philosophy, at the stage at which his philosophical enquires were still incomplete and were still informed by mistakes inherited from his philosophical predecessors, Marx allowed his later work to be distorted by presuppositions which were in key respects infected by philosophical error. (MacIntyre 1998f, 224)

This does not, of course, mean that Marx's *Capital* and other later writings are misleading or useless, but rather that they should be read and used with caution. The analysis of the dynamics and historical development of modern capitalism that constitutes Marx's major work should be understood primarily as an internal critique of modern society.

In stating that Marx's major works should be used with caution, I refer to developments in modern society which, following Hegel, can be called 'cunnings of history', but in a tragic rather than a providential sense. Marx's analysis helped people to understand the dynamics of capitalism, especially the meaning of labour in adding value to products and the related exploitation in relations between labourer and capitalist. These notions gave labourers a better understanding of their conditions and their abilities, and explicated the possibilities of cooperation and organisation. The consequences are well known. Marx was by no means the only theorist whose work aided the labour movement in forming its instruments and strategies. With theoretical and strategic encouragement from Marx and other theorists, labour organisations focused on the acquisition of external goods, such as money, time, and security. Labour unions and socialist parties organised themselves as actors within civil society. Hence Marx's major works in part utilized exactly the civil-society perspective that he also criticised, and they *often* led workers further along the road of alienation by tempting them to focus totally on the acquisition of external goods.

Alienation and Corruption

Could Aristotle have had any conception of alienation? First of all, nothing in Aristotle's works corresponds to or even resembles Marx's views of historical development, nor could it. The Greeks simply did not possess anything like the modern process conception of history (Arendt 1968b). Marx's view of human nature as historically evolving is not his own invention, though he developed the study of human historicity both methodologically and substantially.

The degeneration or corruption of the *polis* from good forms to bad is, of course, a central theme in Aristotle's *Politics*. But the idea of the moral corruption of a person is parallel to and interrelated with this view of political degeneration (Euben 1989). For Aristotle, the aptness for corruption is not a natural tendency of human beings; rather, an individual man can degenerate or become corrupt in certain conditions of scarcity of relevant goods (but cf. also MacIntyre 1988a, 156–58).

A human child ordinarily has a natural tendency to develop into a virtuous being when conditions are favourable. But since these conditions are social and since human beings have a natural capacity to act consciously and rationally, the form of the naturally favourable conditions has to be rationally conceived in order to avoid distorting the conditions by accidents or mistakes. Conscious attempts to secure some of the things that everyone needs for all of the members of a human community is wise, but it requires institutional arrangements, such as the division of labour, a system of taking turns, and centralised decision-making. But institutional arrangements for the delivery of necessary external goods also generate opportunities for exploitation, through so-called free-riding, misguiding or threatening people, embezzlement, and so on. To conceive and establish the right kind of institutions, it is important to identify the kind of conditions that bring opportunities to misuse them.

Human beings naturally have inclinations, which must be directed and partly controlled in order to serve the achieving of the human *telos*, both individual and communal. The vice of *pleonexia* grows from uncontrolled inclinations for external, though natural, goods. But *pleonexia* cannot dominate unless there are conditions which enable one to gain at the expense of someone else, who consequently loses, either knowingly or not. But these kinds of conditions are artificially arranged, established, used, and carried on by human beings themselves. 'The inequality that now is, has bin introduced by the Lawes civill', as Hobbes puts it (*Leviathan* I.15).[7]

In characterising institutions, MacIntyre (MacIntyre 1985a, 194–96) uses the concept of corruption in an ordinary sense: people acting in institutions or institutional settings are very often able to use their status, privileges, or resources in unjust ways to gain private profit at the expense of others. The ordinary concept of corruption clearly indicates that the corrupt person gains something that is good in an instrumental

---

7. Here we have a parallel to the classical question of whether just people make just law or just laws make just people (cf. Plato's *Gorgias* and *Republic* Book 1).

sense, whether fame, status, money, power, information, or material resources. According to MacIntyre, in the case of external goods there are
always winners and losers, and the corrupt person exploits others for
external and typically institutionally defined goods. But, as the ordinary
concept of corruption implies and as the word itself means, in corruption something is always lost or spoiled. According to a claim attributed
to Socrates, the person who fails in his action to meet the standards of
justice in the end does hurt mostly to himself; that is, the corrupted deed
somehow essentially corrupts or spoils the doer.

Plato has formulated the essential question concerning corruption in
the story of the ring of Gyges (*Republic* 360bd): if one could gain something good at the expense of others and without the risk of losing certain other good things (because of punishment, indignation, or the like),
would there be any reason *not* to use the opportunity? Socrates and Plato
answered 'Yes' to this question, and perhaps most of us would intuitively
do the same. By deceiving, stealing, and lying, one supposedly hurts not
only others but also oneself. Plato's argument for this answer, however,
is quite insufficient. Aristotle's argument was better reasoned, and it generated a long tradition of commentaries and attempts at extension. According to Aristotle, an individual or community cannot achieve *eudaimonia,* the *telos* of human nature, without sincere devotion to and the
practice of the virtues, because their claims are essential constituents of
the kinds of human activities and relations whose conscious, intentional
actualisation realises human happiness.

By following MacIntyre's explication of this Aristotelian position
we can reformulate Plato's question in terms of external goods only: if
one could gain some external goods at the expense of others and without the risk of losing other external goods, would there be any reason
not to use the opportunity? For any person, there are reasons to accom-
modate one's actions to the demands of the virtues, even at the expense
of one's relative loss of certain external goods, since without at least a
partial conformity to the virtues one cannot achieve the goods internal
to practices.[8] For in the absence of conformity to and the cultivation of

---

8. I believe that this characterisation is compatible with the internalist account of reasons presented by Bernard Williams (1981).

the virtues, one corrupts or loses one's capacity for objective judgment, subordination of desires, exposure to critique and decisions by others, and stable commitments, even though one may simultaneously achieve a large share of external goods.

The concepts of alienation and corruption refer to a state or a process of deprivation from something good that constitutes the alienated or corrupted person. Alienation, in the first place, is the inability to achieve goods internal to practices, but the concurrent phenomenon of corruption is the loss of one's virtues, and the inability to restrain one's inclinations to pursue external goods at the expense of others. Without the virtues, one distorts one's relations to one's fellow human beings, including mutual recognition, and thus harms oneself, undermining one's possibilities for achieving common internal goods of cooperative practices. A person in the process of corruption is alienating himself from the shared common reality that is recognised and worked out communally, and therefore from his own true good.

Understanding modes of alienation can help us to understand the nature and constituents of the human good, by acknowledging the obstacles and threats it faces. Without Marx's contribution to the critique of modernity, it would be difficult to understand the ways in which modern capitalist society, with its ideologies and institutions, threatens human practices, and with them the virtues, communal living, education, and politics—all things that enable us to live good lives. My argument in this essay is that Marx's critique is insufficient, but that his moral critique of modernity has now been completed by MacIntyre.

7

Leadership or Management

Some Comments on Alasdair MacIntyre's Critique of Marx(ism)

PAUL BLACKLEDGE

The materialist doctrine that men are products of circumstances and upbringing, and that, therefore, changed men are products of other circumstances and changed upbringing forgets that it is men that change circumstances and that the educator must himself be educated. Hence this doctrine necessarily arrives at dividing society into two parts, of which one is superior to society. The coincidence of the changing of circumstances and of human activity or self-change can be conceived and rationally understood only as *revolutionary practice.*
— Karl Marx, *Theses on Feuerbach*

Elsewhere I have argued both that there is a continuity across Alasdair MacIntyre's oeuvre from his early Marxism to his more mature writings, and that over the last decade or so there has been a reduction in the gap between his mature thought and Marx's revolutionary social theory (Blackledge 2005; 2007b; 2008a; 2009). Nevertheless, while MacIntyre continues to draw heavily on Marx's negative critique of capitalism, he remains resolutely critical of Marxism as a positive political project. Thus he would probably continue to accept the claim, made in 1984, that while 'we all still have a great deal to learn' from Marx's historiography, 'the same is not true of [his] politics' (MacIntyre 1984a, 254). In what follows I argue that this perspective assumes a caricatured reading of Marx's politics, and that once we move beyond this misrepresentation we find a significant area of overlap between elements of Marx's revolutionary politics and what Knight refers to as MacIntyre's 'politics of collective self-defence' (Knight 2007, 187). I argue that a dialogue between the two parties would be fruitful. Assuming that Marx, as MacIntyre has argued, did not make fully explicit the ethical dimension of his political project, MacIntyre's own ethical theory includes a similarly tacit non-account of the problem of political leadership. This lacuna in MacIntyre's thought is implicit in all of the examples he cites of virtue fostering local communities, but in this essay I focus on his example in *Dependent Rational Animals*: nineteenth- and twentieth-century Welsh mining communities. Specifically, I argue that beneath MacIntyre's schematic presentation, these communities provide an example of ethical political leadership from which both Marxists and MacIntyre could learn. Whereas Marxists might find in them a model of the kind of political leadership to which they aspire, this model also suggests weaknesses in the comparison, made by MacIntyre in 'Ideology, Social Science and Revolution' (1973a), between socialist revolutionaries and capitalist managers. Further, I argue that this example suggests a more general reappraisal of MacIntyre's critique of Marx's politics. For, despite the fact that there is obviously some truth to MacIntyre's criticisms of some forms of revolutionary leadership, there is also an alternative tradition within both Marxism and the workers' movement which suggests a vision of socialist leadership that is both very much at odds with MacIntyre's model of managerialism and close to the spirit of some of his more positive political suggestions.

MacIntyre and Marx

That MacIntyre's criticisms of Marx deserve serious critical attention is, I think, indisputable. In the 1950s and 1960s he contributed to related attempts both to unpick the real Marxist tradition from Stalinism and to renew this tradition in the face of the new postwar reality. As a militant within, first, the New Left, then the orthodox Trotskyist Socialist Labour League, and finally the heterodox International Socialism group, MacIntyre laid the basis for a fundamentally important contribution to Marxist ethical theory. And his mature thought is best understood, as he himself intimates in the preface to *After Virtue*, as a critical continuation of that project (MacIntyre 1985a, ix−x).

Nevertheless, *After Virtue* ends with a number of related claims, which, when taken together, amount to a seemingly unequivocal rejection of Marxism: first, in the century since Marx's death, insofar as Marxists had taken 'explicit moral stances', they have tended to fall back on either 'Kantianism or utilitarianism'; second, Marx failed to conceptualise the means by which his vision of 'a community of free individuals' was to be constructed; third, Marxists in power have tended to become Weberians; fourth, Marx's political optimism was undermined by capitalism's tendency to morally impoverish the human resources necessary to renew society. Additionally, MacIntyre insisted that anyone who took seriously Trotsky's mature analysis of the Soviet Union would be drawn to embrace a form of political pessimism incompatible with Marxism. Finally, he argued that in conditions of moral impoverishment, Marxists were wont to construct their own 'versions of the *Ubermensch*', for instance, 'Lukács's ideal proletarian' or 'Leninism's ideal revolutionary' (MacIntyre 1985a, 261−62). In a complementary extension of these claims, MacIntyre has more recently argued that while workers may have embodied in their practice a revolutionary ethics of emancipation at certain moments in history, the process of proletarianisation, despite Marx's expectations to the contrary, has simultaneously made resistance a necessary part of the lives of the working class, and robbed this resistance of its emancipatory content. Indeed, proletarianisation 'tends to deprive workers of those forms of practice through which they can discover conceptions of a good and of virtues adequate to the moral needs of resistance' (MacIntyre 1998f, 232).

Whatever the merits of these criticisms of Marxism, they should in no way be taken as evidence that MacIntyre has muted his more youthful criticisms of capitalism (cf. MacIntyre 1968, 146−49; 1985a, 137; 2006i, 39; 2006m, 173). While he no longer subscribes to Marx's positive political project, his 'After Virtue project' is intended both to understand the modern moral wasteland and to search for a map, however fragmentary, which might point beyond it. To this end, After Virtue concludes with a call to construct 'local forms of community within which civility and the intellectual and moral life can be sustained through the new dark ages which are already upon us' (MacIntyre 1985a, 263).

The register of the second half of this sentence recalls the pessimism of Adorno and Horkeimer's Dialectic of Enlightenment and Marcuse's One-Dimensional Man. MacIntyre's call to construct and defend local communities of resistance, however, points beyond the absolute bleakness of their conclusions. In 2006 he commented on the difference between his post-Marxism and that of the Frankfurt School as follows:

> To Adorno my inclination is to respond by quoting Dr. Johnson's friend, Oliver Edwards, who said that he too had tried to be a philosopher, but 'cheerfulness was always breaking in', perhaps a philistine, but also an appropriate response. What grounds then are there for cheerfulness in any social order such as our own about which some of Adorno's central claims still hold true? Those grounds derive surely from the continuing resistance to deprivations, frustrations, and evils that informs so many everyday lives in so many parts of the world, as well as much of the best thinking about those deprivations, frustrations, and evils, including Adorno's and Geuss's. To be good, to live rightly, and to think rightly, it may be said in reply to Adorno, is to be engaged in struggle and a perfected life is one perfected in key part in and through conflicts. (MacIntyre 2006p)

MacIntyre includes, among examples of the struggles through which the good life might be lived, the resistance mounted by some 'rank and file trade union movements'. In fact, his recognition of the radical significance of struggles such as these has long since differentiated his variant of post-Marxist thought from Frankfurt School theory. As far back as 1970 he suggested that if the major thesis of Marcuse's One Dimensional Man were true, 'then we should have to ask how the book came to be written and we would certainly have to enquire whether it would find any readers' (MacIntyre 1970, 62). On a similar note, in Dependent Rational

Animals he suggests that 'Welsh mining communities' should be numbered among those local communities where practices survived in resistance to the market, and which were sustained by, among other 'virtues', those of 'trade union struggle' (MacIntyre 1999a, 143; cf. 2006m, 180).

MacIntyre and the Working Class: Practice and Revolution

MacIntyre's focus on the emergence of virtuous practices 'from below' is a welcome break with the almost willful irrelevance of much of modern political philosophy (Geuss 2008). It is nevertheless unfortunate that his comments in *Dependent Rational Animals* on Welsh mining communities are tentative, to say the least. In a few short lines he writes that these communities were informed by 'the ethics of work at the coal face, by a passion for the goods of choral singing and of rugby football and by the virtues of trade union struggle against first coal-owners and then the state' (MacIntyre 1999a, 143).

Interestingly, although empirical studies of the Welsh mining communities in the nineteenth and twentieth centuries cohere with MacIntyre's general comments on these communities as important foci of virtuous resistance to capitalism, the actual content of this resistance tends to challenge his more general analysis of working-class life under capitalism. In their classic account of the South Wales Miners' Federation (SWMF), *The Fed* (1980), Hywel Francis and Dai Smith point to the intimate links between trade union struggles and the sustenance of these local communities. They argue that it was 'primarily' through the trade union that such 'communities' were constructed from what would otherwise have been mere 'aggregations of work-people'. They claim that 'the totality of commitment to the miners' cause was a form of class consciousness which translated itself into a community consciousness' (Francis and Smith 1980, 55). Their book perhaps also includes lessons for radicals active in the modern global economy. For they show how socialist activists within the SWMF led struggles which overcame divisions within a work force that sprang not only from across the British Isles but also from many parts of Europe as well: Portuguese, Germans, French, Belgians, and Spaniards were brought together in the union, alongside English and Welsh speakers with a multiplicity of local dialects and accents (Francis and Smith 1980, 34, 11). The role of these activists was central to the process whereby communities were formed out of these disparate materials. What is more, there was an important revolutionary voice within both the miners' union and the local communities. Francis and Smith point out that south Wales was 'one of the few areas in Britain where the Communist Party of Great Britain . . . had substantial roots' (Francis and Smith 1980, 28). And the Communist Party in south Wales drew on strong local traditions of Marxism and syndicalism, which stressed, classically in the 1912 pamphlet 'The Miners' Next Step', that the official leadership of the trade unions could not be trusted and that control of the union should be kept as close as possible to the rank-and-file workers (Darlington 2008, 219–32). The militants organised in various revolutionary groups before 1920, and the Communist Party thereafter acted—despite the hegemony of (a left-wing variant of) Labourism in the valleys—in the words of one commentator, as 'a contagious minority which charged the south Wales labour movement with power, internationalism, and colour' (C. Williams 1998, 58). Interestingly, the class-struggle ideology of these activists meant that these communities were built in opposition to the ideology of 'community', which the militants saw as a cover for the subordination of the workers' needs to the needs of capital. In place of the idea of community, the militants proposed workers' solidarity against both the coal owners and the state as their rallying cry (Francis and Smith 1980, 16). And far from being parochial localists, the militants fought for an internationalist interpretation of the concept of workers' solidarity. They acted, one might argue, as Gramscian organic intellectuals (Gramsci 1971, 6), drawing workers together through the ideology of 'proletarian internationalism' in opposition to the attempts of the mine owners and the state to divide and rule over them (Francis and Smith 1980, 31, 351, ch. 10). This ideology was framed by local and national class struggles, but it was also fought for by organised militants in the Second and Third Internationals. And while there was no automatic relationship between the trade union struggles in the pits and the formation of the broader mining communities, neither was there, as MacIntyre's mature critique of Marxism seems to suggest, an unbridgeable gulf between these two processes. The struggle at

the coal face was the backdrop against which local activists played leading roles in building those communities which, MacIntyre claims, fos-
tered the virtues. Moreover, many of these communities paraded their
internationalism by proudly embracing the pejorative name of 'Little
Moscow', which had been applied to them by a hostile press (Francis and
Smith 1980, 53).

This example suggests that the trade union struggles which underpinned the formation of local communities of resistance to capitalism
also informed and reinforced the emergence of an internationalist and
socialist class consciousness within the Welsh working class. At a more
general level, John Kelly has suggested that this relationship was not
peculiar to the south Wales valleys. He points to a relationship between
industrial militancy and the emergence of socialist class-consciousness
within the British working class as a whole in the twentieth century. And
at the close of a detailed comparison of the strike waves of 1915–22,
1968–74, and 1977–79 in Britain, he concludes that although there was
no simple causal relationship between economistic militancy and class
consciousness, nonetheless, there was some relationship between the former and the latter (Kelly 1988a, 127; cf. Robertson 1988 and Kelly 1988b).

The example of the south Wales coal fields suggests that one of the
most important mediating factors between the day-to-day experience of
class struggle and the formation of communities that prized the virtue
of solidarity was the presence of leading local activists (many of whom
considered themselves revolutionary socialists), organised together in
political parties. Given the implicit dependence of MacIntyre's example
of the Welsh mining communities upon a model of political leadership,
it is unfortunate that insofar as he engages with the problem of revolutionary leadership in his mature writings, he tends to conflate such leadership with managerialism (Sedgwick 1982, 264–65).

Leaders and Managers

In one of the most powerful sections of *After Virtue*, MacIntyre develops
Marx's youthful criticisms of mechanical materialism into a devastating
critique of both the theory and practice of managerialism. He argues

that managers, like Weberian bureaucrats, aim at the rational adjust-
ment of means to ends through reference to social scientific laws, which
they believe provide 'a stock of law-like generalisations with strong predictive power' (MacIntyre 1985a, 88). Just as natural scientists aim to extend their control over nature through the manipulation of the known
characteristics of its constituent parts, managers aim at the scientific
manipulation of the managed to meet preconceived ends. They therefore repeat a fundamental mistake of Enlightenment materialism in that
they are 'forced to regard [their] own actions quite differently from the
behaviour of those whom [they] manipulat[e]' (MacIntyre 1985a, 84).
Consequently, and incoherently, managers combine a voluntaristic model
of their own behaviour with a mechanical materialist model of the actions of those they 'manage'. In fact, managerial expertise and materialism are two sides of the same coin: if intentional action is reserved as a
trait of elites, the search for law-like generalisations about human conduct entails dehumanising the managed by denying their actions any
meaningful intentionality. It is this dehumanising method that leads to
failure: because the activity of the managed involves radically unpre-
dictable intentionality, it constantly undermines the pretensions of managerial expertise (MacIntyre 1985a, 89).

This critique of managerialism, interestingly, grew out of MacIntyre's
analysis of Stalinism. Commenting on Marx's third thesis on Feuerbach
in 1960, he wrote,

Marx attacks here one of the doctrines dominant in Europe since
the eighteenth century. According to this doctrine, there are objective causal laws both of nature and of history, knowledge of which
enables men to control their own destiny. So far as social life is concerned, the manipulation of society is possible to those who possess
the secret of these laws. As Marx saw it, this doctrine implies the
sharpest of divisions in society between those who know and those
who do not, the manipulators and the manipulated. Classical Marxism stands in stark contrast to this: it wants to transform the vast
mass of mankind from victims and puppets into agents who are
masters of their own lives. But Stalinism treated Marxist theory as
the discovery of the objective and unchangeable laws of history,

and glorified the party bureaucrats as the men who possessed the knowledge which enabled and entitled them to manipulate the rest of mankind. (MacIntyre 2008f, 119)

Over the next two decades MacIntyre extended this analysis of Stalinism to, on the one hand, the general critique of managerialism noted above and, on the other hand, a more specific critique of classical Marxism. Thus, in 'Ideology, Social Science and Revolution', he argued that just as managers attempt to cloak their actions in a rhetoric of science, revolutionaries tend to justify the 'world-historical significance' of their activity through reference to Marxist theory. Therefore, revolutionaries mimic the 'expertise' of the managers, and, like managers, they are practical anti-democrats whose plans are constantly frustrated by the inadequacies of their model of human behaviour: the contemporary revolutionary consequently 'cannot avoid in himself the very elitism which he attacks in others' (MacIntyre 1973a, 340–42; cf. 1968, 99–101, & 2006b, 136–39). So, MacIntyre claims, both managers and revolutionaries rely on similar pseudo-scientific frameworks to underpin their ultimately futile activities.

One obvious problem with this critique is that it appears to leave little space for nonmanagerial acts of leadership of the kind mentioned by MacIntyre in an early review of Isaac Deutscher's biography of Trotsky. Explicating a key difference between Trotsky's revolutionary interpretations of Marxism and Deutscher's mechanical materialist Marxism, MacIntyre comments that, unlike Deutscher, Trotsky recognised that '[i]f, from time to time, history presents us with real alternatives where my actions can make all the difference, then I am not just part of an inevitable historical progress' (MacIntyre 1971d, 59). If this argument is right, and surely it is, then not only does Marx's critique of mechanical materialism imply something like MacIntyre's analysis of managerialism, but it also implies some model of revolutionary leadership.

In the example to which MacIntyre refers, Trotsky was attempting to explain the decisive role played by Lenin in 1917 by his ability to grasp and shape the dynamic movement of the class consciousness of the Russian workers and peasants (Trotsky 1977, 18). Trotsky claims that Lenin did not impose his will on the situation in some abstract sense. Rather, Lenin was able to influence the historical process because he, more than anyone else at the time (with the exception of Trotsky himself), understood the significance of both the February Revolution and the emergence of soviets as potential organs of workers' power. And he differed from Trotsky in that he had built in the Bolshevik Party a group which became the organisational expression of the most revolutionary sections of the Russian working class and through which he was able both to learn from and to influence the Russian masses. Lenin grasped that the polarisation of society in 1917 had left both the Tsar and the liberals without a social base, while simultaneously creating a potential for either workers' power, on the one hand, or a Russian proto-fascism under General Lavr Kornilov, on the other. His greatness lay in the fact that before 1917 he had played a key role in building a party that was able, in 1917, to act to win hegemony within the Russian working class and across Russian society more generally for the project of soviet power (Trotsky 1977, 343; 1947, 203–5).

Following Trotsky's arguments, Lenin's leadership in 1917 is best understood not as a form of top-down managerialism but rather as a (successful) attempt to articulate the needs and desires of the real movement from below and then to help shape that movement through the Bolshevik Party. Had he not given voice to this movement, he would have become a minor footnote to the history of Russia: one more socialist sectarian who believed in a better world but was unable to do anything about it. It is ironic that Lenin's ability to shape history was predicated on the fact that the form of leadership he practiced had nothing in common with what, as Lars Lih has argued, is the textbook caricature of Leninism as a form of revolutionary elitism (Lih 2006; Blackledge 2006a).

Unfortunately, the hegemony of the textbook interpretation of Leninism has meant that many left-wingers have shied away from discussing the concept of leadership, except to dismiss its elitist connotations (Barker et al. 2001, 1). One consequence of this lacuna is a tendency for management theorists to claim the concept of leadership as their own, colouring it as they see fit. This situation is to be regretted. For all its weaknesses, however, contemporary management theory at least has the virtue of pointing to a distinction, to my knowledge absent from MacItnyre's mature comments on the subject, between leadership and management. Indeed, this distinction has become something of a *leitmotif* of management theory in the decades since MacIntyre wrote *After Virtue*.

In a discussion of the discourse through which the loyalty to capitalism of, primarily, managers is reproduced—what they call the 'spirit of capitalism'—Luc Boltanski and Eve Chiapello provide a comprehensive overview of the transformation of managerial discourse from the 1960s to the 1990s. They claim that over the history of capitalism there have been three 'spirits of capitalism': first, the entrepreneurial spirit, which characterised that period from the nineteenth century until the great depression of the 1930s; second, the spirit which grew out of the crisis of the interwar years and took as its ideal, not the entrepreneur, but the salaried director of the large firm; and, third, the new spirit of capitalism, which evolved from the older spirit as a result of its engagement with the critiques of the 1960s and 1970s. At the center of this new spirit is the idea of 'lean firms working as networks with a multitude of participants, organising work in the form of teams or *projects,* intent on customer satisfaction, and a general mobilisation of workers thanks to their leaders' vision' (Boltanski and Chiapello 2006; cf. Blackledge 2007).

The concept of leadership, with its distance from mere management, has become a fundamentally important ideological trope of contemporary management theory. According to this rhetoric, whereas managers play necessary technical roles within organisations, the role of leaders is to provide the vision of substantive purpose. For instance, Van Maurik approvingly quotes Field Marshall Lord Slim's claim, 'Leadership is of the spirit, compounded of personality and vision; its practice is an art. Management is of the mind, a matter of accurate calculation . . . its practice is a science. Managers are necessary; leaders are essential' (Van Maurik 2001, 2). Developing a related theme, James MacGregor Burns argues that theorists should make an ethical distinction between 'leaders' and 'rulers'. In a critique of Weber's concept of charismatic leadership, Burns argues that 'at best, charisma is a confusing and undemocratic form of leadership. At worst, it is a type of tyranny'. Concretely, he suggests that Hitler deployed his charisma not to lead the German people but rather to 'rule' over them. Apropos the distinction between rulership and leadership, Burns claims that the latter term should include a normative content to differentiate it from the former: leaders, as opposed to rulers, 'define public values that embrace the supreme enduring principles of a people' (J. Burns 2003, 26–29). So, whereas managers have a technical orientation towards some preconceived end, it is the function of leaders to envision this end, and this vision is at its core moral.

Insofar as this shift in managerial discourse has a concrete content behind its self-justifying rhetoric, it merely regurgitates the distinction, criticised by Marx and repeated by MacIntyre, between the active and passive element within history at a higher level. Consequently, the core intellectual failings detected by MacIntyre in an earlier form of management theory remain unaffected. In fact, Burns's ethical delineation between leaders and rulers does not even begin to address MacIntyre's more general critique of the emotivist content of contemporary culture. Any division of this kind must begin by engaging with the claim that in the modern world our judgments on competing moral perspectives can be reduced to 'masks for expressions of personal preference' (MacIntyre 1985a, 19).

Nonetheless, despite these obvious failings, contemporary discussions of leadership—precisely because they admit to the 'essentially contested' nature of this concept (Elgie 1995, 2)—at least open a space to think about leadership as an ethical practice. Moreover, as we have suggested, something like this way of thinking about leadership is implicit in MacIntyre's own comments on local communities that foster the virtues in opposition to capitalism. For not only do these communities provide standpoints from which an ethically justifiable critique of capitalism might be made, but they also assume the activities of practical leaders.

The Dialectic of Workers' Struggles and Socialist Leadership in Marx and Gramsci

Both Trotsky's example of Lenin's role in 1917 (explicitly) and MacIntyre's comments on Welsh mining communities of the nineteenth and twentieth centuries (implicitly) suggest that revolutionaries need not lead like managers, and that in fact they are successful (as revolutionaries) only when they do not. Indeed, these examples imply, in stark contrast to Weber's conflation of leadership with domination and manipulation, that an ability to give voice to real movements from below is the key to successful progressive revolutionary leadership. It is not difficult to excavate a theoretical expression of this type of leadership from within classical Marxism.

Marx considered his scientific account of capitalism not as an ahistorical 'truth' to be handed to the workers from on high, but as a theory that was derived from the standpoint of workers' struggles against their exploitation. Thus, in *Capital* he argues that the truth of the process of exploitation is obscured so long as it is seen from the point of view of atomised individuals, where it appears as free exchange, and becomes fully apparent only when examined from the point of view of workers' struggles, which hold the key to grasping the totality of the capitalist system.

> To be sure, the matter looks quite different if we consider capitalist production in the uninterrupted flow of its renewal, and if, in place of the individual capitalist and the individual worker, we view them in their totality, as the capitalist class and the working class confronting each other. But in so doing we should be applying standards entirely foreign to commodity production. (Marx 1976, 732)

This claim, as I argue elsewhere, is of the utmost importance to an adequate understanding of Marxism, for it provides the point of contact for Marx's scientific, explanatory account of the dynamics of the capitalist mode of production, his theory of history, his normative critique of capitalism, and his politics. If Marx's critique of political economy, his theory of historical materialism, and his condemnation of capitalism all presuppose the collective struggles of the modern proletariat, his political programme is best understood as emerging out of and reacting back onto this process (Blackledge 2008b). The type of leadership implicit in Marx's political theory and arguably realised by Lenin and, to a lesser extent, by some Welsh miners stands in stark contrast to Weber's account of domination. This is what Marx implied when he wrote, '[W]e do not say to the world: Cease your struggles, they are foolish; we will give you the true slogan of struggle. We merely show the world what it is really fighting for, and consciousness is something that it *has to* acquire even if it does not want to' (Marx 1975c, 144). This argument flows from

Marx's claim that the scientific status of his thought derived from its rootedness in working-class struggle. Indeed, far from being an ideology that is presented to the workers' movement from 'without', Marxism is best understood as the theory of the generalised lessons of the struggles of ordinary workers against capitalism. Because these struggles illuminate the inner essence of the capitalist system, Marx's socialism is, in Engels's words, 'nothing but the reflex, in thought', of the social conflicts endemic to capitalism (Engels 1947, 325).

Like MacIntyre, Marx criticises the existing social order from the point of view of real struggles against it. Unlike MacIntyre, he judges that in the present epoch, workers' struggles point towards a fuller realisation of human freedom. George Brenkert has convincingly shown that Marx understood freedom as social self-determination (Brenkert 1983, 88), which itself is underpinned by virtues of solidarity: at first, class-based virtues and then human ones (Blackledge 2008b, 140–45). This is why, as Hal Draper points out, Marx and Engels, rather than using the abstract word 'socialism' to describe their goal, more commonly wrote of workers' power (Draper 1977–90, 2:24).

Marx, as MacIntyre rightly states, did not make the ethical significance of working-class struggle explicit, but it nonetheless is implicit to many of his comments on the issue. Thus, although Marx stressed that socialists should not reify the proletariat as 'gods', he also insisted that even these ungodly folk would tend to feel their alienation as a dehumanisation, against which they would struggle for self-realisation. Marx believed the workers would remake themselves through such collective struggles, as the need for solidarity engendered a more socialistic attitude. For instance, in 1853, Marx wrote that 'the continual conflicts between masters and men, are . . . the indispensable means of holding up the spirit of the labouring classes, of combining them into one great association against the encroachment of the ruling class, and of preventing them from becoming apathetic, thoughtless, more or less well-fed instruments of production' (Marx 1987a, 43). Six years earlier he had pointed out that the struggle to form associations (trade unions), while partially explicable from the point of view of classical political economy as a means of improving wages, became inexplicable once workers began to turn over to the associations, for the sake of association, 'a good part of their wages'. Marx argues that this process is evidence that 'the domination of capital has created for this mass a common situation, common interests'. Consequently, whereas political economy is able only to understand atomised individualism, Marx showed how a new social rationality emerged within the working class (Marx 1987b, 34). Marx accepted that the political economists were right, from their standpoint, to point to the irrationality of workers forming unions, but also that, from the point of view of the working class, workers 'are right to laugh at the clever bourgeois schoolmasters' (Marx 1987c, 35–36).[1] For Marx, therefore, the core of the socialist project is the movement from below, which begins to realise, in however limited a form, the negation of capital: 'in order to supersede the idea of private property, the idea of communism is enough. In order to supersede private property as it actually exists, real communist activity is necessary' (Marx 1975a, 365). Marx thus suggests not only that workers feel compelled to struggle against the power of capital, but that in so doing, they begin to create modes of existence which offer a virtuous alternative to the egoism characteristic of capitalist society generally and of working-class life within that society more specifically.

> When communist workmen gather together, their immediate aim is instruction, propaganda, etc. But at the same time, they acquire a new need—the need for society—and what appears as a means had become an end. This practical development can be most strikingly observed in the gatherings of French socialist workers. Smoking, eating, and drinking, etc., are no longer means of creating links between people. Company, association, conversation, which in turn has society as its goal, is enough for them. The brotherhood of man is not a hollow phrase, it is a reality, and the nobility of man shines forth upon us from their work-worn figures. (Marx 1975a, 365)

By forming and being active within trade unions and working-class political parties, workers create institutions that both register and reinforce the change in themselves: working together in such institutions becomes

---

1. For a discussion of the rationality of striking, see Hyman 1984, ch. 5.

a day-to-day practice, which both presupposes the need for solidarity and engenders a spirit of solidarity within the working class. The virtues thus promoted stand in direct opposition to the competitive individualism of the capitalist market place.

These struggles provide the basis for Marx's involvement in the 'creation of an independent organisation of the workers' party' (Marx 1973b, 324). It has often been argued that the formation of a revolutionary party negates the idea of proletarian self-emancipation. These two aspects of Marx's thought, however, are two sides of the same coin. Because Marx insisted that socialism can only come from below, he realised that it will necessarily emerge out of sectional and fragmented struggles, and it is the sectional and fragmentary nature of the struggle that creates differences between more and less advanced workers, and consequently results in the emergence of socialist leaders (Lih 2006, 556). And, while 'the proletariat tends towards the totality through its practice of the class struggle', this process is necessarily mediated through a revolutionary party (Löwy 2003, 137). This does not mean that it is the role of this party to preach 'the truth' to the working class; rather it aims to 'participat[e] closely in the process of class struggle, helping the proletariat to find, through its own historical practice, the path to communist revolution' (Löwy 2003, 136). As John Molyneux has argued, Marx's conception of the revolutionary party 'absolutely ruled out' both the 'conspiratorial' idea of the party as a small elite acting for the working class and the 'authoritarian view' of the party handing orders down to the working class from above. Against both of these models, Marx firmly established 'the concept of leadership won on the basis of performance in the class struggle' (Molyneux 1986, 17). Whereas socialist sectarians prescribed a set course, deduced from doctrine, to the workers movement, Marx looked 'among the genuine elements of the class movement for the real basis of his agitation' (Marx 1987d, 111–12). In his political practice both in the 1840s and in the period of the First International, he was concerned centrally with the need to foster the struggles of the working class as a class, while simultaneously challenging those forces, for instance, anti-Irish racism in England, which grew out of and acted to reinforce and extend divisions within the proletariat (Collins and Abramsky 1965, 39, 45; Harris 1990, 44–45; Gilbert 1981b).

Among subsequent generations of Marxists, Antonio Gramsci has perhaps developed these ideas most powerfully, in his commentary on Lenin's contribution to Marxism. In the *Prison Notebooks* Gramsci suggested that although the idealist philosopher Benedetto Croce had played a pivotal role in the emergence of European revisionism in the 1890s, his attempt to articulate an 'ethico-political history', which placed individual agency at the center of the historical process, was an understandable and positive reaction to Second International mechanical materialism. Gramsci argued that authentic Marxism 'does not exclude ethico-political history', and that Lenin's revolutionary break with Second International Marxism consisted precisely in asserting the fundamental importance of this moment, the moment of hegemony, to the historical process (Gramsci 1995, 329, 345–46, 357, 360).

In the midst of the struggles of the Turin factory-workers in 1919 and 1920, the group around Gramsci's newspaper, *L'Ordine Nuovo*, sought to provide an answer to the question of how 'the dictatorship of the proletariat' might move from an abstract slogan to a concrete end of action (Gramsci 1977, 68). In answer to the question 'How are the immense social forces unleashed by the war to be harnessed?' Gramsci replied that 'the socialist state exists potentially in the institutions of social life characteristic of the exploited working class' (Gramsci 1977, 65). He proposed that the factory councils, which had emerged out of existing representative bodies (the internal factory commissions), were such institutions (Molyneux 1986, 146). In a self-criticism of early issues of *L'Ordine Nuovo*, Gramsci wrote that these were 'abstract' and that the journal did not read as if it belonged to the local workers: 'it was a review that could have come out in Naples, Caltanissetta, Brindisi', it was an example of 'mediocre intellectualism' (Gramsci, quoted in G. Williams 1975, 94). To overcome this failing, Gramsci quickly reoriented *L'Ordine Nuovo* to address problems that were central to the lives of the local working class, 'the problem of the development' of the factory councils. A consequence of this reorientation was that, in Gramsci's words, the workers came to 'love' *L'Ordine Nuovo* (Gramsci, quoted in G. Williams 1975, 94–95).

Gramsci aspired to learn critically from the Russian Revolution because he believed that Lenin had managed to 'weld communist doctrine to the collective consciousness of the Russian People'. By rooting his political activity within the real movement of workers, Gramsci intended to repeat that success in Italy (G. Williams 1975, 100). He thus aimed at what Gwyn Williams has called the translation of 'the Russian soviet experience into Italian', and he accomplished this by relating his practice to those working-class institutions of struggle that 'arose directly out of the process of production itself' (G. Williams 1975, 102). In thus rooting revolutionary politics in the real movement of workers, Gramsci's Marxism began to realise an ethics that went beyond the antinomies of bourgeois thought.

Whatever the concrete facts of Gramsci's embrace of 'Leninism', many have argued that it undermined the powerful ethical dimension of his earlier Marxism. Indeed, some commentators have implied that there is a tension, at least, between Gramsci's ethical Marxism and his Leninism, and have claimed that Lenin's 'highly centralised conception of the party . . . contradicted all expectations of self-management and democratic participation' (Boggs 1976, 86). This paradox is, however, of their own making; for they tend both to mistake Lenin's Party for Stalin's and to abstract the rise of Stalinism from the awful material conditions that confronted Russian socialists in the wake of the Revolution. Material scarcity at home, alongside failed revolutions abroad, gave rise to Stalinism; and it was from Stalin that the 'Leninist' caricature of Lenin's politics issued. The distinction between Lenin's and Stalin's parties is of the first importance. On this, Marcuse is surely right to argue, in a way that parallels Trotsky's analysis of 1917, that whereas 'during the Revolution, it became apparent to what degree Lenin had succeeded in basing his strategy on the actual class interests and aspirations of the workers and peasants . . . from 1923 on, the decisions of the leadership have been increasingly dissociated from the class interests of the proletariat' (Marcuse 1958, 124). If we follow Marcuse, Trotsky, and others in thinking beyond the Stalinist caricature of Leninism, then Gramsci's increased focus on the importance of the party after 1920 is explicable as a response to his realisation that 'important as workers' control was, it had of necessity to be supplemented by the physical dismantling of the capitalist state' (Gluckstein 1985, 187). As is apparent from The Lyons Theses, Gramsci's last major publication before his imprisonment, his stress on the need to build a party did not mean that he forgot the strengths of

the *L'Ordine Nuovo* period. For this reason he insisted that 'the party organisation must be constructed on the basis of production and hence of
work-place (cells)' (Gramsci 1978, 362). These party cells were designed
not merely to reflect the consciousness of the workers around them, but
to aim at genuine leadership of the class struggle. Thus, in the *Prison
Notebooks,* he insisted that although 'parties are only the nomenclature
for classes, it is also true that parties are not simply a mechanical and passive expression of those classes, but must react energetically upon them in
order to develop, solidify and universalise them' (Gramsci 1971, 227).
The crucial point about Gramsci's conception of leadership is that it es-
capes the common conflation of leadership with domination and manipulation. It did so, as he wrote, by applying 'itself to real men' such
that, from the *L'Ordine Nuovo* period onwards, it was 'not abstract'. Consequently, 'the element of spontaneity was not neglected and even less
despised. It was educated, directed, purged of extraneous contamina-
tions, the aim was to bring it in line with modern theory [Marxism]—
but in a living and historically effective manner' (Gramsci 1971, 198).
Commenting on this argument, Molyneux points out that Gramsci made
a break with the elitist residue of Second International Marxism, without
reverting to a crude dismissal of leadership per se (Molyneux 1986, 157).

In aiming to overcome any abstract—that is, top-down and
managerial—forms of leadership, Gramsci sought to outline an ethical
model of leadership. From this standpoint, the moral dimension of politics is the flipside of the scientific critique of political economy: just
as collective struggles on the part of the working class are the basis for
the latter, they are simultaneously the precondition of the former. As
Löwy argues, 'At bottom what we have here is not even an interpretation
"linked with" or "accompanied by" a practice but a total human activity,
practical-critical activity in which theory is already revolutionary praxis,
and practice is loaded with theoretical significance' (Löwy 2003, 109).

These arguments suggest that Marxists have gone some way towards answering the criticism that they have an underdeveloped model
of the ethical significance of working-class struggle. And the actual content of these struggles bears more than a passing resemblance to the
struggles through which the Welsh mining communities were built and
reproduced.

Democratic Leadership

MacIntyre's contribution to the renewal of Marxism in the 1950s and 1960s involved the attempt to rescue not only Marx but also Lenin from the deadening grip of Stalinism. In a context where both the international Communist and orthodox Trotskyist movements embraced a caricatured top-down model of Leninism, rooted in a superficial reading of Lenin's *What Is to Be Done?*, MacIntyre played an important role in recovering a more democratic tradition of socialist leadership. The practices of the Trotskyist Socialist Labour League (SLL) had seemed to confirm the instincts of the majority of the New Left, who believed that breaking with Stalinism entailed breaking with Leninism. MacIntyre, first as a dissident voice within the SLL and then as an editor of the journal *International Socialism,* drew on Lenin's contribution to Marxism in an attempt to formulate a democratic model of socialist leadership. Thus, just before leaving the SLL for the International Socialists, he posited a dialectical model of socialist leadership, which he counterposed to the SLL's top-down model of the same: 'the only intellectual who can hope to aid the working class by theoretical work is the one who is willing to live in the working-class movement and learn from it, revising his concepts all the time in light of his and its experience' (MacIntyre 2008d, 100). At about the same time, Tony Cliff developed a similar theme on the pages of *International Socialism.* He argued that the need for a revolutionary party followed from the 'unevenness in the level of culture and consciousness of different sections and groups of workers'. From this perspective, Cliff suggested that the function of a revolutionary socialist party was to engage in workers' day-to-day struggles, with the aim of generalising the lessons of those struggles and so winning a majority of workers over to the idea of socialism (Cliff 2001b, 126). It follows from this claim that revolutionary leadership should not be conflated with the top-down practice of either the Communist Party or the SLL.

One can visualise three kinds of leadership that for lack of better names we shall call those of the teacher, the foreman and the companion in struggle. The first kind of leadership shown by small sects is 'blackboard socialism' . . . in which didactic methods take the place of participation in struggle. The second kind, with foreman-worker or officer-soldier relations, characterises all bureaucratic reformist and Stalinist parties: the leadership sits in a caucus and decides what they will tell the workers to do, without the workers actively participating. What characterises both these kinds of leadership is the fact that directives go only one way: the leaders conduct a monologue with the masses. The third kind of leadership is analogous to that between a strike committee and the workers on strike, or a shop steward and his mates. The revolutionary party must conduct a dialogue with the workers outside it. The party, in consequence, should not invent tactics out of thin air, but put as its first duty to learn from the experience of the mass movement and then generalise from it. (Cliff 2001b, 129)

Whatever else one may say of this third model of leadership, it does seem to cohere with the practice of at least some of the militants who built the Welsh mining communities. Conversely, it also follows from Cliff's arguments that without a strike, the strike committee can easily become isolated. If this relative isolation of militants from the real workers' movement reinforces the tendency towards oligarchy in reformist organisations,[2] in revolutionary groups it underpins the danger of sectarianism (Barker 2001, 42). These tendencies towards oligarchy and sectarianism are two sides to the problem of 'substitutionism': the tendency of parties to substitute themselves for the working class. These arguments point to a social basis for the phenomenon noted by MacIntyre in a recent criticism of some of my own comments on Marxism. He argues that both Marx and Lenin, despite their break with mechanical materialism, assumed that 'once [workers] have acquired the relevant understanding' of society they would have 'good reasons' to make the goal of

---

2. Noted by Michels as a characteristic of all socialist parties (Michels 1962; cf. Knight on MacIntyre's broad agreement with this claim, 2007, 127–28, 169), but better understood as a more specific feature of reformist organisations (Barker 2001, 32).

socialism their goal, and that when they did not make this goal their own, Marxists and Leninists assumed that the workers were 'miseducated'. This a priori knowledge, MacIntyre claims, effectively undermines Marxism's self image as the theoretical reflection of proletarian self-emancipation (MacIntyre 2008r, 270). The problem with this formulation is not that it is patently false, but rather that it is one-sided. While it is true that there has been, and continues to be, a problematic tendency towards sectarianism on the revolutionary left, it is also true that many revolutionaries and revolutionary parties have played crucial roles as ethico-political leaders within the workers' movement. The task of contemporary anti-capitalists is to grasp both sides of this reality and to strive to lead in a way that avoids the dangers of sectarianism without becoming mere utilitarian trade-unionists.

A great strength of MacIntyre's early Marxist essays is that they attempted to draw out the (largely implicit) ethical core of Marx's politics (Blackledge 2008a). It was a minor intellectual tragedy that MacIntyre failed to build on this contribution to Marxism to articulate an adequate ethical model of revolutionary leadership (Blackledge 2007b). Nevertheless, for a period in the nineteenth and twentieth centuries, socialists within the Welsh valleys managed to walk this ethico-political line, while Gramsci pointed to the resources necessary to theorise such practice. Indeed, Gramsci and the Welsh miners together suggest not only that proletarianisation has not been an entirely negative historical development but also that it is not beyond the wit of workers to develop organisations whose political practice overcomes the charge, made by MacIntyre, that socialist revolutionaries reproduce modes of activity reminiscent of capitalist managers.

8

—

The Moral Critique of Stalinism

ÉMILE PERREAU-SAUSSINE

Insofar as political thought in the first half of the twentieth century was Marxist, contemporary political thought could be called 'post-Marxist', meaning that it is built upon the failure of the revolution, that is, of Marxist attempts to unite the Real and the Ideal. The situation today is the one recognised by former Communists, such as Alasdair MacIntyre, in the wake of 1956, when the problem of 'having to get your hands dirty' became acute.[1] Much of contemporary political and moral philosophy stems from this dirty-hands problem. In this essay, which focuses on MacIntyre's intellectual journey, I consider the responses offered to this problem by the modern rationalism of neo-Kantianism, the postmodern irrationalism of neo-Nietzscheanism, and the classical rationalism of neo-Aristotelianism.

---

1. 'Essentially, the situation today is as it was at the end of the nineteen-fifties,' notes Castoriadis. 'It is true that, during the nineteen-sixties, different movements (of young people, women and minorities) in France, the United States, Germany, Italy and elsewhere seemed to go against this analysis. But from the mid-seventies onwards, it started to become evident that all this represented one last great upsurge of the movements that had begun with the Enlightenment' (Castoriadis 1996, 88).

The Political Ambiguities of Utilitarianism

Marxism has been refuted by a tribunal it would find difficult to dismiss: history itself. Granted that it is no longer necessary to criticise Stalin, it is nonetheless important to remember the prestige he enjoyed immediately after the war. In 1945 the Soviet Union could bask in the glowing achievements of its armies and its ideas. With Marxist theory to propel it forwards, it remained, or thought it remained, in the vanguard of the history it was bringing to a consummation. As the homeland of all workers, it incarnated or claimed to incarnate the future of a finally reconciled humanity. Several turns of events rapidly darkened this horizon. The Prague coup, along with several others, reminded all those who had not done everything in their power to forget them of the atrocities of the interwar period. In 1956, Khrushchev's denunciation of Stalin, followed by the bringing to heel of Hungary, deprived the Soviet Union of its remaining eschatological privileges. The misdeeds of Communism were being denounced on every side (Furet 1999, 438–77).

The political reasons for this denunciation were all too clear, but its philosophical bases were still uncertain. In his *Autocritique* (Self-Criticism), published in 1959, a former member of the Communist Party summarised the nature of the contradiction in which Marxists who wanted to criticise Stalinism seemed to have become entangled:

> We knew how history plays fast and loose. We knew that history, as Marx said, progresses on its bad side. We knew that the road to hell is paved with good intentions and that, on the other hand, hellish methods can bring about progress. The cunning of reason! . . . We were naturally led to discredit any autonomous morality. Such a morality could only be sentimentality, subjectivism, a fear of the real. . . . 'Abstract', 'idealist' morality could condemn lies, bad faith, the police, murder. But real morality demanded that everything be subordinated to the enterprise that abolished man's exploitation by man. So morality was absolutely identified with politics. . . . Morality was thus the same as efficiency. (Morin 1959, 54–55)

Can efficiency justify the violations of Socialist legality, the systematic lying, the terror inspired by blind repression, the breaking up of families at the behest of the police, a regime of state terror, mass executions—in short, the suppression of the elementary safeguards of justice? The Khrushchev report mentioned torture and minority genocide. The Communists had their pat answer: nothing is achieved in practice by bleeding hearts, and the protesting voice of one's conscience should be rejected as another useless scruple. But many Communists had rallied to the Soviet camp out of indignation against the complacency of the West, and reasons of conscience had not initially been foreign to them—quite the opposite. Many of them consequently felt there was a contradiction between the motives for, and the reality of, their commitment. 'The arrangement whereby the Communist intellectual sometimes stifles the voice of his conscience only works if we forget that this intellectual is a Communist precisely so as to obey the most imperious commandment of his conscience' (Morin 1959, 153). Can one flout morality in the very name of morality? Or commit injustice in the name of justice? Certain Marxists were profoundly convinced of the necessarily moral character of every action carried out by the Party, and could not accept that there might be, within Communism itself, a conflict between ethics and politics. Others criticised morality for its formal, timeless, abstract postulates, and prided themselves on not resorting to such postulates.

A few months after his denunciation of Stalin's crimes, Khrushchev ordered his tanks into Hungary. Morally discredited, the USSR wanted to send a clear message that it was still politically necessary. Even among the Communists most intent on turning a blind eye, there was increasing unease. Here, too, the ex-Communist mentioned earlier summarises the situation well:

> My revolt remained too subjective in my view, and Stalinism remained too objective. I was too afraid I was merely setting my individual drama against History. I would never have dared think that this drama was the drama of history itself. . . . Morally, I rejected the system, but ideologically I rejected my morality. This contradiction fed into my anguish. Any effort to unburden myself of this anguish only intensified it, since it drove even wider apart my ideas and my demands, my theory and my life. I refused to be a 'beautiful soul', but I couldn't resign my self to being an ugly soul. I was afraid

that a moral rejection of Communism would lead me either into an ivory tower, or into 'anti-Communism'. My moral revolt struck me as individualistic, ineffectual, even though I'd already ceased to admire the system as necessary and rational. (Morin 1959, 152–53)

On the one hand, the Marxist is unable to reconcile economic determinism with human freedom. On the other, he has to learn to mistrust his own conscience and the residues of 'bourgeois' mentality whose traces he might still carry around. Even if an action is criminal in nature, it can hasten the emancipation of the human race. Isn't politics essentially a matter of violence, and isn't violence endemic? Doesn't the 'humanism of the future' demand 'terror in the present'?

Isn't the liberation of the human race worth getting one's hands dirty for, even if it means killing innocent people? In *The Rebel* (1951), Camus raised the problem of the ideological justification of violence and argued against the idea that the end justifies the means. Sartre wrote a reply to Camus, whose 'moralism' he criticised, in *Les Temps modernes*, and came to the defence of Stalinism. He accused Camus of staying faithful to an 'outmoded humanism', of wishing to keep his conscience clear, of living with only one foot in the real world, of affirming an empty ideal. Sartre denounced Camus as 'the High Priest of Absolute Morality' (Sartre 1952, 383).

> This Justice, that of some Stoic *grand seigneur,* this anachronistic conception of an Absolute Justice, is one so absolutely absolute that it would be a sin against it to try and bring it into play in the realm of the relative where, despite everything, men have to live and move. This noble demand, which allows real injustices to persist for fear of making them worse, and out of protest against some imaginary Injustice, should surely be characterised, rather, as a mania for absolute purity. The Just Man is the Pure Man: the one who has taken a vow of purity. He is *ipso facto* a naïve man, or an imposter. (Sartre 1952, 366)

In urging Camus to bow to tactical and strategic necessities, and to accept the ambiguities of all action, Sartre had an easy time of it in the postwar context influenced by Marxism. It is impossible wholeheartedly to reject politics for morality or morality for politics. Camus denied that he was moralising and tried to defend himself by pointing out the dangers of a divinization of history and the cult of the *fait accompli*, with all the abdication of responsibility it implies (Camus 1952, 331). Violence unleashed in the name of progress can have no special status unless there is indeed a 'meaning of history'. But is one justified in considering the USSR as the instrument by which the Absolute is being realised?

The critique of Stalinism raised the issue of the nature of moral reasoning. The massacre of the Kulaks, the Moscow trials, the massive deportations, the Gulag, and the split between Eastern and Western Europe could all be defended in the name of the higher interests of humanity. From a Machiavellian or utilitarian point of view (utilitarianism being taken here in the broadest and loosest sense of the term), the interests of the majority justify ignoring or immolating the minority. The moral critique of Stalinism focuses on Machiavellian utilitarianism, on the sacrifice of minorities for the ultimate well-being of the 'majority': it asks, does the importance of the human community justify one in sacrificing scapegoats on its behalf?

In the nineteenth century, the language of 'interests' seemed more favourable to human freedom than did the language of rights. While the language of interests managed to cast a veil over the abysses opened up by modern freedom, the language of rights encouraged the rashest explorations and the wildest and most overblown political promises. But, from the second half of the twentieth century onwards, the situation has been reversed. On the level of principles, what was needed to discredit totalitarianism was less capitalism than human rights. The Nazi and Communist tyrannies again raised the question of the viability of a utilitarian defence of liberalism.

If a calculus of the interests of the greatest number justifies torture, the genocide of minorities, and a regime of state terror, can one still fall back, in the sphere of morality and politics, on instrumental rationality? The Soviet atrocities suddenly raised doubts in the minds of the British and Americans, and seemed to strike a fatal blow at their habitual way of looking at things. Was not utilitarianism akin at least as much to Stalinist Machiavellianism (which they hoped to contain or discredit) as to

capitalism (which they approved of)? The supporters of an individualist interpretation of utilitarianism came to realise that utilitarianism
was not, perhaps, sufficient to condemn a tyranny that boasted a collec-
tivist interpretation of utilitarianism.

In the introduction to the first volume of *Philosophy, Politics and
Society* (1956), Peter Laslett affirmed that political philosophy seemed
to be dead. In 1962, in the second volume, Isaiah Berlin likewise wondered whether political philosophy still existed (Berlin 1962). To put it
mildly, these were strange questions. To be sure, political *science* seemed
to be taking over, in the universities, from political *philosophy*, yet Hannah Arendt, Raymond Aron, F. A. Hayek, Michael Oakeshott, and Leo
Strauss were just coming into their intellectual maturity. But these questions are significant all the same: the horror inspired by Stalinist utilitarianism caused consternation in an Anglo-American world that was
itself traditionally utilitarian.

Classical utilitarian liberalism had rested on two main theses. On
the one hand, men are equal under the law. On the other, this equality
is predicated on property, man being an economic animal, or *homo
economicus*. Marx had shown that, if one stuck to the liberal interpretation, these two theses were at least partly incompatible. If man really is
defined by his economic dimension, then we have to insist that the 'formal' rights to which liberals appeal are not sufficient. Real rights are economic. Real equality includes equality of income and, in the final analysis, the communistic sharing of property. This radicalisation, this Marxist
way of taking things to their logical conclusion, starts out from econo-
mism or liberal utilitarianism, which it turns upside down so as to bring
it more effectively to realisation. But in that case, people must have wondered in the 1950s, how and why should we wage the Cold War, if it is in
the name of utilitarianism that we condemn utilitarianism?

The doctrines of the social contract postulate an essentially asocial
man whom they transform into a good citizen, respectful of law and
the common interest. These doctrines are vulnerable by virtue of their
presuppositions, since it is difficult to show how one can move from pure
particularity to an authentic sense of generality, how man can find in
his nature a reason to obey a law that is foreign to him, and how to deduce disinterest from the most inflexible egotism. This was the problem

of which Anglo-American theorists suddenly became aware in the 1950s, before realising that Kant had come up with a solution to this difficulty when he made Law, which he associated with *respect,* the motive force *par excellence* of action—moral life implying an immediate relation to universality. This was an admirable solution, but its virtue came with a corresponding vice: the notion of contract relies on the social rooted-ness of moral life, which the Kantian sense of the universal does not allow. The categorical imperative focuses on man in his universality and does not take into account the particular political body to which the agent belongs.

The unexpected reception and success of John Rawls's *A Theory of Justice* (1971) was perhaps part and parcel of these debates.[2] Its neo-Kantianism put forward the justification of individualism made nec-essary by the apparent collapse of utilitarianism: Kant had developed the most effective critique of utilitarianism by showing that action could be moral only if men were treated as ends and not as means. Following Kant, Rawls constructed a vast intellectual edifice to argue that freedom cannot be sacrificed to equality, nor can individuals or minorities be considered as mere 'means'. While his work should not be reduced to his answer to the dirty-hands problem, his philosophy offers a critique of the type of despotism made apparently defensible by utilitarianism.

Kantism has been welcomed for its separation of facts and norms, of nature and freedom. It seems to offer an explanation of the failure of philosophies of history: attempts to unite nature and freedom, to 'realise freedom', appear in retrospect condemned to the failure they suffered. The ahistoricism of the original position and, more broadly, of the po-litical philosophy to which Rawls has given such a powerful impetus, skirts the failures of historic materialism, the disappointments which replaced Communists' hope. The Marxist schools, which sought in the Revolution a synthetical end to all contradictions, have been replaced by political philosophy of an analytical type, which tends to call, as its name suggests, for a rediscovery of the importance of liberal separations (the state and civil society, politics and economy, politics and opinion, and so forth).

---

2. Rawls developed his critique of utilitarianism in the 1950s (Rawls 1999).

While the Anglo-American world was pondering the malleability of utilitarianism, German thinkers were pondering the malleability of the thought of Max Weber, the great German theorist of liberalism. The followers of Weber questioned the consequences of his irrationalism and his appeals for a charismatic leader, and brooded over that disciple of Weber who became a Nazi, Carl Schmitt. How could they rely on Weberian liberalism to castigate Nazism, if the teachings of Weber on the ravages of instrumental reason and on the need for recourse to 'charismatic' personalities were used to serve the cause of Hitler? The neo-Kantian philosophy of Jürgen Habermas started out from such debates, and via these Germanic detours it moved close to that of Rawls. The case of the young Habermas is in fact even more typical than that of the young Rawls. The latter did not develop a keen interest in international relations, in spite of his involvement as a young soldier in World War II. In contrast, in the wake of 1956, Habermas has slowly abandoned his own Marxism and become attracted to liberalism in its Weberian and later its neo-Kantian forms.

The solutions of Rawls and Habermas, which echoed that of Camus, did not please everybody, and they particularly displeased the 'fellow travelers' who remained sensitive to Sartre's arguments and had no intention of rallying to liberal individualism, even of a Kantian type. Rawls's solution leads back to the uncertainties of the ex-Communist whose *Autocritique* I mentioned earlier: how can one understand politics by starting from the 'individual'? Hegel's critique of Kant found too attentive a hearing among Communist Party sympathisers for Rawls's neo-Kantianism to rouse any of their enthusiasm. These old-style Marxists—Trotskyists and mavericks of every kind—appropriated for themselves Sartre's critique of Camus, which was akin to Hegel's critique of Kant: namely, the categorical imperative, which places man directly on the level of the whole of humanity, does not enable one to understand action; the concept of rational will, insofar as it is the will of an individual, is ultimately empty; a universal morality is not sufficient to motivate an agent, as he fails to recognise in it his own particular self.

But the fact remained that after 1956, the realisation of Absolute Spirit could no longer be taken for granted, either in its Hegelian or its Marxist form. Already for some time, modern political rationalism had been in a state of crisis. The heirs of the most advanced version of the

Enlightenment could no longer take refuge in Moscow—not even in thought. Have the Enlightenment, science, and technology contributed to the edification of a universal society which will guarantee comfort, security, and equality? The failure of the USSR, which understood itself as the most advanced version of the modern project, seems to show the limits of the project itself. Is it still possible to take this project seriously if what appears to be the deepest attempt to take seriously idealism and constructivism has ruined the very freedom it was supposed to serve?

Postmodernism as a New Style of Marxism

Marx's predictions could not be postponed forever. If the phenomenon of Stalinism were merely a passing anomaly, a marginal phenomenon, it was necessary to show solidarity with the USSR, the first workers' state. But if this phenomenon constituted a new form of exploitation, then Marxism had to be revised and perhaps abandoned.

Lenin distanced himself both from the economic determinism of *Capital* and the democratic spirit of Marxism itself. His political voluntarism had justified the confiscation of power by a minority of professional revolutionaries who in theory had a clear understanding of the 'meaning of history'. The more the leaders of the USSR insisted on political voluntarism, the more they found themselves forced to insist on a dictatorship of the proletariat, as revolution was not the result of a spontaneous realisation, among the working class, of the state of economic forces and relations.

In 1939, Trotsky no longer had any illusions about the Soviet Union. To save Marxism from Stalin's tyranny, he fell back on the language of economic determinism, which he implicitly contrasted with that of political voluntarism. But in availing himself of this language, he took the risk of invalidating the Marxist philosophy of history. While the 1929 crash seemed a final confirmation of Marx's sombre prophecies, giving support as it did to the thesis of the inevitable crisis of capitalism, the progress made by the consumer society during the thirty years of the so-called Golden Age (1945–75) could be explained by Marxism only with the greatest difficulty. In a 1939 essay, 'The USSR at War', written shortly before his death, Trotsky raised the possibility of a new form of oppression. He asked himself whether the Soviet Union was not the first state to represent a completely new type of organisation, neither capitalist nor socialist, and whether there might not emerge, alongside bureaucracy, a new exploitative class that would owe its position less to the economy than to politics—which would in turn throw doubt on Marxist determinism.

> Either the Stalin regime is an abhorrent relapse in the process of transforming bourgeois society into a socialist society, or the Stalin regime is the first stage of a new exploiting society. If the second prognosis proves to be correct, then, of course, the bureaucracy will become a new exploiting class . . . . if the world proletariat should actually prove incapable of fulfilling the mission placed upon it by the course of development, nothing else would remain except to recognise that the socialist programme, based on the internal contradictions of capitalist society, ended as utopia. (Trotsky 1973, 11)

The group Socialisme au Barbarie, which sprang from a split within the French section of the Fourth International, owed a great deal to the disillusioned Trotsky of the end of the 1930s. Claude Lefort and Cornelius Castoriadis, the main figures in the group, took from him a number of their reflections on the nature of the Soviet Union and on bureaucratic society as a radically new social formation (Raynaud 1989). They maintained that the revolution had either to be abandoned or to be rethought. The correct response to Stalinist utilitarianism was not the neo-Kantianism of Rawls but a critique of Enlightenment Reason. Marxism, based on the glorification of rationalism, was abolished in favour of political irrationalism. No longer science, but Life! No longer Reason, but Will! No longer 'Marx', but 'Nietzsche'!

Via the mediation of Socialisme au Barbarie, postmodernism owed much to the Trotsky of the period before World War II. Jean-François Lyotard, the author of The Postmodern Condition, the first manifesto of the genre, was for a long time closely associated with their group (Lyotard 1984; cf. 1957). In his preface to a reprint of the articles he had written for Socialisme au Barbarie, Lyotard observed that 'already [in 1960], there was a dawning suspicion, shared by a significant number in the group, that politics was, or was on the point of, ceasing to be the main arena in which intractable reality showed its presence. We spoke of a 'depoliticisation'. . . . This was more or less what I tried to designate, clumsily, by the term "postmodern"' (Lyotard 1989).[3] Once Marx's predictions on the decreasing rate of profit, the pauperisation of the proletariat, and the inevitable worldwide crisis of capitalism turned out to be false, Marxists were tempted to sacrifice the mechanistic and positivist dimension of Marxism to its 'ideological' dimension. Wishing to affirm their own political voluntarism as against the determinism of *Capital,* the new-style Marxists, reputedly 'postmodern', foregrounded the 'cultural' elements that Marx had deliberately left in the background. But by underlining the importance of this 'ideological' dimension that Marx had resolutely subordinated to the economic infrastructure, they progressively lost Marx's materialist sheet-anchor and preferred the 'will to power' to class struggle.

---

3. Jacques Derrida, who was never a member of Lefort's group, expresses a similar view. 'Many young people today (of the type 'readers-consumers of Fukuyama' or of the type 'Fukuyama' himself) probably no longer sufficiently realise it: the eschatological themes of the 'end of history', of the 'end of Marxism', of the 'end of philosophy', of the 'ends of man', of the 'last man' and so forth were, in the '50s, that is, forty years ago, our daily bread. We had this bread of apocalypse in our mouths naturally, already, just as naturally as that which I nicknamed after the fact, in 1980, the 'apocalyptic tone in philosophy'. What was its consistency? What did it taste like? It was, *on the one hand,* the reading or analysis of those whom we could nickname the *classics of the end.* They formed the canon of modern apocalypse (end of History, end of Man, end of Philosophy, Hegel, Marx, Nietzsche, Heidegger, with their Kojèvian codicil and the codicils of Kojève himself). It was, *on the other hand and indissociably,* what we had known or what some of us for quite some time no longer hid from concerning totalitarian terror in all the Eastern countries, all the socio-economic disasters of Soviet bureaucracy, the Stalinism of the past and the neo-Stalinism in process (roughly speaking, from the Moscow trials to the repression in Hungary, to take only these minimal indices). Such was no doubt the element in which what is called deconstruction developed—and one can understand nothing of this period of deconstruction, notably in France, unless one takes this historical entanglement into account' (Derrida 1994, 14–15).

The USSR for a long time concealed a voracious and tyrannical imperialism behind a theoretical universalism: universality (reason) and particularity swapped their attributes, and Reason was toppled from its pedestal. 'How can a transnational entity, the international organisation of workers, have a historical-political reality when it ignores national proper names?' wondered Lyotard, before discussing 'the difficulties then and thereafter encountered by the workers' movement and its ultimate failure through its collapse back into national communities (at least since the socialist vote in favour of war budgets in 1914)' (Lyotard 1988, 146). Tracing the story back from socialism to the French Revolution, Lyotard denounced 'the authority which the representatives of the French nation arrogate to themselves by speaking in the place of man'. There is a 'differ-end' or incommensurability at work in the politics that emerges from the Enlightenment—an incommensurability that shakes it to its very foundations. How can one behave rationally? For a long time, socialism and communism seemed to provide an answer, by taking the fullest advantage of the premises of the Enlightenment. But after 1956? Didn't the despotic regime in Moscow condemn the political ideologies that drew their resources from the eighteenth century? Meditating on the Soviet experience, Lyotard eventually came to affirm the existence of irreducible forms of incommensurability. The so-called postmodernist school, born in reaction to Stalinism in the 1960s and 1970s, replied to this question with an apparent clarity. 'We have to abandon the Enlightenment, and thus reason, which is fundamentally authoritarian', it exclaimed in enthusiasm and despair.

The postmodern militant, yesterday still fascinated by the future to be desired, is today anxious about the danger to be held at bay. He foresaw the collapse of the walls separating different peoples; now he fears ethnic cleansing. A spectre haunts the postmodern militant: the spectre of crimes against humanity. Yesterday, all the pathos was on the side of the supporters of economic and social rights who based their arguments on the suffering of the most disadvantaged. Today, the pathos is on the side of 'formal' rights, as if the Enlightenment, previously handicapped by its reputation for superficiality, had finally reconciled itself to tragedy and could henceforth gain support by appealing to people's emotions. The principles of 1789 are celebrating their victory in sadness and shame, cutting the optimism of the Enlightenment down to a more sensible size, reminding us that no human effort will suffice to bring heaven down to earth. 'Postmodernism' constitutes in certain respects an extension of the logic of individual rights, in other words, of 'modern' politics itself: in this regard, it is 'on the left'. And yet, the indeterminate darkness of postmodernism can take two contradictory political forms: the one is liberal and even libertarian (authority is bad in itself), the other quite authoritarian (if man is bad, why grant him the freedom to be even worse?). The postmoderns strenuously deny that Nazism is a political Nietzscheanism. Since they reject bourgeois modernity as much as its Rousseauist and Marxist critiques, they are forced to maintain, despite everything, that Nietzscheanism is not Nazism. If the Enlightenment has been sullied by its Communist heritage, postmodernism must not be sullied in advance by disgraceful political consequences. So the postmodern school of thought carefully distinguishes between Nazism and the Nietzschean critiques of socialism, democracy, liberalism, and civilisation.

For fear of falling into 'ideology', Marx had put dialectical and historical materialism before a concern for justice. By rediscovering the 'ideological' element, twentieth-century Marxists and, later, the theorists of postmodernism could have returned justice back to center stage. On the whole, they did not. For they considered that their critique of the rationalism of the Enlightenment swept away with it every theory of rational or natural justice.

The Limits of Individualism

A third philosophical trend, neither neo-Kantian nor postmodern but neo-Aristotelian or even neo-Thomist, also attempts to come to terms with the problem of the moral critique of Stalinism. Like most of the postmodernists, Alasdair MacIntyre considers that it is no longer possible to be a Marxist. Himself an ex-Trotskyite, he takes his inspiration from the Trotsky of 1939, rather like the theorists of Socialisme au Barbarie.

A Marxist who took Trotsky's last writings with great seriousness would be forced into a pessimism quite alien to the Marxist tradition, and in becoming a pessimist he would in an important way have ceased to be a Marxist. For he would now see no tolerable alternative set of political and economic structures which could be brought into place to replace the structures of advanced capitalism. This conclusion agrees of course with my own. (MacIntyre 1985a, 262)

Following Trotsky, MacIntyre turns historicism against Marxism. How can one still be a Marxist, after the failure of most of the predictions made by the ultra-determinist Marx? This difficulty, raised at the end of the nineteenth century by Eduard Bernstein, has become insurmountable, even for the very people who have done everything, or forced themselves to believe everything, in their effort to remain Marxists, revolutionaries, and worshippers of history. In Nietzsche, the most resolute and perhaps the most profound critic of the emancipatory project of the Enlightenment, the author of *After Virtue* finds the diagnosis that enables him to account for the Communist catastrophe: MacIntyre belongs to the same generation as Deleuze, Foucault, or Derrida. But their analyses and conclusions are different. *After Virtue* consists of eighteen chapters. The first nine chapters end with a question, 'Nietzsche or Aristotle?', to which chapter eighteen replies: 'Nietzsche *or* Aristotle, Trotsky *and* St Benedict'. MacIntyre champions Aristotle to avoid being a postmodernist. His thinking springs from the conjunction of two phenomena—the crisis of modern political idealism and the rediscovery of classical rationalism.

In Germany, but also in Great Britain or the United States, the last several decades have witnessed a renewal of Aristotelianism, brought about by growing dissatisfaction with neo-Hegelian or neo-Kantian solutions. In Germany, the disciples of Husserl and Heidegger—Gadamer in particular—have seen in the Aristotelian theory of practical reason a means of avoiding the trap of positivism, without thereby yielding to the charms of postmodern irrationalism or nihilism. In Great Britain, those who have reread Aristotle in the light of Wittgenstein have argued that the *Nichomachean Ethics* was capable of renewing a moral philosophy that had become anaemic. These philosophers relate the questions raised by ancient philosophy to the problems studied by analytical philosophy (Anscombe 1959, 13). Among the figures prominent in this movement,

Elizabeth Anscombe is one of the foremost. In the wake of Anscombe, MacIntyre develops Wittgenstein's arguments in a direction Wittgenstein himself carefully avoided, and takes further Wittgenstein's remarks on action.

In an essay that originally appeared in the winter of 1958–59, MacIntyre criticised the Polish revisionist Leszek Kolakowski, often considered one of the heroes of 1956. Deploying, probably without being aware of it, some of the arguments that Sartre had already leveled against Camus in *Les Temps modernes*, MacIntyre argued:

> The reassertion of moral standards by the individual voice has been one of the ferments of Eastern European revisionism. But, because of the way in which it is done, this reassertion too often leaves the gulf between morality and history, between value and fact as wide as ever. Kolakowski and others like him stress the amorality of the historical process on the one hand and the moral responsibility of the individual in history on the other. And this leaves us with the moral critic as a spectator, the categorical imperatives which he proclaims having no genuine relationship to his view of history. One cannot revive the moral content within Marxism by simply taking a Stalinist view of historical development and adding liberal morality to it. (MacIntyre 1998a, 34)

The direction taken by MacIntyre's later works was already here in a nutshell, for at this point he took stock of the impossibility of a morality based on an abstract universal. He argues that the individual cannot place himself directly on the level of humanity as a whole without the mediation of some form of particularity—party, civic life, or Church. MacIntyre counters abstract individualism with the image of a human being fully 'set' within his environment. He thus opposed Kolakowski, to begin with, but also, twenty years later—in a context that was not greatly different—he opposed Rawls (MacIntyre 1985a, 215–23; cf. Kolakowski 1990). The moral critique of Stalinism, in the manner of Kolakowski, had left an impotent individual wrestling with a tyrannical state. MacIntyre belongs to the school which, from the 1950s onwards, has reflected on the modern forms of tyranny and, foreseeing the individualist reaction to which the phenomenon has given rise, has judged that reaction to be inadequate. He warns both against totalitarianism and against the indefinite multiplying of the rights of the individual. At the same time (and here lies the rub), one has to ensure that one has the means of criticising the community, if it happens to go astray—hence the problem of the moral critique of Stalinism. It may have been necessary for Sartre to criticise Camus's pamphlet; but Camus assuredly had good reasons not to yield to Soviet propaganda. It is not enough unilaterally to affirm the importance of community. It still has to be shown to what extent man cannot be reduced to his forms of belonging.

MacIntyre feels that Marx remained too dependent on utilitarianism and individualism, and made the mistake of placing his hopes in a 'socialist Robinson Crusoe' (MacIntyre 1976, 180–81; cf. 1985a, 261–62). Individualism does not constitute the solution to Stalinism because, in the final analysis, individualism (in its methodological form) is responsible for the failure of Marxism! Should the failure of the Soviet Union be considered a victory for the supporters of moral individualism? This MacIntyre denies. The 'fear of 1984' must not be allowed to 'revive the politics which glorified 1688', he wrote at the end of the 1960s (MacIntyre 1971j, 11).

It is useful to compare the reactions of MacIntyre and Habermas to the events of 1956. They belong to the same generation, being born in the same year (1929). Both strove to remain Marxists in spite of Stalinism, and indeed managed to do so until the middle of the 1960s. But the student revolts, far from filling them with enthusiasm, made them fear the worst. Habermas came to a sombre conclusion: Marxism did not enable him to say whether the students were on the extreme left or the extreme right. It offered him no way to guide the students *enragés* away from what he called, in 1967, 'left fascism'. Marxism, which until recently had been the politician's infallible guide, no longer allowed one to distinguish between saints and sinners. Around 1970–71, the ideas of MacIntyre and Habermas changed course perceptibly so as to avoid the postmodernism which they sensed was in the offing. At the very moment when people started to suggest that we were entering postindustrial society, a 'society of knowledge', they both offered an analysis in terms of *logos koinos*, of a common language, in place of one in terms of 'interest'.

But Habermas moved towards neo-Kantianism, whereas MacIntyre became a neo-Aristotelian. By developing the thinking of the Trotsky of 1939, MacIntyre became in his own way a 'postmodernist', but he finally called for a more radical reaction: a return to the moral philosophy of Aristotle. According to MacIntyre, the collapse of the Enlightenment project, largely a polemic against Aristotle, pointed to a return to classical rationalism.

MacIntyre's *Three Rival Versions of Moral Inquiry* (1990) could be described as an analysis of the post-1956 situation. MacIntyre maintains that the failure of Rousseauism and Marxism leads one to appeal either to the modern descendants of Locke and Montesquieu, or to those of Nietzsche, or to those of Aquinas and Aristotle. For him, we now have the choice between three possibilities: postmodern Nietzscheanism, a return to the Enlightenment, or Thomist neo-Aristotelianism. With these alternatives, MacIntyre aims to offer an alternative to the contrast commonly drawn these days: between a rationality of the neo-Kantian kind and the subjective irrationality of the postmodern kind. In the wake of the crisis produced by the denunciation of Stalinism, the great hope of a reconciliation of humanity with itself, as embodied in the progressive wing of the Enlightenment, had ended up losing any real substance.

Habermas and Rawls appeal to a separation of the Right and the Good (or a priority of the Right over the Good) to clarify the moral neutrality of the liberal state: on the one hand, the good man, on the other, the just citizen. They do not deny that individual freedom has to be related to a truth or a metaphysics, but for them this truth and this metaphysics can and must be subordinated to political life. Anxious to reach a minimal consensus, they want to prevent moral disagreement from creating political discord. But MacIntyre insists on the inevitability of disagreement. The just cannot be addressed prior to the good. In order for a rule to be properly understood, properly applied, properly interpreted, or even properly transformed when necessary, moral and intellectual virtues are required. Political science cannot isolate itself from moral philosophy, from the question of individual 'character'. MacIntyre relates political life to moral life. In his eyes, nothing represents Victorian England more aptly than the figures of the Explorer, the Engineer, and the Headmaster; and nothing is more characteristic of Wilhelmine Germany than the Prussian Officer, the Professor, and the Social Democrat. The twentieth century is represented, in his view, by the Bureaucrat and the Psychoanalyst (MacIntyre 1985a, 23–35). He relates politics to anthropology, and the organisation of city and state to certain human types.

MacIntyre's intellectual journey, which has brought him from Marx to Thomism, is intelligible only in the light of an ever deeper concern to question the Machiavellianism from which Marxist doctrine provided no escape. One reason for this concern is based on the belief that modern reason has a self-destructive character. The other derives from the critique of democratic individualism. MacIntyre orchestrates and links these two themes. The desire to find a balance between absolute democracy and a sense of excellence, or between consent and wisdom, leads either to a theory of natural law or a theory of natural rights. In *Whose Justice? Which Rationality?* he compares different theories of natural right and defends premodern theories of natural right simultaneously against modern or individualist approaches, and against the adversaries of natural right as such—sophists, positivists, and irrationalists. The book's title could equally well be, *Which Natural Law?*

The collapse of Marxist idealism rebounds on the Enlightenment as a whole. And the crisis of modern rationalism means that at the very moment liberalism triumphs, it risks losing its foundations. The political response that the cruelty of the twentieth century requires does not merely involve techniques of government, a sort of constitutional engineering, and a systematic circumventing of human nature. It also involves, no doubt on a deeper level, nature itself and man himself.

9

Alasdair MacIntyre and Trotskyism

NEIL DAVIDSON

Alasdair MacIntyre began his literary career in 1953 with *Marxism: An Interpretation*. According to his own account, in that book he attempted to be faithful to both his Christian and his Marxist beliefs (MacIntyre 1995d). Over the course of the 1960s he abandoned both (MacIntyre 2008k, 180). In 1971 he introduced a collection of his essays by rejecting these and, indeed, all other attempts to illuminate the human condition (MacIntyre 1971b, viii). Since then, MacIntyre has of course re-embraced Christianity, although that of the Catholic Church rather than the Anglicanism to which he originally adhered. It seems unlikely, at this stage, that he will undertake a similar reconciliation with Marxism.

Nevertheless, as MacIntyre has frequently reminded his readers, most recently in the prologue to the third edition of *After Virtue* (2007), his rejection of Marxism as a whole does not entail a rejection of every insight that it has to offer. MacIntyre's current audience tends to be uninterested in his Marxism and consequently remains in ignorance not only of his early Marxist work but also of the context in which it was written. MacIntyre not only wrote from a Marxist perspective but also belonged to a number of Marxist organisations, which, to differing degrees, made political demands on their members from which intellectuals were not excluded. Even the most insightful of MacIntyre's admirers tend to treat the subject of these political affiliations as an occasion for mild amusement (Knight 1998, 2). By contrast with this dismissive perspective, during the period from 1953 to 1968 he seems to have treated membership of some party or group as a necessary expression of his political beliefs, no matter how inadequate the organisations in question may ultimately have been. An introductory note to an early piece in *International Socialism,* evidently written by MacIntyre himself, cheerfully recounts his 'experience of the Communist Party, the Socialist Labour League, the New Left and the Labour Party' and reports his (unfortunately over-optimistic) belief 'that if none of these can disillusion one with socialism, then nothing can' (Blackledge and Davidson 2008, xxxv). In other words, his was not the type of academic Marxism that became depressingly familiar after 1968, in which theoretical postures were adopted, according to the dictates of intellectual fashion, by scholars without the means or often even the desire to intervene in the world. On the contrary, at some level MacIntyre embraced what a classic Marxist cliché calls 'the unity of theory and practice', particularly in the Socialist Labour League (SLL) and International Socialism (IS).

These were Trotskyist organisations; and readers of *After Virtue* will recall that Trotsky first features there as one of MacIntyre's 'exemplars of the virtues', along with fellow-Marxists Frederick Engels and Eleanor Marx, but also with St. Benedict, St. Francis of Assisi, and St. Teresa (MacIntyre 1985a, 199). When MacIntyre reintroduces him in the final chapter, it is to use Trotsky's intellectual integrity to illustrate the inability of Marxism to help achieve human liberation. MacIntyre clearly still admires Trotsky as an individual for his moral qualities and literary abilities, but to what extent was he ever a 'Trotskyist'? During the 1930s, after all, an entire generation of leading intellectuals and artists in the United States strongly identified with Trotsky without, in most cases, ever fully understanding his politics (Wald 1987, 91–97; N. Davidson 2004, 110–11). One possible interpretation of this phase in MacIntyre's career, therefore, is that it was a late recurrence, under British conditions, of this type of attitude. This was certainly the conclusion drawn by some of his erstwhile comrades in the SLL (Baker 1962, 68). I will argue, however, that it would be wrong to see MacIntyre simply as the British equivalent of

James Burnham (who incidentally began his literary career as a neo-Thomist), albeit one with a rather more intellectually reputable post-Marxist output. I want to suggest instead that MacIntyre's attempt to critically engage with Trotsky and Trotskyism, if ultimately a failure, was nevertheless a productive failure from which there is still much to be learned by those who continue to stand in that tradition.

MacIntyre's Early Marxism

One characteristic of *Marxism: An Interpretation* is the way it accepts the dominant view of the Marxist tradition, in which there is an unbroken succession from Marx and Engels to Lenin and from Lenin to Stalin. This was almost universally accepted, not only by both sides of the Cold War (although liberals and Stalinists ascribed different and opposing values to the lineage), but also by any surviving anarchists who took neither side. Only Trotskyists continued to insist on the existence of what Trotsky himself had called 'a whole river of blood' separating Lenin and the Bolsheviks from Stalinism (Trotsky 1978, 423). Insofar as there was a commonly held alternative to the continuity thesis on the political left, it placed a break after Marx, so that Lenin and the Bolsheviks bore sole responsibility for initiating the descent into totalitarianism. Ironically, Trotsky's earlier writings, together with those of Rosa Luxemburg, were frequently quoted, in a necessarily decontextualised manner, as prophetic warnings about the likely outcome of Lenin's organisational innovations (Trotsky n.d., 77; Luxemburg 1970, 114–22). According to this tradition, the former succumbed to the Leninist virus and the latter heroically, if tragically, maintained her faith in the democratic role of the working class until the end (see, e.g., Borkenau 1962, 12–13, 39–56, 87–89). And, sure enough, the sole reference to Trotsky in *Marxism: An Interpretation* invokes the passage from *Our Political Tasks* in which he allegedly foresees the emergent dictatorship of the party over the class (MacIntyre 1953, 103).

Nonetheless, in most other respects MacIntyre's work is not a conventional account. Where he differed from most contemporaries on either side of the Cold War was his view that both the positive and the negative aspects of Marxism arose from within Marx's own work. In particular, as befits his own Christian orientation at this time, he saw the problem as arising in the Marx's shift from prophecy to theory, or more precisely, from prophesy to theoretical prediction. In this respect MacIntyre takes up entirely the opposite position to that later developed by Louis Althusser, in whose work an 'epistemological break' around 1845 marks the passage from mere ideology to science (Althusser 2005, 31–38). For MacIntyre the problem is precisely that Marx after 1845 is attempting to fuse science with a fundamentally religious attribute, with the result that both are diminished: 'Thus in Marx's later thinking, and in Marxism, economic theory is treated prophetically; and that theory cannot be treated prophetically without becoming bad theory is something that Marxism can teach us at the point where it passes from prophecy to science' (MacIntyre 1953, 91).

MacIntyre was prepared to praise Marx as an individual thinker (MacIntyre 1956, 266). But as late as 1956 he was still dismissing all contemporary Marxist theory as largely 'fossilised' (MacIntyre 2008a, 25). What did MacIntyre consider 'Marxism' to be at this point? Although he was clearly aware of several key debates within the Marxist tradition— the debates between Eduard Bernstein and Karl Kautsky on socialist morality and those between Georgi Plekhanov and Lenin on the nature of the revolutionary party are both mentioned—he did not distinguish between any tendencies or traditions, still less claim that one of these might be more authentically Marxist than another. There was nothing unusual in his lack of engagement with Trotsky. The fact that Trotskyism later became the dominant tendency on the British far left has tended to obscure the fact that, before 1956, most people in the labour movement had never read anything by Trotsky or personally encountered any of his followers (N. Davidson 2004, 109–10). Indeed, even today it is not unknown for prominent left-wing intellectuals to admit to ignorance of his work (Hardt 2003, 135). Only a few years later, MacIntyre himself acidly suggested in an open letter to a Gaitskellite that 'you are perhaps slightly disappointed to find that those who denounced Trotskyism among your friends had never actually read Trotsky' (MacIntyre 2008m, 215).

The events of 1956 meant that the encounter with Trotsky's thought could no longer be averted. MacIntyre did not respond immediately to Khrushchev's revelations, the suppression of the Hungarian Revolution, or the thwarted reforms in Poland, but as someone involved in the emergent New Left he would quickly have become aware that Trotskyists offered an explanation for the realities of Stalinism which did not simply rely on abstract moral categories. MacIntyre made his first reference to Trotsky or Trotskyism in 1958, in one of his first articles for the socialist press, but it was not complementary. In a review of Raya Dunayevskaya's *Marxism and Freedom* for the journal *Universities and Left Review,* he wrote of the author, 'She has been repelled by the arid, seminary textbook Marxism of the Stalinists and the Trotskyists (who share all the dogmatism of the Stalinists without any of their achievements)' (MacIntyre 2008b, 43). Yet, less than a year later, MacIntyre had joined one group of Trotskyist 'dogmatists', the newly formed SLL. And, as one member recalls, 'He was at first full of enthusiasm; he spoke at meetings, sold papers, wrote articles and pamphlets' (Baker 1962, 65, 68). Why had he taken this apparently unexpected step?

MacIntyre as an Orthodox Trotskyist

MacIntyre began his career as a Trotskyist by adhering to the most 'orthodox' position then available. His initial move was assisted by his position on the nature of the USSR and the other Stalinist regimes, namely, that they represented more advanced forms of society than those of the capitalist West—not yet socialist, of course, but at least in the process of transition to socialism. He had criticised Dunayevskaya's belief that society had entered 'the age of state capitalism, a form of economy common to both U.S.A. and U.S.S.R', because it involved 'a fantastic undervaluation of socialist achievement in the Soviet Union' (MacIntyre 2008b, 43). In a sense, then, his initial organisational affiliation to the SLL was unsurprising, since this was precisely the position they also held, albeit in the special terminology of the Trotskyist movement (the USSR was a 'degenerated worker's state', the later Stalinist countries were 'deformed worker's states'). His first published work after joining the organisation was a review of Herbert Marcuse, in which he praised the author for rejecting alternative interpretations, such as state capitalism (MacIntyre 2008c, 78).

However, there were other reasons why the SLL might have seemed attractive to a young militant seeking an organisational framework. Given the sectarian dementia for which the SLL (and its later incarnation as the Worker's Revolutionary Party) became infamous on the British left, it is important to understand that it initially presented itself as an open organisation, keen to encourage debate and facilitate the exchange of views in SLL publications such as the weekly *Newsletter* and the monthly *Labour Review,* both of which were launched in 1957 (Hallas 1969, 30; Ratner 1994, 207). This stance obviously held attractions for those who had found the regime in the Communist Party of Great Britain (CPGB) intolerable. Furthermore, the SLL was able to provide an explanation for the degeneration of the CPGB, which—unlike the explanations on offer from the New Left—did not see the problem as lying with the Original Sin of democratic centralism.

Much of what MacIntyre wrote for the SLL was focused on the question of revolutionary organisation. In a talk delivered—incredible as it now seems—on the BBC Third Programme and later reproduced in *The Listener,* he identified the key factors behind the decline of the CPGB as the 'rise of Stalinism in the Soviet Union' and 'the defeat of the British working-class in the General Strike' (MacIntyre 2008f, 116–17). This is possibly the most 'orthodox' statement of his career, although there is little in it with which members of any other Trotskyist grouping would disagree. But, moving from historical analysis to the contemporary scene, it is clear that MacIntyre was conscious of the need to balance the ability to reach out to the existing audience for socialist politics— whether or not they possessed the correct proletarian credentials—with the need for a revolutionary organisation. In his discussion of the New Left, for example, he objected to the dismissive tone adopted by SLL theoretician Cliff Slaughter, but MacIntyre saw his more positive approach as a way of winning activists in the New Left to a more fully revolutionary politics and party commitment, not perpetuating its amorphous approach to organisation (MacIntyre 2008e).

The internal SLL debate over the nature of revolutionary organisation reached its highest level in an essay by MacIntyre, 'Freedom and Revolution', published the following year. In part, this seems to have been an attempt to defend the theory of the revolutionary party embodied in

the SLL against those who—in response to its increasingly undemocratic practice—had either left or been expelled from it. But it was also
an attempt to think through his own perspective, which was beginning
to diverge markedly from that of his comrades. MacIntyre argues from
first principles, starting with the position of people in capitalist society,
not with quotations from Lenin and Trotsky (although the discussion of
ideology in 'What Is to Be Done?' forms a ghostly backdrop throughout).
Indeed, the only thinkers he mentions are Hegel and Marx. He begins his
case for a revolutionary party with the apparently paradoxical notion
that such a party is essential for the realisation of human freedom—not
the usual starting point in Leninist or Trotskyist discussions: 'To assert
oneself at the expense of the organisation in order to be free is to miss
the fact that only within some organisational form can human freedom
be embodied' (2008g, 129). But the role of the vanguard party is not itself to achieve freedom, 'but to moving the working class to build it'. In
order to 'withstand all the pressures of other classes and to act effectively
against the ruling class', it has to have two characteristics (2008g, 132).

The first, the need for constant self-education, is relatively unconten-
tious. But the second, which returns to the paradox of vanguardism and
freedom, is more interesting. MacIntyre begins conventionally enough,
noting that 'one can only preserve oneself from alien class pressures in a
vanguard party by maintaining discipline. Those who do not act closely
together, who have no overall strategy for changing society, will have neither need for nor understanding of discipline' (2008g, 133). Appeals for
'discipline' by themselves were unlikely to win over members of the New
Left, who were only too conscious of how this strategy had been used by
Stalinist parties to suppress discussion, but their alternative tended to
emphasise personal choice. MacIntyre was able to show that there was an
organisational alternative to both bureaucratic centralism and liberal
individualism:

> Party discipline is essentially not something negative, but some-
> thing positive. It frees party members for activity by ensuring that
> they have specific tasks, duties and rights. This is why all the consti-
> tutional apparatus is necessary. Nonetheless there are many socialists
> who feel that any form of party discipline is an alien and constraining

force which they ought to resist in the name of freedom. The error here arises from the illusion that one can as an isolated individual escape from the moulding and the subtle enslavements of the status quo. Behind this there lies the illusion that one can be an isolated individual. Whether we like it or not every one of us inescapably plays a social role, and a social role which is determined for us by the workings of bourgeois society. Or rather this is inescapable so long as we remain unaware of what is happening to us. As our awareness and understanding increase we become able to change the part we play. (MacIntyre 2008g, 132–33)

The knowledge required to identify our social role is not, however, a personal but a collective possession. 'So the individual who tries most to live as an individual, to have a mind entirely of his own, will in fact make himself more and more likely to become in his thinking a passive reflection of the socially dominant ideas; while the individual who recognises his dependence on others has taken a path which can lead to an authentic independence of mind' (MacIntyre 2008g, 133).

Whether the SLL was the type of party that MacIntyre advocated was less clear. The leadership responded obliquely with an article by Cliff Slaughter, 'What Is Revolutionary Leadership?', not criticising MacIntyre by name, but identifying what Slaughter evidently saw as an inadequate conception of the revolutionary party (Slaughter 1960, 103). Slaughter's response was itself a serious contribution, which brought into the debate arguments not only from Lenin but from the early Georg Lukács and Antonio Gramsci, both of whom were virtually unknown in the English-speaking world at this time. Lukács in particular was to be important in MacIntyre's development, although there is no evidence that he had read Lukács before this point. Nevertheless, Slaughter's essay also contained warning signs of the SLL's future development, notably in his insistence on the need to raise 'discipline and centralised authority . . . to an unprecedented degree' (Slaughter 1960, 107, 111).

In the course of an earlier debate in *The Listener*, MacIntyre had written that 'whether the SLL is or is not democratic or Marxist will be very clearly manifested as time goes on. I myself have faced no limitation on intellectual activity of any kind in the SLL' (MacIntyre 1960, 500).

Ironically, within months of writing these lines, MacIntyre was expelled from the SLL, along with a number of other prominent activists who refused to act as mere puppets of the leadership. In a letter to SLL leader Gerry Healy, MacIntyre observed that it was clearly impossible for a minority to exist within the organisation because of his personal dominance and the fact that he effectively owned it as private property, since the assets were in his name. His conclusion, however, was not that these problems stemmed solely from Healy's personal malevolence—real though that undoubtedly was—but because of the small size of the Trotskyist organisations, which allowed individuals to play this role (Callaghan 1984, 78). Nevertheless, he quickly joined another even smaller organisation, albeit one with—as Knight would have it—a 'less dogmatic' attitude to Trotskyism. Of his attitude towards Trotsky himself, however, there was no ambiguity. In the conclusion to 'Breaking the Chains of Reason', an essay written while he was still in the SLL but published only after his departure, MacIntyre concluded with an incandescent passage establishing his admiration for Trotsky as a model for radical intellectuals:

> Two images have been with me throughout the writing of this essay. Between them they seem to show the alternative paths for the intellectual. The one is of J. M. Keynes, the other of Leon Trotsky. Both were obviously men of attractive personality and great natural gifts. The one the intellectual guardian of the established order, providing new policies and theories of manipulation to keep society in what he took to be economic trim, and making a personal fortune in the process. The other, outcast as a revolutionary from Russia both under the Tsar and under Stalin, providing throughout his life a defence of human activity, of the powers of conscious and rational human effort. I think of them at the end, Keynes with his peerage, Trotsky with an icepick in his skull. These are the twin lives between which intellectual choice in our society lies. (MacIntyre 2008h, 166)

Having rejected Trotskyist orthodoxy, MacIntyre had two organisational choices if he wanted to remain an active revolutionary. One was International Socialism (formerly the Socialist Review Group) which had been formed out of a much earlier split—in fact, a series of expulsions—

from the last unified British Trotskyist organisation, the Revolutionary Communist Party, back in 1950. The central position of the IS, elaborated by the group's founder Tony Cliff in 1948 on the basis of his reading of the Marxist classics, was the very view of Stalinist states that MacIntyre had earlier rejected, namely, that they represented forms of state capitalism. The other was the post-Leninist, post-Trotskyist, and ultimately post-Marxist organisation established by other former SLL members, initially called Socialism Reaffirmed, then (from 1961) Solidarity. This group also rejected the view that the Stalinist regimes were in any sense socialist, but were far less specific than the IS in giving them a positive characterisation, referring to them instead as examples of 'bureaucratic society'. Another difference was important for MacIntyre's later theoretical and political development. Whereas for the IS, the postwar boom was underpinned by the arms economy, to Cliff and the other major IS theoretician, Mike Kidron, this boom did not lead to permanent stabilisation but rather would ultimately produce its own contradictions. Solidarity, on the other hand, drawing on the work of the one-time Greek Trotskyist known at the time as Paul Cardan (i.e., Cornelius Castoriadis), argued that capitalism had definitively overcome its tendency to economic crisis (compare Kidron 1970, ch. 3, with Castoriadis 1988, 233–57). In terms of how these organisations understood their relationship to the working class, however, there appeared to be far fewer differences, as can be seen by comparing the statements of their respective leading thinkers (Brinton 2004, 19; Cliff 2001b, 129). Cliff continued to talk about leadership, a notion which Maurice Brinton consciously avoids, but both groups had clearly distanced themselves from the kind of bureaucratic machine-Leninism practiced by orthodox Trotskyist organisations such as the SLL. Solidarity and IS coexisted in a relatively fraternal manner, and the early issues of *International Socialism* contained material by prominent Solidarity members, including Brinton (under the name of Martin Grainger) and Bob Pennington. It also published material by both Cardan and other members of his group, Socialisme au Barbarie, including the later prophet of postmodernism, Jean-François Lyotard (Cardan 1961; Lyotard 1963).

What was the relationship of IS to Trotskyism at this time? In 1965 the American author George Thayer reported an interview with Kidron:

'He claims that his group is not Trotskyist but Trotskyist-derived, point-ing out that Socialism is his first concern and that his conclusions may only incidentally incorporate the thoughts and conclusions of Trotsky. He adds that he welcomes all Socialist thought—from Marx, Lenin, E V Debs, or anyone else—if it can be of assistance to him' (Thayer 1965, 142).

As a one-time member of the Fourth International, Cliff identified more closely with Trotsky and the classical Marxist tradition he had done so much to preserve. There is no reason, however, to think that Cliff was not being perfectly honest in his 1959 assessment of the best model for a revolutionary party: 'For Marxists in advanced industrial countries, Lenin's original position can serve much less as a guide than Rosa Lux-emburg's, notwithstanding her over-statements on the question of spon-taneity' (Cliff 2001a, 113).[1] MacIntyre, therefore, would have regarded himself as having joined a group which had developed out of Trotskyism, while rejecting some of Trotsky's specific theoretical and organisational conclusions.

MacIntyre's Heterodox Trotskyism

The most complete statement of MacIntyre's attitude towards Trotsky and Trotskyism during this period was given in his review of the final volume of Isaac Deutscher's biography, *The Prophet Outcast* (1963). In this essay he argued that Trotsky never succumbed to the theoretical con-servatism that later overtook most of his followers: 'Throughout his life Trotsky was prepared to reformulate Marxism. The theory of permanent revolution bears striking witness to this' (MacIntyre 1971d, 58). Conse-quently, it was entirely in keeping with Trotsky's own theoretical bold-ness to seek to understand the limitations of his positions, where neces-

---

1. Cliff's subsequent revision of this and another passage in the 1969 edi-tion of *Rosa Luxemburg* was the result of his reconsideration of the nature of the revolutionary party in the aftermath of the French events of May 1968. The ver-sion in Cliff's *Selected Works* contains both original and revised passages. See Cliff 2001a, 113. For the impact of the May events on his thought, see Birchall and Cliff 2001, 209–13, and Cliff 2000, 98–104.

sary, and to move beyond them. MacIntyre now accepted Cliff's version of the theory of state capitalism as an attempt to do this and raised the possibility that Trotsky himself might have come to share this view, had he been faced with the evidence that private capitalism and socialism were not the only available alternatives; there was also 'the collective class rule of the bureaucracy'.

> For the Trotsky of the 1930s, as for Marx, socialism can be made only by the workers and not for them. It is in part because of this that Trotsky, had he lived, would have had to treat his predictions about the aftermath of the Second World War as falsified. He could not but have concluded from his own premises that Russia was in no sense a workers' state, but rather a grave of socialism. . . . He could never have accepted Deutscher's analysis, which has only one thing in common with his own: the use of nationalised property as a criterion for socialism. (MacIntyre 1971d, 55, 57)

The failure of more orthodox Trotskyists to make comparable theoretical reconsiderations condemned them to sterility. Consequently, his attitude towards these parties in some senses reverted to an earlier dismissiveness:

> So-called Trotskyism has always been among the most trivial of movements. It transformed into abstract dogma what Trotsky thought in concrete terms at one moment in his life, and canonised this. It is inexplicable in purely political dimensions, but the history of the more eccentric religious sects provides revealing parallels. The genuine Trotskyism of [Alfred] Rosmer or Natalya [Sedova] must have at most a few hundred adherents in the entire world. (MacIntyre 1971d, 59)

It is perhaps worth noting that, since MacIntyre was still active in IS at this time, he presumably did not regard himself as belonging to the political equivalent of a 'religious sect'. But, when all due recognition is granted to Trotsky's intellectual achievements, was there some connection between the chronic irrelevance of Trotskyist organisations and his own thought? MacIntyre hinted at an answer in a review of Trotsky's *Literature and Revolution,* in which he wrote that Trotsky's literary criticism revealed the 'unity of greatness and weakness' in his thought: 'The greatness lies in the grasp of actual social connections.... The weakness comes out in the substitution of an *a priori* scheme of things for the actual complex reality whenever he comes to a point made difficult by his own theory' (MacIntyre 1962b, 33). In another context MacIntyre gave a specific example of this weakness:

> When, in the early 1930s, Trotsky was confronted with the facts of this growth [in working-class standards of living] by the Marxist economist Fritz Sternberg he remarked that he had no time recently to study the statistics; that on the truth or falsity of the statements involved much else that he was committed to depended he does not seem to have noticed. Nor was this attitude restricted to Trotsky, whom I select here as the most honest, perceptive and intelligent of post-1939 Marxists. (MacIntyre 1968, 90–91)

This is less than fair to Trotsky, who wrote (in a series of notes not intended for publication), 'The dialectic does not liberate the investigator from painstaking study of the facts, quite the contrary; it requires it' (Trotsky 1986, 92). And this scrupulousness with 'the facts' is attested to, for example, by his handling of source material in *The History of the Russian Revolution.* What is of interest here is less the accuracy of MacIntyre's judgment than the source he identifies of Trotsky's theoretical weakness: 'Trotsky is as helpless as anyone else imprisoned in the categories of Leninism' (MacIntyre 1962b, 33). As this suggests, MacIntyre takes a far more ambivalent position towards Lenin than towards Trotsky. He noted that Wright Mills regarded himself as a Leninist without being a Marxist (MacIntyre 2008n, 244). What would a non-Marxist Leninism involve? In a discussion during which he accused Sartre of effectively holding this position, he accused him of lacking Lenin's 'practical realism' (MacIntyre 2008l, 206). But is that all Leninism is? The core of Marxism is summed up in the phrase Marx wrote into the Provisional Rules of the International Working Men's Association: 'That the emancipation of the working-class must be conquered by the working-class themselves' (Marx 1974, 82). From this perspective, the problem with Sartre (and Wright Mills) is more that the working class has no independent role to play in the revolution, and consequently will simply end up exchanging one set of masters for another. A non-Marxist Leninism would therefore be the elitist, conspiratorial affair that Liberals and Anarchists always accused actually existing Leninism of being.

This highlights the ambiguity in MacIntyre's position. In certain places he implies that the charge of elitism falsely identifies Lenin's politics with those of Stalin, whereas he instead links Trotsky and Lenin together as proponents of socialism from below: 'Trotsky's emphasis that socialism can only be built consciously and Lenin's that it cannot be built by a minority, a party, together entail that a pre-condition of socialism is a mass socialist consciousness' (MacIntyre 2008j, 189). In other places, however, he suggests that Lenin's politics were genuinely elitist, in other words, non-Marxist, and he invokes other Marxists to remedy this apparent defect in Lenin's thought. In particular, he claims that James Connolly had been truer to Marx's notion of political movement of the working class arising in the 'transition ... from the trade union movement concerned with purely isolated economic issues to the trade union movement concerned with the political issue of class power' (MacIntyre 2008i, 172–73). Here MacIntyre retreats from his own earlier insights in 'Freedom and Revolution'. The party cannot be an expression of the class because the class itself is uneven in terms of consciousness; instead, it is a political selection of individuals to develop and maintain class consciousness (Harman 1968–69).[2] A trade union cannot fulfill the function of a party precisely because it has to include all eligible workers regardless of

---

2. The essay by Harman referenced here was the most significant advance in the discussion of the revolutionary party since the MacIntyre/Slaughter contributions eight years earlier. Harman was the first British Marxist since Slaughter to make serious use of Gramsci in this context, and it is regrettable that MacIntyre does not seem to have encountered his work. This is particularly frustrating since, in several articles written during his membership in IS, MacIntyre raises themes that were later to be popularised with the partial translation into English of the *Prison Notebooks*, notably that of contradictory consciousness. 'All sorts of facts may limit social consciousness', wrote MacIntyre in 1963; 'But false consciousness is essentially a matter of partial and limited insight rather than of simple mistake' (MacIntyre 2008o, 252–53). Compare Gramsci 1971, 333.

their politics. Consequently, unions can be more or less militant in their behaviour, more or less progressive in their policies, but inevitably they must embody rather than overcome unevenness. Since MacIntyre does not accuse Trotsky himself of elitism, this reading suggests that the sole problem of Trotskyism was its attempt to maintain organisational forms that perpetuated bureaucratic elitism. Whatever there is to be said for this, it is quite clear that, from the point at which Trotsky became convinced of Bolshevism in 1917, he never wavered in his insistence that a revolutionary party was required for the success of the socialist revolution.[3] There may be circumstances in which building the party may not be immediately feasible, there may be examples where attempts to build revolutionary parties reproduce Stalinist rather than Leninist norms, but it would be difficult for anyone claiming fidelity to Trotsky's thought to rule out building a vanguard party as a matter of principle. Paraphrasing his own judgment on Wright Mills and Sartre, we might therefore say that MacIntyre regarded himself as a (idiosyncratic) Trotskyist without being a Leninist—a position whose coherence Trotsky would have questioned.

The problem that MacIntyre thought Lenin and Trotsky had in common was what he came to describe as their voluntarism. This position was explicable, he acknowledged, as a response to the Mensheviks' 'mechanical view of social development', but it did not provide a coherent alternative since it did not take account of 'the objective limitations of possibility'. So, Menshevik automatism led to Bolshevik voluntarism; Stalinism's mechanistic philosophy to Trotskyism's voluntaristic talk of crises of leadership; and even the orthodoxy of the British Communist Party to the voluntarism of the New Left (MacIntyre 2008o, 255). In some circumstances it is, of course, correct to say that the 'possible alternatives' are limited. Earlier in the same essay MacIntyre had discussed these in general terms: 'We may become conscious of the laws which govern our behaviour and yet be unable to change it; for there may be no alternative to behaving in the way that we do. Or again there may be alternatives, but not ones that enough of us would prefer to the present social system' (MacIntyre 2008o, 252). And later he pointed to a specific example from the degeneration of the Russian Revolution: 'The key lies in

---

3. Compare Trotsky 1975, 252, with Trotsky 1973, 215.

the nexus between Stalin's economic policies—which were directed toward problems for which, as Trotsky never fully understood, there were no *socialist* solutions—and the political need for purges created by the failure to acknowledge that socialist theory had perforce been left behind when these policies were adopted' (MacIntyre 1971c, 50).

By contrast, in his earlier writings MacIntyre had emphasised precisely how the subjective intervention of revolutionaries helped shape what would, in due course, become a new set of objective conditions:

> The Marxist standpoint starts from the view that this question is not a question about a system outside us, but about a system of which we are a part. What happens to it is not a matter of natural growth or mechanical change which we cannot affect. We do not have to sit and wait for the right objective conditions for revolutionary action. Unless we act now such conditions will never arise. (MacIntyre 2008d, 102)

What he is proposing here is far from a 'voluntarist' belief that any set of obstacles can be overcome by an act of will. The existence of circumstances in which alternatives are restricted or even nonexistent does not mean that they apply in every case. Furthermore, in his critique of Deutscher, MacIntyre gave perhaps the greatest example of the opposite situation in twentieth-century history, involving Lenin and Trotsky! (MacIntyre 1971d, 59).

Reading MacIntyre's work during this period can produce a dizzying effect, as the author moves back and forth between one assessment and other, often in quick succession, suggesting at the very least some uncertainty on his part as to his own conclusions. What is interesting about MacIntyre's positive reading of an 'activist' reading of history, in the passage quoted above, is how closely it echoes some of the positions taken by Lukács in *History and Class Consciousness* and *Lenin: A Study in the Unity of His Thought*. MacIntyre was soon to revisit the theme, decisively, in the terms set out by Lukacs and his pupil, Lucien Goldmann.[4]

---

4. *International Socialism* reprinted several works by Lukács and Goldmann in the 1960s.

In Goldmann's outstanding study of Pascal and Racine, *The Hidden God* (1964), he wrote:

> Marxist faith is faith in the future which men make for themselves in and through history. Or more accurately, in the future that we must make for ourselves by what we do, so that this faith becomes a 'wager' which we make that our actions will, in fact, be successful. The transcendental element present in this faith is not supernatural and does not take us outside or beyond history; it merely takes us beyond the individual. (Goldmann 1964, 90)

MacIntyre expanded on the parallel drawn by Goldmann between 'Pascal's wager' and the Marxist understanding of the relationship between theoretical understanding and action in the world:

> If tragic thought and dialectical thought differ in . . . crucial respects, they also resemble each other at key points. Both know that one cannot first understand the world and only then act in it. How one understands the world will depend in part on the decision implicit in one's already taken actions. The wager of action is unavoidable. . . . Not eternity but the future provides a context which gives meaning to individual parts in the present. The future which does this is as yet unmade; we wager on it not as spectators, but as actors pledged to bring it into being. (MacIntyre 1971f, 81, 84–85)[5]

Other Marxists, unknown to MacIntyre, had framed the issue in similar terms, notably Gramsci and Walter Benjamin (Gramsci 1971, 438; Löwy 2005, 4, 114, 137). But it is important to understand that when MacIntyre invokes the notion of tragedy in this context, he means this quite literally, for what seems to be entering his work at this point is a view

---

5. Compare the famous aphorism by MacIntyre's hero James Connolly—a favourite of Cliff's, incidentally—which makes precisely this point: 'For the only true prophets are they who carve out the future which they announce' (Connolly 1987, 263).

that the basis of the Marxist wager—the revolutionary capacity of the working class—might have been mistaken. Consequently, Marxists tended to invest the actual working class with characteristics it does not possess, at least to the extent that would allow the revolutionary project to be realised. MacIntyre sees this as a major theoretical reason for Lukács's collapse into Stalinism (MacIntyre 1971g). But why were the working class—whose self activity MacIntyre had hailed only a few years before—now deemed to be incapable of successful revolution?

Goodbye to All That

The emergent differences between MacIntyre and his comrades surfaced in a public meeting on June 5, 1965, organised by Solidarity. Ostensibly it was a debate between MacIntyre and Cardan on the latter's book, *Modern Capitalism and Revolution*. Solidarity had asked MacIntyre to represent the IS position without formally approaching the other organisation. The outcome of the debate seems to have surprised everyone, as the account of the meeting in Solidarity's own journal stated: 'The two main speakers, although approaching the problem from different angles, did not disagree on fundamentals. The similarity of many of their views led one comrade, who had come "expecting a debate", to deplore the presence of "two Cardans"' ('Cardan Debate' 1965, 22). The comrade was Kidron, whose contribution was actually one of the more measured from IS contributors. In his response to the discussion, MacIntyre detected 'a very bad tone in what Kidron and Cliff had said . . . because it was translated from the Russian, about the year 1905': 'The crucial difference between those who managed capitalism in the 19th century and those who manage it today was that the latter had achieved a degree of consciousness as to what they were doing' ('Cardan Debate' 1965, 23).

It was clear from this discussion that MacIntyre's own position was far closer to that of Solidarity and Socialisme au Barbarie than it was to the organisation to which he ostensibly belonged, but with one crucial difference: whereas Brinton and Cardan still maintained that the working class was a revolutionary force, this position was precisely what MacIntyre was increasingly coming to reject. His starting point was Lukács's claim that 'historical materialism both can and must be applied to itself' (Lukács 1971). Cardan made similar claims in a series of articles first published between 1961 and 1964, which were gradually translated by Solidarity throughout the 1960s and 1970s (Cardan 1971; Castoriadis 1987). But for Cardan, the self-investigation called for by Lukács would reveal that Marxism had to be abandoned, not least because of the ways in which it treats as permanent aspects of human society those which are particular to capitalism. MacIntyre appeared to converge on this version of the argument as the 1960s drew to a close:

> It would be inconsistent with Marxism itself to view Marxism in any other way: in particular, what we cannot do is judge and understand Marxist theory as it has really existed with all its vicissitudes in the light of some ideal version of Marxism. It follows that by the present time to be faithful to Marxism we have to cease to be Marxists; and whoever now remains a Marxist has thereby discarded Marxism. (MacIntyre 1970, 61)

The failure of Marxism was that it had accepted the division of the economic, political, and social that was characteristic of capitalism and was reproduced in the categories of liberal theory. This failure led most Marxists to misunderstand how a class could arise in Russia which had apparently abolished capitalist property relations and which used Marxist vocabulary to cover their continued exploitation of the working class (MacIntyre 1968, 100–104). MacIntyre argued that, hitherto, Marxists had explained away the failure of Marx's predictions either by claiming that the time scale was simply longer than Marx had supposed, or by asserting a series of 'supplementary hypotheses', including those of the labour aristocracy and 'doctrinal corruption', but that these were ways of avoiding two painful facts: 'The first of these was that the working class—not just its leadership—was either reformist or unpolitical except in the most exceptional of circumstances, not so much because of the inadequacies of its trade union and political leadership as because of its whole habit of life' (MacIntyre 1968, 90–91). The point was not that Marxism had never been true, but that it no longer was true:

[O]ne might write the history of the age which Marxism illuminated so much more clearly than any other doctrine did, the period
from 1848 to 1929, as one in which Marx's view of the progress of
capitalism was substantially correct, but at the end of which when
the Marxist script for the world drama required the emergence of
the European working-class as the agent of historical change, the
working-class turned out to be quiescent and helpless. (MacIntyre
1970, 42, 43)[6]

The second painful fact, which had contributed to the 'quiescence', was
that living standards had generally improved, if unevenly and incon-
sistently, especially after 1945, when 'the ability of capitalism to innovate in order to maintain its equilibrium and its expansion was of a radically new kind. Consequently, not only has the future crisis of capitalism
had—for those who wished to retain the substance of the classical Marxist view—to be delayed, there had to be additional explanations why, in
the new situation, capitalism is still liable to crisis in the same sense as
before'. The resulting degeneration can take two main forms. On the one
hand are those who 'flee from the realities of that society into the private cloud-cuckoo lands of Marxist sectarianism where they tilt at capitalist windmills with Marxist texts in their hands, the Don Quixotes of
the contemporary left'. On the other hand are those who 'embrace what
Lenin called the worship of what is . . . allowing Marx's notion of revolutionary working class power to be confused with that of the administrative manoeuvres of the Soviet bureaucrats' (MacIntyre 1968, 105).

As a result of these changed conditions, those who describe themselves as 'revolutionaries' are, according to MacIntyre, likely to have five
main characteristics. First, theirs is an 'all-or-nothing existence', whose
activities allow them, second, to 'sustain a plausible social existence'.
Third, they must believe that their activities have 'world-historical significance', which provides the justification for their revolutionary beliefs,

---

6. Open statements of working-class incapacity are actually quite rare in
the writings of ex-Trotskyists, but for an earlier rejection of Marxism on these
grounds by Trotskyists in the United States, see Vannier 1948.

despite their apparent lack of significance in the world: 'In this way miniscule Trotskyist groups can represent their faction fights as a repetition of the great quarrels of the Bolshevik party'. Fourth, the tension between activity and aspiration gives their lives an inevitable precariousness: 'Joseph Conrad understood this; so did Henry James; so, in his own way, did Trotsky'. Fifth, and finally, revolutionaries must believe that their activities are justified by both history and their own activity, but both are refutable by counterexamples: 'This requirement is in obvious tension, however, with the revolutionary's commitment to make the predictions derived from his theory come true'. MacIntyre claims that a comparable elitism links the revolutionary with the industrial manager and the professional social scientist: 'The ideology of expertise embodies a claim to privilege with respect to power'. Consequently, the 'contemporary revolutionary' is 'antidemocratic' (MacIntyre 1973a, 340–42).

Examples of 'antidemocratic' revolutionaries abounded in the late 1960s, of course, not least in the Third World. Yet even at this stage, MacIntyre still counterposes Trotsky the revolutionary democrat against such revolutionaries and their sympathisers in the developed world: 'One can well understand why Trotsky's ghost haunts Sartre and Debray. For both Sartre and Debray have a peculiar conception—far more elitist than that of Leninism—of an inert mass of, be it workers, be it peasants, who need a leadership of particular gifts to rouse them to revolutionary activity'. But on this view, Trotskyism is not an alternative strategy for revolutionaries in the Third World, but an analysis which identifies why they are bound to fail and, in doing so, bound to endlessly repeat the experience of Socialism in One Country, in other words, of Stalinism (MacIntyre 1971e, 73).

MacIntyre's essay title 'Marxism of the Will' indicates that for him, the Marxists he is criticising have succumbed to the illusions of voluntarism. Yet in some contexts he had accused Trotsky of the same failing that he now invokes against these Marxists. MacIntyre is not, of course, arguing that Trotsky was a secret gradualist, but rather, claiming that he is the supreme realist in the Marxist tradition. In effect, MacIntyre is arguing that Trotsky has demonstrated that there can be nothing beyond capitalism. This general conclusion is brought out with the greatest clarity in the closing pages of *After Virtue*:

[I]f the moral impoverishment of advanced capitalism is what so many Marxists agree that it is, whence are these resources for the future to be derived? It is not surprising that at this point Marxism tends to produce its own versions of the *Übermensch*: Lukács's ideal proletarian, Lenin's ideal revolutionary. When Marxism does not become Weberian social democracy or crude tyranny, it tends to become Nietzschean fantasy. One of the most admirable aspects of Trotsky's cold resolution was his refusal of all such fantasies.

A Marxist who took Trotsky's last writings with great seriousness would be forced into a pessimism quite alien to the Marxist tradition, and in becoming a pessimist he would in an important way have ceased to be a Marxist. For he would now see no tolerable alternative set of political and economic structures which could be brought into place to replace the structures of advanced capitalism. This conclusion agrees of course with my own. (MacIntyre 1985a, 262)

But is it legitimate to infer this conclusion from Trotsky's last writings? A passage that seems to have had particular importance for MacIntyre occurs in Trotsky's last sustained discussion of the nature of the USSR before his assassination:

The historic alternative, carried to the end, is as follows: either the Stalin regime is an abhorrent relapse in the process of transforming bourgeois society into a socialist society, or the Stalin regime is the first stage of a new exploiting society. If the second prognosis proves to be correct, then, of course, the bureaucracy will become a new ruling class. (Trotsky 1973, 11)

This is how MacIntyre interpreted these words in 'Trotsky in Exile':

Although Trotsky continued to defend the view that in some sense the Soviet Union was a workers' state, he had committed himself to predictions about the results of the Second World War, the outcome of which would for him settle the matter. If his view were correct, the Soviet bureaucracy after a victorious war would be overthrown as a result of proletarian revolution in the advanced countries of the West. If the view of those Trotskyists who held that a kind of bureaucratic state capitalism existed in Russia were correct, they would be vindicated by the failure to occur of such a revolution and such an overthrow. (MacIntyre 1971d, 55)

And here is how he interprets it in a superficially similar passage from *After Virtue*:

Trotsky, in the very last years of his life, facing the question of whether the Soviet Union was in any sense a socialist country, also faced implicitly the question of whether the categories of Marxism could illuminate the future. He himself made everything turn on the outcome of a set of hypothetical predictions about possible future events in the Soviet Union, predications which were tested only after Trotsky's death. The answer they returned was clear: Trotsky's own premises entailed that the Soviet Union was not socialist and that the theory which was to have illuminated the path to human liberation had in fact led to darkness. (MacIntyre 1985a, 262)

Between these two texts, the position MacIntyre derives from Trotsky has shifted from one in which the outcome of the war decides whether or not the USSR was a form of bureaucratic state capitalism, to one of deciding whether socialism is possible. The first vindicates Marxism because it is capable of explaining this outcome; the second condemns Marxism as being responsible for it. Given that in 'Trotsky in Exile' MacIntyre dismissed those Trotskyists who transformed 'into abstract dogma what Trotsky thought in concrete terms at one moment in his life', there is a certain irony in the fact that this is precisely what he does in *After Virtue*. Trotsky's position towards the USSR in the last years of his life is clearly bound up with his 'now or never' attitude to the entire world situation on the eve of the Second World War—a perspective which also included the irreversible decline of the capitalist economy, the collapse of Social Democracy, the impossibility of Third World development, and many other predictions which turned out to be false. The source of MacIntyre's error actually occurs in the first quoted passage above, for Trotskyists who identified the USSR as a form of state capitalism did not argue that revolution was impossible in Russia. Rather, they simply argued that the state was not an unstable, temporary formation, which would shatter under the impact of war, as Trotsky and his orthodox epigones claimed. Indeed, Cliff ended his initial statement of the state capitalist case by predicting 'gigantic spontaneous upsurges of millions' in a forthcoming revolution (Cliff 2003, 130).

AT THE END OF WORLD WAR II, ORTHODOX TROTSKYISTS FOUND THAT reality did not correspond to what their theory had predicted. Their initial response was to deny reality, then to revise their theory to such an extent that it lost contact with the notion of working-class self-emancipation that had been at the heart of both Trotskyism and the classical Marxist tradition it sought to continue (Callinicos 1990). MacIntyre, in effect, did the opposite. He too understood that the world had changed, but he was too intellectually honest to produce endless 'auxiliary hypotheses' to protect the theory. If MacIntyre had simply overestimated the extent to which these changes signaled permanent shifts in the nature of capitalism, reality would soon have provided a check with the onset of crisis from the mid-1970s. Yet this was not the only or the main reason why MacIntyre abandoned Trotskyism and, with it, Marxism as a tradition. Rather, it was the source of individual insights. He has restated that second reason, namely, working-class incapacity, on several occasions since, most recently in 'The *Theses on Feuerbach*: A Road Not Taken'.

In this essay, MacIntyre discusses the world of the hand-loom weavers, as documented by E. P. Thompson in *The Making of the English Working Class*, and of the Silesian weavers whose struggle Marx himself noted in 1844, and contrasts the militancy of both of these with the situation of the contemporary working class: 'But [Marx] seems not to have understood the form of life from which that militancy arose, and so later failed to understand that while proletarianisation makes it necessary for workers to resist, it also tends to deprive workers of those forms of practice through which they can discover conceptions of a good and of virtues adequate to the moral needs of resistance' (MacIntyre 1998f, 232). This does not mean that MacIntyre has become reconciled to capitalism. According to his current Aristotelian position, 'the costs of economic development are generally paid by those least able to afford them', but politics offers no alternative:

Attempts to reform the political systems of modernity from within are always transformed into collaborations with them. Attempts to overthrow them always degenerate into terrorism or quasi terrorism. What is not barren is the politics involved in constructing and sustaining small-scale local communities, at the level of the family, the neighbourhood, the workplace, the parish, the school, or clinic, communities within which the needs of the hungry and the homeless can be met. (MacIntyre 1998i, 265)

'I do not see any prospects of overthrowing the dominant social order', MacIntyre has written. 'But perhaps it can be outlived; and even if it cannot be overthrown, it ought to be rejected' (MacIntyre 1984a, 252). The difficulty is that it looks increasingly likely that the dominant social order may not allow us the luxury of outliving it. If we do not succeed in overthrowing it, then things will not simply continue in the old oppressive way, getting perhaps a bit better, perhaps a bit worse. Socialism is necessary simply to remove the threats to existence for millions from starvation, epidemics, and war, and for everyone, including the capitalists themselves, of environmental catastrophe. It may be that one of the other Marxists who understood revolution as a form of 'wager' was belatedly right in his assessment. 'Marx says that revolutions are the locomotive of world history', wrote Walter Benjamin in 1940: 'But perhaps it is quite otherwise. Perhaps revolutions are an attempt by the passengers on this train—namely, the human race—to activate the emergency brake' (Benjamin 2003, 402). In these circumstances, revolution appears, not as a sectarian indulgence, but as the only serious option, so we had better find a way to make it work without reproducing the very forms of oppression which make it necessary. In periods of crisis and social upheaval, Marxism, or rather, Marxisms, always experience a revival in interest. The variants which attain the greatest popularity are not always those which embody the emancipatory heart of the tradition. And if MacIntyre's critique, of which his engagement with Trotsky was such a central part, cannot be accepted as a whole, it may still alert us to potential dangers and indicate the roads not to take.

10

MacIntyre and the Subversion of Natural Law

SANTE MALETTA

In this essay I aim to test MacIntyre's claim that the natural law is *subversive* of *liberalism*. What is natural law, according to MacIntyre? MacIntyre opens his essay 'Aquinas and the Extent of Moral Disagreement' with a consideration of the major aspects of ordinary moral experience: 'Characteristically and generally human beings first encounter judgments about goods as small children in situations in which what is for their good is sharply contrasted with what they are about to do or have just done at the immediate prompting of some desire. . . . And the same contrast is also central when the young are later initiated into a variety of practices as students or apprentices'. So, he argues, 'everyone of us initially brings to the practices in which we engage a set of motivations grounded in our antecedent desires. . . . But what successful initiation into every particular practice requires . . . is that one should come to recognise the goods internal to that practice and the standards of excellence necessary to achieve those goods. So our desires have to be redirected and transformed' (MacIntyre 2006k, 70). We learn, therefore, to distinguish between what is good to do or to achieve and what we currently happen to want, and this distinction 'is one that is primarily embodied in our everyday practice, including our practical discourse, and only secondarily in our theoretical reflections about our practice. And it is also at the level of everyday practice that we face the question of what place to give in our lives to the multifarious kinds of good that we have learned that it is possible for us to achieve' (MacIntyre 2006k, 70).

It is impossible to answer this question without referring to some conception of human flourishing and to some single final end, which is revealed in the way in which we organise the multiple goods we pursue. And in doing so, we realise that there is deep disagreement about what constitutes the final end or human flourishing. We face the case of fundamental moral disagreements, which are a 'matter for theoretical, philosophical enquiry, just because in such moral disagreements each contending party presupposes a view of human nature for which *truth* is claimed' (MacIntyre 2006k, 72). MacIntyre holds that in these cases, when we encounter moral disagreement 'in the course of *deliberation* about what to do here and now . . . what rationality requires is that we deliberate further with others about how such disagreement should be resolved, including among those others those with whom we mostly disagree' (MacIntyre 2006k, 72, emphasis added).

In order to understand MacIntyre's view, we need to reflect on what deliberation is: 'deliberation is by its very nature a social activity . . . when my relationships with others are in good order, my conclusions as to how it is best for me to act will often be one of a set of decisions, by others as well as by myself, which give expression to a common mind that we have arrived at together in our shared deliberations' (MacIntyre 2006k, 72–73). Deliberation as a social activity is helpful to overcome the one-sidedness of each individual's point of view, but it is essential in order to distinguish between genuine goods and objects of desire in the concrete circumstances: 'it is when the goods that we are pursuing are genuine goods that we are least able to recognise that we are pursuing this or that not so much because it is good as because its achievements will satisfy our desire for, say, power. This is when we most need the ruthless correction of our judgments by others who can see in us what we cannot see in ourselves' (MacIntyre 2006k, 73–74). Of course, in order to be a source, not of deliberative corruption, but of deliberative correction, we need from others the exercise of the virtues of objectivity.

Before considering the relation between the natural law and the ordinary moral experience, we need to take another step. Following Aristotle and Aquinas, MacIntyre holds that deliberation is about means and not about ends. If this is true, 'how is it possible for engagement in deliberation to involve reflection upon our ultimate end, whether in agreement or disagreement?' We should recall that first we have a *practical,* not a theoretical, knowledge of our ultimate end: 'We do not begin, as theoretical enquiry does, with some partly articulated, highly general conception of that end that can be stated in propositional form. It is rather that we begin by discovering a directedness in our particular actions and in our particular deliberations, so that we find ourselves inclined, first by nature, then by habituation acquired through education by others, to move towards certain types of goal, ordered and understood in certain specific ways' (MacIntyre 2006k, 75). We can discover a disagreement with others on a particular judgment or choice, and this disagreement can be superficial or basic. In the latter case, we are pushed to raise questions of a theoretical kind (assuming that we have the moral and rational virtues to do this). Here we face the possibility that shared deliberation with others is no longer possible, namely, that the community already produced by the participation in 'joint rational decision-making' disappears. We have three chances to make communal decision-making possible. The first is to rely on 'inherited patterns of authority that are endowed with non-rational legitimacy'; the second, to base communal decision-making 'on some implicit or explicit social contract whereby individuals and groups, each trying to maximize their own advantage, arrive at some arrangement about the allocation of costs and benefits'. The negative aspect common to these first two chances is that in both of them, 'it will be inequalities of power that determine the outcomes of decision-making processes' (MacIntyre 2006k, 76). The third chance is to rely on enquiry in company with the opposing others, together trying to discover the truth about the flourishing of human nature. Enquiry is a *practice*: it has an internal good to be achieved and internal rules to be respected. Shared participation in the practice of enquiry presupposes agreement on the following two truths: 'no account of the human good can be adequate that is not vindicated and sustained by continuing enquiry that takes truth to be its end and good', and 'the good of truth must be a constitutive part of the human good' (MacIntyre 2006k, 77).

Such a progress towards truth is achieved only if three conditions are satisfied: 'we have to accord to the good of truth a place that does not allow it to be overridden by other goods'; 'enquiry has to find *some* continuing and significant place in our lives' (MacIntyre 2006k, 77), by following its own rules and by exercising its own virtues; and we have to become disinterested. In particular, the first two identify the rules of the ethics of enquiry, while the third is the major condition of a form of intellectual and moral asceticism that can counter the influence of material and psychological interests.

If we are disinterested, then 'our relationship to those together with whom we are engaged in argumentative enquiry will have to be governed by norms that afford to each participant the best opportunity for considering the rival theses and arguments that have been presented impersonally and impartially'. First, 'a precondition of rationality in shared enquiry is mutual commitment to precepts that forbid us to endanger gratuitously each other's life, liberty or property' (MacIntyre 2006k, 78). 'So the precepts by which we will be bound, insofar as we are rational, will forbid us ever to take innocent lives, to inflict other kinds of bodily harm on the innocent, and fail in respect for the legitimate property of others'. Moreover, 'we can expect the other to speak the truth, as she or he understands it. There must be no deceptive or intentionally misleading speech. And each of us must be able to rely upon commitments made by the others' (MacIntyre 2006k, 79).

It is now evident that *the precepts of practical enquiry are the precepts of natural law.* We do not acquire them as a result of enquiry, but we find out that 'we have already—implicitly, characteristically, rather than explicitly—had to accord them authority' in adopting the attitudes of rational enquiry (MacIntyre 2006k, 79). In summary, we can say with Mark Murphy that the precepts of natural law are standards of justice common to all communities. They are both substantive and procedural. The precepts of natural law are presupposed and naturally known in every circumstance where we have a common learning and a common research about the individual and the common goods on behalf of a group of rational individuals (Murphy 2003).

II

What are the major consequences of the refusal of the natural law? These consequences are clearly outlined in MacIntyre's commentary on the papal encyclical *Veritatis Splendor* (MacIntyre 1994a), where he claims that certain errors, popular in liberal culture, are at the same time philosophical and moral errors. First, 'there are those mistakes which derive from distorted conceptions of the freedom and autonomy of the individual self. . . . One expression of these conceptions is attachment to some notion of the self as constituted in key part by its pre-rational and pre-moral choices. . . . Another expression . . . is the conferring upon the individual conscience of a sovereign independence of *any* standards external to its own judgments' (MacIntyre 1994a, 191).

Secondly, 'there are those mistakes which derive from the tendency in our culture to conceive of all practical situations as ones in which it is appropriate for rational agents to weigh benefits and costs. . . . This generally has two bad consequences. If and whenever changing social circumstances alter the balance of costs and benefits, so that what was hitherto a profitable principle for me to live by becomes an unprofitable one, then it also becomes, on this view, rational and right for me to exchange that principle for another' (MacIntyre 1994a, 191). Therefore, he argues, 'unconditional trust in another becomes form of moral superstition. Temporariness becomes a crucial feature of the moral life and the virtue of integrity, of a willingness and an ability to stand by one's central commitments, whatever the consequences, becomes thought of not as a virtue, but as a piece of moral irrationality'. Another consequence of reducing practical rationality to a calculation of benefits and costs is that 'what is in fact incommensurable is too often treated as though it were commensurable and . . . what is presented in the guise of rational calculation in fact conceals . . . an underlying set of evaluative judgments of quite another kind. The apparently rational may thus disguise . . . arbitrariness of preference and power. And the self is once again injured by such concealment and deception' (MacIntyre 1994a, 192).

A final consequence of the refusal of natural law is *relativism*, because the natural law embodies the standard that makes it possible to have a 'conversation with the representatives of alien cultures in which we might learn how to see ourselves from their point of view and so learn further about ourselves' (MacIntyre 1994a, 193). In summary, 'each of these three kinds of error turns out to be an attachment to something which in the end deprives us not only of our good . . . but also of something crucial in ourselves, something without which we will become

incapable of achieving that which alone in the end gives point and purpose to our activities ... we become *self-frustrating beings*' (MacIntyre
1994a, 194, emphasis added).

III

The expression 'self-frustrating beings', I believe, is at the core of Mac-
Intyre's criticism of liberalism. It allows us to go beyond MacIntyre's
explicit critique to the possibilities inherent in his revision of the natural law tradition. To do so, let us recall the major features of MacIntyre's
criticism of liberalism.

If we consider liberalism as a political doctrine—that is, as a doctrine whose major issue is the juridical limitation of political power and
the defence of individual liberties—there is nothing wrong with it. The
problem, of which the supporters of political liberalism are seldom aware,
is that it almost always joins with moral and economic doctrines that are
not fully consistent with its own message (see MacIntyre 1971i, 281–83).
In particular, in modern times, political liberalism has embraced the view
that the individual is the unique source of moral value, in juxtaposition
with the idea that the realm of facts is deprived of any axiological dimension. Politics is represented as a market, where responsible individuals can rationally choose the best offer among available offers. There
are two major negative aspects of this situation. First, the political offers
are determined by the elites, who hold the power in politics and in the
media—a situation that leads to a rising apathy among the electorate
(see MacIntyre 2006l, 153). Secondly, the responsibility and the rationality of individuals in the political market are understood exclusively in
terms of strategic action.

Political liberalism of this type is inconsistent with its own core mis-
sion, the defence of individual liberties. This becomes evident when we
consider the theories of action that underlie the most popular moral and
political concepts of liberalism (the second part of MacIntyre's *Against
the Self-Image of the Age* is devoted to this topic). Against these theories,
MacIntyre first recalls that 'rational action is structured very differently
in different times and places' (MacIntyre 1998d, 120). Secondly, we must
not forget that rational action has a hermeneutic nature: it is formed by

practical reasoning, which has at the same time an individual and a social character, because it shapes how I understand others' actions and how others understand my actions. Moreover, as MacIntyre holds, every rational action is a practice, which *After Virtue* defines as a 'coherent and complex form of socially established cooperative human activity through which goods internal to that form of activity are realised in the course of trying to achieve those standards of excellence which are appropriate to, and partially definitive of, that form of activity' (MacIntyre 1985a, 187).

Liberals, on the contrary, understand practical reasoning in terms of satisfying agents' preferences, where these preferences are considered independently of any conception of the good and of any rational justifications of those preferences (see MacIntyre 1998d, 129). 'So it is not human individuals as such, bearing with them the complexities of belief and circumstance, including their allegiance to some theory of the good and their membership in social groups espousing such a theory, who are the agents who appear in modern practical reasoning. It is individuals *qua* individuals of whom I am speaking, individuals viewed by themselves and by others as inhabiting the role of "the individual"' (MacIntyre 1998d, 130). Thanks to the often implicit and even unconscious anthropological and psychological assumptions underlying the liberal view of social action, individuals are allowed to use the statement 'I want/desire this' as the major premise of a practical argument, that is, as a valid reason to act—independently of any assessment of that particular will or desire. In summary, we can say that, according to liberalism, the subject always reasons assuming the viewpoint of a third person, because she avoids assessing the will or the desire that underlies her own practical reasoning and action. She takes them as positive data. We face the case of *an alienation of the subject from her desire and her will,* that is, *from her own self.*[1]

Not only within liberalism but in every form of social life there is a close interdependence between the theory of action and the conception

---

1. For the distinction between 'first person' and 'third person' ethics, see Abbà 1996.

of practical reasoning. This is not a relativist view. On the contrary, it is the starting-point for 'understanding relativism and perspectivism historically, as arising from and giving expression to the standpoint of a particular type of social and cultural situation', that is the situation in which

> the individual has been able to or has been compelled to free him or herself from any fixed identity which would impose a standpoint. . . . It can only be the individual whose distinctive identity consists in key part in the ability to escape social identification, by always being able to abstract him or herself from any role whatsoever; it is the individual who is potentially many things, but actually in and for him or herself nothing. And this may well be someone whom it is very difficult to be outside the arenas of philosophical and literary discussion. (MacIntyre 1998d, 135)

MacIntyre provocatively describes the standpoint of an individual of this kind through an expression borrowed from A. A. Zhdanov: 'rootless cosmopolitanism'.

Every form of practical rationality and every enquiry about practical rationality are thus bound to a particular standpoint, which has been 'developed within the kind of tradition which has been able to embody itself to the necessary degree in the kind of social relationships, in the forms of community which are necessary for its exemplification' (MacIntyre 1998d, 135). Therefore, the rootless cosmopolitan speaks 'from a standpoint dictated by a stage in the dissolution of social traditions at which no form of practical rationality is any longer possible' (MacIntyre 1998d, 135). This is the most negative aspect of liberalism and the most alarming cultural feature of our own age.

Three examples taken from sociology may clarify the crisis of practical rationality. We are already familiar with the first, namely, the tendency to conceive of all practical situations as ones in which it is appropriate for rational agents to weigh benefits and costs. The second is the *professionalisation of procedures*: 'Ours is a culture dominated by experts, experts who profess to assist the rest of us, but who often instead make us their victims'. The most notable case of professionalisation of procedures is embodied by lawyers, 'who will proceed to represent you by words that are often not in fact yours, who will utter in your name documents that it would never have occurred to you to utter, and who will behave ostensibly on your behalf in ways that may well be repugnant to you' (MacIntyre 2000a, 91–92). '[T]he plain person in search of a remedy is thereby to a significant degree *alienated from the words and actions* which are thus legally and bureaucratically imputed to her or him, and is able in any case to speak and act in this guise only as the more or less instructed and obedient client of someone whose professional expertise has officially licensed her or him to behave as required' (MacIntyre 2006d, 115, emphasis added). But even if the plain person obtains the remedy he wanted, he or she will find out that

> through the process of obtaining this remedy ... *the original relationship has been transformed into something quite other than it at first was,* so that the outcome of the complaint and its bureaucratic sequels cannot be the once hoped for restoration of the original relationship of trust, but must be instead a relationship informed by rules mandating an enforceable respect, rules away and only to be correctly grasped through dependent reliance upon someone else's professional expertise. (MacIntyre 2006d, 115–16, emphasis added)

The most important negative aspect of the professionalisation of procedures is the erosion of the social capital of mutual trust: individuals increasingly will rely on procedural rules and professional expertise, and this reliance will alter the character of the original personal engagements. The final effect is paradoxical: a social order built to defend the value of the individual and her own liberties produces a new form of dependence and alienation.

The third example is the compartmentalisation of roles. This is the one MacIntyre stresses most, because it involves the possibility of a concrete exercise of the virtues. Such compartmentalisation occurs when 'each distinct sphere of social activity comes to have its own role structure governed by its own specific norms in relative independence of other such spheres' (MacIntyre 2006n, 197). The precepts of the virtues are understood as prescriptions for the development of habits that make an individual more efficient in his or her role-playing. Virtues lose the subjective dimension that they have from an Aristotelian or a Thomist viewpoint: they no longer support the development of an awareness of the goals included in one's social role and therefore the possibility of criticising them. The outcome of the compartmentalisation of roles is a divided self, who lacks the two virtues basic to the exercise of his moral responsibility—integrity, which sets limits to one's adaptability to social roles, and constancy, which sets limits to flexibility of character (MacIntyre 2006n, 192). In summary, the compartmentalisation of roles produces an uncritical and therefore irresponsible moral agent.

Generally, the liberal subject is unaware of her condition. On the one hand, she flatters herself on being able to disengage from any social role, and on the other hand, she totally identifies with the social roles she happens to play. *After Virtue* calls this situation 'bureaucratic individualism'. In both cases we have an inauthentic solution, because the individual is encouraged to shy away from responsibilities. The liberal subject has an *ideological* consciousness—in the Marxian sense of the word 'ideology', which means a false consciousness. As MacIntyre claimed in his book on Marxism, alienation in capitalist societies lies in the fact that individuals as social actors 'do not recognise the source of this frustration as residing in the forms of their own activity; in this consists their *alienation from themselves*' (MacIntyre 1968, 89, emphasis added). This is possible because social practices and institutions are not mere objects or positive data, but are in part shaped by the beliefs and the concepts of those individuals involved in them. Social tensions and conflicts influence the theoretical vocabulary used to represent those social practices and institutions. In other words, sociological doctrines are related to social conflicts. In this situation, 'social victory . . . is the achievement of inducing those who participate in the practice to agree in conceptualising their activities in such a way that one of the contestable interpretations no longer appears contestable, but simply how things are—"the facts". It is when a social theory serves this form of social practice that it functions as an ideology' (MacIntyre 1998b, 59). Ideology tends to present a partial truth so that in practice it is protected against any possible confutation. Therefore ideology conceals social conflicts, it censors other possible interpretations, and it presents what actually occurred as necessary. Hence, in practice ideology works as a prohibition upon asking questions (MacIntyre 2006j, 42).

From this viewpoint, liberalism is an ideology playing two incompatible roles: it is one of the conflicting parties, and it governs the public debate about the good by determining the theoretical vocabulary and the questions of this argument.

IV

How can the natural law subvert liberalism? Before answering this question, we need to ask if and how it is possible for an individual living in a liberal society to avoid false consciousness. This issue is approached by MacIntyre from a Thomist viewpoint in chapter 10 of *Whose Justice? Which Rationality?* '[T]he acquisition of practical knowledge and the exercise of good practical reasoning cannot occur without some development of the moral virtues and that in turn cannot occur without education; yet it must be the case that those not yet educated and those deprived of the possibility of such education possess sufficient practical knowledge to do and be what justice and the divine law require' (MacIntyre 1988a, 177). The solution to this problem can be found if we consider the fact that

> every human being has within him or herself the potentiality of formulating those principles which constitute the most fundamental precepts of divine law, *as it is presented to human reason by human reason,* and of rendering this knowledge actual in such a way and to such a degree as to make every individual responsible for not acting upon it. This actualisation of potentiality is part of the development of a natural aptitude for virtue, which needs to be trained. Such training is generally given to the young within the household. . . . What then are the resources of those deprived of such training . . . ? Their resource . . . lies in their intelligence. (MacIntyre 1988a, 179, emphasis added)

This consists primarily in asking moral questions of this kind: 'What is my good?', 'What precepts must I follow in order to learn what it is?' (MacIntyre 1988a, 177). As MacIntyre argues, 'The attempt to answer these questions will at the very least make it clear to such persons that they cannot pursue their good . . . in isolation and that the relationships into which they enter in order to secure their most obvious goods need to be such as will enable them to improve their knowledge of what their good is. . . . What the person deprived hitherto of adequate moral education has to discover is that what he or she needs is a friend who will also be a teacher in the approach to the virtues' (MacIntyre 1988a, 179–80). It follows that 'those human relationships through which alone anyone can hope to learn the nature of their good are themselves defined in practice as well as in theory by the standards set by the natural law. So the natural law is discovered not only as one of the primary objects of practical enquiry but as the presupposition of any effective practical enquiry'. Therefore, 'confrontation with the natural law is inescapable for anyone who persists in the enquiry as to what his or her good is' (MacIntyre 1988a, 180). We should also recall that this moral education has nothing automatic or necessary about it: it depends on the will, 'a will which being free to choose not only can choose to do evil but can give to that choice an endurance and a commitment which it would not otherwise possess' (MacIntyre 1988a, 181).

When an individual participates in social practices and tries to accomplish the precepts of the natural law, and at the same time carries on his own enquiry about the good and the goods, a new possibility arises for a rational discourse about the common good. This person will realise that, beyond the goods that are pursued individually by people, there are goods 'in key part constituted by cooperative activity and shared understanding of their significance'. In these cases, 'excellence in activity is of course often a means to goods other than and beyond that excellence. . . . But it is central to our understanding of a wide range of practices that excellence in the relevant kinds of activity is recognised as among the goods internal to those practices'. Moreover, 'without virtues skills lack the direction that their exercise requires, if excellence is to be achieved'. Therefore 'it is characteristic of such practices that engaging in them provides a practical education into the virtues' (MacIntyre 1998g, 240).

In "Politics, Philosophy and the Common Good," MacIntyre elucidates the relationship between moral experience and politics and the primacy of the natural law in shaping this relationship:

[F]or individuals who are so educated or are in the course of being so educated two questions arise inescapably, questions that may never be explicitly formulated, but which nonetheless receive answers in the way in which individuals live out their lives. For each individual the questions arises: what place should the goods of each of the practices in which I am engaged have in my life? . . . Yet any individual who attempts to answer this question pertinaciously must soon discover that it is not a question that she or he can ask and answer by her or himself and for her or himself, apart from those others together with whom she or he is engaged in the activities of practices. So the questions have to be posed: what place should the goods of each of the practices in which *we* are engaged have in *our* common life? What is the best way of life for *our* community? (MacIntyre 1998g, 240)

In such a community the common good is therefore founded on common learning; this stimulates that rational practice which is identical with the common good itself, namely, the ordering of individual goods and social goods. What generates the social bond is consequently the question of the order of the goods, because it is impossible to tackle this problem without involving others who take part in the practices. This is a model of political community that relies on a bond which is not cultural, ethnic, or linguistic, but rather *rational*: 'although this type of political society . . . does indeed require a high degree of shared culture by those who participate in it, it is not itself constituted by that shared culture and is very different from those political societies whose essential bonds are bonds of a shared cultural tradition'. It is not a *Volk* but a *polis*:

A *polis* is indeed impossible, unless its citizens share at least one language . . . and unless they also share modes of deliberation, formal and informal, and a large degree of common understanding of practices and institutions. And such a common understanding is generally derived from some particular inherited cultural tradition. But these requirements have to serve the ends of a society in which individuals are always able to put in question through communal deliberation what has hitherto by custom and tradition been taken for granted. . . . A *polis* is always, potentially or actually, a society of rational enquiry, of self-scrutiny. (MacIntyre 1998g, 241)

It is practical rationality itself that has a political dimension, because it is 'a property of individuals-in-their-social-relationships rather than of individuals-as-such' (MacIntyre 1998g, 242). From this point of view, the legitimisation of any political authority comes from the relationship between the individual good and the common good, and this relationship develops through the exercise of practical rationality, that is, through the enquiry and the discussion about the good and the goods.

All problems with the modern state originate in the fact that it cannot guarantee, except in a 'deformed and fragmented' way, the exercise of that common practical rationality which constitutes the common good. In the modern state, 'politics, far from being an area of activity in and through which other activities are rationally ordered, is itself one more compartmentalised sphere from which there has been excluded the possibility of asking those questions that most need to be asked' (MacIntyre 1998g, 243).

We can say now that, according to MacIntyre, politics is the activity of answering questions about the ordering of practices in ordinary life (Murphy 2003, 163). Politics is a *second-order practice.* Therefore, the internal goods of politics considered as a practice relate to deliberation about the practices. Politics is the common practical reasoning about the common life. It is consequently basic for the individual good and essential for the development of rational skills. In summary, politics itself, considered as a rational practice and as an exercise of practical rationality, embodies the common good. So MacIntyre succeeds in rephrasing the question about the common good, going beyond the limitations of the Marxian solution. MacIntyre's strategy—similar to other neo-Aristotelian contemporary approaches—is to point out within ordinary human praxis those practices that cannot be included in the category of *poiesis,* in which the products of practices are goods *external* to the practices. Within these practices, 'those engaged in [them] transform themselves and educate themselves through their own self-transformative activity, coming to understand their good as the good internal to that activity' (MacIntyre 1998f, 231). We can find examples of this in history,

MacIntyre argues (e.g., the hand-loom weavers of Lancashire and York-shire in the period around 1800), and these examples are revolutionary because these people refused to shape their own minds and lives according to individualist modern ideologies.

We can now answer our basic question as follows: The natural law is subversive because its precepts, though negative, enable the individuals to accomplish their own goods, and therefore they have a liberating function; the natural law 'frees us from a variety of hindrances and frustrations that would otherwise bring to nothing the pursuit by each of us of our positive good and that of the others' (MacIntyre 1994a, 177). To understand this, of course, we need to abandon as illusory and deceptive the liberal idea of moral freedom as the power to make our own pre-moral choice of norms and values. We must welcome a more detailed and sound conception of freedom:

> What freedom is for human beings depends upon what their capacities are, upon what difference it makes to them how they set about actualising those capacities, and upon what success they are able to have in so doing. To have become free is to have been able to overcome or avoid those distractions and obstacles which frustrate or inhibit the development of a capacity for judgments by standards whose rational authority we are able to recognise for ourselves and for action in accordance with such judgment. To have failed to become free is to have rendered oneself subject to frustration or inhibition in respect of such development. And the exercise of choice as such may contribute as easily and as often to failure as to success in becoming free. What we all have to learn is how to make right choices, on the basis of judgments that are genuinely our own, so that our choices contribute to the development and exercise of our capacities. The virtue which we need if we are to become capable of right choice is the Aristotelian virtue of *phronesis, prudentia*. The acquisition of the virtues is impossible without a recognition of the rational authority of the precepts of the natural law, most of all perhaps the negative exceptionless precepts. Thereby we become able to choose in a way that is not self-frustrating, but liberates our capacities for judgment and action directed towards our good. This is

why the negative precepts are . . . enabling, and why acknowledgment of their rational authority is a constitutive element of human autonomy. (MacIntyre 1994a, 183)

On the contrary, as we have seen, 'any attempt to locate human freedom in a freedom to make choices which are prior to and independent of the precepts of the natural law is bound to be not only theoretically mistaken, but also practically misguided'. From a theoretical point of view, 'those who accept such a view understand law as primarily a constraint upon, rather than an enabling condition of freedom'. And this erosion of rules practically leads to 'a surrender of human relationships to competing interests' (MacIntyre 1994a, 185).

V

It is finally possible to outline MacIntyre's political proposal. The first issue is the restoration of a conception of justice that allows us to formulate concerns about both desert and needs in terms of an overall idea of community, which is informed by a shared conception of the ultimate human good (MacIntyre 1991a, 107). Within such a community the law is considered, as we have already seen, an enabling resource. Since this conception of the law is integral to a conception of justice that 'requires that no one be excluded from the claims upon them to participate in the tasks of this kind of community', then the second issue is that law must have 'the structure of the precepts and arguments of the natural law' (MacIntyre 1991a, 108). The third issue requires us, first of all, to abstain from the controversies of large-scale public debate, since they lack a common standard, independent of the preferences and wills of the conflicting parties, to which appeal can be made in trying to show why one standpoint is rationally superior to the others. The natural law perspective must be communicated to those who are unfamiliar with it or hostile towards it 'by constructing the types of institutionalised social relationship within which it becomes visible'. Second, we must formulate disagreement within institutions (such as schools, clinics, or workplaces) 'in concrete terms at the level of practice. . . . At this level, such disagreements will be local and specific, concerned with the ends and thus the goods of particular types of policy, practice, and institution. These ends provide precisely the kind of context needed for an elaboration of what justice requires for its implementation, both in the enforcement of law and in the construction of institutions, in detailed and concrete terms' (MacIntyre 1991a, 110). In this form of social life, toleration is not a virtue, since each of us is required not simply to tolerate those who disagree, but to establish with them a rational debate and to accept the possibility of changing one's own mind. We should recall that in fact, every community is first of all a community of *research*.

This political prospect is utopian in the sense that it embodies the condition for solving political questions in modern times. As we have seen, the exercise of politics is basically the same as the exercise of practical rationality. Consequently, 'community' serves as the condition of solubility for both political and moral questions. Only within a communitarian form of life is it possible to avoid the alienation peculiar to the liberal subjects who are unable to question their own desires and wills, since they consider them as positive data. The community is the condition of possibility of the *humanum*.

If this is true, then MacIntyre's political prospect is somehow paradoxical, since it cannot be translated into a political platform. The final appeal to Saint Benedict in *After Virtue* is not merely a rhetorical device, but an acknowledgment that the generation of communitarian forms of life goes beyond the possibilities of human political planning. Borrowing from Jacques Derrida, we can say that *community is impossible*.

We can look at the paradoxical nature of community from the perspective of the so-called dilemma of Böckenförde: 'The free secular state lives according to presuppositions that it cannot itself guarantee' (see Böckenförde 1967, 93). MacIntyre does not reject the liberal state; on the contrary, he defends it from any organicist tendency that, according to him, is essentially totalitarian. Nevertheless, not only does he recognise that this kind of political regime is based on prerequisites that it cannot generate, but he is also aware that, as Émile Perreau-Sassine argues, 'the liberal political regime is dependent on pre-liberal dispositions, it presupposes habits that it continuously destroys' (Perreau-Saussine 2005, 126). The political is based on a pre-political entity—the community— which it unhappily undermines. The most evident case of this is the professionalisation of procedures, in which, as we have seen, human beings are alienated from their own words and actions. What is threatened here is something essential, that *original relationship* from which morality is generated, together with law and politics. In the professionalisation of procedures, in fact, law loses its own relational character, to the point that it can no longer generate the desired remedy (restoration of the original mutual trust), but instead produces a relationship governed by rules whose understanding depends on professional expertise.

MacIntyre implicitly opens up the possibility of new philosophical research that is strongly connected with the concept of natural law and the possibility of resisting evil. We have already noted his stress on the compartmentalisation of social roles peculiar to liberalism, which produces a divided subject, one unable to take a critical view of the standards that govern his or her social roles. This is an irresponsible individual, unable to take a firm stand, since he or she lacks the virtues of constancy and integrity. Such an individual cannot resist evil. MacIntyre therefore opens up the possibility of a new and interesting interpretive perspective on contemporary history, which is characterised by its inability to resist evil, especially when this evil has the deceptive but persuasive appearance of an ideology. It is not the case that constancy and integrity are the two virtues peculiar to those 'righteous' who, in the last century, could resist ideological evil (see Grasselli and Maletta 2006). From the point of view of MacIntyre, constancy and integrity arise and develop through the exercise of discourse—of that *logos* that never stops to ask questions about the order of the goods within a community of research. And this fact points to the prospect of an intelligent revival of the tradition of the natural law, when this is understood as a *rational* law, as a law that enjoins the achievement of the human good as *bonum rationis*; that is, as the good of reason, for reason, and formulated by reason.[2]

---

2. For such an approach, see Rhonheimer 2000.

11

Troubling Oneself with Ends

ANTON LEIST

Much contemporary normative thinking within ethics and politics falls either into thinking about ethics or into thinking about politics, but not both. This is due, in part, to apolitical conceptions of ethics and ethically neutral conceptions of politics. MacIntyre's work has never allowed for an easy categorisation into the one or the other field, and his more recent approaches decidedly neglect such conceptual and disciplinary restrictions. His programme of an Aristotelian-Thomist renewal of ethics is decisively anti-liberal and thereby critical of restraints of all kinds, especially those of politics as opposed to ethics. His central idea that human lives and communities are teleologically structured seems to provide the possibility of elaborating human goods in a way that transcends the restraints entrenched in modern thinking.

In this essay I distinguish different versions of a normative teleological theory, with the aim of investigating which version MacIntyre might be prone to defend himself against. In doing so, I will attempt to show that neither the Aristotelian nor the Thomist version of his programme is compatible with important liberal convictions constitutive of contemporary political visions. We are better off, I contend, giving up on the concept of a substantial ethical 'telos'. Either this concept, noncontroversially, can be substituted by 'ends', or it proves to be inconsistent with political ideas such as liberty, autonomy, and equality. Teleological theory is, in short, misleading at best, and an initiative to renew metaphysical humanism at worst.

Teleology in Ethics

Philosophical theories of action and theories of morality must be teleological in a sense, even if for different reasons. Theories of action have to reconstruct the intentionality and end-directedness of most, if not all, kinds of action. Theories of morality have to include an awareness of teleology, since the typical function of morality is to direct, motivate, or restrict individual actions. Morality thereby has to focus on the ends of actions, whether in terms of intentions or of factual outcomes. Even the strictest and simplest deontological morality—as, for example, David Ross's conception of *prima facie* duties—is teleological in the sense that it is an order either to do or to avoid doing something. However, it would be an error to conclude that all ethics and politics must be 'teleological' in a more interesting sense.

In order to be teleological in a more substantive sense—the sense commonly identified with 'teleological ethics'—normative reference to a good has to be made. Such a reference seems to be unavoidable within nonauthoritarian forms of morality, given that duties and rights, if not accepted outright, have to be explained and justified by appealing to what is good. Nonauthoritative versions of morality invite a teleological form, and since ethics per se is a kind of critical reflection on morality, it could be concluded that ethics per se has a teleological form.[1] General form al-

---

1. Contrary to this statement, the distinction between 'teleological', 'deontological', and 'virtue' ethics is prominent in many introductory texts. But these distinctions might be better read as signifying different interests, that is, interests in goods and values, duties, rights, and virtues. As Nussbaum (1999) shows for the misleading stereotype of 'virtue ethics' as a 'theory' separate from the other traditions, ethics comprises these different topics within a single overall structure.

lows for different interpretation, however, and in the following I will distinguish three versions of teleological ethics, and then concentrate on what I take to be the most important one.

The three versions are distinguished by what could be called a 'utilitarian', a 'rationalist', and a 'perfectionist' *telos*, yielding a utilitarian, rationalist, or perfectionist teleological view of morality. Given the many terminologies and taxonomies available in the literature, my distinctions are certainly not original, and hopefully they depart only slightly from what has been covered under different terms. I define the three kinds of *telos* as follows:

Utilitarian telos: maximisation of *good states*, with an open category of what counts as good.

Rationalist telos: striving for the right in terms of *reason*; doing what is right because of its being right, the right being nonreductive in relation to the good.

Perfectionist telos: striving for *actor* conceptions of the good.

Crucial to these three views is the difference between *good states, reasons*, and *actors*. If one begins teleological thinking of morality with any one of these concepts and tries to be coherent, one will be caught up in a general logic that lies behind utilitarianism, rationalism, and perfectionism. I will not try to prove the conceptual self-sufficiency and distinctness of the three ideas here. Nor is it possible to do justice to the pros and cons of each of these views, or to the wealth of developed subpositions in each of the three families of excessively detailed theories.[2] Nevertheless, it is intuitively clear that to set oneself the end of a good in terms of states, one will have to transcend one's personally related good (including the virtuous dispositions one might achieve) and become involved in an argument concerning how to organise one's life under

---

2. This is especially true, as is well known, of the utilitarian and rationalist positions. The former differentiate into act-, rule-, and other types of utilitarianism, the latter into contract- and consent-readings, with (for example) Gauthier and Scanlon as representatives.

the perspective of maximising good states 'in the world'. The utilitarian and the perfectionist *telos* fall apart, since the latter transcends the perspective of the agent only in combination with further suppositions. The rationalist *telos*, finally, suggests transcending the alternative of the first-person and the third-person points of view inherent in perfectionism and utilitarianism.

The many counterintuitive consequences of maximising good states are well known. Thus, such a perspective requires strong arguments. As for the rationalist *telos*, one also needs extensive arguments as to why one should abstract from other forms of the good and rest content with the very special good of rationality. But would it be possible, if such arguments were available (for example, by way of a plausible scepticism towards the more concrete goods), to isolate the good of rationality from the goods one wants to achieve by reason? Both the conceptual and the justificatory isolation of rationality seems rather implausible and requires more explicit argument. I will return to this problem later, in the context of how to make sense of 'community' as implied in the perfectionist account. For the present we are left with the third option, the perfectionist-conception. In the rest of this section I will specify what this might mean.

The family of ethical views under inspection follows principles such as these: the 'priority of the good before the right' (in contrast to the converse relation), 'agent-centeredness' (in contrast to act- or rule-centeredness), and 'plurality of agent-qualities' (in contrast to a monism of such qualities). All perfectionist views need to fulfill these conditions. In addition, there is space for alternatives concerning the function and role of agent-qualities, concrete interpretations, and lists, especially for the social conditions these qualities presuppose.[3]

For a better perspective on ways in which this space can be filled, it is helpful to distinguish the following four positions: the 'intuitionist'

---

3. I purposely talk of 'agent-qualities' instead of 'virtues', as some think the virtue terminology antiquated and not compatible with modern societies. I think there is something to this point, but will not try to avoid virtue terminology in the following.

conception, the 'human-requirement' conception, the '*telos*' conception, and the 'community' conception. The intuitionist conception is favoured by Bernard Williams (1973; 1997) and Annette Baier (1985, ch. 2); the human-requirement conception has been voiced by Philippa Foot (1978) and then developed by Martha Nussbaum (1992; 1993)[4] and, in a different way, by Christine Swanton (2003); the *telos* conception is explicitly stated by MacIntyre (MacIntyre 1985a, ch. 14) and in some versions also by Foot, Rosalind Hursthouse, Nussbaum, and many commentators on Aristotle (and of course Aristotle himself); the community conception is most prominently endorsed by MacIntyre (MacIntyre 1985a, ch. 14), but also by Baier. As we will see, the *telos* conception is the most complex one, giving itself space for diverse interpretations and distinct subpositions. Depending on how strictly one uses the term, '*telos*' could be understood as an over-arching concept for all positions sketched here, but that would miss important differences and should be avoided.

The motive behind an intuitionist understanding of good action is (Humean) scepticism about rationality and rationalism, including the rationalism of Aristotle. The intuitionism favoured by Williams is a methodological one in line with John Rawls, but without the supposition that 'coherence' will somehow improve the moral quality of the outcome, or even make it more 'reasonable' in a way. Rather, Williams wants to rely on the cognitive power of the emotions, and this in a rather direct and unmediated way, made possible by literature and poetry instead of philosophical reflection. Scepticism about all general theories leads the intuitionist to a multitude of local ethical solutions instead of a 'theory' of virtues. In the following discussion I leave open the question of the importance of this sceptical conception, but the position in which I end up is fairly close to that of Williams.

What I call the 'human-requirement conception' springs from Foot's idea that the virtues are answers to human weaknesses (1978) and results from the way Nussbaum describes her list of virtues as functioning within correlative spheres of experience, imbued with typical human

---

4. Without being as detailed as she is, in large parts of this overview I follow Nussbaum (1999).

weaknesses and problems (1993).[5] In related publications Nussbaum is interested in an anthropologically representative list of 'capabilities', to be considered within a general (in part, Rawls-like) theory of social justice, thereby expanding justice disproportionately in relation to the other virtues (1992). This move can be read as introducing a private/public distinction and separating public from private justice—ideas at which Nussbaum hints in many places by referring to public interests, liberalism, civic policy, and so forth. Nussbaum attaches great importance to defending the universality or, as she prefers to put it, the 'essence' of specific types of human functioning, thereby attacking postmodernist cultural relativism (1992). To label her programme as a 'human-requirement conception' seems apt, insofar as she does not rely on the metaphysical dogmas of an Aristotelian ethics, including a substantive idea of *telos*.[6]

One simple reason why the capabilities approach need not be read teleologically is that it is, or can be, introduced negatively by anthropological challenges rather than by positive reference to something like the 'human good', implying reference to the latter only indirectly. All positive attempts, by contrast, could be summarised as *telos* conceptions. There are different versions of how to relate to the human good, and accordingly, different versions of this family of ethical argument. All of the following ideas seem to be part of the human good, but since the latter is both a vague and a complex concept, people have developed different strategies for approaching it. These strategies are oriented, first, to 'human nature' (Nussbaum 1995) or 'human kind' (Hursthouse 1999, chs. 8–11;

---

5. Another title could be the 'human deficiency' or the 'corrective' conception. See also Swanton (2006), who characterises Aristotle's search as one that asks 'what are the fundamental flaws to which humans are subject, inhibiting their prospects of living a good life' (2006, 172). Statements such as these (regarding functional explanations of virtue) should, however, be seen as extending to humanly typical social and collective situations, as done in classical political theories (see Oakeshott 1991, ch. 2). Except for some remarks in the last section of this essay, I make no attempt to engage in this task here.

6. Reference to some of these dogmas, to be mentioned shortly, is part of Nussbaum's defence of Aristotle's handling of 'human nature' (Nussbaum 1995).

Foot 2001, ch. 5); second, to 'human activities', 'excellences' or 'aretais', or the *kalon* to which they are directed (Korsgaard 1996; Lear 2004, ch. 6); and third, to the classical idea of the human good, '*eudaimonia*' (Foot 2001, ch. 6). In a sense, especially following Aristotle, these elements depend on each other. But the task of clarifying the relations between them opens up various possibilities, thereby giving priority to one or the other, and perhaps even getting rid of one or the other.

Let us start with human nature. Why should we believe in a substantial concept of human nature, that is, believe that such a substance has content and is normatively binding? Human nature is a sortal concept that has to be contrasted with what real and individual humans do in, and with, their lives. Humans seem to be extremely capable of circumventing any nonbiological content that might be claimed as 'human nature'. Lives marked by disastrous deeds are still human lives. The best way to account for this observation is to bring human activities into play, namely, to explain the normative content of human nature by human capacities or activities. This move wavers, however, between trying to achieve some informative coherence between human nature and human capacities, and shifting the argument fully to the second strategy mentioned above. In order to hold on to the first alternative, human nature must have a normatively relevant content of its own, and even when this is suggested on the basis of sociobiology, it is difficult to see what this content could be, if it is understood as individually binding and not merely biologically descriptive.[7] In addition, if one tries to 'biologise' human nature, obviously one creates a conflict with what humans are capable of, a problem that underlies long-standing debates on the conflict between naturalism and freedom.

The second strategy of a *telos* conception typically runs into the problem of presenting a hierarchy of human capacities, in order not to depart from the debate on the general anthropological level that is typical of the human-requirement conception. Unavoidable, nasty problems arise here in determining the role of practical reason in contrast to the

---

7. See the argument by Williams against Nussbaum: (B. Williams 1985, ch. 3; 1995, 192–202; Nussbaum 1995).

other virtues, and especially the role of reason in relation to morality (understood in the modern sense). In order to prove something like the absolute dominance of practical reason or wisdom, as is inherent in Aristotle's idea of *eudaimonia,* one would need a quasi-Kantian transcendental argument, and that is hard to come by. And in order to prove the urgency of moral behaviour for the living of a good life, one must resort to psychological material and the plausibility of typical cases—for example, as Foot has done (2001, 94–98)—which are notoriously contested.[8] In general, it is plausible to think that our lives should be oriented to 'excellences', but less plausible to think that these excellences do not contradict themselves, that there is unity rather than disunity, and that wisdom constitutes the highest end.

The third strategy overlaps the second, given that Aristotle's active idea of *eudaimonia,* in distinction to a passive-hedonist one, is roughly convincing; human activities and excellences are its most important part. However, there are at least two problems here that are not solved by Aristotle's own teleological suggestions. First, it is not clear what to say in refutation of the occasional hedonist who refuses to let his enjoyment be rationally categorised under a valuable activity. Even if we accept the tediousness of living one's whole life within an 'experience machine' (a contraption giving constant pleasure), the question of what we should think of part-time visits to such machines remains open. Second, it is not clear how to trade off or adjudicate between ethical and contemplative activities, if we cannot (with Aristotle) unconditionally and absolutely esteem the latter. We find ourselves at a point, then, where we concede much of the overall picture in Aristotle's ethics, but lose a grasp on the specific finality it purportedly claims. Even if, as I think is unproblematic, we accept the overall picture, including decisions concerning the whole of an ethical (as opposed to an unethical) life, the idea that all

---

8. 'It is also a problem for any program that wants to connect the ethical life with psychological health through notions of integration, or reduction of conflict. These psychological aims in themselves carry no ethical weight unless they are already defined to do so; the best way of integrating some people would be to make them more ruthless' (B. Williams 1985, 47).

human activities, lives, and ends can be streamlined into a *telos* worthy of its name seems to me rather depressing.

The last approach I consider here, the community conception, can again, in a sense, find its motivation in Aristotle's notion of self-sufficiency (*autarkes*), which includes living in a community.[9] The first thing to ask, however, to take the most extreme version of this approach, is whether communities can have a *telos* of their own, thereby allowing a distinction between virtuous and nonvirtuous communities. Aristotle was surely not of this opinion, since he thought of communities only as a means of enabling humans to become virtuous. To achieve this result, a *polis* need not be of an ideal kind; most of them are 'deviant' ones, and even deviant, non-ideal societies, for Aristotle, can provide the conditions under which the virtues can develop. Also, even if Aristotle believed friendship to be very important for a virtuous life, he did not present the ideal city as a form of collective friendship. Rather, and more realistically, he thought of large political communities as being conflictual both in interests and ideas. The kind of friendships that can be achieved within such communities, on an impersonal level, are those of interest only, namely, the least good ones on the tripartite list of kinds of friendships. Aristotle, then, cannot be enlisted for a strong community conception of collective or individual *telos* (see also Yack 1993, chs. 1–2, which distances Aristotle from Rousseau and modern communitarians).

One reason for this merely indirect interconnection between virtue and the *polis* can be seen in Aristotle's appreciation of *phronesis* among the virtues and his reckoning with a pluralism of excellences (in addition to his realism concerning political and social harmony). Whatever we think of Aristotle's own position, the importance of community seems to be in conflict with the importance of practical reason. The latter can only be understood individually, and if community in terms of coherence, sharing of values, or identification is considered to be so important, this

---

9. 'By self-sufficient I mean not for the person himself, leading a solitary life, but for the person along with parents and children and a wife (!) and in general his friends and fellow citizens, since the human being is by nature a political being.' (*NE* 1097b7–11)

idea of community will have to cohere with a kind of reason that is not self-sufficient. Or rather, community as an individual *telos* harmonises with the minimisation of reason, whereas a strong conception of reason displaces the practical relevance of communal identity.

Let me pull this overview together by pointing to a general problem underlying most of the troubling queries at the door of the *telos* variants of perfectionism. These queries have their source in the very idea of teleology when it surpasses the constraints of intentional action and is, instead, meant to follow from objective structures inherent in human acting and living in a wider sense. The obvious initiator of this kind of project is, of course, Aristotle, who extended the teleological project far beyond the confines of single actions into the realm of 'human goods', and especially into a hierarchy of these goods. Once one reconstructs human acting teleologically, one is invited to accept two tendencies, namely, that ends are independent of human desires, and that there must be a single highest end which is somehow the 'best' and finally orienting end. Both tendencies can be found in Aristotle, who, against a background of general teleological metaphysics, is pushed into the problem of how 'middle-level ends', such as the moral virtues of friendship or honour, relate to the 'highest end', *eudaimonia*.[10] If, on the one hand, *eudaimonia* is constituted by these middle-level goods, as famously suggested by John Ackrill (1974), then the teleological structure is relinquished— but once questioned, the entire system is seriously diminished. If, on the other hand, the highest end keeps functioning as a guide for how to balance between middle-level ends, many critical questions remain open with no obvious answers to be found.

On a lower and more applied level, another problem arises for the teleologist, which concerns the link between the crafts and the virtues.[11] If the crafts are thought of teleologically, the interests of craftspersons are shaped and oriented by the ends of the craft. Bridlemakers have a

---

10. The term 'middle-level ends' is from Lear (2004, ch. 1). Her treatment elaborates extensively on the problem of how *eudaimonia* could be linked with the concrete goods.

11. Here I am following Lear 2004, 36–37.

reason for making good bridles through the ends to which horses are put, for example, achieving victory in a battle. But there are always alternative ends, and it is implausible that the ends relevant to a craftsman can be grasped by him without reference to his interests. Only in an extremely harmonious or static society do ends and interests cohere; in most real societies, different ends (given by conflicting crafts) and different interests conflict with each other. Aristotle's answer may be, for bridle-makers, that these people wish to achieve honour and that only their virtuous behaviour is the reason for this. But unless we assume a predetermined harmony between ends and ends, and between ends and interests, it is quite open as to how to achieve this.

The upshot of these remarks on teleology is that the teleological project is unstable. If put under pressure, it either deteriorates into a vaguely teleological scheme that is compatible with the human-requirement conception of perfectionism, or it must do further work on the highest end, its necessity, quality, and function. Aristotle may have found a version of teleology that was balanced in this latter sense, although one may doubt this, given the distance of his ideal system from the Greek society of his time. However this may be, in the remainder of this essay I will try to show that MacIntyre, who set out as a vague teleologist in *After Virtue,* developed into a fundamentalist one, pushed into an arcane metaphysics by the logic of teleology.

From *After Virtue* to Rival Traditions

MacIntyre's short sketch of the *Nicomachean Ethics* in *After Virtue* is, in retrospect, refreshingly 'liberal': that is, aware of the normative relevance of the historically altered conditions for the appropriation of such a text. And it is rather critical towards some of Aristotle's assumptions, once again at least in a modernist sense. Most importantly, MacIntyre distances himself from the kind of 'metaphysical biology' (MacIntyre 1985a, 148) touched upon earlier in connection with the human-kind variant of virtue ethics and criticised as giving an insufficient description of human conflicts. He diagnoses Aristotle's fixation on types and natures as underlying his moral blindness towards slaves and barbarians, and he points out, in an illuminating way, the consequences of a species-oriented kind of science, the most important being the lack of a sense of individuality and, correspondingly, of history.[12] Aristotle is chided heavily for being an ahistorical thinker who, due to his historic blindness, neglected the potential for conflict over the virtues in his culture, instead suggesting their unity. 'The absence of [something like Sophocles'] view of the centrality of opposition and conflict in human life conceals from Aristotle also one important source of human learning about one important milieu of human practice of the virtues' (MacIntyre 1985a, 163). In other words, MacIntyre suggests that opposition and conflict are important as a 'milieu' for human learning, a fact overlooked by Aristotle and so much more important in a 'world in which there are no city-states' (MacIntyre 1985a, 163).

In *After Virtue* MacIntyre famously set out his description of contemporary Western moral and political culture as disastrously conflictual—a diagnosis regularly repeated, from an increasingly one-sided negative perspective. Even in *After Virtue,* the diagnosis of moral conflict in modern societies plays no role within MacIntyre's constructive efforts. Central to these efforts is his extensive use of the idea of 'practices', an adaptation of the Aristotelian concept of *technai* (or even more generally, *energeiai*).[13] Practices are taken to outline a wider class than crafts, and include the sciences, the arts, politics, and family life (MacIntyre 1985a, 187 f.). Practices characteristically involve 'internal goods', which are to the advantage of a community of practitioners, whereas 'external goods', such as honour, power, or money, are divided and competitively struggled for among individuals. Internal goods and excellences can only be had

---

12. 'History indeed is not a reputable form of enquiry—less philosophical than poetry because it aspires genuinely to deal with individuals, whereas even poetry, in Aristotle's view, deals with time. Aristotle was well aware that the kind of knowledge which he takes to be genuinely scientific, to constitute *epistêmê*—knowledge of essential natures grasped through universal necessary truths, logically derivable from certain first principles—cannot characteristically be had of human affairs at all' (MacIntyre 1985a, 159).

13. *Energeiai* (activities) have their ends in themselves, in contrast to *kineseis* (processes).

by taking part in practices: for example, in the goods (and not merely skills) of medicine. But goods are acquired not only through practices but also through the virtues, especially in the forms of justice, truthfulness, courage, or patience. The virtues are actualised in relation to the practices, but are not to be thought of as internal to them, as are the goods. In contrast to Aristotle, MacIntyre reckons with a multitude of practices and therefore with incompatible claims from practices, which cannot be reduced to flaws of individual character (MacIntyre 1985a, 196–97). And he expects external goods to compete with internal ones, which can regularly endanger a practice by corrupting the internal motives for the practice. The virtues are burdened with these diverse requirements to negotiate, not only inside but also outside the practices. Given that the virtues are not wholly, and perhaps not even importantly, internal to practices, an explanation is needed as to how they can fulfill the role they are supposed to play.

In an early critique, David Miller pressed this question by distinguishing two kinds of practices: *self-contained* ones, such as chess, and *purposive* ones, such as medicine. The latter type has a wider social purpose, for example, the just distribution of hospital beds or the equal treatment of rich and poor (D. Miller 1984). He rightly, in my view, pointed out that the socially more important practices, such as medicine, are less self-contained, and are better seen as socially purposive ones. With them, the virtues can only do their work if they are oriented to the wider social good or to a vision of the whole of society. Even if MacIntyre did not think, as suggested by Miller (1984, 53), that the virtues are wholly regulated from within different practices, he gave no convincing answer as to how the virtues should work in the context of purposive practices, if the internal goods model of practices is meant to be constitutive of the virtues.

What was MacIntyre's answer to the problem that the virtues transcend concrete practices? He helped himself out with the concept of a 'narrative quest' and the idea of the virtues being oriented to this quest (MacIntyre 1985a, 219). For human actions to be intelligible, according to MacIntyre, it is necessary to see them as embedded within a narrative of lengthier parts of life. The reason seems to be that persons are normally 'accountable' for their lives, and being accountable means to make intelligible how different parts hang together (MacIntyre 1985a, 217–18). There is, obviously, a gap between something like a 'narrative quest' and making intelligible the linkage of one's actions. Actions and happenings can be made intelligible even if they happen by chance and when they are heavily contingent. Even if the human quest can be characterised by the question 'What is the good for me?', it is not at all plausible (as Mac-Intyre states without further argument) that someone interested in his own individual good has to have an interest in some 'conception of the good for man' (MacIntyre 1985a, 219). And it is even less plausible that 'the good life for man is the life spent in seeking the good life for man' (MacIntyre 1985a, 219), which is a possible rephrasing of Aristotle's intellectual *telos,* can step in for the individual good. By way of making narrative sense of personal history, MacIntyre wants to achieve what he criticised in Aristotle as part of his 'metaphysical biology', having obviously forgotten his own objection that history (being interested in the particular) and biology (being interested in the type) do not go together. No one interested in writing his autobiography needs to first come up with a theory about 'the life and good of humans'—and the danger of becoming involved in speculative theory is too obvious.

One can see why MacIntyre, by thinking he had secured an argument for the importance of the 'human good', also thought he had a strategy for answering the question of the social directedness of the virtues. The purposive virtues refer to the common social good in the widest sense, a point that MacIntyre himself alludes to, in connection with the virtues of justice and patience.[14] This reference needs explication, but not in terms of the statement 'the good life for man is the life spent in seeking the good life for man' (MacIntyre 1985a, 219). Here the most

---

14. In *After Virtue* MacIntyre thinks of justice as desert-oriented, and for that reason he considers 'the goods internal to the practice of making and sustaining forms of community' (MacIntyre 1985a, 202)—leaving open, however, how extensively he wants to think of communities. The practices of medicine or work in a Western society, for example, are under permanent discussion in political struggles and conflicts, even if hardly concerning the whole of society and not in the interest of any 'kind', be it society or man. We observe a pluralism of practices and communities, not one teleologically pointing to the good of 'man'.

difficult questions regarding Aristotle's understanding of his highest good in relation to the middle-level goods (not to mention material goods) surface again. Should one philosophise instead of saving a drowning child? Is the life of the philosopher the best life, and should we 'maximise contemplation and for the rest act well' (Keyt 1983, 370)? Is the best society one of philosophers? These excerpts are sufficiently absurd not to be taken literally, but nevertheless there is a spiritual ring to the message that good communities might devote themselves to lives 'spent in seeking the good life for man'. Good communities, that is, devote themselves to the good 'for Man', written with a capital 'M', and not for a workable account of the good of many single lives.

A well-known pattern of explanation in cultural anthropology is the functional one. Its strategy seems very plausible: to explain social norms and part of individual behaviour by what furthers the well-being of social organisations, be these families, tribes, or larger social collectives. MacIntyre's story of Western morality coheres well with this strategy of functional explanations, especially in the transition from the Homeric role-constituted morality to Aristotelian teleology (reading the latter as a philosophised version of Homeric role-models [MacIntyre 1985a, 59]). The 'Enlightenment project' had to fail, according to MacIntyre, because its strongest proponents lost every sense of both social functionality and of teleology; and, as we saw, his proposal in *After Virtue* was to win back teleology by way of considering the importance of social collectives, as depicted by practices. Given the barrenness of large parts of analytic normative ethics and meta-ethics, this strategy is an intriguing one, but in the hands of MacIntyre it suffers from being pressed into rigid and exclusive alternatives. To start ethics with practices is surely more promising than starting it with moral sentences or deontic operators or decontextualized rights or duties, that is, with highly abstract concepts. Practice-integrated actors do not need to orient themselves to final ends, whether individual or generic, where 'final' is interpreted in an absolute sense. How they are able to accomplish that, however, is in need of explanation. At this point, let me refer to one way out of the problem of how to distance oneself from practices and how to judge practices through another practice as the 'liberating' one. MacIntyre, by contrast, in his further and latest development did not take this way out. Instead, he radicalised finality, definitely siding with something akin to 'biological metaphysics'.

Before looking at MacIntyre's reason for this move, let us ask whether there is an obvious answer to the problem of conflicting practices and of how to integrate local practices into a larger whole—either of one society or of encompassing different societies. Given the overview on different positions of perfectionism in the last section, the human-requirement conception suggests itself.[15] If we work with this conception, we think that there is a nontrivial 'human nature', which is not merely biological but informatively universal, and which provides a basis for answering the problems outlined. This 'universal human nature' has its basis in shared characteristics, such as fear and bodily desires, and shared requirements, such as our need for resources in conditions of scarcity, for security of property, for effective coordination of actions, and so forth. These provide—or at least one might rationally think so—a sufficient shared background of interests to achieve consensual results. Could this be a fully convincing answer to the problem of diverging practices and virtues? I do not think so, and in this conflict I side with MacIntyre's historicism: that is, human requirements are always historically embedded (which is what makes them human) and transformed requirements, their 'universality' being embedded in historically different interpretations. The virtues surface, therefore, as answering requirements within different 'historic situations', and we should try to distinguish epochally differentiated forms of virtues. MacIntyre grasps these forms in terms of 'traditions', and, taking traditions to be divergent, he must think that any simple reference to universal requirements misses the point. In doing so, I take him to be right, and the bare universalist conception of the virtues is mistaken.[16]

---

15. Nussbaum (1989) actually makes use of it in her critical review of MacIntyre's *Whose Justice? Which Rationality?* She appeals to her own list of requirements and virtues and points out that Aristotle had a much more optimistic idea of reason than MacIntyre.

16. In her extensive writings, Nussbaum does not, to my knowledge, confront the task of a sensible historicism, in part motivated by fear of moral relativism and its political drawbacks (see Nussbaum 1992). One need not fully relinquish, on the other hand, the idea of universal human requirements, as shown by articulating their different cultural interpretations.

This point in favour of the historicist position having been made, and given the elementary alternative of a universalist/historicist view of the virtues, it remains unclear how one should interpret MacIntyre's answer to the problems arising in *After Virtue* by way of a historicist reading of the whole of European history of morality—an answer given in *Whose Justice? Which Rationality?* and in later essays and books. Despite what readers of *After Virtue* might have expected, MacIntyre never again devoted himself to a systematic treatment of the central concepts in chapter 14 of this book, namely, 'practices' and 'narrative quest', save for an increasingly fine-grained description of 'traditions'. His writings develop a taxonomy of four traditions, covering antiquity, the Middle Ages, the Scottish Enlightenment, and the liberal age. The reason why I, for one, am puzzled by this taxonomy is the conflicting interpretations MacIntyre gives to it. His history of four stages is largely formulated in purely descriptive terms. It is subsumed under the unmediated historicist idea that in history there is nothing but a succession of historic stages of thought, and the later stages are not clearly 'better' than the earlier ones, since each stage answers different problems and stages are difficult to relate to each other.[17]

As we can learn from MacIntyre's critical stance towards the liberal tradition (see MacIntyre 1985a, chs. 5–6; 1988a, ch. 17), his historicism takes narrative stages neither to be contingently ordered nor to approach the culture of the day, as the one representing 'truth'. MacIntyre thinks that Aquinas achieved a synthesis between Aristotle and Augustine, which Hume, as a representative of liberalism (and the liberal economic man), did not surpass. On the face of it, especially for an historicist, such an idea is deeply implausible. If one thinks of history as incorporating something like a process of collective learning (even if not

---

17. In an essay first published in 1977 (2006q), MacIntyre sided with a nonradicalised version of Kuhnian history of science: a history avoiding incommensurability between paradigms and finding truth in narratives of these paradigm changes. Overall the essay favours a 'standpoint of an approach to truth' (2006q, 21), backed by the better understanding of flaws in the earlier ones through the paradigm of the day. Applied to political theory, this would make liberalism the hero of narratives—not something favoured by MacIntyre!

mysteriously approaching 'truth'), it would make much more sense to think of liberal culture as achieving a synthesis between Aristotle and Hume, which could not be achieved by Augustine and Aquinas. It is fair to say that there is some collective learning underlying different stages in the development of traditions, but more difficult to see why the upshot of this learning should be Christian faith or belief in absolute truth instead of in liberal culture. Liberal culture has achieved the social coexistence of believers and nonbelievers, of people clutching to dogmas and people floundering between ideologies, and it is difficult to see why this is not a more impressive product of collective learning than returning to 'first principles' and a community in the style of the Catholic Church.[18]

MacIntyre's historicism is incoherent, it seems to me, if it takes (as historicists should) the present conditions as unavoidably shaping judgments on earlier stages of historical development. We can always write a history of collective learning leading up to the present, given the normative conditions of the present. MacIntyre obviously tries to avoid this, or he would not be able to arrive at his esteem of Aquinas as the preferable moral thinker to Aristotle, Hume, or Mill. There is only one move I can think of which would make MacIntyre's devotion to Aquinas plausible: one coherent with Aquinas's own natural law theory, but still hardly historicist. To end one's narrative at the site of an absolutist thinker, one somehow needs an absolutist premise in one's story. Put slightly differently, one needs some sort of transcendentalist argument to breach the gap between traditions. Historic development only leads to a thinker upholding absolute truth if historic development is read from the point of absolute truth. Starting from a liberal culture that is sceptical towards absolute truth, an argument must be found for it, to the extent that absolute truth is necessary in order to understand history. It is difficult to see MacIntyre giving such an argument. It will not do, for example, to ask for absolute truth as a precondition of historic understanding. A Davidsonian

---

18. Comparisons could also be made on the level of the different thinkers favoured by MacIntyre. Think, for example, of the different treatment of sexual morality in Aristotle and Aquinas, differences due to the Christian doctrine of guilt working in the one but not in the other. Nussbaum (1989) points this out, as well as other contrasts in favour of Aristotle.

reading of historic changes within an exhaustive 'conceptual scheme' is sufficient to give sense to explaining the conceptual differences within a common 'human' horizon of understanding, and this reading tallies well with a minimalist conception of truth.[19]

So far these remarks are devoted, in a very general sense, to the strength of MacIntyre's historicist argument concerning the *telos* conception of morality. His most important general argument is derived from inspection of the stages of development of our present view, and *Whose Justice, Which Rationality?* is intended, with the help of the conflicting succession of traditions, to answer the problem of divergent practices in *After Virtue*. Given the breadth of this narrative and the complexity (and sometimes vagueness) of MacIntyre's reconstruction of it, my reading by way of systematic argument may well have missed something important within it. Given MacIntyre's regular references to teleological structure in his writings up to the present, and especially in the context of his opposition to liberal standpoints (see MacIntyre 2008r, 262), the contrast between an idea of absolute finality and our present liberal culture seems to me, rightly, to be a crucial one, even if it works to the detriment of MacIntyre's argument. Even if one were convinced of a morality in line with Aquinas, one would need to be aware of a surrounding society which is normatively shaped by the liberal argument. In the remaining two sections of this essay, I expound on what I have so far mentioned only sketchily concerning the conditions within liberal culture for a transformation of the virtues, and, briefly, on how these conditions express themselves normatively in politics. The larger society, oriented to forms of communities, can and must be put back into the picture that MacIntyre sketches.

---

19. MacIntyre's methodological statements on matters such as relativism, commensurability, narrativity, and so on are difficult to discern, since they do not openly promote an absolutist or transcendentalist position. His missing vote for incommensurability could be read in a Davidsonian manner (see 1988a, ch. 19), in comparison with, for example, Ramberg (1989, ch. 9). This, however, would be a mistake, as his realist reading of Kuhn (in MacIntyre (2006q) and his later votes for a teleological programme make clear (see, for example, 1998e). In a sense MacIntyre is not an historicist at all, since he reckons with an 'approach to truth' (2006q, 21) that does not correspond with actual history.

Transcending Practices

Let us look again at practices, the undeveloped concept of *After Virtue*. As I have said, if one thinks of practices as hermetic socialising vehicles for the virtues, the problem emerges of how to think of purposive practices, not to mention virtuous behaviour outside any guiding practice. If the chance bystander (not a neighbour, fellow citizen, or police officer) witnesses a crime in the street and thinks about helping the victim, there is no practice save general morality or humanity to guide him in either springing into action or shirking it. The sociologically informed concept of practices could and surely can be helpful in analysing specific moral role-behaviour; but if practices are not constitutive of the virtues throughout, more basic ethical questions concerning the virtues cannot be read from the social structure of practices.[20] MacIntyre ingeniously quipped that every moral philosophy 'characteristically presupposes a sociology' (MacIntyre 1985a, 23), but the sociology of practices does not exhaust the virtues. Insofar as it exhausts the narrower role-bound virtues, this is, as will become clear in a moment, to the damage of the role player. What else is necessary? The human-requirement conception again gives us a clue, even if it leans too far to the other side, to existential human experiences that are neutral with respect to historic and social conditions. To improve this conception, human requirements have to be understood as historically situated; the 'human situation' always must be read historically. Studies of practice-bound virtuous behaviour may be helpful for this reading, but we are in need of a more extensive understanding of the virtues in a historical context.

Despite an overwhelming interest in 'virtue ethics' during recent decades, thorough work on the conflict between the ancient logic of the virtues or specific traditional virtues and the requirements for virtuous

---

20. This makes itself shown, I think, in controversies on the applicability of the 'practice' construct to managerial and medical activities, or on whether or not teaching is a practice: see Brewer (1997); Beadle (2001); Dawson and Bartholomew (2003); Hoogland and Jochemsen (2000); MacIntyre and Dunn (2002).

behaviour under modern conditions is, I find, fairly rare. This harsh judgment becomes plausible if one steps away from the different *telos* conceptions I have mentioned and regards Nussbaum's list of virtues as insufficiently historicist.[21] Two ways to grasp what could be meant by a transformation of the virtues under conditions of modernity are, first and obviously, trying to find out about typical 'liberal virtues', that is, virtues working under conditions typical for a liberal society; and second (and perhaps less easily), orienting oneself to a radically modern moral thinker and asking what his or her perspective would do for the virtues. In this section I make some remarks akin to the second of these approaches, while in the next section I will follow the idea behind the first. The most radical modern figure is, of course, Nietzsche, and bringing his perspective to bear on the virtues is one possible method by which to modernise them.[22]

The most inspiring recent work on Nietzsche's relation to the virtues, to my mind, has been done by Christine Swanton (2003; 2005; 2006). Swanton brings out clearly why it is important to engage with Nietzsche if one's aim is to renovate or refurbish the structure and content of the virtues according to the conditions of modernity. Nietzsche is the most consistent anti-religious philosopher and therefore is least prone to recycling metaphysical ideas under the guise of secular formulas. His concept of goodness is genuinely based on *aretais*: virtuous behaviour is not the realisation of 'values', but values at best are abstractions

---

21. Foot's and Hursthouse's treatments, in addition to being metaphysically imbued by an idea of human nature, are too far removed from contemporary moral problems. Driver's (2001) conception is unacceptably consequentialist, but symptomatic in the sense of pressing thinking about the virtues into either a Kantian or a utilitarian scheme. Any successful revitalisation of the virtues would have to make them see actual difficult situations of life anew, instead of rephrasing what is already well known.

22. Conservative friends of the virtues, such as Foot, Hursthouse, and MacIntyre, typically make use of Nietzsche only as a stand-in for the 'amoralist'/'immoralist', alongside Thrasymachos or Ayn Rand: see Foot 1991; Hursthouse 1999, 253–56; MacIntyre 1985a, ch. 8; 1990a, ch. 2. For criticism of Foot with regard to Nietzsche, see Swanton 2005.

from virtuous behaviour. Behaviour is not dominated by anything like 'values'. And, more importantly in the present context, he develops a non-teleological idea of perfection, a perfection not oriented towards an already fixed, given end. Self-realisation ('self-overcoming') is at the center of Nietzsche's ethics, but it is meant not as an improvement according to an external end, but as an improvement of activity-patterns already in one's possession (Swanton 2005, 190). A famous expression of his non-teleological thought is the subtitle of Nietzsche's autobiography, *Ecce Homo*: 'How One Becomes What One Is'. Instead of discovering a pre-given, albeit deeply embedded (Freudian) self, and instead of perfecting oneself according to a pre-given cultural ideal, 'true' development for Nietzsche means the ever more extensive elaboration of who one is in one's beginning, after the subtraction of culturally virulent idols. To find out what one is, is at least a twofold task, necessitating first getting rid of beliefs and desires that are not one's own, not akin to one's abilities and leanings, and second, improving and developing one's abilities. Nietzsche works with a psychology that is less one of a hidden (Freudian) self and more one of a notion of persons being constructively put together by their deeds. To discover one's abilities and to improve on them is the first task he thinks one has to face, and to 'become oneself' is the first virtue, the virtue to 'empower' oneself.[23]

It is difficult and perhaps impossible to figure out one underlying 'human requirement' that could produce the set of virtues typical in Aristotle, and Nussbaum's procedure, with the help of a list and without excessive attempts at unification or at weighing one virtue against the others, is therefore apt. There is, of course, a strong focus in Aristotle on the human tendency towards hedonism and (as regularly stressed by Nussbaum) a strong confidence in reason, developing into the notorious bent towards the intellectual virtues. Due to the traditional setting of Aristotle's writings, his virtues are not driven by what has become the mark of our modern moral behaviour, and which is most visible in Nietzsche, as well as twentieth-century existentialists: namely, the concept of a 'problematic self', or the agent becoming a problem for himself. Due

---

23. For more elaborate descriptions of these points, see Nehamas (1983); Swanton (2005).

to the loss of communal traditions, the loss of (authoritative) religion, and the naturalist dissolution of secular philosophical substitutes, humans become mysteries to themselves. If we hold on to the general definition of the virtues, as generalised demands on human acting, then the modern historical situation surely puts forward quite different demands compared to those of antiquity or the scholastic Middle Ages, and a historicist reading of our current understanding of virtues should take these demands into account. Nietzsche's central exhortation to 'empower oneself' is not a proto-fascist longing for social and political power, but the compressed expression of a deep and generalising insight into the multitude of demanding concrete situations, all of which have in common the idea that a form of self-construction has to take over tasks that have earlier been solved by unquestioned cultural habits. Self-overcoming is the organising virtue in the Nietzschean perspective; commitment is a solution suggested by Kierkegaard; fear in view of death is Heidegger's answer; and decisive integrity is the solution of Sartre in his well-known description of decision problems. Fear and anxiety are deeply woven into many life situations, and to become aware of this and to respond to it as competently as possible constitutes the first sign of the modern virtuous individual—in distinction from the Aristotelian intellectual of the *polis*.

Given that one accepts this very sketchy profile of modern demands on the virtues and the analogously sketchy characterisation of an answer in terms of self-empowerment, commitment, integrity, or truthfulness, what does this mean both for the single virtues and for a virtue ethics? Again, a more extensive answer is needed than is possible to give here, but enough can be said to do justice to the task of suggesting an alternative to MacIntyre's idiosyncratic vision of a virtue ethics. From the historical situation sketched above, I draw three conclusions concerning the content of 'modern virtues', and three further conclusions concerning a meta-ethical view of the virtues. For the sake of discussion, I associate the terms 'authenticity', 'self-love', and 'creativity' with the three virtue-centered conclusions, and 'pluralism', 'conflict', and 'extension' with the three meta-ethical ones.

Aristotelian virtue, according to standard interpretation, is eudaimonistic; the virtues are contributing to and guided by *eudaimonia*. This teleological link to *eudaimonia*, with *eudaimonia* somehow given and presupposed, perhaps explains why 'demands of the world' or 'typical human requirements' find no mention in Aristotle's general statements on the virtues. According to the requirement-conception of virtues, a reference to *eudaimonia* is not necessary, and in fact it is highly implausible that virtuous behaviour inherently leads to *eudaimonia*.[24] This is perhaps a problematic statement, in that it is difficult to find consensus on the good ends in life in the present, and therefore the virtues lacking them cannot be elucidated, either. Present thinking is still Aristotelian, in that a 'developed' personality definitely encompasses all speculations on the good ends of life, but again, conflicting opinions about such a developed personality are abundant. In contrast to Kant's metaphysical idea of 'self-worth', Nietzsche was the first and most original thinker to delineate the aspects of psychologically 'healthy' individuals, and authenticity, self-love, and creativity are different dimensions of such an individual (see Swanton 2006, 183–87).[25]

Authenticity can be seen as courage towards oneself, combined with a reflective distance towards common opinion. Given the multiplicity of conventional roles and practices of authenticity, it is an ongoing task to find oneself in this multitude. Self-love is a 'healthy' acceptance of oneself, which in its optimal form, according to Nietzsche, is not to the detriment of love of others, but instead able to include this love in a form that does not involve pity. Creativity is the opponent of laziness and combines with authenticity and self-love. Together, these attitudes form a kind of perfectionism, a striving or excellency, albeit not one oriented at an end as something outside oneself. This kind of perfectionism does not fol-

---

24. For the relation between virtue and *eudaimonia* in Aristotle, see Julia Annas's stress on the importance of the external goods (Annas 1999); for a more extensive argument in favour of a non-eudaimonistic understanding of the virtues, see Swanton 2003, ch. 4.

25. A turn to a psychological and deep psychological reflection on the virtues should not be understood as handing over the normative competency of ethics to empirical science, that is, as arbitrarily naturalising ethics; but instead as the unavoidable alternative to the conceptual fetishism of standard ethics. Swanton gives excellent references to psychologists such as Karen Horney, Abraham Maslow, and Mortimer Adler on the health/disease structure of the virtues.

low social rules or forms, or realise 'values', but instead produces itself on the basis of the psychological structures of individual personalities.

Let me add some short remarks on the meta-ethical profile of this view of the virtues. 'Pluralism' here refers to a state in which different virtues cannot be systematised into a whole by establishing a hierarchy among them. Different interpretations of this state are possible. Corresponding to each interpretation is a specific attitude towards this state of pluralism. Pluralist virtues require a further response to the state of being pluralist. I first give a general reason for virtue pluralism and then return to the consequence in terms of an attitude in the face of pluralism.

The most basic reason for virtue pluralism is easily seen, I think, once one fully gives up the idea of a 'unifying' concept or capacity, such as first principles, knowledge, reason, including *phronesis,* or values.[26] If one treats the virtues as correcting answers to human frailties and forgoes the work of the unifying entities mentioned, it is obvious that nothing forces a unification. The different virtues are as different as are their demands, not part of 'one' kind of virtue. Swanton makes use of the helpful concept of 'bonds' as targets of the virtues—bonds with oneself, others, living beings, and things (Swanton 2003, 93–94, 216–19). Since the demands of the world are different and have to be answered piecemeal, by bonding with excellent aspects in oneself and others, there will always be different virtuous solutions that cannot be unified into standard answers that are normatively binding for others. In the absence of overarching concepts, and with reason powerless to give solutions which are authoritatively binding for all agents, it is obvious that moral conflict is endemic, as are the conflicting aims in everyone's personal life. As self-development and a widening of one's perspectives are possible

---

26. Or, narrativity. According to *After Virtue,* one's life would not have a narrative unity if it were not tellable under two conditions: first, the quest-oriented impetus to seek something good and true in one's life; and second, the consciousness of one's being sociohistorically embedded within a larger story of a non-individualist sort: the story of one's family, religious community, or nation. Both ends are not unifying, though, if the quest is missing a unifying end and if traditions can always be interpreted differently from the individual standpoint, as they must be.

only through conflicting views, a conflictual sensitivity is actually more virtuous than one of rigid harmony.

'Extension' signifies that the virtue perspective is not to be restricted to 'the practical', as distinguished from 'the empirical' or 'the theoretical', but that objectivity, as the master epistemic quality, arises from an adequate cooperation of the virtues, be it in (more) practical or (more) factual matters. All knowledge should be regarded as embedded in, and arising from, a psychological and indeed passionate personal standpoint, which is to be corrected not by simple detachment but by the competency of a 'right' involvement with the demands of the world. Swanton (2003, ch. 8) suggests a helpful method—in the spirit of the doctrine of the means—by identifying objectivity as the middle ground between the vices of 'hyper-objectivity' and 'hyper-subjectivity', the first marking the view from nowhere and the second a purely aesthetic or personal view. Objectivity is a first epistemic virtue by circumnavigating the two corresponding vices.

MacIntyre, as attested to by his Weberian vignettes of the ideal-types of the manager, the aesthete, and the therapist in *After Virtue*, is fully aware of the details of modernity, which have been addressed by Nietzsche and are important for present-day virtue ethicists such as Swanton. Unfortunately, he ignores the relevant message in the reverse of his quip that every moral philosophy presupposes a sociology. That is, every sociology demands its own moral philosophy and forsakes developing a view on the virtues that responds to modern societies.

Communities and Liberal Societies

If we ask what a 'Nietzschean politics' would look like, there is a breadth of possibilities. However, we need not be interested here in the historic or systematic details of such a politics. I take Nietzsche to be a renovator of virtue ethics under the conditions of modernity, who helps give us an idea of how to rephrase most of the virtues. Again, continuing this strategy, let us consider the consequences of a modernised virtue ethics for politics. In this concluding section I ask in what sense the conditions of modernity force us into an at least partially liberal politics, thus forgoing a 'perfectionist' politics as suggested by MacIntyre.[27] The disadvantages of a perfectionist politics will then become more apparent.

One could speculate that Nietzsche, by stressing individual development, would have to be a liberal of sorts, who favoured freedom and even, through the idea of freedom for all, a mild form of equality. One could also speculate that, due to his vote for conflict and plurality, he might be a defender of pluralism of the good life on the political level. There are avenues into different families of liberalism, however, depending on how one thinks about pluralism within the political sphere. Before addressing different kinds of liberalism, first let us be clear what the alternatives to liberalism are. 'Perfectionism' is an alternative if, by this term, we mean that achieving a common moral good is part of the aims of politics, and that both the historico-empirical fact of pluralism is neglected and a normative ideal of pluralism excluded. A perfectionist community is anti-liberal, then, as Aristotle's *polis* surely was. Second, there is an understanding of pluralism that is more radical than what is usually meant by 'liberal pluralism', and which formulates either a radical version of liberalism or no liberalism at all. This position has been defended most cogently by Chantal Mouffe (1993). She sometimes calls her position 'democratic liberalism', in that effective equality and participation are put into the place of the 'rational foundations' suggested by present-day liberals. Mouffe's position seems to me a stringent one (and, incidentally, one akin to Nietzsche), since she makes plain the fact that 'rational groundings' of liberalism, as found in Rawls, Jürgen Habermas, or Charles Larmore, collide with the principle of pluralism and are, in the absence of something like a 'transcendental force' of rationality necessarily binding on everyone, nothing other than hidden power

---

27. MacIntyre's remarks on politics per se are rare, which may be read either as an attitude of abstention or as expressing a vote for perfectionism concerning politics, where 'political perfectionism' means the unrestricted relevance of morality for politics. Liberalism concerning politics, on the other hand, strictly separates the common political and the common moral good. Given MacIntyre's excessive criticism of liberalism, my guess is that he definitely, even if ultimately unconvincingly, favours the second alternative.

moves. Mouffe accordingly suggests that the only convincing concept of the political is its attempt not to resolve but to organise the conflicts between parties. Forms of rational liberalism fail under this idea of the political, since they, in combination with the misleading idea of 'reasonable agreements', treat politics as achieving harmony and consent, thereby non-harmoniously excluding those who are not 'reasonable' or 'rational'.

The problem with Mouffe's position is that the source of her optimism regarding radical democracy is unclear.[28] Democracy, as distinct from liberalism, means the will of majorities, and such majorities can be (as, among others, one of Mouffe's inspirers, Carl Schmitt, pointed out) distinctly illiberal. We have to resign ourselves, therefore, to less far-reaching forms of liberalism, but to a liberalism nevertheless. I agree with Mouffe that the different forms of rational liberalism are misleading attempts at foundationalism—and that Rawls's handling of the term 'reasonable' is a bad rhetorical method to back up what are merely more or less widely shared moral intuitions. Mouffe is right that liberalist principles are not 'universalist rational' ones but rather are locally effective, just as MacIntyre is right that liberalism is another tradition and not something like a meta-tradition or end of traditions (MacIntyre 1988a, ch. 17). The minimalism that structures and restrains the pluralism suggested by rationalist liberals is, in reality, a historically contingent local minimalism. Rationalist liberals make use of 'reason' and 'rationality' devoid of moral content, but actually assume ideas of 'equality' or 'dignity' or 'autonomy' or 'authenticity', which they translate into a more

---

28. Sometimes she rephrases 'radical democracy' in moral terms presupposing freedom and equality, even if not as a specific understanding of these values (1991, 70). Either one presupposes, then, a morally given idea of democracy, or every 'new' and 'innovative' reading of freedom and equality by hitherto marginalised groups, such as blacks, women, or ecologists, provides the normative ideal of how to think of radical democracy. My hunch is that the second alternative is the only one possible, and that the only safe logic is the historical one of a new reading being burdened by the old one. It has to prove itself better in the light of the older one. If democracy is somehow in place, the new reading will not be able to turn it against itself.

impressive terminology. Rational liberalism is thus not entirely true to liberalism's elementary principle of distinguishing between morality and politics, and in any event, to keep the first out of the second is not something that should be done.

There are two objections at this point, both voiced by MacIntyre and others. First, if political liberalism is understood as moral minimalism and is not backed by 'universal rationality', how can politics be possible, given the social fact of moral pluralism? Second, all the central liberal political values, such as equality and autonomy, articulate forms of individualism. And as such, they are conjoined with unrealistic normative abstractness and, in practice, with a rather apt social pathology (Durkheim's anomie, or Marx's alienation being just two expressions of this). This second criticism touches upon one of the most contested strands in the controversy between liberals and 'communitarians'. MacIntyre, to be sure, continually distanced himself from communitarianism, but he seems to favour the pessimistic thesis that social structures define the potentiality of individual attitudes and creativity. Individualist institutions must first be changed in order to set free a better form of society than the liberal one.

The first objection can be answered only by detailed empirical analyses, which concentrate on specific topics such as medicine, science, education, and so forth. What should we think of MacIntyre's diagnosis—to some extent surely correct—of endemic moral conflict and pluralism?[29] In my opinion, this diagnosis is somewhat exaggerated and, in its dramatic message, oriented to a wrong, because consensual, idea of liberal politics. Surely, at least for the time being, partial types of consensus exist about how to treat the unborn, the dying, animals, and children, about how to distinguish morally between animals and plants and other parts of the environment, and the like. These are partial understandings of

---

29. Much less convincing, I think, is the purported dominance of an 'emotivist' moral culture in present societies (MacIntyre 1985a, chs. 1–3). MacIntyre himself, in other publications, makes use of the experience that moral statements are couched in assertoric sentences and thereby truth-oriented (see MacIntyre 2006r).

the boundaries of morality. It is true that in a sense they are 'overlapping', that is, not fully shared, and that political concepts of freedom, equality, solidarity, and justice are much more greatly contested than opinions concerning the limits of morality. The reason for this difference could be the inherently conflictual structure of politics. In summary, there is a form of 'common morality' in Western society, even if it is a diffuse and constantly changing one.

An overly dramatic view of factual pluralism may result from a too abstract idea of how modern society coheres. Pluralism can be expressed, and expresses itself, not so much by a multitude of opinions but rather within a multitude of social and political 'spheres'. Michael Walzer (1983) was the first philosopher to take up this perspective, and his method is still, I believe, the most congenial one regarding how attempts for normative reconstructions should address normative reality. According to Walzer's method, as is well known, equality is not an abstract value but is contextualised according to different spheres, which again are determined by the function of distributing different types of goods. No attempt has been made — and it would be impossible to make one — to build an overarching normative sphere of all functional spheres, and there is no general encompassing value of equality to speak of. Also, a positive state of pluralism must remain, insofar as the goods to be distributed by different spheres are pluralist: political power, wealth, honour, and offices have to be appropriately diversified and distributed. The ideal state is one of evenly distributed conflict, not of synthesis or harmony.

If one accepts this model of social spheres, MacIntyre's second objection to individualism also can be accepted in part. MacIntyre orients himself to the one-sided, Kantian versions of liberal philosophy when he criticises liberal democracies for their individualism. If one takes heed of social spheres, both empirically and ideally, this excessive critique of individualism diminishes. People can be seen instead as integrated in different spheres, and thus to the good and bad within these spheres. The flexibility to transcend particular spheres and to participate in more than one sphere (which MacIntyre criticises in the form of role theory [MacIntyre 1985a, 32, 204]) is a functional necessity of modern society, of which modern individuals are proud. Politics is tied to the functional aims of spheres, including the continuous reformulation of the spheres' ends and aims. Individuals organise themselves politically, not as abstract citizens, but rather as doctors and nurses, teachers and parents, pilots and air-traffic controllers. There is surely a strong economic streak to all their interests and conflictual exchanges, but insofar as they are organised professionally, their historic professional roles and implied morality are not lost and forgotten.[30]

MacIntyre's orientation to practices as described in *After Virtue* is, however, implausible for a liberal understanding of politics. The central reason, as I have argued in this essay, is the nonexistence of 'inherent goods' in an uncontested way. There is no uncontested *telos* of any given practice in modern societies; all 'inherent ends' of practices are prone to pluralist interpretation. Practices modeled on the classic professions are typical of this, if one only thinks of the healing/enhancing debate in medicine, of plea-bargaining in the judicial arena, or the conflict between risk of human life and making a profit. There simply are no 'inbuilt' aims and norms in professions in modern conditions, and the analogue of playing chess is therefore highly misleading (MacIntyre 1985a, 188). Given the non-teleological structure of most representative social practices, a teleological idea of practices cannot provide a model for the reconstruction of non-individualist forms of politics in liberal societies. Accordingly, the political strategy at which MacIntyre has hinted since giving his diagnosis in *After Virtue,* that of trying to find or revitalise pockets of teleology at the level of smaller communities and practices, is a fundamentally misguided one. Endemic pluralism in the modern world effectively does away with all forms of teleology, whether we are talking about a nation, a political party, a school, or a marriage. Practices with definite ends can at best (and for some time) be conducted privately, such as religious practices; but in public they are illusionary at best and, of course, totalitarian at worst.

---

30. 'Practices' play a role within social spheres, but it seems appropriate to distinguish between practices and fields of their realisation. In *After Virtue,* MacIntyre could think of the 'outside' of practices in economic terms only, and therefore he did not inquire into the relevance of integrating social fields and spheres as also politically relevant.

Mouffe reminds us of an important distinction made by Michael Oakeshott between *universitas* and *societas,* the former indicating an engagement in the collective pursuit of a common good, the latter the participation in a civil association whose members have the single unifying motive of sharing a common concern and of being loyal to each other in the light of shared interests and problems (Mouffe 1993, 66–69; Oakeshott 1991). It seems much more adequate, both descriptively and normatively, to think of professions, clubs, universities, and even religions and churches in terms of Oakeshott's idea of *societas* rather than in terms of teleologically oriented practices. Oakeshott also suggests thinking of an entire society as a *societas*; membership in different associations is not to the disadvantage of participation in the larger *societas*. On his model, society is at a distance both from the premodern community and from a liberal politics that instrumentalises the state into a promoter of interests and a guarantor of the rule of law. Mouffe again, rightly I think, suggests combining this teleologically thin conception of *societas* with the (Hobbesian and Schmittian) axiom of an ineluctably conflictual form of political life, thereby neutralising the harmonist and consensualist tendency in Oakeshott's republican politics. Since there are no 'fundamental ethical values', nor is there a 'foundational reason' basic to such a conflictual politics, it is in the end the most active and successful democratic party, or the most active and engaged politicians, those identifying themselves most strongly with political affairs, who determine the outcomes in a field of conflicting views and interests.

It seems to me that this antagonistic reading of civil associations is the best answer that one can give to MacIntyre's criticism of liberalism. It shares in part his critique of liberalism, but it deduces from the thesis that liberal politics is 'civil war carried on by other means' (MacIntyre 1985a, 253) not the unrealistic vision of favouring premodern communities, but the more hopeful and realistic interpretation that this war is conducted under the conditions of a given, albeit multiply diversified and only minimally shared, understanding of freedom and equality. As long as MacIntyre and others point to the ideological character of reason and the illusionary quality of rationalist liberalism, and instead refer to the psychological mechanisms underlying political engagement, their advice is fully welcome. It is not taken, however, as a necessary part of a convincing argument for a renewed vision of the common good. Instead, the most basic elements of liberalism, the ethics of freedom and equality and the important identification with local causes and projects, have to be taken together in a different way in order to avoid the total loss of politics—either in the form of MacIntyre's absolutist new reading, thereby privatising the common good, or in building illusionary rationalist theories of justice.

12

Compartmentalisation and Social Roles
MacIntyre's Critical Theory of Modernity

PETER McMYLOR

The moral theory of philosophers is almost always pursued at
a level of abstraction from the concreteness of everyday life which
is exhibited only in the strategy and tactics of those general staffs
whose armies are about to be defeated.

> —Alasdair MacIntyre, 'Moral Philosophy and
> Contemporary Social Practice'

Ask about your cultural and social order what it needs you and
others not to know.

> —Alasdair MacIntyre, 'Social Structures and
> Their Threats to Moral Agency'

The resources provided by the social sciences, broadly conceived, have
always been important for Alasdair MacIntyre. The early and in certain
respects continuing significance of Marx in his thought is obvious, and

no one who goes back to read 'Notes from the Moral Wilderness' (MacIntyre 1998a), with its powerful Marxian inspiration—written, we may recall, in the late 1950s—can fail to see the strong continuities as well as significant innovations that have characterised MacIntyre's intellectual development up to the present. However, MacIntyre's use of the social sciences is much wider than his use of Marx. Indeed, although I am concentrating here on MacIntyre's use of and significance for sociology, he ranges far beyond that discipline, as is clear from the historical, anthropological, and psychological materials in much of his work (cf. MacIntyre 1990b). Nor does MacIntyre use the social sciences merely as sources of illustration or as the raw material for a problem-solving technical philosophy. On the contrary, as he put it in the preface to *After Virtue*, 'The notion that the moral philosopher can study *the* concepts of morality merely by reflecting, Oxford armchair style, on what he or she and those around him or her say and do is barren' (MacIntyre 1985a, ix).

In seeking to understand MacIntyre, we must always recall that in producing *After Virtue*, he was not simply providing an account of moral philosophy with some social context. Despite the book's subtitle, 'A Study in Moral Theory', he in fact set out to write two books: one on the fate of morality in the modern world and another on the philosophy of social science. In the process he discovered that the arguments of one book required the arguments of the other. For, as he argues, 'a moral philosophy . . . characteristically presupposes a sociology' (MacIntyre 1985a, 23), that is, some way of socially instantiating its moral concepts. Therefore a successful sociology of a place or period may well have something to teach us about the nature of that place's or period's moral philosophy, and of course the moral philosophy of a period, especially as it relates or fails to relate to social practice and social relationships, may well tell us important things about that place's or period's social organisation.

In this essay I argue that MacIntyre's mature work in moral philosophy is, to quite a remarkable degree, dependent upon a critical sociology of modernity and that if his arguments are correct, then they provide important resources for a sociological understanding of the present. I also suggest that key aspects of what appear to be intellectual issues and problems in a variety of areas that MacIntyre's work addresses—the failures of contemporary moral philosophy, the related failures of social actors to be able to sustain consistent moral practices, and the apparent processes of religious disbelief or secularisation—are all understood by MacIntyre to be rooted in the distinctive pattern of contemporary social organisation, that is, the pattern of social organisation he calls compartmentalisation, and this is a matter that he clearly understands as primarily a sociological issue.

The significance of sociology for MacIntyre lies not only in its insights into the modern world but also in the way in which it provides a mode of modernity's self-interpretation. The significance of this self-interpretation for MacIntyre became very clear in *After Virtue*, where he made use of two of the most significant figures of sociology: Max Weber and Erving Goffman. These two are, of course, the theorists and documenters of key aspects of the modern social order, an order that has as one of its crucial aspects the compartmentalisation of different areas of social life. Weber or, perhaps more accurately, versions of Weberianism are understood as having been used to underpin modern thought about organisations and bureaucracy, including the thought of those who run and work in these organisations. As MacIntyre has noted, one of the most significant, though frequently ignored, effects of the social sciences is the way in which they change that which they seek to study, so that they bring 'into being new ways of thinking, feeling, acting and interacting' (MacIntyre 1985b, 897). He also notes, surely correctly in reference to psychology, but by extension to sociology as well, that 'actual and aspiring managers systematically read works of social psychology about the behaviour of managers' (MacIntyre 1985b, 898).

MacIntyre's famous deployment of characters to exemplify social forms is best understood within this context of the broader social sciences as potential providers of scripts of social behaviour. These characters help us see the moral dramas enacted before us and by us; 'the Manager', for example, appears as the key figure in the public realm of modernity. As MacIntyre puts it, in relation to Weber's influence on management and organisational studies: 'Weber's thought embodies just those dichotomies which emotivism embodies, and obliterates just those distinctions to which emotivism has to be blind. Questions of ends are questions of values, and on values reason is silent; conflict between rival values cannot be rationally settled. Instead one must simply choose—between parties, classes, nations, causes, ideals' (MacIntyre 1985a, 26).

If the manager obliterates the manipulative/non-manipulative distinction at the level of the organisation, the therapist obliterates it at the personal level. The manager treats ends as given and is concerned principally with technique, that is, how to transform the resources at his/her disposal into a final product, such as investment into profits. The therapist also has a set of predetermined ends to which to apply technique. Mental illness, frustration, dissatisfaction, and so forth are to be transformed to create 'healthy', namely, self-directed, organised, contented individuals. But, neither the manager nor the therapist can meaningfully argue about the moral content of their ends.

It is here that Goffman's work becomes significant for MacIntyre. Goffman gives us a concept of the self which seems to be no more than a ghostly presence in the multiple roles inhabited by the modern social actor. The self for Goffman is a spectral one that flits from role to role, being no more than ' "a peg" on which the clothes of the role are hung' (MacIntyre 1985a, 32). But the self has not disappeared in Goffman; rather, it stands over and against each of its roles. Its sense of 'freedom' seems to reside in its relative indifference to any particular role and in an awareness of the ultimate contingency of each situation. Such a self is at home in the conceptions of a therapeutic vision of society.[1] If Weber is the theorist who conceptualises the activities of the manager, then Goffman displays a self that may often require the managerial ministrations of the therapist, whether directly or in the myriad of self-help texts characteristic of our era (Lasch 1979; 1985). In his later work MacIntyre suggests that the ultimate value or skill prized by modernity is that of

---

1. The key source for MacIntyre here is the work of Philip Rieff, who developed the notion of a therapeutic culture most fully in his work *The Triumph of the Therapeutic* (1966, new edition 1987). Rieff knew and admired MacIntyre's work and stated in his new preface to the 1987 edition that 'on our "emotive" value civilization and on its ruling unholy trinity, the finest philosophical work yet to appear is Alasdair MacIntyre's *After Virtue*' (Rieff 1987, x). For a good survey of the issue of our therapeutic culture, owing much to Rieff and not a little to MacIntyre, see Imber 2004.

adaptability, and adaptability is implicitly what the practice of therapy promises to deliver for the self.

MacIntyre's use of these two sociologists and what might be termed their distinctive sociological visions to illustrate the nature of the moral practices of modernity has not gone unchallenged. His use of Weber to illustrate emotivism has been criticised (see, e.g., Tester 1999). Given the principal focus of this essay on compartmentalisation and social roles, however, I will not pursue this question here except to note that the most thorough reconstruction of Max Weber's moral thought, by Rogers Brubaker, seems to confirm completely MacIntyre's characterisation (Brubaker 1984, 113).

MacIntyre's use of Goffman, however, does call for comment, for the latter is without doubt the most important modern theorist of role analysis. MacIntyre's use of role analysis throughout his later work is dependent in many respects on the evidence and plausibility of Goffman's account of the modern self and its roles (MacIntyre 2000b). The use of Goffman's work as evidence of the moral texture of contemporary social relations and practices has been challenged. This challenge has come, perhaps surprisingly, not from those who oppose the significance of what is often called micro-sociology, but from some of its strongest advocates. For example, some argue, in response to sociological critics of Goffman who see his work as promoting a cynical view of human nature that celebrates selfishness and egocentricity, that Goffman is not attempting 'a characterisation of daily life as we all know it' and that 'he is not concerned to picture the self as "the person in the round"' (Anderson, Hughes, and Sharrock 1985, 151). Instead, Goffman was engaged in producing a 'naturalistic' sociology concerned with information flows and was 'trying to make the self a visible sociological phenomena' (Anderson, Hughes, and Sharrock 1985, 152). Critics point out that Goffman uses images and analogies drawn from aspects of human activity such as stage performances, or participation in ceremonies, to organise and analyse the behaviour that he observes 'naturalistically'. Goffman's interest is solely in the observed behaviour, how it is accomplished, and how it displays meaning, but only within the context of the particular interaction. There is no point, on this view, in being interested in what might lie behind the behaviour displayed or in its broader social significance.

So, Goffman's is purely a sociological project of exploring the conditions that maintain the interaction order as a social order.[2]

Does this sort of critique mean that MacIntyre's use of Goffman as a reliable source for understanding modernity is illegitimate? If Goffman brackets out much of reality for specific intellectual purposes, then does this mean that the picture of the modern self that MacIntyre draws—admittedly partly from Goffman—is, in some respects, suspect?

In my view the answer is no. MacIntyre, I believe, has three possible and convincing responses to this particular set of academic disciplinary objections to the use of Goffman's apparently specialist work in his analysis. In the first place, consider the sheer popularity of Goffman's work. In Britain and the United States his works have been sold in popular paperback formats and distributed widely in bookshops across the country and thus have reached a much larger audience than that of sociology students. The novelist Jenny Diski recalls her encounter with his work in the 1960s: '[Goffman's] *Stigma* told me about the nature of outsiders, ways of not belonging which redeemed my sense of not belonging, and *The Presentation of Self in Everyday Life* made sense of more or less everything, but especially the overwhelming sense of phoniness I perceived in all my encounters with the world, which Goffman defined neatly (too neatly, perhaps) as performance. . . . I read entirely subjectively and Goffman wrote towards that subjectivity' (Diski 2004).

The second reason is, perhaps, more significant: Goffman's work is required reading in numerous applied courses and training programs, ranging from business schools to basic vocational training in the service industries, such as sales and other occupations requiring face-to-face interactions with the public (Hochschild 2003; cf. Steinberg and Figart 1999). What may have begun as the specialist reports of a sociologist concerned with understanding the interactional order was, it seems, recognised by a wider public as, at least in some respects, providing accurate or 'useful' accounts of key aspects of contemporary social life.

---

2. But see the fascinating essay by Paul Creelan for an argument about the moral seriousness and even anger that underpins Goffman's work, especially in relation to how power-holders manipulate moral codes (Creelan 1984).

A third reason, which in a sense encompasses the first and second, is the fact that the concept of social roles is much more than a sociologist's conceptual device. One can argue that the emergence of the concept of the *social role* in social thought signals wider social changes. As the German sociologist Heinrich Popitz put it, 'Roles are not inventions of sociology, but are an invention of society. . . . Underlying the sociological abstraction is a social abstraction' (cited in Arditi 1987, 587).[3] The conventional wisdom behind this conception is that the primacy of social roles is a consequence of the social complexity that emerges with the radical deepening of the division of labour within modern industrial capitalist societies. While this is correct, what is not normally acknowledged in this standard sociological description is the cultural dimensions of the phenomena, which makes the concept of *role* more than simple social description. A key aspect of the cultural dimension of *role* is, as Arditi has noted, the significant sense and reality of 'detachment' from any one particular role; and, as Arditi suggests, an important dimension of the culture and ideology of contemporary individualism stems from this social reality (Arditi 1987, 587). This, as we see below, is a central aspect of the matter for MacIntyre.

It seems clear, therefore, that there are good reasons for thinking that MacIntyre's sociological intuitions are sound and that there is a good case to be made for the significance of role theory as a key element in a descriptive sociology of modernity. How, then, does this vision of social role relate to the process of compartmentalistion, and how, together, do they produce their profound effects? One way to get at some aspects of the processes involved is to consider how this vision illuminates the issue of secularisation. It is useful to choose secularisation as

---

3. Arditi's essay 'Role as a Cultural Concept' provides an important account of the development of role theory and an interesting contrasting analysis of the development by George Simmel and the early Chicago School of the concept of the social type, in the form of 'the Stranger', 'the Miser', and so on, which has intriguing parallels with MacIntyre's use of 'characters' to explore contemporary social life. Some may argue that this presentation seems close to Weber's Kantian-based ideal type constructions, but this does not seem fair; these forms seem to owe more to forms of dramatic narrative than to abstract constructions of the ideal type (Arditi 1987).

an example, in part because it is not a well-known aspect of MacIntyre's work, and in part because it illustrates very clearly the priority of sociological explanation in what appear to be matters of intellectual belief.

In a lecture delivered at Manchester University in 2001, entitled 'Four Kinds of Atheism', MacIntyre sets out to examine the development of atheism from the early modern period to the present and, alongside the various expressions of atheism, the corresponding theistic responses to them. The key distinction that he elaborates in the lecture is between three types of atheism that can collectively be understood as the atheisms of 'active denial', brought about by their 'explicit and detailed rejection of the theist's central claims', and a fourth, contemporary form of atheism, which he terms the 'atheism of secular indifference'. The fourth is the one that concerns us here.

This contemporary form of atheism has the character it does, not because it possesses any great intellectual force based on reasons and propositions, but rather because of sociological factors. The atheists of secular indifference, as he puts it, 'inhabit the constructed social world of the contemporary bourgeoisie . . . [and] lead significantly compartmentalised lives, moving between such distinct spheres as those of home, the workplace, the school, the clinic, the arenas of leisure activities, and the milieus of politics, each with its own roles for the individual to play and its own norms by which the role-playing is evaluated'. This pattern of life offers, he suggests, little opportunity for individuals to stand back from the variety of roles they play, 'so they might view their lives as a whole and ask how they should . . . evaluate them'. Thus, it is increasingly the case that there is no place where questions about the whole shape and direction of a life can be raised, that is, the type of questions to 'which theists and impassioned atheists offer rival answers'. Crucially important, he argues, is that religion—apparently traditional theistic religion—is not absent from this kind of social order. Rather, ' "religion" has become the name of one more compartmentalised area, one type of activity for the hours of leisure, just like golf and aerobics . . . [and] whether one engages in it or not is a matter of individual choice. Such religion does not put in question either itself or the social world in which it is embedded.' So the relationship between who does or does not participate in religion is often implicitly understood as a difference 'between those who have alternative consumer preferences, not as one giving rise to metaphysical questioning and conflict'. In practice, then, according to MacIntyre, what emerges as the religious forms of much of modernity are in reality parodies of their traditional pattern.

Much could be said about this argument, but for my purpose, its significance lies in the way that sociological considerations are treated as having the power to determine apparently intellectual and cultural outcomes. This is not an isolated example. We can find almost exactly the same structure of explanation at work in MacIntyre's account of the contemporary failures of moral philosophy to gain a serious purchase and influence on contemporary ethical practice.

In a range of essays, several now published in MacIntyre's two-volume *Selected Essays,* he sets out the sociological reasons for the central significance he gives to what he calls 'the compartmentalisation of role-structured activity'. He also adds two other subordinate sociological theses, referred to as 'the professionalisation of procedures' and 'the negotiated aggregation of costs and benefits' (MacIntyre 2006d).

In essence, rights-based appeals within modernity, rooted in the intellectual and institutional triumph of various forms of Enlightenment liberalism, encounter in contemporary practice a professional and bureaucratic translation of these rights into technical legal definitions at work in specialised institutional settings. This phenomenon has been well described by one sociologist as the 'sequestration of [moral] experience' (C. Smith 2002), where legal definitions colonise moral judgments within an internally referential system of legal understandings (Luhmann 1985). In the process, what is often produced is again a parody of the original concepts, in the form of alienated dependencies that this rights-based liberalism in its historical origins had sought to overcome. We should note, however, that this process is necessarily carried out by professionals who are, themselves, moving through role-based compartmentalised practices, and who collude to avoid consideration of the wider 'moral' or 'political' aspects of the cases with which they are faced.

MacIntyre presents what is perhaps his key contemporary sociological observation as to how this process works. It deserves to be quoted in full, not because of its absolute originality, but because it articulates what many 'plain persons', as MacIntyre might put it, seem to sense is wrong with the scale and anonymity of modernity:

This relative autonomy of each demarcated sphere of activity is re-inforced by the degree to which in contemporary advanced societies individuals encountered in each particular sphere are often not the same as those whom one meets elsewhere. When one encounters each individual only within some particular sphere, in some role that is a counterpart to one's own role in that particular sphere, then one's responses are increasingly only to the-individual-in-this-or-that-role rather than to the individual who happens to be occupying this role at this time. So individuals as they move between spheres of activity, exchanging one role for another and one set of standards for their practical reasoning for another, become to some important extent dissolved into their various roles'. (MacIntyre 2006n, 197)

The character of a typical moral agent in such a context is best ex-plored, MacIntyre argues, by examining what moral characteristics and virtues they lack. They lack, in particular, a standpoint that can pass judg-ments upon their performances in their various roles, and they lack the virtues of integrity and honesty necessary for exercising the power of a moral agent. This moral agent, he argues, 'cannot have integrity, just be-cause its allegiance to this or that set of standards is always temporary and context-bound. And it cannot have the constancy that is expressed in an unwavering directedness, since it recurrently changes direction, as it moves from sphere to sphere' (MacIntyre 2006n, 200).

The vision of what would constitute virtue in this environment is likely to be one that focuses on excelling in role performance, and natu-rally this may mean excelling very differently in different role perform-ances in various social contexts. Insofar as the self has successfully dis-solved itself into its various social roles it would experience no conflict between these differing valuations of excellences, as in being, say, a lov-ing father in the domestic sphere and the successful manager of a land-mine production facility in another.

A significant parallel analysis, which reinforces that of MacIntyre's, can be found in the work of the sociologist Bryan Wilson on role theory and moral behaviour (Wilson 1985; 2001). Wilson explores the Durk-heimian concept of de-moralisation in modern Western societies via a contrast he draws between the intensive moralisation, of a public and institutionalised kind, of nineteenth-century social actors—especially, but not only, the working class—and the relative absence of such public-sanctioned morality within the social order of postindustrial capitalism. In essence, the argument turns on the significance of our increasingly differentiated social and technical division of labour, in which carefully delineated social roles within the economy, in particular, provide new refined techniques of role compliance. As Wilson notes, 'Control could become more specific: there is less need for the blanket effect of total socialisation and moralisation. The good worker need not now be 'the good man'; indeed his moral quality as a man could now be regarded, in-dustrially and commercially, as a matter of indifference' (Wilson 1985, 321). Modern social roles within modern capitalism require what is called 'professionalism' and technical skill, and these can be understood in Wil-son's terms as a 'harness' in which the role players are asked to cast aside all irrelevant competencies and skills, including moral ones, to perfect their core professional abilities. Any wider moral concerns about the di-rection and purposes of their particular lives must be left at the door of the workplace.

Consider MacIntyre's second subordinate thesis, 'the negotiated ag-gregation of costs and benefits', which has roots in the conceptual inheri-tance of utility theorists and aims at impersonal and interest-neutral forms of collective social assessment. These organised processes of as-sessment are faced by groups and organisations with incommensurable types of aspirations and needs. Thus, they only appear to produce just resolutions via a translation process into the bureaucratic and political forms of contemporary modernity. Answers to controversial and con-tested issues are constructed via negotiation, commissions, reviews, tri-bunals, committees of inquiry, and so forth. We now have abundant em-pirical research—not referred to by MacIntyre, but the bread and butter of sociologically informed policy analysis—in support of the view that such methods produce results based upon the differential power and influence of those who access them (cf. Domhoff 2005; Lukes 2005). As MacIntyre concludes, 'Once again it is not the moral philosopher's the-oretical concepts that have found application but . . . a mode of practice which assists in preventing the intrusion of those theoretical concepts' (MacIntyre 2006d, 121).

In this context, MacIntyre is pointing to the relative futility of con-temporary debates about the significance of the Enlightenment—for and against—for contemporary practice, and he would surely endorse Dan Hind's argument that 'the institutions that claim collectively to embody the Enlightenment, above all the state and the corporations, pose the most serious threat to reasoned understanding of our time' (Hinds 2007, 5).[4] It is also worth noting, in this context, the extraordinary growth in significance of the public relations industry in assisting both the state and private corporations to 'manage' public opinion—almost always in the interests of those with power and wealth (cf. Miller 2008; Miller and Dinan 2000; 2007).

MacIntyre's account of these obstacles and problems is not a piece of sociological determinism that points towards a Weberian pessimism about our contemporary fate. Rather, MacIntyre points to the threats to moral agency within modernity, not to its complete obliteration. Moral agency remains possible, and if it fails, it is we, as moral agents, who collude in that failure. A key indicator of this collusion, MacIntyre notes, is to be found in the newest entrant into the catalogue of the virtues, namely, the distinctive modern virtue of 'adaptability'. This, he observes, is often understood not just as a feature of this or that particular role, but as a feature of the individual as such. Indeed, it is difficult to think of a more frequently applauded modern trait, alongside the traits of being innovative, motivated, and naturally blessed with that wonderful capacity 'to move on'. The emergence of 'adaptability' as a virtue is significant because it reveals, not the complete dissolution of the self into its various social roles, but rather the skillful management of a series of transitions by a still capable 'self', who is engaged, 'when well-managed, [in] a dramatic feat, an expression of the actor as well as of the roles enacted' (MacIntyre 2006n, 201).

It remains possible to ask questions about the role one is playing: to ask, 'How should I play the role?' and 'By what standards do I judge my performance?' and indeed, 'Should I continue to play the role at all?'

---

4. Hinds, whose book is a much-needed polemic, refers to a 'folk Enlightenment' that is deployed ideologically by primarily Western intellectuals to demonise a wide range of dissenting and oppositional opinions, from those of evangelical Christians to those of environmental campaigners and political Islamists. See especially Hinds's account of 'the party of modernity', which differentiates strands of opinion but notes their cumulative impact (Hinds 2007, ch. 1).

These are all questions that the role player can and should ask. Not to do so is to be actively complicit in the formation of the divided state of one's life. So, although the structures of the compartmentalisation of social roles and their enacted structures of bureaucratic domination are real, they nonetheless cannot exclude the possibility of critical reflection and action. Such actions would include the creation of social spaces for reflection on the moral significance of the social roles we all inhabit.

As I have argued, institutionalised forms of modern society have increasingly featured in MacIntyre's accounts of the frustrations and conceptual confusions that seem to bedevil moral argument. This is in part a consequence of MacIntyre's recognition that many problems within academic moral philosophy are debates between positions that not only never seem to be able to finally vindicate themselves against their opponents, but also seem to have little relevance to the ethical practices of social life. However, this recognition of the importance of social structure should not lead social scientists to simply congratulate themselves on finding that they have a perhaps surprising relevance to philosophical thought. They should rather recognise a point that I have completely ignored until now in this essay: namely, it is MacIntyre's Aristotelian-Thomist conception of human nature and its place in the order of things that gives their work a potential critical significance, which can take it beyond the Weberian pathos I mentioned above (MacIntyre 1999a). But if they do acknowledge this, then they may well be forced to recognise that their empirical work on the forms of social and organisational life provides the material for exploring the conditions from which the contemporary forms of human estrangement spring. They will then have to raise the possibility in their analyses that without some substantial rejection of the institutional forms of modernity, human flourishing will be systematically frustrated. For without this rejection, the lessons of MacIntyre's work on our moral culture could be summed up in the title of Niklas Luhmann's famous essay, 'The Future Cannot Begin' (in Luhmann 1984). If social scientists are open to such arguments, they will find in MacIntyre's work the basis from which a genuinely critical social science can renew itself.

13

Virtue, Politics, and History

Rival Enquiries into Action and Order

KELVIN KNIGHT

After Virtue's conclusion is notorious.[1] It is that 'barbarians . . . have already been governing us for quite some time' and that, like 'the Roman *imperium*' before it, our present order is not worth 'shoring up' (MacIntyre 1985a, 263; cf. 2007, xv–xvi). This conclusion is frequently cited in allegations that the book's author, Alasdair MacIntyre, presents a 'thoroughly "pessimistic" account of the possibilities for Aristotelian politics' (Fives 2008, 151–52). Such pessimism is often contrasted with the claim that the modern state is a political community of citizens, and that this state therefore affords ample scope for an Aristotelian politics of the common good. Claimants typically add that the same liberalism which MacIntyre opposes has long been opposed by a republican tradition, and suggest that MacIntyre's 'pessimism' should therefore be replaced by a republican politics.

---

1. I thank Ron Beadle, Ronnie Beiner, Caleb Bernacchio, Alasdair MacIntyre, Cary Nederman, Jeff Nicholas, Niko Noponen, John Pocock, and Manjeet Ramgotra for helpfully commenting on drafts of this essay.

This essay brings MacIntyre's Aristotelianism into critical engagement with republicanism, as well as liberalism. Each of these three positions is understood by its protagonists as a tradition in rivalry to others. Republicanism is represented here by the historians J. G. A. Pocock and Quentin Skinner. Historically, republicans shared Aristotelianism's concern with human character, intention, and action. Liberals, by contrast, are characteristically concerned with general rules as constraints on individuals' actions. Enforcement of these rules is the task of the state. Even so, the central argument of the liberal theorist who had much the most political influence in the late twentieth century, F. A. Hayek, was that the rules which most beneficially constrain individuals' actions have evolved apart from the state, and that the state cannot be allowed to contravene these rules. This argument he traced back to the eighteenth-century Scottish Enlightenment, making Adam Smith's famous 'invisible hand' emblematic of the idea that social order necessarily exists 'spontaneously' and independently of any particular or shared intention. Accordingly, rules are justified by reference to their present consequences, *not* by reference to any authorial intention. As Pocock concedes, this idea undermined republicanism's conception of politics as the virtuous activity of intentionally creating and maintaining order. Whereas republicans identified ethics with the public activity of citizens, liberals privatised morality.

In *After Virtue: A Study in Moral Theory*, MacIntyre contested this privatisation of morality by advancing an historically informed account of the intentional and social nature of action. Reason motivates action by identifying desirable ends, as well as means to their actualization. Action is therefore to be understood teleologically, as directed towards those intentional objects which Aristotelians call goods. The greatest good to be achieved through action is actors' own habituation into such excellences of character as courage, truthfulness, and justice towards others. These propositions constitute an Aristotelian justification for following moral rules, according to which moral action is the means by which human potentiality is actualised (MacIntyre 1985a, 52–53). For a good to be morally educative, it must possess objectivity relative to the actor (MacIntyre 1993), as do those goods which are internal to social practices (MacIntyre 1985a, 187–94). Because such goods exist prior to, and independently of, any individual actor, they possess an objectivity that is irreducible to subjective reason, motivation, or action. It is by being socialised into shared practices and kinds of reasoning, by conforming one's desires to the pursuit of practices' common goods, and by acknowledging the authority of practices' standards of excellence over one's own actions, that one best internalises the virtues.

As I have argued elsewhere, MacIntyre's argument reforms traditional Aristotelian ethics and politics. The theoretical presuppositions of Aristotle's own practical philosophy (and not just what he said of women and slaves) are incompatible with an inclusive idea of political community. Specifically, what Aristotle said (in *Physics* II and *Metaphysics* I–II, V.1–2, VII.7–9) about production in distinguishing final from efficient causality, and what he said (in *Nicomachean Ethics* VI) in isolating practical from theoretical and technical kinds of knowledge and reasoning, has needed to be reconceptualised. This, I argued, has now been done by MacIntyre (Knight 2007). Therefore, a contemporary Aristotelian politics should begin from MacIntyre's work.

Republicanism may be understood to share something with Aristotelian practical philosophy insofar as republicanism is concerned with virtue, which it identifies with citizens' pursuit of the good of their republic. It shares still more insofar as republicans understand that virtue is *learned* through pursuit of common goods, but that character and action can also be institutionally corrupted. Pocock identifies a historical continuity from the concept of corruption to that of alienation, making the ethical point that alienation from one's own action prevents one's cultivation of character. What nonetheless opposes republicanism to MacIntyre' Aristotelianism is its identification of virtue and politics with action in an exclusively public sphere. Virtue, for republicans, contrasts with activity that is self-interested and private. This, from the perspective of MacIntyre's Aristotelianism, is a false distinction, because virtue is cultivated in a wide range of social kinds of good-orientated action and expressed in all of one's activities. A genuine excellence of character is not something displayed in one area of life but not others. Republicanism's conceptual and institutional compartmentalisation of 'private life from public' (MacIntyre 1985a, 204) has become a presupposition of liberalism. From an Aristotelian perspective, this compartmentalisation should be rejected. Instead, politics should be reconceptualised and re-institutionalised as the intentional coordination of social practices towards a comprehensively common good.

This argument is advanced in seven stages, corresponding to the following sections of this essay. First, I summarise Pocock's concept of republicanism and compare his approach to the history of ideas with those of Skinner and MacIntyre. Secondly, I relate MacIntyre's politics to republicanism. Thirdly, I explore Skinner and Pocock's historical concern with conceptual innovation, focusing upon the eighteenth century. Then, I turn to Hayek's use of the eighteenth-century's innovative idea of order. Fifthly, I summarise Skinner's reconceptualisation of republicanism's rivalry with liberalism, after which I conclude my case that republicanism is a source of, rather than a rival to, liberalism. Finally, I summarise MacIntyre's innovative alternative to both republicanism and liberalism.

Republicanism as an Aristotelian Tradition

The idea that an early modern republican tradition revived an Aristotelian politics of citizenship was influentially expressed in Pocock's *The Machiavellian Moment: Florentine Political Thought and the Atlantic Republican Tradition,* originally published in 1975. The continuing philosophical importance of 'the Aristotelian tradition' throughout the Renaissance had already been established by Paul Oskar Kristeller, while others had highlighted the importance of a newly 'civic' humanism in Renaissance Florence (Baron 1966) and, controversially, rewritten the history of American political thought to emphasize the importance of Anglophone republican ideas in the neo-classical 'founding' of the United States. Pocock expressly combined the latter two historical arguments and silently followed Kristeller in arguing that Renaissance Aristotelianism led to an Atlantic republican tradition that based politics in citizens' virtuous pursuit of the good of their republic.

Pocock's republican 'tradition of thought . . . is Aristotelian'; the role in it of Aristotle's *Politics,* 'the earliest and greatest exposition of it', was 'vast and all-pervasive'; and 'the Aristotelian polity [was] the ultimate paradigm of all civic humanism' (Pocock 2003, 67, 478). For Pocock, traditions or temporal 'paradigms', as linguistic and conceptual schemes, exercise 'authority' over individual authors, conceptualising the problems to be addressed and providing the terms in which to do so (Pocock 1973, 3–41, 233–91). Such is the case with Aristotelianism, on the account of Pocock, for whom a properly historical approach to texts involves, first, returning them 'to the contexts in which they were first written', and then, tracing 'the fortunes' of them and of 'the discourses they may be said to have conveyed, as they travel from one context to another' (Pocock 2003, 554). Pocock therefore proposes that, as Aristotle's *Politics* traveled through history, it continued to exercise authority over participants in that republican tradition for which it was paradigmatic.

There are, however, grounds to doubt the authority of Aristotelianism over republicanism, even on Pocock's account. He initially presents republicanism or 'civic humanism' in the 'teleological and ethical terms' of 'the development of the individual toward self-fulfillment' and, further, of 'the distinction between a universal good . . . and the multiplicity of particular goods'. This distinction expressed a 'solution' to what he presents as 'problems of particularity', temporality, and change that posed endemic challenges to 'the medieval conceptual scheme'. Aristotelianism's solution was that particular goods should be politically subordinated to the universal and 'static', or atemporal, good of the self-sufficient republic. 'The integrity of the polity must be founded on the integrity of the personality, and . . . the latter could be maintained only through devotion to universal, not particular goods', so that 'the concept of the citizen or patriot was *antithetical* to that of economic man' (Pocock 1973, 85–90, emphasis added; cf. 2003, ix).

In interpreting this account we should refer to another source of Pocock's republican synthesis, because it owed something of considerable importance to Hannah Arendt and, via Arendt, to Martin Heidegger. On their account, time is the existential problem for human being, and Aristotle attempted to elide this problem by reconciling Plato's atemporal universals with the particularity of human action. He did so by elaborating the metaphysical concept of a *telos,* as a good of potentiality that is internal and universal to all particular individuals of a specific, natural kind. This concept was repudiated by Heidegger and Arendt, and by

Pocock, and its repudiation returns us to the Platonic issue of temporal particularity and *a*temporal universality. Having rejected Aristotelian theory, Arendt focused upon the concept of action, the 'greatness' of which lies 'only in the performance itself and neither in its motivation nor its achievement' (Arendt 1958, 206). On her account, Aristotle continues a tradition of 'political *philosophy*', which, following Heidegger (Knight 2008b; 2008c), she accused of directing individuals' gazes away from their own, political acts (Arendt 1968a). Although, like Arendt, and unlike Aristotle, Pocock is keen to separate politics from philosophy, he is far too much of a historian to accept Arendt's way of dealing with temporality. Unfortunately, his resistance to philosophy is nonetheless sufficient for him to accept Arendt's presentation of Aristotelianism in terms that ignore the radical way in which Aristotle revised Platonism.

In *The Machiavellian Moment* Pocock retained the language of 'universality' and 'particularity' (e.g., Pocock 2003, 3–9, 20–24, 62–78), but now in a curiously anachronistic combination with the term 'values' (e.g., Pocock 2003, 3, 67–71, 73–76). The term 'value' (like *Wert*) entered modern philosophy from economics, serving to undermine Aristotelian teleology and virtue ethics by juxtaposing values to facts, 'ought' to 'is'. We may, in any case, suspect that Pocock's apparently ontological terminology of 'particularity' and 'universality' was a surrogate for more political concerns, as when he writes of 'private' rather than 'particular' goods (Pocock 1973, 86; 2003, 74). Like Arendt, he disregarded what Aristotle said at the beginning of the *Ethics* about a hierarchical ordering of goods 'for the sake of' greater goods, and he interpreted what Aristotle said about *polis* and *oikos* at the beginning of the *Politics* in terms of an 'antithetical' opposition of what is 'public' to what is 'private',[2] of what is universal to what is particular, and therefore of the *res publica* to the 'private' sphere of 'economic man'.

---

2. This juxtaposition could also be accused of anachronism. Scholars routinely translate *idios* and *demosios* as 'private' and 'public' (e.g., Nagle 2006, 11), and the concepts of *demosios* and politics might have been peculiarly close in Aristotle's Athens. His *Politics* nonetheless distinguishes the concepts of village (*kome, deme*) and people (*demos*) from that of political community.

Even if Pocock is insensitive to conceptual change in ancient philosophy, the same can certainly not be said of his treatment of political thought in the Renaissance. However we understand Aristotelianism, it would seem that Machiavelli represents a moment in the history of political thought in which there is a revolutionary paradigm shift away *from* Aristotelian practical philosophy. This is not what Pocock argues, but he *does* say, in 1975, that with Machiavelli 'the material basis for civic personality . . . shifted . . . from [Aristotle's] notion of the household to that of arms' (Pocock 1975, 65). The central message of the central part of *The Machiavellian Moment* is that Machiavelli effected a conceptual innovation in the political understanding of virtue. This innovation would appear to have two aspects. First, Machiavelli isolated *virtù* from 'particular' values, private goods, or, in more modern language, 'interests'. Secondly, Machiavelli presented political virtue as a matter of skill more than of character or morality. Indeed, for Pocock, Machiavelli's innovation was to redefine *virtù* as itself 'that by which we innovate' (Pocock 2003, 167).

The Machiavellian moment is also, on Pocock's account, that in which political time came to be understood in the new way of *fortuna*. *Fortuna* has nothing to do with either Christian eschatology or Aristotelian teleology. Aristotle (in *Physics* II.4−8) had consigned to 'chance' those events, those unintended consequences of action, that lie beyond the causal necessity of nature or of artifactual production, and beyond the causal power of intentional action, even when informed by excellent practical judgment. Chance was marginalised by Aristotle's explanatory scheme. For Machiavelli, in contrast, *fortuna* was the contingency that felled republics. Even *virtù* could not be counted upon to prevent destruction. Indeed, 'the self-destructive nature of virtue' (Pocock 1975, 75) was an ineradicable problem. In conquering a territorial empire, the military effectiveness of virile Roman citizens' martial virtue unintentionally destroyed the political community that generated that very virtue. Unlike the decline and fall to barbarian invaders of its imperial successor, the death of Roman republicanism was, on this view, caused by an entirely endogenous pathology. The veritably pessimistic inference is that republics can never survive history. Machiavelli's politics here reflect Pocock's historiography. Rather as 'the uncontrolled act' of Machiavelli's innovative prince has 'uncontrolled consequences in time' (2003, 156), so too, Pocock's more knowing 'historian . . . intend[s] to make statements that have unintended consequences and that situate practice in the unintended and unpredicted universe of history' (Pocock 1996, 111).

The final part of *The Machiavellian Moment* is centrally concerned not simply with politics but with 'political economy'. This idea has nothing to do with that which is traceable back to the second book of the pseudo-Aristotelian *Oeconomica* (Aristotle 1935). Rather, it is a 'neo-Machiavellian' idea in that civic virtue and the unity of personality are based materially in the self-sufficiency supposedly gained from the ownership of land (for which reason Pocock also calls it 'neo-Harringtonian') and of arms, as in Fletcher's argument for a militia of the Scottish gentry. This political economy is republicanism's final form. It succumbs, like its Roman predecessor, to internal corruption, but a corruption that takes the new form of commerce.

Pocock's work has been assimilated with that of Skinner, John Dunn, and others in a so-called 'Cambridge School' of the history of political thought.[3] The unifying intention of this school is to understand texts in the historical contexts in which they were first authored (but not also, as for Pocock, to understand those texts' subsequent 'fortunes'), rather than in relation to the supposedly ahistorical questions of philosophy. Skinner is the pivotal figure in this school, and his methodology is informed by a kind of philosophy that is thoroughly analytic and linguistic. Accordingly, individuals' utterances, even in the writing of philosophical texts, are to be understood as linguistic 'usages' and therefore as 'actions', rather than as straightforwardly propositional, so that texts can be more illuminatingly understood as exercises in rhetorical persuasion than in logical reasoning. This thought might have disturbed an Enlightenment *philosophe,* but it would hardly have offended a Renaissance humanist or Thomas Hobbes and it is their texts which have remained Skinner's

---

3. Pocock's greatest opus is no longer *The Machiavellian Moment* but the ongoing project of *Barbarism and Religion*. This, too, concerns the modern reception of the West's classical heritage, but the project's elaboration of a plurality of historiographical perspectives exceeds anything else in the Cambridge School, and Pocock has not related this study of the fall of the Roman *imperium* to his study of republicanism's modern fate.

principal subjects. Skinner is therefore more alert than Pocock to individual intentions and, still more than Pocock, to the possibility of individuals' conceptual innovation.

Skinner temporalises his understanding of language-use by combining it with R. G. Collingwood's idea of human history as the record not of causal events but of the enactment of intentional thought, and with Collingwood's interpretation of the intentions of actors through a 'logic of question and answer' (e.g., Collingwood 1939, 30–42, 66–72; cf. Skinner 1988a, 233–34; 2001). Past thought can be understood through the study of texts, and those texts can be understood by understanding the questions that they were intended to answer (Skinner stipulating that the context in which those questions are to be understood is that of other texts, with which authors may be presumed to have engaged).

> The history of political theory is not the history of different answers given to one and the same question, but the history of a problem more or less constantly changing, whose solution was changing with it. . . . Just as the Greek *polis* could not be legitimately translated by the modern word 'State' . . . so, in ethics, a Greek word like *dei* cannot be legitimately translated by using the word 'ought'. (Collingwood 1939, 62–63; Greek transliterated)

Skinner has acknowledged his indebtedness to Collingwood—and also to MacIntyre, whose work 'on the philosophy of action as well as on the history of moral concepts' he admired (Skinner 1978a, x; see also 1974, 282; 1984, 193; 1988a, 327–28). In the philosophy of action, MacIntyre argued that actions are only intelligible in their particular contexts. Regarding the history of moral concepts, he elaborated upon what Collingwood indicated was the modernity of 'ought' (MacIntyre 1967; 1971k through 1971p), while Skinner elaborated upon the modernity of 'state'.

Although there is evidently a certain Collingwoodian complementarity in the projects of MacIntyre and Skinner, when MacIntyre writes of rival traditions of 'enquiry' (e.g., MacIntyre 1990a) he extends Collingwood's logic of question and answer far beyond the methodological bounds of Cambridge. The traditions he traces are unified by the questions their participants ask, and by what Collingwood called the metaphysical 'presuppositions' of those questions. For MacIntyre, the most elemental presupposition of any tradition of enquiry must be some concept of truth, and Aristotelianism's 'desire to understand' imbues it with a concept of truth as the *telos* of enquiry. Whereas Pocock demands 'a separation of functions' between the disciplines of philosophy and history (Pocock 1979, 97; cf. 1962; 1973, 4–13; Skinner 1988b, 64–67), MacIntyre considers it an 'unacceptable implication' that 'the study of the past will have been defined so as to exclude any consideration of what is true or good' (MacIntyre 1984a, 39; cf. 1985a, 265–72).

Despite this basic methodological difference, MacIntyre's *After Virtue* concurred substantively with Pocock's *Machiavellian Moment* in several respects. MacIntyre cast Cicero, Machiavelli, and Adam Ferguson alongside Aquinas as members of a tradition that he called 'classical' as well as 'Aristotelian', he invoked Machiavelli's *fortuna* in criticism of positivist facticity (MacIntyre 1985a, 93, 105), and he proposed that 're-publicanism in the eighteenth century *is* the project of restoring a community of virtue' (MacIntyre 1985a, 236, MacIntyre's emphasis). Like Pocock, he followed the republican tradition to both America and Scotland, opposing those, such as David Hume, 'who define the virtues in terms of their relationship to the passions [and therefore] treat of society as nothing more than an arena in which individuals seek to secure what is useful or agreeable to them' (MacIntyre 1985a, 236). Finally, he shared Pocock's concerns with an uncompartmentalised personal integrity and a virtue that is unafraid of conflict. Nonetheless, it does not follow that MacIntyre's Aristotelian tradition was, even then, the same as that which Pocock postulated. If the Machiavellian moment is that in which politics was isolated from ethics, this sets Pocock's republicanism in opposition to MacIntyre's Aristotelianism.

Republicanism as a Rival to Liberalism

The historical context in which Pocock completed *The Machiavellian Moment* was, as he presciently noted, that of 'a profoundly counter-revolutionary point in time'. His statement that his 'study of the quarrel between virtue and commerce' made a contribution to 'the conservative side of the ledger' (Pocock 2003, 551) is illuminated both by what he said earlier of the authority of paradigms and by his recent proposi-

tion 'that all historical narrative, all written historiography, is by its nature conservative-liberal in its intention and effects' (Pocock 2004, 549).
It is 'liberal in the sense that it tells the state, conservative in the sense
that it tells the revolutionary, that there is always more going on than either can understand or control, and that to believe otherwise may have
consequences that are terrible because totalising. We know this lesson by
heart' (Pocock 2008, 27). As we will see, this is a lesson taught by Hayek.
Nonetheless, Pocock intended his revival of the Aristotelian 'image of
the citizen' as a 'criticism of [his] own world' (Pocock 2006a, 42).

Pocock's republican idea of a specifically civic virtue was, irrespective of the intentions of its author, soon adopted as a post-totalitarian
response to the commercial and decidedly uncivic individualism promoted by the new, Hayekian right. This is certainly how the republican
side in the conflict of virtue with commerce was understood by MacIntyre when completing *After Virtue,* which was originally published in
1981.[4] He first proposed that 'the barbarians . . . have been governing us
for quite some time' and 'that our own age resembles more than any other
that in which the fall of the Roman Empire began to be recognised as an
inevitability' in a review of Dunn, written in the aftermath of Margaret
Thatcher's election as prime minister in his former home, the United
Kingdom. Capitalism, MacIntyre asserted, 'violates all defensible conceptions of a rational moral order', and 'the modern Western state is today
moving towards bankruptcy' since its 'palliative measures' threatened a
fiscal crisis and 'its economic base, capitalism, continuously generates
forms of disorder' (MacIntyre 1979, 6, 4). Given this analysis, the Western *imperium* once again appeared to be heading for a fall, but this time
not because of any external threat but because of contradictions that were
entirely internal. Whereas Pocock's eighteenth-century republicans had
feared that public debts to private interests threatened corruption, the
fear of many American Republicans and others in the 1970s was that the

---

4. MacIntyre's 'Notes from the Moral Wilderness' has been described as a
Marxist critique of a republicanism that has been stretched back to 1960s Britain and across its political spectrum (Foot 2006; see 43–45 on MacIntyre 1998a),
but historians with a longer view could accuse such conceptual elasticity both
of anachronism and of underestimating the influence of their own texts.

state had grown so big that it would destroy its own fiscal bases in private capitalism. Such systemic bankruptcy was also anticipated by Marxists (e.g., O'Connor 1973), and by MacIntyre. To this economic analysis he added the moral point that a politics based only in self-interest, and not in any common good, is 'barbaric'. As he now reminds us, when he attacked 'eighteenth century claims, whether American or French', for individual rights, his intention was to attack bases of 'Thatcherite conservatism, epitomised by Margaret Thatcher's brash assertion that there is no such thing as society' (MacIntyre 2008r, 272–73).

Following Thatcher's election, and just two days after Ronald Reagan's election as president of MacIntyre's new home, the United States, MacIntyre's public attack on 'the contradictions of America ... and of the American idea' was launched.[5] America's contradictions are reflected in the 'contradiction ... at the heart of the principles of American intellectual conservatism', which 'combines the political liberalism of an 18th-century Whig with the economic liberalism of a 19th-century Manchester businessman' (MacIntyre 1980a, 14). How contradictory these principles really are is debatable, and I shall suggest below that eighteenth-century Whigs helped prepare commerce's progress to nineteenth-century capitalism, but this is inessential to MacIntyre's accusation that 'if the United States is founded upon an idea, it is an idea that involves theoretical contradiction and practical incoherence' and, therefore, 'is false'. As evidence, MacIntyre cites Thomas Jefferson's statement that he intended the Declaration of Independence as 'an expression of the American mind', and that this mind was informed by 'Aristotle, Cicero, Locke, [Algernon] Sidney, etc.' (MacIntyre 1980a, 14, quoting Jefferson 1999, 148; cf. 1980b, 67; 1984b, 159–60). America's founding was, on this evidence, legitimated in terms taken from the rival and incompatible traditions of classical republicanism and modern liberalism.

Here, MacIntyre applies to the culminating act of Pocock's Atlantic republican tradition the historiographical principle informing the cen-

---

5. This attack (MacIntyre 1980a) contrasts strikingly with an essay written earlier (MacIntyre 1980b), in which some of the same material is used in a way that is far less critical.

tral *historical* argument of the about-to-be-published *After Virtue*. This argument is that Aristotelianism's 'tradition of the virtues' combined moral theory with social and political practice, and that this tradition's modern decline allowed the conceptual separation of values from facts. The historiographical principle is that theory and practice must still be combined. 'There ought not to be two histories, one of political and moral action and one of political and moral theorising, because there were not two pasts, one populated only by actions, the other only by theories', and because 'every piece of theorising and every expression of belief is a political and moral action' (MacIntyre 1985a, 61).

For Pocock, 'the paradox of American thought', like 'the essence of socialist thought', lies in 'a constant moral polemic against the way in which' history 'bring[s] about incessant qualitative transformations of human life' (Pocock 2003, 551). The United States has 'the only political culture which recurrently laments the corruption of its virtue . . . and then sets about renewing' it. Calvinism's ethical individualism 'blend[ed] perfectly' with 'the republican paradigm', and 'European historians whose deepest wish is that America should never have existed . . . are driven to the unconvincing strategy of condemning the paradigm as ideology precisely because it works as historiography' (Pocock 1983, 239). Here, though, we see the disjuncture between Pocock's republicanism and contemporary American reality, as he himself admits. The nostalgic 'persistence of Jeffersonian values' of an 'agrarian republicanism . . . is a major fact of intellectual history', and, it seems, a fact that persists unchangingly across time and across contexts, so that 'what America might have been remains a standing instrument of criticism of what it is' (Pocock 1983, 244). As for MacIntyre, so for Pocock, the American idea appears inherently contradictory. They concur in valuing Jefferson's agrarianism, observing that Jefferson 'saw the preconditions of virtue as agrarian rather than natural' (Pocock 2003, 533) and proposing 'that the small working farmer is the social type of the virtuous man' (MacIntyre 1985a, 239). However, there is a difference between their appraisals. For Pocock, Jefferson continued the Anglophone and 'transatlantic' tradition of neo-Machiavellian political economy that based civic and military virtue in landed property, and it must be remembered that Pocock's republican paradigm is intentionally political, not philosophical. Since the republican 'ideal type ... was the citizen, not the farmer' (Pocock 1987a, 340), it is the citizen who embodies Pocock's normative ideal of 'the unity of personality'. This ideal is the opposite of what MacIntyre, too, condemns as the compartmentalisation of the self (MacIntyre 1988a, 337; 2006a), but MacIntyre differs from Pocock in contending that farming has sustained 'virtues that are central to all human life, and not just to farming'. Although this contention is not strongly causal, because he acknowledges that 'farming societies have sometimes been mean-spirited and oppressive' (MacIntyre 1998g, 237), he goes so far as to commend Jefferson, the agrarian, for advancing well beyond Aristotle, who 'would have found it difficult to acknowledge any close connection between the nature of the occupation in which someone engages and that individual's likelihood of developing the virtues' (MacIntyre 2000c, 132). Aristotle, MacIntyre argues, now 'needs to be corrected' by a tradition of 'agrarianism'—the 'charter document [of which] is Xenophon's *Oeconomicus*—which has understood that the virtues of the farmer and of the fisherman are the same virtues needed in the politics of small-scale community' (MacIntyre 1998g, 250–51). Here, MacIntyre claims a political significance for the ethics of household economy, or *oikonomia*, of exactly the kind that (as we will see) was attacked by Hayek.

In the heyday of the Thatcherite and Reaganite 'new right', MacIntyre was often assimilated to a 'communitarian critique of liberalism' that was said to be the republican tradition's contemporary expression. Such a stance continues to be exemplified by Michael Sandel (e.g., Sandel 1998). Accordingly, liberalism is equated with individualism and selfishness, and republicanism with a regard for the common good. This is a position to which MacIntyre sometimes appeared close in the early 1980s. As he then told a patriotic American audience:

> There is a long tradition in the past of our own culture, stretching from the best theorists of the ancient Greek city-state to those of eighteenth century republicanism, according to which politics is itself a form of practice, in the sense in which I have used the word. It is one of a whole species of practices concerned with the making and sustaining of forms of human community, whose end product is the living out of a certain mode of human life. (MacIntyre 1984c, 154)

MacIntyre therefore took 'eighteenth-century republicanism to be a . . . serious claimant for moral allegiance' (MacIntyre 1985a, 238), and, like Pocock, he added that there even remained 'important features of American public life in the first half of the 19th century which sustained the ideal of public virtue' (MacIntyre 1982, 14). Republican values are, apparently, even sustainable under federal government. That there are limits to their sustainability under modern political conditions is, however, a 'lesson' to be learned from those other eighteenth-century republicans, the French Jacobins, who were among 'the last great representative[s] of the classical tradition of the virtues' (MacIntyre 1985a, 243). The negative lesson they taught was 'that you cannot hope to invent morality on the scale of a whole nation when the very idiom of the morality which you seek to re-invent is alien', and, further, that state power cannot successfully 'impose . . . the ideal of public virtue' (MacIntyre 1985a, 238).[6] In combining these lines of reasoning, *After Virtue* concluded that republicanism is now 'exhausted as a *political* tradition' (MacIntyre 1985a, 262, MacIntyre's emphasis). MacIntyre may have agreed with Pocock, and with Hannah Arendt, that eighteenth-century republicanism was more successful in America than in France, but nowhere can republicanism now rightly claim moral allegiance.

MacIntyre soon extended the idea that the American state was legitimated by reference to contradictory principles into a critique of all modern states. He argues that the state requires legitimation in terms both of self-interested normality and of occasional patriotic defence. In the former, liberal mode, the state is legitimated by its protection of individuals' right to pursue their private goals; in the latter, republican mode, the state claims a legitimacy that requires individuals to sacrifice their private interests, and perhaps their lives, to a common or public good. Philosophically, the liberal position presupposes that individuals' interests are fundamentally prepolitical, whereas republicans seem to presuppose something like the Aristotelian idea that humans are political animals. Because claims of state legitimacy and of individuals' 'political obligation' to obey the state necessarily take both theoretical forms,

---

6. For a similar lesson from Irish republicanism, see MacIntyre 2006f, 167–71.

because these forms are in theoretical contradiction, and because theory necessarily informs practice, it follows that modern citizenship involves practical incoherence. Therefore, as Ronald Beiner has observed, whereas Sandel's 'civic republicanism' expresses the hope that 'local allegiance and experiences of nationwide civic allegiance will work together', MacIntyre 'opts decisively for the local', rejecting the state as 'a monstrosity of liberal-bureaucratic impersonality' (Beiner 2003, 68–69). On MacIntyre's account, 'bureaucratic authority is nothing other than successful power' or '*effectiveness*' (MacIntyre 1985a, 26, MacIntyre's emphasis).[7]

Interpretation, Legitimation, Alienation

The question of why individuals are obliged to obey the state is foundational to most liberals' understanding of their tradition. The converse of this question is that of the state's sovereign right to author and enforce laws and 'policies'. If individuals are to enjoy private liberty in matters of faith, commerce, and morality, then it is necessary for some separate, public power to issue general rules so as to ensure order. Reasoning about laws and policies is what liberals call 'politics', but, before liberals can rightly reason about what laws to enforce, what policies to administer, and what taxes to extract, it is first necessary for them to legitimate a power capable of those political actions. Liberal politics therefore presupposes the authority of the state, and the first task of liberal political philosophy is, logically, that of justifying the state's claim to authority as *the* political actor.

---

7. MacIntyre's principal subsequent elaboration upon *After Virtue*'s 'core conception of the virtues' (MacIntyre 1985a, 186 ff.) is in his contrast of 'goods of excellence', or virtues, with instrumental 'goods of effectiveness' (MacIntyre 1988a, especially 31–39; Knight 2008a). The prioritisation of each of these two kinds of good, one over the other, is the origin of two rival traditions of politics. Aristotelianism is the tradition that prioritises goods of excellence over goods of effectiveness, whereas liberalism continues the tradition that prioritises goods of effectiveness over goods of excellence. In these terms, the argument of this essay is that republicanism is on the same side as liberalism.

The Cambridge School originated in work (first of all, by Peter Laslett) that undermined liberals' interpretation of their history, as originating in an intentional modification by John Locke of Hobbes's contractarian solution to an elemental problem of political obligation. Such self-understanding might make good philosophical sense in attempting to isolate a first principle from which to deduce a coherent theory, but logical or philosophical priority cannot be read into history. Pocock and Skinner join Dunn in insisting that a properly historical interpretation demonstrates that Locke's intentions were other than those retrospectively imputed to him by liberal philosophers. Nonetheless, as Skinner indicates in the second volume of his *The Foundations of Modern Political Thought,* the question of political obligation originates in a real, historical problem, caused by both the individualism and the confessional conflicts that arose from the Reformation.

In answering the question of 'why *ought* I to obey the *state?',* liberals understand themselves to offer a moral solution to a political problem. Following Collingwood, and following both MacIntyre and Skinner, we may say that this foundational question of liberal philosophy is preeminently modern. While MacIntyre elaborated on the modernity of 'ought', Skinner investigated the modernity of 'the state'. The 'central thesis' of *Foundations* is that we 'enter the modern world' with the conceptualisations 'of the state as an omnipotent yet impersonal power' and 'of "politics" as the study of statecraft' (Skinner 1978a, x; 1978b, 358, 350). Although 'any attempt to excavate the foundations of modern political thought needs to begin with the recovery and translation of Aristotle's *Politics*', this reception only constituted a *pre*condition 'for the modern concept of the State'. It was a 'precondition' because it enabled 'the sphere of politics [to] be envisaged as a distinct branch of moral philosophy' (Skinner 1978b, 349), but the concepts of state and politics could only become fully 'modern' once divorced from Aristotelian ethics. Once the question of political obligation has been answered and individuals' obedience to state law morally justified, then individual morality is privatised. Both of the foundations of modern political thought that Skinner has laid out—first, the Renaissance, Machiavellian, and republican foundation, and second, the Reformation and Hobbesian (but not, on his Cambridgean account, liberal) one—are constituted historically by freeing politics from the concerns of wider practical, and not just theoretical, philosophy.

Skinner's conception of the state in *Foundations* was 'essentially Weberian' (Skinner 2006, 248; cf. 1978a, x), and here we must note his second philosophical 'allegiance'. This is to the 'tradition of twentieth-century social thought' that may 'be said to stem from Nietzsche' but which he first encountered 'in the social philosophy of Max Weber' (Skinner 2002a, 176). That this is not the sole source of his interpretivism we have already noted, along with the priority of his allegiance to analytic philosophy. What he owes to Weber and Nietzsche specifically is his interpretive idea of the *ideological* and manipulative 'use' of concepts, and, most especially, the Weberian idea of legitimation. When Skinner speaks of 'ideologies' he does so genealogically and perspectively, using 'the term not in a Marxist sense to refer to distortions of social reality, but rather in a Weberian sense to refer to discourses of legitimation' (Skinner 2006, 242). Legitimation is effected by manipulating the terms of existing discourse to create new meanings. In the tradition of Nietzsche and Weber, no goods are objective, so all values must be created subjectively.

For Skinner, Weber's 'Protestant ethic' thesis is an account of the 'rational choice' of 'a powerful legitimising device' by 'those who spoke for' 'early capitalists', in 'manipulating the speech act potential of certain evaluative terms' (Skinner 2002a, 150–51).[8] Their trick was to use the language of personal devotion and vocation to legitimise the accumulation of capital, which for Catholics (in part, for the Aristotelian reason that material wealth is only an instrumental or 'external' good and not an end in itself) was a sign of the vice of greed. This was a second ideological innovation in the concept of virtue, following that effected by Machiavelli. It would seem that, in Skinner's view, modern moral theory, like modern political thought, has its twin 'foundations' in the Renaissance and Reformation.

Pocock also considers the Protestant ethic as a conceptual and legitimatory innovation, even though he has long viewed Western intel-

---

8. MacIntyre, in contrast, understands the thesis to be about historical causality (e.g., 1962a; 1972, 435–38).

lectual history as pivoting upon the eighteenth century. Accordingly, he has made the surprising claim that, in 'a real sense', the legitimation of entrepreneurial activity by 'the Protestant ethic was invented' in early eighteenth-century England (Pocock 1975, 81; 2003, 446), and that, as the century progressed, this Protestant 'ethic of frugality was compelled to take second place to the ethic of self-interest'. This shift was due to the increasing 'concern with constructing systems of rationality based directly upon passion' (Pocock 1975, 81; cf. 2003, 446). The most enlighteningly innovative figure here is Hume, and Pocock's history of the eighteenth-century legitimation of commerce is that of 'a widening gap between facts and values'. Self-interested commerce became a rational 'strategy for those who accept that the movement of history is away from virtue and towards corruption' (Pocock 1975, 76, 82). For Pocock, as for Kant, martial virtues were bound to be undermined in time by the allure of the polite commerce of civil society. When a new theory appeared to explain how market values and 'mechanisms would ensure all the ends of virtue though individuals were not virtuous themselves', then it appeared 'that under modern conditions the notion of virtue itself became obsolete' (Pocock 1987a, 340). 'Public benefits', it seemed, could be more surely achieved by the free exchange of opinion and of material 'goods' or commodities than through the exercise of either public or private virtues. In the Machiavellian view, the unintended consequences of even virtuous action could hardly be anything but detrimental and, eventually, fatal to the republic, but in the new perspective of eighteenth-century commerce, rule-constrained action, even when viciously self-interested, could, in aggregate, hardly be anything but beneficial to society as a whole. Now, Hume is eclipsed by Smith.

We may agree that the Scottish Enlightenment 'brought to secular maturity the deeply familiar separation of human decision and consequent effect which had been implicit in orthodox Calvinist and Stoic discussions of causality offered by previous Scottish scholars', thereby causing 'the final and widespread success of a doctrine of unintention' (Allan 1993, 213). The success of this doctrine was what proved fatal to republicanism, in the form of Pocock's neo-Machiavellian political economy. Invoking Newtonian principles of causation, protagonists of the 'social theory of the Scottish Enlightenment' (Berry 1997) explained social order in ways that divorced actors' intentions from actions' effects. This was modernity's greatest conceptual innovation. From this point onward, moral theory would progressively cease to be concerned with virtue, however conceptualised. Instead of being a matter of character and intention, ethics increasingly became a matter of evaluating the consequences of actions and, still more, of evaluating the rules that coercively constrain action. Public morality was therefore replaced by policy, law, and rights.

For Pocock, all of this represents the corruption of republican citizenship. He locates another eighteenth-century Scot, Ferguson, 'at the point where the classical concept of corruption merges into the modern concept of alienation' (Pocock 2003, 502), having already proposed that 'Aristotle was anticipating features of the modern concept of alienation' at the very beginning of the republican paradigm (Pocock 2003, 72). Alienation's full conceptualisation began in Scotland's age of military professionalisation, cultural anglicisation, philosophical 'enlightenment', and economic 'improvement'. This moment involved 'what the classical and civic tradition presented as the crucial and disastrous instance of specialisation of social function', making urgent for Ferguson what 'for all Aristotelian theorists' was 'the problem . . . of deciding when the particular or private goods should be seen as contributing to the universal or public good, when as competitive with it'. Republicanism's 'concept of civic virtue staked everything on an immediate relation between personality and republic', and therefore condemned and excluded more particularistic goods as divisive to the body politic. The division of labour led to 'the specialisation of personalities' and to a mutual dependence that undermined 'the citizen as amateur, propertied, independent, and willing to perform in his own person all functions essential to the polis' (Pocock 2003, 499–502). Certainly, Marx regarded Ferguson as Adam Smith's 'teacher' about the demoralising effects of a deskilled division of labour (e.g., Marx 1976, 220, 474, 483–84), and Pocock echoes words of Ferguson made famous by Marx when he states that 'society as an engine for the production and multiplication of goods was inherently hostile to society as the moral foundation of personality' (Pocock 2003, 501; cf. Ferguson 1995, 174; Marx 1976, 483). This was no accident, and (following his temporal relocation of the Protestant ethic) Pocock advances a second paradoxical claim for the intellectual magnetism of his long, Anglophone eighteenth century. On his account, 'the history of Marxism . . . . began' around 1698, when the Scottish patriot Andrew Fletcher of Saltoun, wishing to maintain 'the search for liberty in self-sufficiency', elaborated neo-Machiavellian political economy (Pocock 1975, 83; 1985, 253).

None of this makes Pocock a friend of Marxism. He consistently emphasises that republicans' idea of an expressly *political* economy was articulated on behalf of aristocratic owners of real estate, not of mobile capital. Dismissing the view of intellectual historians who are 'so obsessed with their hostility to a Lockean "modern" or "bourgeois" "liberalism" that they can see nothing on the stage of history but the arrival and triumph of their antagonist' (Pocock 1983, 239–40), he attempts to reduce Marxist argument to a linguistic confusion. 'The *polis* and the *bourg, Burg* or borough were profoundly different places, and it is hard to estimate the amount of confusion caused by the circumstance that the German word for "citizen" is *Bürger*' (Pocock 1985, 103, cf. 47, 40). This is curious. Greek and Latin are assimilated in a way that is necessary for Pocock's own assimilation of Aristotelianism to republicanism, but these classical languages are then opposed to the barbaric German of 'the ancient constitution', 'the common-law mind' (Pocock 1987b) and, indeed, of republicanism as a 'Harringtonian' and 'transatlantic' tradition. Elsewhere, Pocock consistently contrasts the republican language of what is 'civic' to the jurisprudential language of what is 'civil', and this corresponds to the contrast he draws between the political economy of republicanism and the apolitical economy of civil, commercial, or indeed, bourgeois society. His deeper objection to Marxism may be that its history really began in 1843, with Marx's condemnation of the republican idea of the 'free state' as a 'bourgeois' ideology that hid workers' alienation and exploitation behind an equality that was merely legal and 'abstract' (cf. MacIntyre 1998f, 228).

Pocock's understanding of the eighteenth century apparently owes less to Marx than to Arendt. He uses 'the language of Hannah Arendt' in describing it as the period when 'the social rose up against the political, and the image of human action was replaced by that of human behaviour' (Pocock 2003, 550, 573; cf. Arendt 1958, 38 ff.), but what is 'missing' even from Arendt, he proposes, is an adequate account of *homo faber*, man as maker (including, we might add, man as Jeffersonian farmer). He admits that it remains unclear 'how the emergence of this figure is related to the European debate between virtue and commerce' and to the eighteenth-century 'quarrel between civic virtue and secular time', which ended by subordinating virtue and politics to the progress of prosperity. For Pocock, this quarrel between virtue and history still continues because it is 'anchored in a concern for the moral stability of the human personality', and Marxism's eschatological ideal is the ahistorical one of 'personality as awaiting redemption from the alienating effects of specialisation' (Pocock 2003, 550–52). In a way partially redolent of Arendt, for whom Marx stands at the end of a Platonic and Aristotelian tradition of political philosophy, Pocock has long contended that Marx 'hoped to restore to his universality' the 'Aristotelian citizen, participant in all the value-oriented activities of society'. Certainly, as Pocock says, Marx did speculate about unalienated individuals within communist society being able to play the parts of 'hunter in the morning and critic in the afternoon' (Pocock 1973, 103), but this perhaps misses what is central to Marx's critique of the social division of labour. What Marx objected to was not the proliferation of different industries requiring different skills but the division of labour from ownership, of work from its control, and of productive activity from the activity of its management. What is objectionable is this kind of *class* division of labour—of those who control from those who are controlled—and *not* the social division of labour between those engaged in different kinds of productive activity. It is the alienation of workers from owners and managers that is the social cause of the demoralising alienation of workers from their own action, from their own causal powers, and therefore from their own humanity.

Between Hume, Smith, and Ferguson and the later figure of Marx stands Hegel. Even if we were to agree with Skinner that with the state we 'enter the modern world', we should acknowledge the importance of Hegel's conceptual differentiation of the state from civil institutions and order, including within civil society what Hegel presented as the impersonal rationality of 'the system of [material] needs'. Marx's use of Scottish political economy was indebted to this Hegelian distinction, and he also owed his use of the Scots' post-Aristotelian stadial history 'of the progress of society toward commerce' and alienation (Pocock 2005a, 158–62; 2006b, 284) to Hegel, who (following the 'unsocial sociability' of Kant's *Idea for a Universal History with a Cosmopolitan Aim*) attempted with his 'conception of the *cunning of reason*' to turn the tables on Hume's account of practical reasoning by postulating how 'reason uses passion itself as its tool in bringing about its ends' (Collingwood 1946, 116, Collingwood's emphasis). Hegel's schematic philosophical aim was to overcome the modern individual's alienation from the universal through the educative mediation of particularity. The antithetical middle term is crucial to Hegel's triadic logic, and the particularity of civil society and its division of labour necessarily mediates between the subjectively free individual and the universally rational state. Crucial to his politics, therefore, is representation not of individuals *qua* individuals but, universalising the Protestant ethic, *qua* members of particular vocations. In this, we might think, Hegel poses an answer to Pocock's 'Aristotelian' question of how to reconcile particular and universal 'values', but it is an answer that Pocock rejects, along with Hegel's historicism. He rejects 'representation, the one great invention in politics that had been made since antiquity' (Pocock 1988, 70), because 'every theory of corruption, without exception, is a theory of how intermediaries substitute their own good or profit for that of their supposed principals', and 'if *partecipazione* was distributed according to socially specialised needs and nothing else, there would . . . be no *res publica* . . . no *polis*' (Pocock 1985, 122, 42). Like 'market mechanisms', representation renders citizens' virtue 'obsolete'. From Pocock's 'point of view it does not matter much whether the state regulates the economy or leaves it to the invisible hand' (Pocock 1990, 128).

Liberal Social Theory

Hayek's liberalism differed significantly from that of John Rawls, and his understanding of the liberal tradition also differed from that of most liberal academics. His is what, as we have seen, MacIntyre calls an '*economic* liberalism', and Hayek was far less a specifically political philosopher than (notwithstanding his dislike of the terms) a *social* and *economic* theorist. He nonetheless remains the greatest theorist of what is widely called 'neoliberalism', which allied with conservatives in the 'new right' that found its leaders in Thatcher and Reagan. Although MacIntyre would protest that their policies have caused much inequality and injustice, those policies do appear to have rescued the liberal and capitalist order from the fall that many predicted thirty years ago.

Hayek no more questioned the existence or legitimacy of the state than did Rawls, but he did question the efficacy and extent of its powers. Social order, Hayek argued, does not originate in the sovereign state, and extension of state power therefore threatens not only individual liberty but the very order that is constituted by individuals' conformity to entirely general, or 'abstract', rules of conduct. These rules are not simply posited by the state, even if they are defined by legislatures and interpreted by judges. Rather, they have evolved through usage.

Individual liberty under the rule of an impersonal and prepolitical law is, on Hayek's account, a necessary condition of any prosperous and, indeed, sustainable social order. He first identified this argument with a jurisprudential tradition of both natural and common law. This tradition, which 'goes back to classical antiquity, to Aristotle and Cicero, which was transmitted to our modern age mainly though the work of St. Thomas Aquinas' (Hayek 1967, 94), includes an 'English Whig doctrine of government limited by general rules of law' (Hayek 1978, 123–24) that he frequently claimed was exemplified in Harrington's famous identification (following 'Aristotle and Livy') of 'the empire of laws and not of men' (Harrington 1992, 8; see, e.g., Hayek 1960, 166). Hayek's idea here was that, when free from arbitrary domination and subject only to the rule of law, individuals will naturally order their relations to one another in a way that is spontaneous, civil, and mutually beneficial. Progressively, he shifted from this idea of nature.

Like Pocock, Hayek came to accord the eighteenth-century Scots a pivotal place in intellectual history. 'Smith's work marks the breakthrough of an evolutionary approach', to which 'the Aristotelian tradition' was blinded by Aristotle's 'naive and childlike animistic view of the world' (Hayek 1988, 146, 143, 47) that equated outcomes with intentions. On the evolutionary view, 'practices which had first been adopted for other reasons . . . were preserved because they enabled the group in which they had arisen to prevail over others' (Hayek 1973, 9). What he intended

by 'practices' is the same kind of conventionally ordered activity, in conformity to abstract rules of conduct—rather than to commands, aiming at some single end—that was conceptualised by his second cousin,
Ludwig Wittgenstein. Language, for Hayek, as for Wittgenstein, is paradigmatic of the kind of order that evolves, unintentionally, through the
usage of individuals in pursuit of their multifarious ends.

Hayek elaborated upon the Scottish Enlightenment's 'doctrine of
unintention' alongside a normative consequentialism that is resolutely
nomological and anti-teleological. Individual action conforming to rules
*'of the stability of possession, of transference by consent, and of the perform-
ance of promises'* (Hayek 1960, 158, quoting Hume; Hayek's emphasis)
is said to sustain a materially beneficial and geographically extended social order, whereas action that conforms to shared purposes is likely to
be detrimental. Hayek's presupposition was that of a general scepticism
about the scope of human reason to construct explanatory knowledge
or predict the consequences of actions. This 'critical rationalist', Humean
(*and* Kantian) scepticism shares with Hobbes the belief that the only
real causes are 'efficient' ones, but, according to Hayek's revised intellectual history, it opposes Hobbes's tradition of 'constructivist rationalism'
in denying that we can have certain knowledge of the workings of such
causes. There are necessary limits to our understanding, notwithstanding 'the fatal conceit' (Hayek 1988) that can arise from philosophers' desire to understand.

Hayek agreed with Hume's anti-Aristotelian claim that practical reason is instrumental, in that it concerns only means, but he eschewed the
central tenets of Hume's moral psychology: that passions dictate goals,
and that virtues are either 'natural' or 'artificial'. Hayek's own exploration
of 'the sensory order' (Hayek 1952) of the human mind may have moved
him toward a general distinction between 'complex' and simple kinds of
order, and, therefore (Caldwell 2004), towards the Scots, but it had begun
from other sources. Hume, in any case, never quite conceptualised '"unintended consequence" phenomena' as 'a third category between natural
and artificial' (Haakonssen 1981, 24). Hayek argued that such a conceptual innovation was achieved by Ferguson and Smith, frequently expressing his own idea of 'spontaneous' or 'self-organising' order in terms of
Ferguson's reference to 'establishments, which are indeed the result of

human action, but not the execution of any human design' (Ferguson 1995, 119; e.g., Hayek 1967, 96–105). What he disregarded was the extent to which Ferguson's conception was of 'spontaneous order as [a providential] teleology' (Hill 2006, 117; cf. Chen 2008). Smith's 'invisible hand' best exemplifies the eighteenth-century aspiration to move from empirical description to causal explanation of secular order, in conceptually separating the aggregative effects of rule-governed actions from the intentions of individual actors. His proposition is that under conditions of free trade 'every individual necessarily labours to render the annual revenue of the society as great as he can', even though the individual 'neither intends to promote the publick interest, nor knows how much he is promoting it' (A. Smith 1976, 456). This is what interested Hayek in Smith's economics and not, for example, Smith's theory of value. Hayek's own conception of goods, or economic values, was thoroughly subjectivist.

What interested Hayek in the history of ideas, still more than Skinner and Pocock (but without their sensitivity to historical context), is not philosophical coherence but conceptual innovation. He therefore has no interest in resolving the 'Adam Smith problem' of interpretive reconciliation between *The Wealth of Nations* and *The Theory of Moral Sentiments,* or any interest in the ethical speculations of either Ferguson or Smith. His own basic claim about morals was that they are among the practices and rules that are selected for, in the sense of a temporal process of survival of the fittest *society.* The morality of general rules that fits the extended market order is different from the morality of virtuous solidarity and altruism towards known others, which evolved when humans lived in small groups. An Aristotelian ethics and politics that rationally directs individuals to a common good may therefore have suited small communities (although Hayek denied that it suited an Athenian *polis* financed from maritime trade), but disaster must now follow when such an obsolete ethic is imposed by a state (Hayek 1976, 133–50; 1979, 153–76; 1988).

On Hayek's account, the *unintended* consequence of rule-governed human action is the maintenance of the spontaneous and 'extended order of human cooperation' commonly 'known as capitalism' (Hayek 1988, 6). Monetary values function communicatively, enabling self-interested entrepreneurs—Hayek's equivalent of the princely innovator—to ascertain the demand for commodities by unknown others, and giving those entrepreneurs self-interested reasons to act to meet those needs. In this way, the epistemological problem of dispersed knowledge of individuals' subjectively determined needs is overcome, as is the problem of how to order action to meet those needs. Hayek came to dislike calling this order an 'economy' (still less a *political* economy) because, etymologically, this implies the purposive directing of individuals to the common good of a community, as in a household. Instead, he proposed that it be called a 'catallaxy' (Hayek 1976, 108–9), indicating how wrong things went in the Greek beginnings of philosophical reflection upon practice. Although this attempt at linguistic innovation has been ignored even by his disciples, his (and Thatcher's) similar objection to the term 'society' has proven notorious. On his late account (Hayek 1988), it is a fallacy to suppose that there is such a thing as society. This is the presupposition of 'socialism' and, more generally, of those constructivist rationalists who suppose their knowledge of this imaginary entity to be sufficiently scientific to enable them to effect its political reorganisation. Against this, Hayek argues that rules and order have evolved. They are authored neither by God nor the state, but by human history. Therefore, on Hayek's hyper-Humean account, authority is a function of untheoretical tradition.

For Hayekian liberals, then, the fundamental problem of order is not one of political obligation but of the 'coordination' of action. Only when individuals' actions can be efficiently coordinated so as to produce and distribute goods to meet needs can order be extended beyond small groups. This coordination problem can only be solved by market rules, not political direction, and this because the order's complexity requires that action be 'governed not by shared purposes but by abstract rules of conduct' (Hayek 1988, 112). In this argument, we find a fully theorised consequentialist justification of that commercial order which first undermined republican political economy and has now defeated state socialism.

Republicanism as a Neo-Roman Theory

In contemporary political philosophy, republicanism is increasingly presented as a rival to liberalism. This is primarily due to Skinner. Although still posing republicanism as the renaissance of classical politics, he has never called it 'Aristotelian'. Instead, as Pocock says, Skinner is involved in 'setting Cicero', assisted by Livy and Tacitus, 'in the place of Aristotle' (Pocock 2003, 557). Skinner emphasises that 'the vocabulary of Renaissance moral and political thought was derived from Roman stoic sources' (Skinner 1978a, xiv). MacIntyre concurs, recognising that republicans wrote 'in an idiom inherited from Roman rather than Greek sources', an idiom that was Stoic rather than Aristotelian, making 'virtue primary and the virtues secondary' (MacIntyre 1985a, 236–37). Skinner is more emphatic. For him, still more than for Pocock, Machiavelli was 'revolutionary' in the way he drew a 'sharp distinction between *virtù* and the virtues' (Skinner 1978a, 156).

What has proven revolutionary about Skinner's reinterpretation of republicanism is his claim that, from Machiavelli onward, its fundamental idea and value has not been virtue but *liberty*. Pocock happily concedes that 'two conceptualisations of citizenship existed in history', but he also observes 'an ideological dimension to the works of those scholars who are so determined to maintain the primacy of rights over virtues that they deny the latter any autonomous presence in history' (Pocock 2008, 10). Conversely, Skinner's allies oppose 'the language of republicanism . . . to the language of political Aristotelianism' (Pagden 1987, 7) and even allege that 'the interpretation of republicanism as an intellectual tradition derived from Aristotle is a gross historical error' (Viroli 1995, 170–71).

Skinner himself calls the tradition's characteristic theory of liberty 'neo-Roman'. If applied to the republican tradition, the term 'neo-Roman' would have the merit of drawing attention to that tradition's historical and conceptual presupposition in the Roman law distinction of what is 'private' from what is 'public'—the *res publica*, public being, *status reipublicae, status civitatum,* or state (cf. Skinner 1989, 91–95). However, despite acknowledging the significance of Roman law for medieval and early modern republicanism (e.g., Skinner 2002b, 13–15), this is not what he intends by the term. Instead, as we have seen in his study of 'the foundations of modern political thought', he stresses the state's modernity. He also paid much attention there to the Renaissance 'ideal of liberty'. Only later did he risk the charge of anachronism by referring this ideal to the famous differentiation of 'two concepts of liberty' proposed by an older and philosophically inclined historian of political and social ideas, Isaiah Berlin (Berlin 2002).

Berlin's 'two concepts' have often been juxtaposed by Pocock, for whom 'republican vocabulary . . . articulated the positive conception of liberty' (Pocock 1985, 40; cf., e.g., Pocock 2006a, 43). As Skinner argues, this 'positive' conception derives from 'the ultimately Aristotelian suggestion that we are moral beings with certain true ends and rational purposes, and that we are only in the fullest sense in possession of our liberty when we live in such a community and act in such a way that those ends and purposes are realised as completely as possible'. This concept of liberty is thus based in 'an objective notion of *eudaimonia* or human flourishing' (Skinner 1984, 196–97). Accordingly, 'it is rational to be moral' because 'we have an interest in morality', to which we are 'committed by our very natures' (Skinner 1986, 234). In this conclusion, Skinner apparently echoes the moral theory of *After Virtue,* but he implicitly rejects that theory, together with the positive concept of liberty, because he rejects Aristotelian naturalism. Rather, he agrees with Berlin and other proponents of the contrary, 'negative' concept of liberty that individuals pursue a plurality of 'ends and purposes' and that they should be free to choose those ends, privately. What *is* by nature is, and ought to be, conceptually separated from consideration of what individuals *ought* to do.

Initially, Skinner identified the liberty of the moderns—republicans as well as Hobbesians and liberals—with the 'ordinary theory of negative liberty' (Skinner 1986, 237). His only disagreement with Berlin's case for negative liberty was then over means, not ends. Whereas Berlin held that it is 'a dangerous error to connect individual liberty with the ideals of virtue and public service' (Skinner 1984, 197), Skinner argued that negative liberty entails duties, and not just rights. As we have different ends, we have no necessary 'interest in morality', but, he argued, it follows that we *do* have an interest in each other's virtuous performance of specifically public duties. This is because such performance is a necessary condition of maintaining a 'free state', which is, in turn, a necessary condition of our individual freedom to pursue our private ends. 'It is only possible to be free in a free state' (Skinner 1998, 60), and therefore public liberty is a prerequisite of private liberty.

We have noted Skinner's 'allegiance' to Nietzsche and Weber, and he shares their rejection of any basing of liberty in natural necessity, whether Thomist or Hobbesian. His 'essentially Nietzschean' (Skinner 2006, 244) standpoint opposed him to *After Virtue*, given its critique of Nietzsche and Weber and its assimilation of Nietzsche to liberalism in contending that 'the crucial moral opposition is between liberal individualism ... and the Aristotelian tradition' (MacIntyre 1985a, 259). In writing on liberty, Skinner first merely noted this contention (Skinner 1986, 249). Later, in reorganising his text, Skinner made his dissent from MacIntyre's contention a hook upon which to hang the 'significance' of 'the "republican" theory of political liberty' and, indeed, 'of the republican tradition' (Skinner 1990, 293; cf. 1992, 222). He objected that his republicanism, being neo-Roman and Machiavellian rather than Greek or Aristotelian, comprises a third tradition in rivalry to both Aristotelianism and liberalism.

At this point, Skinner accepted the offer of what has proven an enduring alliance from the philosopher Philip Pettit. Pettit, who was aware of the Cambridgean separation of history from philosophy, hoped that he would 'not offend historical sensibilities too grossly' in writing of 'a republican theory of the state', 'which liberalism superseded' (Pettit 1989, 163). His ethics are consequentialist, and one way in which he has accommodated republicanism to this perspective is by making liberty, understood in a peculiarly republican way, the political goal to be effected by means of state power, policy, and law (e.g., Braithwaite and Pettit 1990; Pettit 1997). On this republican understanding of liberty, it means the individual's 'non-domination' by others, and Pettit followed Skinner in attacking 'MacIntyre's mesmeric dichotomy' in the name of republicanism as a third 'alternative' (Pettit 1994).

It was only after supplementing Berlin's dichotomy with MacIntyre's that Skinner insisted on distinguishing the neo-Roman understanding of liberty as *non*-domination from the 'ordinary theory of negative liberty' as '*non*-interference'. In specifying non-domination as 'a third concept of liberty', he was 'convinced' by Pettit (Skinner 2002c; 1998, 70). He also now maintains that it is only under Pettit's influence that he calls the neo-Roman theory of liberty 'republican'. He does so with regret because this name problematises his own attempt to claim for it such non-republicans as Locke (Skinner 2008a, ix), who perceived 'the foundation of all Law' in the subordination of 'a dependent intelligent being' to 'the power and direction and dominion of him on whom he depends' (Locke, quoted in Dunn 1969, 1).[9]

Skinner and Pettit have tried long and hard to establish that there is something of fundamental importance at issue between the liberal or Hobbesian idea of liberty as non-interference and the republican idea of liberty as non-domination,[10] that is, as 'the absence of arbitrary power' or of subjection to another's will, as the public, rule-governed protection of private life, and as the antonym of slavery (e.g., Skinner 2008b; Pettit 2008b; on slavery as antonym, see, e.g., Pettit 1996, 314–16; 1997, 31–35; Skinner 2002b, 286–307, 339–42). The republican idea is understood in the language of Roman law, as independence from another's *dominium*. Pettit bases this idea of non-domination in a moral psychology of agency (Pettit 1996; 2001), arguing that it is best protected and promoted by the separate, sovereign agency of the state. However, to conceive of the state as such a unitary agent is hardly to conceive of it as a public collectivity of participating citizens, and this is the dilemma with which Skinner is now grappling in bringing his history of ideas of the state up to the present. Although he emphasises that republicans have often conceptualised the state in a different way from that of Hobbes's sovereign actor, he does not equate their concept with a public *imperium* that is protective of private *dominium* over things (and, originally, over persons as things, slaves). 'What is the state?', he continues to insist, is a specifically modern question, concerning the identification of a superhuman actor successfully exerting its sovereign will over mortal others, and not a matter of jurisprudential juxtaposition. Having met with great success in establishing the amoral distinctiveness of this modern political concept, he now emphasises that his own answer is not purely 'historical', factual, or 'genealogical'; rather, it is also significantly 'normative', evaluative, and, indeed, 'moral' (Skinner 2008c).

---

9. Dunn explains Locke's sensitivity to the issue of domination by reference to the precariousness of Locke's social situation. A similar claim is often made about Hobbes and, still more, Machiavelli.

10. Pettit was keen to oppose republicanism to 'liberalism', but now prefers to substitute 'libertarianism'. His willingness to follow Skinner's identification of Hobbes as republicanism's principal opponent is now nuanced in Pettit 2008a.

We might follow Skinner here in asking what the republican concept of liberty was intended to legitimate and, especially, what was intended by the contrast of liberty to slavery. The approach of Skinner is here as ahistorically analytic as that of Pettit, and it may be instructive to draw historical insight from Pocock. In historical reality, liberty and slavery were not opposed; on the contrary, 'freedom was what slavery was for' (Pocock 1996, 105), and Pocock admits the charge 'that republicans were necessarily slaveholders, and . . . slaveholders were generally republicans' (Pocock 1993, 291; cf. 1985, 163). The Roman ideal was that of possessing women and slaves within the *dominium* of one's household and estate, as a precondition of participating in *imperium;* that is, of acting as a citizen, freely and independently of other citizens. But what could be intended by the insistent contrast of liberty to slavery when (notwithstanding Fletcher's novel proposal that slavery be reintroduced as a remedy for famine; Fletcher 1997, 56–70), as in early modern Europe, a society without slave-holding was the context? As an ex-student of Skinner's has noted, the 'basic position' of 'Roman republican values' differs from the Greek in that it 'views property as a trump against the power of the community, and insists that the *respublica* was originally constituted in order to protect private property'. Following this, the early modern 'neo-Roman view . . . rejects any political interference in property distribution as a violation of the principle of justice' (Nelson 2004, 17, 16). It therefore seems that Roman republicanism may be the original legitimatory expression of a possessive individualism. However, there must be more to legitimate than private property because republicanism, unlike Calvinism, concerned *public* activity. What the widespread contrast of liberty with slavery legitimated was the public activity of a few, the political exclusion of the many, and the private domination of the many by the few. Cicero himself had extended the contrast to 'all those workers who are paid for their labour and not for their skill', because 'in their case the very wage is a contract to servitude' (Cicero 1991, 58), and modern republicans were to use this contrast to exclude from citizenship those who, because they did not own land, had to earn their living by working for another. In (neo-)Roman terms, workers were under private domination. The contrast of liberty to slavery was therefore grounded in that of *imperium* to *dominium,* of the republic as the sphere of non-domination to the rightful domination exercised within private spheres. Understood in these terms, Skinner and Pettit's concept of liberty as universal non-domination, implying the absence of spheres of 'private', domestic, or corporate domination, *contradicts* rather than continues the Roman concept of citizens' liberty.

The contrast of citizenship to slavery drawn from Roman history in Renaissance and early modern Europe told people nothing of local social relations between proprietors and their employees. Citizens wished *not* to have to deal on any equal footing with their wives, servants, or tenants, and their wish was legitimated by the distorting dichotomy of liberty and slavery. Later, the dichotomy was used in a contrary cause. The idea that waged work is tantamount to ('wage-')slavery was used by socialists, as an argument not for workers' exclusion from citizenship but for the subjection of capital in the cause of civil equality. However, when Marx compared the commodification of labour to slavery, he stressed that 'free wage labour' renders capitalism an entirely different mode of production and surplus-extraction from that found in Greece or Rome. What Marx here intends by 'free' corresponds with 'non-interference', not 'non-domination'. Workers are dominated by their employers so long as they are employed, in that their labour-time is managed by their employer and is no longer their own. Nor is the product of their labour, or its 'value', theirs. This is what Marx primarily intended by 'alienation', and by 'exploitation'. The efficient working of capitalism requires that workers be free to leave the employment of any individual or corporation, to work for another. It therefore requires that coercive power be taken away from employers and monopolised by the state under the rule of law, so that political power be separated from economic power, the public from the private.

Many liberals have argued against Skinner and Pettit that liberty as non-domination is fully compatible with liberty as non-interference. This is also arguable if the neo-Roman theory is compared with that of Hayek. Hayek, too, drew an 'elementary contrast between freedom and slavery', pointing out that 'the courtier living in the lap of luxury but at the beck and call of his prince may be much less free than a poor peasant or artisan, less able to live his own life', and so too may be a managerial 'director' who has 'to change all his intentions and plans at a word from a superior' (Hayek 1960, 19, 17). Hayek certainly opposed liberty to 'interference' (Hayek 1976, 128–29), but what should be free from interference is one's own 'domain' (Hayek 1973, 106–10; 1976, 123–24), so that non-interference is justifiable in terms of non-domination. Admittedly, also, he opposed liberty to 'coercion', which Skinner and Pettit say is too restrictive, but what Hayek intended by 'coercion' is not reducible to 'the threat of physical force', and what he regarded as important is that coercion be subject to general law so that it is 'independent of the arbitrary will of another person' (Hayek 1960, 135, 21). He admitted that under extreme conditions, 'the manager may well exercise an entirely arbitrary and capricious tyranny over a man to whom he has taken a dislike', but he seemed to oppose such 'tyranny' in the same way as do our republicans. Like them, Hayek disagreed with Marx's contention that workers are dominated. For him, so long as a worker can choose to work for any one of a plurality of employers, she is free from domination. On his account, it is only 'in periods of acute unemployment' or where (as 'in a mining town' or 'a fully socialist state') there is a 'monopoly of employment' that a worker may really be subject to arbitrary managerial will (Hayek 1960, 136–37). Although he differentiated the 'individual liberty' that he extolled from 'what is commonly called "political freedom"', he clearly favoured the latter, 'in the sense of absence of coercion of a people as a whole', insofar as it is (as Skinner argues) a precondition of the former (Hayek 1960, 13–15). Unsurprisingly, then, Hayek applauded 'the tradition derived from the Roman Republic' and the 'spirit of the laws of free Rome' as transmitted by Livy, 'Tacitus and, above all, Cicero', whom he called 'the main authority for modern liberalism' (Hayek 1960, 166). Hayek's concept of liberty therefore resembles that of our modern republicans (cf. Pettit 1997, 89); it is, in a 'time-honoured phrase . . . "independence of the arbitrary will of another"' (Hayek 1960, 12).

Classical republicans understood order as extending no further than could be explained by reference to intentional action. Beyond that, they saw only *fortuna*. Pettit has a conception of order as constituted by rule-following that shares far more with Hayek.[11] Both he and Hayek are con-

---

11. There are obvious limits to Hayek's scepticism, and these largely coincide with Pettit's rejection of the sceptical interpretation of Wittgenstein on rule-following (Pettit 2002, 26–48; 2007, 243–46).

sequentialists. As noted, one way in which Pettit has rendered republicanism consequentialist is by positing non-domination as the goal of state power, policy, and law. Despite Hayek's fondness for liberty as non-domination, this is, of course, a radically un-Hayekian kind of consequentialism. A second, more Hayekian way in which Pettit renders republicanism consequentialist is by entertaining the idea of beneficial social orders operating in the 'spontaneous' manner of what he calls an 'invisible hand', and adding that a second kind of 'spontaneous order' may be described in terms of an 'intangible hand'. On his account, both kinds of order can be created politically; 'spontaneity' refers to an order's mode of operation, and does not imply that the order has unintentionally evolved. Such orders may therefore be the results of human action *and* design. The rules in accordance with which Pettit's spontaneous orders operate may be fully intended, and so too may be the public benefit of those orders, even though this is not intended by those many individual actors who sustain such orders when well designed.[12] In the case of the 'invisible hand' kind of market order, individuals act in accordance with their own material self-interest, whereas 'intangible hand' mechanisms operate by exploiting individuals' desire for 'esteem', by bringing others' estimation to bear upon their actions. Pettit appeals to Adam Smith in distinguishing the two, proposing that Smith describes the first kind of order in *The Wealth of Nations* and the second in *The Theory of Moral Sentiments*. If the first kind of order is straightforwardly commercial, the second kind allows the coexistence of republican norms. This is because the desire for external goods of status, honour, or glory is that sentiment which classical and Machiavellian republicans exploited in their own constitutional designs, which were intended to combat the threat of corruption and to induce citizens and, especially, officials to conform to norms of civic virtue. Fletcher's neo-Machiavellian political economy has, for Pettit, been replaced by an altogether more sustainable 'economy of esteem' (see especially Brennan and Pettit 1993; 2004; Pettit

---

12. Again, much of this should be allowed by Hayek, who, even in *Law, Legislation and Liberty,* was willing to speculate about institutional design (1979, 105 ff.), and still more so in earlier works.

1996; 1997; 2002, 308–43; 2007, 334–35; cf. 1989, 163–64). Here, Hayek would once again agree. On his account, 'all morals rest on . . . esteem', and it is esteem 'which makes moral conduct a social value' (Hayek 1979, 171). It therefore seems that the two kinds of order and tradition—first, civic humanist or republican; secondly, jurisprudential and commercial, or liberal and capitalist—which Pocock set in opposition, and which Pettit also originally thought existed only in historical succession, might coexist, in manageable contradiction, within the social order of the modern state and market.

The Question of Liberal Origins

The reality of a liberal tradition has always been questioned by Pocock, who has consistently challenged any metanarrative of liberalism's rise to hegemony. Even though an increasing number of writers have identified themselves as liberals over the past two centuries, he regards such metanarratives as creations of their opponents, whether Marxist or Straussian (cf. Dunn 1969, 5, 205, 221–22). 'The main historical weakness in the antiliberal position', he long proposed, 'is that it is impossible to locate any 'moment at which economy became emancipated from polity and market man, productive man, or distributive man declared that he no longer needed the *paideia* of politics to make him a self-satisfactory being'. It is, he claimed, impossible even to identify such a moment 'in the eighteenth century' (Pocock 1985, 70).[13]

Liberalism, indeed, has no single origin in the way and to the extent that Aristotelianism originates in the work of Aristotle, Marxism (contra Pocock) in that of Marx, or Straussianism in that of Leo Strauss. Clearly,

---

13. Donald Winch, who, by claiming Smith for republicanism, had been Pocock's greatest ally in denying that the eighteenth century was such a moment (Winch 1978), appears to have since identified the moment of liberal origin in the early-nineteenth-century 'context of the controversy provoked by Malthus' (Winch 1996, 228). Thomas Malthus's idea of order may be more theologically providentialist than that of Smith, but it otherwise possesses Hayek's qualities of 'spontaneity' and beneficence.

also, capitalist economy has never been entirely 'emancipated' from politics; on the contrary, capitalism requires a state for its legal constitution and protection. Conversely, the 'market man' motivated by a Calvinist ethic certainly *did* declare 'that he no longer needed the *paideia* of politics to make him a self-satisfactory being' (even if, under certain conditions, he then found reason to legitimate political resistance or to participate in founding new polities, in Geneva or America). As Hayek said, 'this ethos regards it as the prime duty to pursue a self-chosen end as effectively as possible without paying attention to the role it plays in the complex network of human activities' (Hayek 1976, 145). Self-satisfaction can be found in modern, privatised religion and in privatised work, just as self-alienation can be experienced in such work, quite irrespective of the trappings of modern, liberal citizenship. The fact that liberalism has no single origin does not entail that it has no origins and, therefore, no reality.

The eighteenth century's innovative attempt to emancipate 'market man' from moral censure and political domination is one crucial moment in the genealogy of that liberalism which has thrived since the nineteenth century. An earlier moment was the seventeenth century's similarly innovative, contractarian justification of individuals' obligation to obey state law. Skinner problematises this second moment by posing Locke as a 'neo-Roman', but this idea should, rather, point us to a still older presupposition of contemporary liberalism: the separation of a private realm of *dominium* and 'subjective right' from the public realm of the state.[14] I have argued that republicanism was itself the major source of this conceptual presupposition.

Pocock would have us oppose a continuing jurisprudential tradition to the tradition of republicanism, and therefore the modern legacy of Roman lawyers to that of Roman (and Graeco-Roman) historians. For Pocock, it was only with Smith and his contemporaries that jurisprudence was 'organised into history' (Pocock 1999, 313). Here I would agree

---

14. The expression 'subjective right' is borrowed from one of Skinner's closest followers, Annabel Brett (1997), who, like Hayek, argues that Spanish scholasticism was another route for Roman jurisprudence.

with Skinner that the legacy of Roman jurists—and of Roman philosophers and historians—almost totally eclipsed any legacy of Aristotelianism within the republican tradition (e.g., Skinner 2006, 258). The original
presupposition of republicanism was the legal one that the *res publica* is
distinct from private *dominium* over private things. One need not agree
with Hegel that this Roman 'moment' logically entailed either individual
political obligation or a commercial social order, but it is no fallacy to see
these later ideas as historically conditioned by the conceptual juxtaposition of 'public' to 'private'. This condition was due to languages of both republicanism *and* of a non-republican jurisprudence. I therefore agree
with Pocock that there is something wrong in simply opposing republicanism to liberalism, not, however, because of any unreality of liberalism as a coherent discourse, but because republicanism was a historical
condition of liberalism.

Pocock is a historian, not a moral or political philosopher. His sympathy for Machiavelli's republicanism and Fletcher's political economy
is not sufficient for him to argue that these should be revived. Even when
he detects a resurgent Jeffersonian spirit in America, he advances no argument in its support. Rightly so. If republicanism was ever a cosy communitarian politics of a common good, then the common good it promoted was that of land-owning (and often slave-owning), exploiting,
patriarchal imperialists. The good life for them depended, as an absolute precondition, on their domination of others, and the good of their
politics was concerned, essentially, with that common dominance. Republicanism's ethical ideal was more than this, but it was the ideal of a
self-sufficient individual who took pride in denying the fact of his dependence upon others. If, as Pocock proposes, socialism was in some
sense the successor of republicanism, then that succession was a vast ethical advance. Socialists presuppose that there is such a thing as society,
and that individuals within it necessarily depend upon one another. This
is a presupposition not of republicanism but of its opponents, such as
Hume, for whom politics presupposed that people are 'united in society,
and dependent on each other' (Hume 1969, 43). Against Pocock, I have
argued that republicanism's successor is not socialism but liberalism. Socialists proposed that property may be justly expropriated for the common good, because it is a product of socially divided labour. Liberals

responded that private life must be independent of politics, so that politics will be independent of particular interests, and they claimed that in extending equal legal rights to all individuals they universalised republicanism's ideal of personal independence.

This claim has perhaps now been conceded by Pocock, in substance. We have already seen him concede to Skinner that 'two conceptualisations of citizenship existed in history'. Now we can add that he concedes the existence, in historical succession, of two conceptualisations of republicanism. He allows that there was in the eighteenth century 'a hinge moment', in which swung open 'a new, modern understanding [of republics] that was both commercial and individualist', according to which 'the purpose of a republic' is to increase citizens' 'freedom—often defined as their right—to engage in a great variety of social behaviours (many of them acquisitive) which need not be directly political at all' (Pocock 2005b, 53). Let Pocock call this another conceptualisation of republicanism; it is what others call liberalism.

MacIntyre is now (cf. MacIntyre 1967, 157 ff.) aware of the Cambridge critique of any proposal that Hobbes, Harrington, and Locke be simply understood as originators of a liberal theory of possessive individualism, and this is perhaps a reason why he does not identify any single moment as liberalism's origin. In *Whose Justice? Which Rationality?* he suggests that liberalism has origins, first, in Athens' division of its 'post-Homeric inheritance', secondly, in the philosophical failure of Scotland's Calvinist inheritance, which was itself inherited on both sides of the Atlantic, and thirdly, in Germany's post-Lutheran and post-Kantian subjectivisation of values. In *After Virtue* he conjoined Weber's 'irreducible plurality of values' to that of Berlin (MacIntyre 1985a, 109), and, although he has nothing substantive to say about Berlin's bifurcation of the value of liberty, we may observe that MacIntyre, like Berlin and Hayek, regards the negative concept of liberty as central to whatever liberalism truly is. As Skinner still agrees, 'the concept of liberty is essentially a negative one' in that it is 'marked by an absence', whether of 'dependence' or 'interference' (Skinner 2003, 21) or, as Hayek would say, of both. Even though, as Skinner says, Berlin's contrary, so-called 'positive concept of liberty' is, at its base, teleological and Aristotelian, MacIntyre has concentrated upon more innovative concepts than that of liberty.

Before proceeding to MacIntyre's conceptual scheme, we should re-call what he shares with Pocock and Skinner. He is a philosopher but also, like them, a historian. Both the Machiavellian and Hobbesian moments were ones in which Aristotelian philosophy was rejected. For Machiavelli, cosmos and polity were alike in their subjection to *fortuna*. For Hobbes, the only way for colliding human bodies to be ordered was through state power. Neither Machiavelli nor Hobbes accepted Aristotle's presupposition of an order awaiting explanation. In the moment represented by Adam Smith, order was once again presupposed, but it was now conceptualised in very different terms. MacIntyre rejects some of these terms, but not others. The Smithian moment was that in which 'history became a narrative of contexts as well as of actions' (Pocock 1999, 9), and MacIntyre conceptualises order in terms of such narrative. He explains human intentions and actions in the context of practices, institutions, and traditions, and social order in terms of practices and institutions as well as intentions and actions.

MacIntyre's Renovation of Aristotelianism

Skinner's republicanism has been criticised by Marilyn Friedman for failing to 'acknowledge that some capacities for arbitrary interference in the lives of others are also capacities for benefitting those others in ways that are necessary for their survival and flourishing', and because 'everyone is dependent on some others for at least some stages of life and few if any human beings are ever completely self-sufficient at any stage' (Friedman 2008, 254–55). MacIntyre would agree with this criticism, as is clear from his *Dependent Rational Animals*. Capacities for 'interference in the lives of others' should be exercised in conformity with the shared rationality of social practices. It is, MacIntyre argues, through being educated in traditions of practical rationality that one learns to become an independent practical reasoner, able to make sound judgments both for oneself and, when necessary, for those who genuinely lack the capacity for independence. Moreover, we are *all* social animals before we can be veritably political beings.

MacIntyre's understanding of our mutual dependence was basic to the argument of *After Virtue*, motivating its critique of Nietzsche in the name of Aristotle. Still more basic to the book was MacIntyre's innovation within Aristotelianism's teleological scheme in reconceptualising the social nature of action and order, and MacIntyre now admits that Aristotle, too, had a false ideal of individual self-sufficiency (MacIntyre 1999a, 7, 127). As I have suggested elsewhere, it may be no accident that Aristotle's basic accounts of the metaphysics and physics of causality, and of the different kinds of rationality involved in theory, production, and *praxis,* can serve to justify the domination of those who regard themselves as the best over those upon whom they are, in social and material reality, dependent (Knight 2007). Hume, Smith, and Ferguson did much to theorise this mutual dependency, and more was then done by Hegel and Marx. MacIntyre has critically reworked the insights of Marx, and also of Wittgenstein, into an innovative social theory, and has elaborated this theory as a reformation of the Aristotelian tradition of the virtues.

The innovation that MacIntyre has brought to Aristotelian theory is not akin to the kind of innovation that Skinner imputes to Calvinist entrepreneurs and to Machiavelli. That kind of innovation is in the usage of the vocabulary of the virtues, so as to legitimate activities which would previously have been considered vicious. In contrast, MacIntyre's innovation is not semantic but theoretical; it is concerned not with changing linguistic usage in order to legitimate new kinds of activity, but rather with justifying the languages of goods and excellences spoken within past and present social practices. He has elaborated a moral theory of such socially particular goods, and has therefore expressed a justification of those goods and practices in the language that has become particular to the academically institutionalised practice of philosophy.

Within other shared practices, no such innovation is necessary. Such practices are the contexts in which individuals' actions are most readily intelligible and justifiable—to their fellow practitioners, to knowledgeable others, and even to themselves. Actions performed within the context of a practice are intelligible to others precisely because the practice includes shared goals or goods and, therefore, shared reasons for action. In the absence of shared kinds of reasoning about action, no sound judgment of other's motivation or character is possible. Practices are the contexts in which judgments of excellence or virtue may most readily and authoritatively be expressed, because they include shared standards. In the absence of any shared and objective standard, no sound judgment as to one's own or another's excellence is possible.

The modern separation of social theory from philosophy presents a problem that is addressed by MacIntyre. For academic philosophy, the problem is precisely the 'particularity' (to use the language of Pocock, and of Hegel) of those practices, and of the internality or specificity of their goods. This particularity has excluded such goods from the universalist concerns of philosophy (and, also, from the 'public' concerns of politics).

MacIntyre's project has been that of combining social science with practical philosophy. In *After Virtue,* he proposed that 'a moral philosophy . . . characteristically presupposes a sociology. For every moral philosophy offers . . . [some] conceptual analysis of the relationship of an agent to his or her reasons, motives, intentions and actions, and in so doing generally presupposes some claim that these concepts are embodied or at least can be in the real social world' (MacIntyre 1985a, 23). His concern with the intentionality informing action brings him close to Kant's account of practical reason. What makes him an Aristotelian is his refusal of any absolute separation of 'ought' from 'is', values from facts, and, also, of the intentionality informing action from action's empirical motivation and consequences. Reasons are causes of action and, therefore, causes of the social order that results from action. Different traditions of rationality therefore correspond to different kinds and, indeed, traditions of social order.

The concept of tradition is rather 'more complex' than MacIntyre supposed in *After Virtue,* he now tells us. There, he argued that traditions, like social practices and individual lives, are best understood in pursuit (or 'quest') of some good, but he appeared ambivalent as to whether 'tradition' should be understood philosophically or sociologically. Now he tells us that 'the tradition of the virtues was at once a social tradition and a tradition of enquiry embedded in that social tradition'. The 'conception of the virtues' that is 'articulated, reflected upon, enlarged, criticised, and sometimes revised' by the Aristotelian tradition of philosophical, political, and moral enquiry is a conception that is 'embodied in the practices of everyday life' (MacIntyre 2008r, 278; cf. 1994b, 291–93; 1988a passim; 1998d). This position is more clearly realist, and less apparently interpretivist, than that which he proposed in 1981.

The historical reasons why both modern philosophical and social theory have excluded the ordinary, moral language of 'plain persons' (MacIntyre 1998h) are set out in the first half of *After Virtue*. They are well understood by Dunn, our third member of the Cambridge School. As he says, 'the core of MacIntyre's message is that the way in which the theory of how to know better [than plain persons] has developed in the West in recent centuries has disintegrated at a theoretical level all our conceptions of how men can have good reason to strive to live well', which 'grossly slights [human] creativity and capacity for agency' (Dunn 1985, 146).[15] This message is indeed 'thoroughly pessimistic'. It is that the Enlightenment's theoretically innovative epistemological project (with Hobbes and Locke taking the place of Descartes in *political* philosophy) has caused profound demoralisation, not least by legitimating managerial domination of workers.

Crucially, however, this is the message of only one of the histories recounted in *After Virtue*. In the book's second half, and in subsequent writings, MacIntyre conveys a historical, sociological, and ethical message that is altogether more sanguine. It is that we, as ordinary actors and social practitioners, *can* and *do* see good in our capacity for creativity and agency, that we often *do* attempt to emulate standards of excellence, and that therefore, to a considerable extent, and necessarily, our society *is* ordered by our shared ethical agency. MacIntyre therefore proposes that 'institutions and practices characteristically form a single *causal* order', and that 'the integrity of a practice *causally requires* the exercise of the virtues' (MacIntyre 1985a, 194–95, emphases added). The history recounted in the first half of *After Virtue* is, therefore, a history of how 'individuals came to conceive of themselves as other than they are' (MacIntyre 2008r, 266). It is, in other words, a history of modern alienation.

---

15. John Searle's increasingly influential philosophy of mind may be understood as exemplifying a new kind of theory of how to know better. Although MacIntyre refuses to characterise his position as constructivist (e.g., MacIntyre 1994c, 37), he has never engaged critically (cf. 1999a, 35) in print with Searle. A preliminary contrast between the two (which, though sympathetic, misrepresents MacIntyre's position) is drawn in Rust 2006, 142–82, and it is to be hoped that MacIntyre's work in the philosophy of intentionality (e.g. 2006a; 1999a, 11–79) will provide grounds for further opposition.

For MacIntyre, Aristotelianism is not a 'theory of how to know better' than plain persons but a theory of what plain persons know. What he seeks to legitimate is the cooperative reclaiming by plain persons of their own creativity and capacities for agency. His theoretical innovation, introduced in the book's second half, is that the kind of intentional object which Aristotelians traditionally call a good should be extended to include those goals that are internal to many of the everyday practices of ordinary actors, and that are therefore common to practitioners. As he has since emphasised, these include the goods internal to productive practices that are necessary to others' survival and flourishing. Practices require and express the virtues, so that the Aristotelian tradition should now be understood to generalise the kind of purposive, good-oriented, and teleological reasoning familiar from, and learned in, particular practices. These different forms of practical reasoning should all inform the political activity that directs them to a comprehensively common good.

MacIntyre now urges that this theoretical innovation be followed by empirical research into the reasoning internal to various practices (MacIntyre 2010; cf. Beadle and Könyöt 2006; Beadle 2008), designed to show how the concepts of virtue, practice, and institution 'are embodied . . . in the real social world'. Even in *After Virtue* he looked for some 'empirical counterpart of the conceptual account of the virtues which I have given, a sociology which aspires to lay bare the empirical, causal connection between virtues, practices and institutions' (MacIntyre 1985a, 194). Having learned from reading Collingwood that the study of philosophy is inseparable from the study of its past, he first looked to the past for an empirical and sociological counterpart of his conceptual account of the virtues.

We have seen that MacIntyre looked to the republican tradition, perhaps in part because of what others had recently said of the educative importance of practice for *virtù* (e.g., Skinner 1978a, 178–80). However, MacIntyre now tells us that those philosophers whom he (like Kristeller) regards as having continued Aristotelianism through the Renaissance treated virtue as something to be taught from books. They thereby reduced virtue to a subject of theory uncaused by action and habituation, as something more applicable *to* practice than learned *in* practice (MacIntyre 1999b; 2006e). Therefore, in addition to (what I have proposed as) Aristotelianism's political supplanting by Machiavellianism, the Renaissance was, on MacIntyre's account, a moment in which Aristotelianism faltered as a *moral* tradition. The Jacobin failure to impose virtue through the state followed an earlier Aristotelian failure to impose it through texts.

Despite already having reservations about republican politics, MacIntyre wrote in *After Virtue* that the sociological counterpart of his philosophical innovation could be found in 'Ferguson's type of sociology' and, albeit 'with a good deal [less] sophistication', in Jefferson (MacIntyre 1985a, 195–96). What he said of practices is redolent of Ferguson's ethical analyses of the different 'arts and professions' (Ferguson 1995, 161–93; 1792 vol. 1, 189–316, vol. 2, 407–512), while Ferguson's feared alienation and 'corruption incident to polished nations' (Ferguson 1995, 235–47) anticipate what MacIntyre intended by a 'causal connection between virtues, practices and institutions', and his argument that an 'essential function of the virtues is' to 'resist the corrupting power of institutions' (MacIntyre 1985a, 194). Since then, he has looked more closely at eighteenth-century Scotland. He has posed 'Andrew Fletcher, David Hume, Adam Smith and Adam Ferguson' as offering 'a variety of mutually incompatible answers' to the questions of whether 'the values of small communities' could and should 'be preserved in a period of commercial and industrial expansion' (MacIntyre 1987, 18). Fletcher offered the Aristotelian answer that those values should be preserved, but he thereby 'presuppose[d] a kind of state and a kind of economy far too alien' (MacIntyre 1987, 27) so that, by Ferguson's time, Fletcher's 'social and intellectual program . . . had been decisively rejected' (MacIntyre 1988a, 256). (If this suggests the Pocockian thought that Fletcher was defeated by 'the movement of history', it should be added that the kind of 'enthusiasm' with which he had famously advanced his proposals became subject to increasing criticism.) In this context, the 'pressing' question for Fletcher's successors, 'Hume, Smith, and Ferguson', was 'What is the effect of an expanding economy upon the moral and intellectual life?' (MacIntyre 1988a, 258–59). Now, though, MacIntyre no longer poses Ferguson as offering any real alternative to the kind of answers advanced by Smith and Hume. 'What is important about Hume is that his arguments and insights were such as to defeat his philosophical opponents' (MacIntyre 1994b, 299). It transpires that eighteenth-century Anglophone republicans had no better answers than did Jacobins to demoralizing effects of capitalist development.

We should hardly be surprised if we fail to find in any past works, even those of Ferguson or Jefferson, an 'empirical counterpart' to Mac-Intyre's 'conceptual account of the virtues'. The concepts of practice and institution that MacIntyre articulates are his own innovations, having been formed in his sociological extension of Aristotelianism's conceptual scheme of theoretical, ethical, and political philosophy. The counterpart required by these innovations cannot be one informed by any ideal of self-sufficiency, or of domination, or of any other singular moral identity. Rather, it must be informed by the facts of humans' interdependence and by the multiplicity of ways in which the human good can be actualised in social practice.

As Pocock has observed, 'the appeal . . . from the political to the social is itself a political act', 'designed to empower those hitherto disempowered, to admit them to the political, and to change the structure and even the concept of the political in the course of doing so' (Pocock 1998, 224). MacIntyre's innovative appeal to the social is designed to empower those previously alienated from their own human capacities, and therefore to reconceptualise and restructure politics. It is another attempt, following social democracy's statist failure, to overcome what Dunn has pessimistically called 'the economic limits to modern politics' (Dunn 1990; cf. Dunn 1994). In the past, veritably *political* community has been local. Athens was once a political community, albeit only of property-owning patriarchs. So too was Rome, but Rome could no longer be a political community when its frontiers extended to the Rubicon. Scale must remain a political issue so long as the ethical issue is character. Confronted with Hayek's argument that an Aristotelian ethic can only be practiced in small communities and not in any extended order, MacIntyre replies that 'a local political community with its own economy can be of considerable size'. As examples, he still cites 'the larger city-states of the past in the periods of their maximal flourishing', alongside 'the municipality of Bologna under Communist rule' (MacIntyre 2008r, 268).[16] Against

---

16. For an attempt to relate what MacIntyre says of the political potential of agrarian communities to the idea (in Wickham 2005, 383–588) of a 'peasant mode of production', see Knight 2010.

Hayekian claims that there is no alternative, MacIntyre has always argued for the desirability and possibility of alternative orders.

What is ethically important about *local* community is that it enables action to be related to social order in a way that is fully intentional. That is, within a local community one's own actions and shared practices can be readily understood as effective parts of a concrete order, with known effects, including both observable benefits to known others and conflicts with others over external goods. Within such a community, action can be ethically educative in a way that may be impossible when its effects are unknowable. Actions here can also be veritably political, in that they can be purposefully coordinated towards finite and knowable common goods.

Following his acknowledgment that republicanism is of no help in replying to liberalism's challenge, MacIntyre has readdressed from Hume to Marx the question of 'whose justice?' At first, he proposed that we should 'guide our present actions in moving towards . . . institutionalisation' of 'a highly determinate kind of community in which each person can play his or her due part' by reversing 'the sequence which Marx foresaw in the movement from socialist to communist justice' (MacIntyre 1991a, 107). More recently, he has agreed with Marx's own sequence, saying that we should 'move from the maxim "From each according to her or his ability, to each according to her or his contribution"' to 'a revised version of Marx's formula for justice in a communist society, "From each according to her or his ability, to each, so far as is possible, according to her or his needs"' (MacIntyre 2006l, 154; 1999a, 130). He differs radically from Marx, however, in proposing that such a principle ought to guide our actions now, rather than either be entrusted to the state or put off until 'an as yet unrealisable future' (MacIntyre 1999a, 130). What is of most interest in Marx is, for MacIntyre, epitomised in the third of his 'theses on Feuerbach', and is incompatible with the claim of any 'vanguard' party to possess a 'theory of how to know better' than ordinary practical reasoners and actors (MacIntyre 1998f).

The search for new possibilities for Aristotelian politics must start in a recognition of what is already known and done by plain persons within social practices. MacIntyre takes seriously Aristotle's proposition that we are political animals, and argues that acting as such beings is incompatible with the modern understanding of politics as a 'compartmentalised, specialised area of activity' (MacIntyre 1998g, 248). He therefore takes seriously, as republicans never have, what Aristotle said at the beginning of his *Ethics* about the rational and political ordering of goods and practices for the sake of greater, more common goods. On this account, there can be no institutionalised isolation of the universal from the particular, of a *res publica* from productive and other social and economic activities. Hegel understood something of the educative importance of intentionally ordering particular activities politically, but his conception of history nonetheless committed him to accepting the rationality of the Roman and modern state. MacIntyre urges us to reject any idea that there is a rational order inscribed in history. He also urges us to reject the state's *imperium*. If people really are to participate actively and educatively in politics, and if politics really is to be about ordering goods of practice for the common good, then new possibilities have to be found apart from the institutions of corporate capital and the bureaucratic state.

Where Hayek claimed to perceive unintentional but *de facto* coordination or 'cooperation', MacIntyre sees ideologically masked conflict. This conflict is between those who are institutionally alienated from control over their own activity and those who (with varying degrees of success) manage that activity, between exploiters and exploited, and between those pursuing goods of excellence internal to practices and those pursuing institutionalized goods of effectiveness that are external to any practice. States are loci of conflicts over legal authority and coercive power. Markets are loci of conflicts over surplus value. Individuals, in identifying those common goods that they share with others, have to ask what kinds of relationships with others foster and which obstruct the achievement of their common goods. Since every social order is the historical outcome of struggles in which those with power and resources are apt to threaten and endanger the achievement of common goods, political and economic orders are often despotic and exploitative. Liberal order, insofar as it is real, is not spontaneous but organised and imposed. The kind of managerial oppression that Hayek admits only as exceptional within a world of rule-abiding entrepreneurs is, for MacIntyre, essential to an order in which corporate domination (legally institutionalised in such forms as the joint-stock, limited-liability company) by private management meshes into public bureaucracy, from which it requires ever tighter regulation. Where Hayek sees the invisible hand of self-interested calculation according to conventional rules, MacIntyre sees the integration and mutual reinforcement of managerial, financial, and governmental structures.

For all its historical importance, the distinction between public and private may be counted among liberalism's moral fictions. Against those fictions, MacIntyre insists that 'the range of present possibilities is always far greater than the established order is able to allow for', and that ordinary actors can rationally order their practices into veritably cooperative 'projects that challenge the limitations of the existing order' and 'bring into being types of community through which we are liberated from compartmentalisation, from distorted desires, from inequalities, and from the lawlessness of the present order' (MacIntyre 2010). What he implies by 'lawlessness' is that the rules enforced by the state lack either the necessity or the authority of natural law. Such authority only pertains where law is intentionally directed to the common good; that is, where rules are, and are understood to be, directed to the common good by their subjects. This is the basic limitation on the scope of political community.

MacIntyre's innovative rejection of the state is entailed by that innovation which he has effected in Aristotelianism's traditional ideas of action, causation, and order. For him, it entails nothing pessimistic about possibilities for Aristotelian politics, since neither a modern republic nor a capitalist state can constitute a political community. The possibilities for such community are to be found elsewhere.

14

Alasdair MacIntyre and the Lithuanian New Left

ANDRIUS BIELSKIS

Although Alasdair MacIntyre rejected Marxism as early as 1968, he never rejected Marx's critique of the capitalist social order. The moral and theoretical criticism of the social and economic injustice generated by market capitalism is an important theme and a commitment that MacIntyre inherited from Marxism and has never abandoned.[1] Ever since the publication of Kelvin Knight's essay 'Revolutionary Aristotelianism', scholars have consistently moved from a communitarian interpretation of MacIntyre's philosophy towards a more accurate one that can be broadly described as a revolutionary Thomism. This postcommunitarian reading of MacIntyre not only acknowledges the central importance of Marxism in his early, pre-1968 works, but also seeks to show the centrality of Marxism in his mature work (Knight 2007; Blackledge 2005; McMylor 1994). In this essay I explore some of the reasons for MacIntyre's rejection of Marxism and ask whether, and if so how, his post-Marxist ethical theory, which is nonetheless informed by Marx's critique of capitalist

---

1. MacIntyre has repeatedly stressed this in a variety of his later works, for example, MacIntyre 1999 and 2007.

modernity, can be utilised in reviving the political left in Eastern Europe after the collapse of Soviet Marxism.

The socioeconomic development in Eastern Europe following the 1989 revolution has been marked by neoliberal reforms. They were welcomed by the general public and especially by pro-American elites in Eastern Europe, including Lithuania. Today critical intellectuals and the general public alike are far more skeptical about these reforms. The gap between the rich and the poor has grown considerably, public services are left unreformed, social exclusion is soaring, and public spaces are being privatised on a grand scale. A related fact may be that the suicide rate in Lithuania, as of 2005, was the highest in the world (Gailienė 2005). Hence the importance of alternative politics in Lithuania and in other East European countries as a means of addressing issues of social exclusion and social injustice. The fundamental question for any left-wing intellectual and political movement is how a strong political left is possible after the enormous changes that European politics have undergone in recent decades: that is, the weakening of the labour movement, the transition to consumerism and postindustrial society, and the collapse of the Soviet Union together with the Soviet Marxism. I argue here that Alasdair MacIntyre's mature ethical theory can provide us with some of the answers to these questions. In so doing, it can enable us, or so I hope, to revive the New Left—which of course would be very different from the British New Left of the 1960s and 1970s.

MacIntyre's Rejection of Marxism

MacIntyre's preoccupation with Marxism in 1950s and 1960s ended with his rejection of Marxism, although without rejecting Marx's thought. As an active participant in a variety of Marxist organisations (the Communist Party of Great Britain, the Socialist Labour League, and the International Socialists), he also rejected Marxism as someone who knew it from the inside. This prefigures his mature philosophical position as elaborated in *Whose Justice? Which Rationality?*, where he argues that the philosophical criticism and rejection of a theory is possible only if it is advanced from the inside, that is, by someone who knows the subtleties of the language of tradition as his or her own. It was on the basis of this that MacIntyre did not consider the critiques of Stalinism by Labour Party leaders or the Catholics of *The Catholic Herald* as very important, implying that their critique is not morally and philosophically significant (MacIntyre 1998a).[2]

MacIntyre's critique of Marxism rests on his philosophical claim that Marx and Marxism should be understood historically. There is a continuity between Hegel, Feuerbach, and Marx, as well as a remote continuity between Marx, Engels, Lenin, and Stalin. Thus an attempt to dismiss Hegel's and Feuerbach's influence on Marx, including their influence on his mature work, leads to misunderstanding of the subtleties of Marx's thought (MacIntyre 1968). One of Marx's key concepts, which he inherited from Hegel and Christianity, according to MacIntyre, is the idea of human alienation. MacIntyre argues that even *Capital* is informed by the notion of human alienation, and thus Engels's reading of Marx's idea of political economy and his analysis of capitalism as a thoroughly scientific theory is misleading. It misses the fact that there is a tension in Marx's thought between his scientific theory of capitalism and a general philosophy of history (MacIntyre 1968, 64). Furthermore, MacIntyre argues, if Marx's analysis of capitalism is to be treated as a scientific theory, then it has to acknowledge its conditional character. Following Karl Popper's distinction between a law and a trend, MacIntyre claims that 'in so far as Marx's theory of the workings of capitalism is part of science, his predictions are bound to be conditional. Yet at more than one point Marx appears to predict *unconditionally* not merely the intensifying crisis of capitalism but the transition to socialism' (MacIntyre 1968, 66).

---

2. It is possible to argue that Marxism as described in MacIntyre's *Marxism and Christianity* can be understood as a tradition in his sense, if we read that book in the light of *Whose Justice? Which Rationality?* Of course, in the late 1960s and early 1970s, MacIntyre had not yet used the notion of tradition. In *Against the Self-Images of the Age* (1971), he uses the term 'ideology', which, nonetheless is conceptualised in a strikingly similar way to 'tradition' in his later works. The question we should bear in mind is this: Why is Marxism, as a philosophical and moral tradition, excluded from MacIntyre's later work? One of the possible answers lies in the fact that MacIntyre sought to distance himself from Marxism, not least because it gradually lost its practical relevance.

A deterministic reading of Marx and its allegedly scientific predictions is problematic, according to MacIntyre, for at least two reasons. First, there is far too much rhetoric in Marx when he writes about the transition to socialism. Second, the main Marxist predictions about capitalism's systemic inability to expand and adapt to new historical circumstances have failed. And they failed not only because capitalism showed its ability to expand, but also because the workers' movement in advanced industrial societies has been domesticated and has become unable to produce a revolutionary class with wide support among ordinary working men and women.

Marx himself was never explicit about the nature of socialism. He saw it as the self-activity of the working class, and thus socialism could not 'be accomplished for or on behalf of them [workers] by anyone else' and therefore could not be objectively predicted (MacIntyre 1968, 71). MacIntyre's interpretation of Marx, then, appears at odds with that of Engels and other 'deterministic' interpreters of Marx, who dismissed the Hegelian conceptual scheme. But Engels, Karl Kautsky, and Stalin are not the only critics who have provided a one-sided reading of Marx. Another school of Marxism, most notably embodied in Georg Lukács's humanist interpretation of Marx, has faced problems as well. The philosophical argument of Lukács's *History and Class Consciousness,* together with his emphasis on class consciousness and revolutionary activism, led Lukács, one of the most original Marxists, to put his revolutionary faith in the Communist Party. But philosophical and political commitment to the party required obedience to its decrees, which included disapproval of his 'subjectivist' reading of Marx. This eventually led Lukács to denounce his earlier views in favour of Stalinism (MacIntyre 1968; 2006b).

Thus, on both sides there are fundamental problems, which originate, so MacIntyre argues, from the very work of Marx itself. The Hegelian notion of alienation from human nature, which is so significant in early works of Marx, ceases to be important for Marx later on. MacIntyre argues that Marx's sociology of the workings of capitalism would have been far more fruitful, had Marx developed his Hegelian legacy into a moral theory that could provide the ethical grounding for an emancipated human practice. This point is confirmed and reiterated in MacIntyre's criticism of R. H. Tawney's socialism, where he argues that one of its intellectual shortcomings was that the 'moral denunciation of British capitalism took its content and its interest not from the morality of socialism but from the immorality and evil of capitalism' (MacIntyre 1971a, 39).

MacIntyre takes up this theme in his essay 'The *Theses on Feuerbach*: A Road Not Taken'. Here, MacIntyre's position, as opposed to that in *Marxism and Christianity*, is expressed in Aristotelian rather than Hegelian terms. He argues that Marx's error was not so much his rejection of Hegel and Feuerbach as his rejection of philosophical enquiry that could be incomplete. In so doing, 'Marx allowed his later work to be distorted by presuppositions which were in key respects infected by philosophical error' (MacIntyre 1998f, 224). What are these errors? My suggestion, although MacIntyre does not explicitly claim this, is that these errors were the presuppositions that Marx inherited from Hegel and his philosophy of history. This interpretation gains credibility in light of MacIntyre's claim that the philosophical difficulties which Marx faced when he wrote his *Theses on Feuerbach* could not have been understood or articulated in Hegelian terms (MacIntyre 1998f, 226). The Hegelian presupposition in Marx was his belief that large-scale revolutionary changes and the transition to a technologically more advanced socialist society were universal and necessary. Thus, Marx inherited from Hegel an overly abstract idea of human history, which he understood in terms of a progressive development inevitably moving towards a fully liberated society. He therefore missed the moral importance of more traditional human practices and local forms of community, such as those embodied, as MacIntyre argues, in the lives of hand-loom weavers of nineteenth-century Britain or Germany. Marx's mistake was similar to the mistakes of Hegel, whom Marx accused of philosophical abstractions, abstractions which Marx himself later committed. These Hegelian abstractions led him to a quasi-scientific analysis of the workings of capitalism, while assuming the Hegelian conception of progressive history which Marx thought he had scientifically proved. Instead, MacIntyre argues, Marx should have engaged in philosophical analysis of and reflection on human practices and how these practices could morally transform individuals so that they can collectively achieve their ends and, in doing so, flourish.

MacIntyre withdrew from the revolutionary left in the late 1960s because it was dominated by a type of Marxism which, he believed, lacked the philosophical and moral resources to articulate a positive moral alternative to the individualism of market capitalism. One of the failures of Marx was his refusal to formulate an alternative ethics, that is, one different from moral theories that were at home with, and sprang from, the individualistic ideas and practices of civil society. Thus, Marx and Marxists failed theoretically to formulate the moral resources that would be needed for the self-activity of working men and women in a socialist society. Similarly, MacIntyre, at the end of *Marxism and Christianity*, argues that Marxism, being unable to articulate an alternative ethical theory to Kantianism and utilitarianism (which are essentially the theories of nineteenth-century bourgeois society), has become a theoretical stance that individuals choose arbitrarily. The failures of Marxism can be understood only historically, and these failures are partly the failures of Marx himself. In the early 1970s, already living in the United States, MacIntyre concluded, 'It follows that by the present time to be faithful to Marxism we have to cease to be Marxists; and whoever now remains a Marxist has thereby discarded Marxism' (MacIntyre 1970, 61).

The Old and New Left: The Case of Lithuania

The argument that the intellectual and political left, especially after the collapse of the Soviet Union, is in crisis is all too familiar. Steven Lukes, for example, claims that there were at least three distinctive 'lefts' in history (the anti-monarchists of the French Revolution, the nineteenth- and twentieth-century left of workers' movements, and the late-twentieth-century left of single-issue movements), and that the third left has lost its electoral base and its coherence—especially after the second left gradually ceased to be politically important. Thus, according to him, the question of how the left can regain its influence and whether socialism can still be seen as a feasible alternative to capitalism remains unanswered (Lukes 2003, 625). In a similar manner, Duncan Thompson (2007) and Slavoj Žižek (2007) have recently argued that the left not only failed to act, but that it also lacks any viable position that would enable it to challenge the dominance of global capitalism.

Not surprisingly, following the collapse of the Soviet Union, East European countries such as Lithuania advanced their reforms under the banner of free-market capitalism. The general public of Lithuania in the early 1990s tacitly accepted the aggressive neoliberal economic policies promoted by local intellectuals, right-wing American think tanks, and the World Bank and International Monetary Fund. Of course, an important factor contributing to this development was the total distrust of all forms of Marxism, which was associated with the repressive socioeconomic system of the Soviet Union. The consensus of the general public in Lithuania was to privilege the liberal-democratic-capitalist-West over the socialist-authoritarian-East. This unarticulated distinction—the pro-Western, capitalist patriotic Lithuania versus the pro-Russian communist Lithuania—has become so prevalent since the early 1990s that even today, any authentic attempt to revive the ideas of the European left is met with great resistance and suspicion.

The political landscape of postcommunist Lithuania is telling in yet another, far more important, respect. It illustrates MacIntyre's claim that the Stalinist Soviet Union had created a bureaucratic state capitalism, which oppressed ordinary workers generally, and the intelligentsia especially (teachers, lecturers, social workers, and so on). As is widely known, the leaders of the Communist Party in the Soviet Union, including Soviet Lithuania, were the most privileged social class, enjoying wide access not only to external goods, such as prestige, money, power, and status, but also to a wide range of social benefits (the best summer resorts free of charge, legal and political immunity, apartments in the most prestigious parts of towns, trips abroad, and so on). The directors of state-owned industry were appointed by the Communist Party and had to be members of the Communist Party. After the collapse of the Soviet Union, the former Communists, who still held key management positions in state-owned companies, welcomed the political decision to privatise these companies. The result of this neoliberal policy (often called, in Russian jargon, '*prichvatizatsia*'; an English equivalent would be something like '*grabisation*') has been that the former Communists, most often through corruption, became the new owners of the largest privately owned companies. At the center of this process was the supposedly left-wing political party LDDP (Lithuanian Democratic Labour Party). The former Lithuanian Communist Party in 1990 turned into a European 'labour' party (LDDP), and then in 2001 it became the Lithuanian Social Democratic Party (LSDP), after a successful merger with the smaller and far more socially conscious Social Democratic Party.[3] Thus from the very beginning and to this day, the main ruling political party (LDDP and later LSDP), although representing the social democratic values of the Old Left in its rhetoric, has been the main supporter of big corporate business and capital. The economic and political ties between the LSDP and capital is symbolised by the friendship between Algirdas Brazauskas,[4] a longtime prime minister, and Bronislovas Lubys, the second richest man in Lithuania and the majority owner (51 percent) and director of the Achema Group.[5] Lubys, together with his business associates, illegally privatised the state owned company Azotas in 1994 by means of a grand scale money laundry while the government, then controlled by LDDP, turned on this its blind eye. Ever since then Lubys, who is also the president of the Confederacy of Lithuanian Industry, has been financially supporting Lithuanian political parties (especially LDDP and then LSDP) in return for convenient silence and the tacit agreement not to raise the issue of nationalisation.

Consequently, the need for an alternative left-wing intellectual and political movement in Lithuania is evident. There have been virtually no significant political actors who could seriously stand for social justice, oppose the concentration of capital, or defend ordinary working men

---

3. LDDP won a landslide victory in 1992 following the unsuccessful reforms of the National Front, a right-wing nationalist public movement which won Lithuania its independence from the Soviet Union. Although LDDP lost the next parliamentary election in 1996, through successful political negotiations, bargaining, and its ability to enter into coalitions with other political parties it managed to stay in power for eight successive years, by supporting Algirdas Brazauskas and Gedeminas Kirkilas as prime ministers.

4. Algirdas Brazauskas (1932–2010) was a leading politician of Lithuania who was the first Secretary of the Lithuanian Communist Party, a longstanding leader of LDDP and then of LSDP, the president of Lithuania from 1993 to 1998, and the prime minister from 2001 to 2006.

5. Achema Group is a consortium of forty companies which controls the fertiliser industry, a significant part of the Lithuanian media, construction and sea transportation industries, the hotel and entertainment business, and publishing and advertising companies. Its annual turnover in 2006 was 2.5 billion litas, approximately 1 billion U.S. dollars.

and women. The current leaders of LSDP have been the former bureaucratic state capitalists who promote unfettered neoliberal market capitalism. Trade unions still lack the political power to challenge the exploitation of workers because of the legacy of the Soviet Union, when
unions were organised from above by the Party. The practice of imposing the structures of a 'labour movement' by top management, where
trade union 'leaders' are appointed by CEOs and are financially dependent on management, still often occurs in Lithuania.

The ideological misbalance and the corrupt transition from bureaucratic state capitalism to market capitalism have prompted young intellectuals and activists to launch an alternative intellectual and political
movement. The Lithuanian New Left was born after the declaration of
New Left 95 Manifesto in May 2007. Based on its members' conviction
that political activism should be understood first of all in terms of discourse formation rather than the power game of *Realpolitik,* the Lithuanian New Left sees itself as primarily an intellectual movement that
seeks to change people's beliefs and the social practices that accompany
those beliefs, thus challenging general apathy, public disappointment,
and the dominant neoliberal thinking. As one of its members, Linas
Eriksonas, wrote in 2007:

> During the period of formation a virtual, email list-based, organisa-
> tional form was adopted as the most suitable for the formed commu-
> nity of practice. The group now lists around 35/40 activists who each
> extends the reach of NK95 [New Left 95] to many other groups and
> formally established organisations in Vilnius and other cities, thus
> sustaining a nation-wide network for the New Left public actions or-
> ganised and coordinated by self-appointed and group-approved ini-
> tiators of individual actions on an ad hoc basis which may involve
> also organisational gatherings, if required. Main forms of actions un-
> dertaken by NK activists are: formal statements (letters of opposition
> or support, declarations, signed public statements, group petitions
> or other group statements), communications with a wider audience
> (press releases, posters, interviews, website, etc.). The main objective
> of NK95 (outside the most obvious—popularisation of its 45 theses
> from the manifesto) is to galvanise the political life in Lithuania by

bringing to the fore of public debate leftist political values and ideas, with the hope that sooner or later the whole political thinking and with it political practice would shift leftwards. (Eriksonas 2007).

The Lithuanian New Left embraces elements of poststructuralism. Calling on the work of Jean François Lyotard, Michel Foucault, and Jacques Derrida, such philosophers and social critics as Nida Vasiliauskaitė, Audronė Žukauskaitė, and Gintautas Mažeikis tend to interpret the social world in constructivist terms (Mažeikis 2005; Vasiliauskaitė 2006; Žukauskaitė 2006). The social world is to a large extent discursively constructed, and thus to understand thoroughly the dominant discourses, we must critically engage in analysing them. Since language and discourse are world-forming, rather than mere reflections of the world, the aforementioned social theorists treat critical engagement with the dominant socio-discursive order as part of their attempt to construct alternative world-forming discourses. Such a philosophical approach is instructive inasmuch as it enables one to understand politics in far broader terms than the traditional Machiavellian or Weberian approaches. That is, politics does not only include attempts to win and maintain political power through a competitive process in order to form an active government of one's country. It also includes all processes that structure people's beliefs, their thinking, their self-understanding, and their actions. Since the social world cannot be distinguished and separated from language and discourse, discourse creation is seen as essentially political. It is in this sense that the Lithuanian New Left is able to claim to be both an intellectual and a political movement, by maintaining that social criticism and alternative discourse formation are political activities *par excellence*.[6] Above all, it believes that political battles are battles between competing ideas and beliefs, and between conservative and progressive mind-sets and values, a point of view that has been dramatically marginalised in the contemporary landscape of Lithuanian politics.

Such an extended conception of politics has many advantages. It allows intellectuals and social critics to take an active part in political life by

---

6. See its manifesto on www.nk95.org.

galvanising public debate on marginalised social and political issues and by challenging the ideological status quo, which is employed to justify the existing power structures. However, it also has the potential danger of reducing politics to mere discourse. That is, it can blur the difference between mere discourse as a never-ending sterile academic discussion, and meaningful political action (Bielskis 2007).

To counter such a conception of politics, it is instructive to look at Aristotle's understanding of political *praxis*. From an Aristotelian point of view, the link between *praxis* and *phronesis* is at the center of any political action. Meaningful political action is impossible without the two components of *praxis* and *phronesis*—practical wisdom is achieved through public *discourse* which ends in the right *action*. But *praxis* as political action is essential in yet another respect. By blurring the distinction between discourse and reality, one runs the danger of not recognizing the important economic and political distinctions that have been important for the politics of the European left. One of these is Karl Marx's conceptual distinction between capital and labour, a distinction that cannot be reduced to mere discourse. I argue in the remainder of this essay that this distinction, important as it is, needs to be reworked in the light of MacIntyre's distinction between practices and institutions.

Capital and Institutions versus Labour and Practices

The importance of the distinction between practices and institutions in MacIntyre's work has been rightly emphasised (see Knight 1996 and 2007; Murphy 2003). What has been often overlooked is the conceptual and thematic link between MacIntyre's distinction between practices and institutions, on the one hand, and Marx's distinction between labour and capital, on the other. That such a conceptual link is plausible will become clear if we take a look at how Marx understood labour and capital.

For Marx, labour and capital were two opposite but at the same time reinforcing components of capitalism. Labour is represented by working men and women who have nothing to exchange in the market but their ability to work, and thus are forced to sell it for a wage. Capital is the means of production, which is the result of labour's ability to produce

surplus value through the production of commodities and their circula-
tion in the market:

> Productive labour, in its meaning for capitalist production, is wage-
> labour which, exchanged against the variable part of capital (the part
> of the capital that is spent on wages), reproduces not only this part
> of the capital (or the value of its own labour-power), but in addition
> produces surplus-value for the capitalist. It is only thereby that com-
> modity or money is transformed into capital, is produced as capital.
> Only that wage-labour is productive which produces capital. . . .
> Consequently, only that labour-power is productive which produces
> a value greater than its own. (Marx 1969, 152)

Thus, despite the fact that labour and capital need one another, the process of capital accumulation, according to Marx, always favours those
who own capital and exploits those who live off of their wage-labour.[7]
Thus, in the very structure of the capitalist mode of production there
is an essential element of exploitation of wage-labour, which is bound
to produce a self-conscious working class through the organised labour
movement. As we know from the history of the labour movement, gross
inequality and social injustice did produce an organised resistance to
capitalist exploitation, reaching its peak with the Second International.
However, the labour movement failed on the brink of the First World
War 'in its self-assigned task of uniting the international struggle for
socialism', since it was unable to produce a socialist revolution in Western Europe (Geary 2003, 238). This did not mean the failure of the labour movement in general, since precisely due to its political struggles,
the democratisation of European societies, as well as the advancement of

---

7. Marx defines capital accumulation in terms of a circular process: on the
one hand, the conversion of money into the means of production and labour-
power, which can and does take place only in the market; on the other hand, the
process of production of commodities, which then are sold to obtain surplus
value, which in turn is transformed into the means of production (Marx 1976,
711–57).

policies of social provision and welfare, was gradually achieved. However, a consequence of the welfare state since the Second World War, as MacIntyre has rightly observed, has been the gradual domestication of effective trade union power (MacIntyre 2006l, 153). And although MacIntyre claims that this domestication has led to the further erosion of trade union power, it is certain that the past struggles of trade unions are still present in the legislation that governs the industrial relations of most European societies and protects workers from the type of exploitation which they suffered in the nineteenth century. Nonetheless, it is true that consumer capitalism, together with policies of social welfare, has destroyed the collective movement of organised labour—partly because of improved standards of living and the growth of general welfare produced by consumer capitalism. In enabling workers to participate in capitalist prosperity, the trade union movement gradually eliminated the very reason for its existence. Thus, the opposite of what Marx predicted has happened—the expansion of capitalism co-opted the workers.

This does not mean, as Daniel Bensaïd has rightly argued, that the structural opposition between labour and capital ceases to be important. If anything, the opposition is more apparent than ever, not only because the gap between the richest and the poorest has grown, but also because two-thirds of the population in advanced capitalist societies live off of wage-labour and thus formally fall under Marx's description of the proletariat (Bensaïd 2002). I argue, however, that the formal Marxist definition of labour (that is, productive labour producing surplus value, which is invested in and serves capital) is not sufficient. It should be conceptually revised in the light of those moral characteristics of human labour that we find in MacIntyre's conception of social practices. Without them, we lack the moral and intellectual resources needed to renew the self-consciousness of those who represent labour as practice, rather than representing capital and institutions. In this sense, the formal distinction between capital and labour is useful in order to draw the line between the left and the right: all those who represent labour are on the left, whereas those who support and serve capital are on the right.

The social-democratic movement in Europe began in the nineteenth century and was advanced by the trade union movement, while the bourgeoisie were represented by the liberals. Today, a revival of an alternative New Left is possible only if we rethink Marx's conception of labour, which was originally identified with manual labour. Today, the so-called working class is no longer homogeneous and cannot be defined in the narrow nineteenth-century sense. And this is due to the well-known social transformation from an industrial to a postindustrial consumer society. The binary opposition between the working class of manual labourers involved in heavy industry, on the one hand, and on the other hand, the bourgeoisie consisting of highly skilled professionals such as doctors, lecturers, teachers, information technology specialists, and so forth, is no longer tenable. This becomes immediately evident if we look at the traditional understanding of the working class through MacIntyre's conception of practices. All highly skilled professionals, who genuinely pursue the internal goods of their practices through hard work and who do not serve the institutional structures of capital, can legitimately be perceived as members of the working class.

For MacIntyre, a practice is a cooperative activity that requires technical skills and moral virtues, as well as, necessarily, work. A practice is a coherent, 'socially established human activity' through which shared understanding of goods are realised in order to achieve the standards of excellence of such activity (MacIntyre 1985a, 187). The examples of practices usually provided by MacIntyre are farming, football, chess, medicine, architecture, portrait painting, and the enquiries of philosophy, biology, or physics. It is important to note, however, that a practice is necessarily a cooperative activity, and thus whoever enters one already finds a community, which is necessary for the functioning of the practice. He or she also finds standards of excellence, which are always external to the arbitrary desires of the self. Thus an activity, which does not involve cooperation with others and has no potential for the moral transformation of the self, cannot be considered a practice. We therefore find the Aristotelian threefold structure of the moral transformation of the self within MacIntyre's conception of practice: (1) an understanding of myself as *I am in this* particular situation; (2) the standards of excellence of a practice, which cannot be achieved without necessary skills *and* virtues such as truthfulness, justice, courage, and wisdom; and (3) practical rationality, which is essential to achieving the internal goods necessary for the overall human good.

MacIntyre draws two important distinctions between internal and external goods, on the one hand, and practices and institutions, on the other. External goods such as wealth, fame, and power are not the goods of a particular practice, since there is no direct connection between these external goods and the standards of excellence of the practice. External goods cannot define a practice because they are common for all practices. Thus, a practice can be defined only in terms of its internal goods. To be a good chess player is to pursue skills and virtues necessary for playing good chess. However, practices need institutions, which are the bearers of practices by providing ways to secure external goods of money, power, status, and other material goods. One of the characteristics of external goods is that they are scarce and cannot be easily shared, that is, 'the more someone has of them, the less there is for other people'. In contrast, internal goods, although achieved through a competition to excel, bring 'a good for the whole community' (MacIntyre 1985a, 190). Thus, internal goods allow the communities of practices to achieve a common good, while institutions, provided that they are subordinated to practices, secure the necessary external goods without which practices would not be able to survive for any length of time (MacIntyre 1985a, 194). The problem with institutions is that practices are vulnerable to the effects of institutional corruption; practices can easily become subordinate to the acquisitiveness of institutions and their attempts to accumulate money and power.

Here, we come back to the legacy of Marxism in MacIntyre's mature work. The institutional corruption of practices and other human activities is especially evident within the socioeconomic context of advanced capitalism. Like Jürgen Habermas, MacIntyre argues that the symbiosis between the state and the market in advanced capitalism makes the Old Left nearly impossible, because a simple nationalisation of private capital does not immediately mean that the corrupting character of state-owned capital and the acquisitiveness of institutions will be easily resolved. In the command economy of the Soviet Union, the issues of democratic governance of publicly owned companies and of the pursuit of the internal goods of practices together with people's ability to realise a common good, were far more pressing than they had ever been under market capitalism. The bureaucratic dictatorship of the Communist Party in Eastern Europe was far more oppressive towards communities of practices than the order of advanced capitalism in the West. Thus capital, whether state-owned or private, has the power of co-opting practices and, inasmuch as it functions in the economic order of market capitalism, corrupts. Hence the vices of capital and of institutions are the same: acquisitiveness and the subordination of activities and practices to the external goods of money, status, and power. A remedy against this corrupting power is our daily attempt to resist it, through our commitment to honest work in order to sustain cooperative practices and their communities, within which the realisation of a common good is possible.

A possible objection can be raised here. One might argue that to understand Marx's concept of labour in terms of MacIntyre's concept of practices is to overlook the fact that labour for Marx was predominantly an economic activity. At least in *Capital*, Marx, as discussed above, conceptualised labour in terms of productive activity which produces a value that can be used or exchanged in the market. Bricklaying, digging, or sewing, which are not practices for MacIntyre, are the prime examples of labour for Marx. In answer to this objection, I point not only to the fact that Marx understood emancipated labour in a socialist society in terms of the self-activity of the working class, but also to the teleological aspect of both Marx's and MacIntyre's thought. That is, the aim of organised political movement is to promote socioeconomic reforms in our societies in such a way that as much human labour as possible becomes an intrinsic part of cooperative practices, where individuals engaged in labour are able to realise their human potential. The rebirth of the international New Left in postindustrial societies could start from a renewed faith that such changes are possible, not so much through a global revolution seeking to overthrow capitalism from above, as through a network of attempts to resist deformed power structures within local institutions and practices.

ALASDAIR MACINTYRE'S CONCEPTION OF PRACTICES ENRICHES MARX'S conception of labour because it gives to the idea of labour a moral character. It also enables us to look at the working class in far broader terms than those in which it was traditionally understood by the Old Left. Labour, insofar as it involves practices, seeks internal goods and embodies standards of excellence which are unachievable without the cultivation of intellectual and moral virtues. The exhaustion of the trade union movement, whose main objective was external goods (better pay, shorter working days, unemployment benefits, and so on), was partly inevitable once these goods were more or less achieved. Today, a New Left and the labour movement should concentrate on the internal goods of practices in which working men and women are engaged. Thus understood, the working class includes all wage-labourers (from manual labourers to 'middle-class' professionals) who are engaged in a variety of practices and jobs, not only in order to meet the ends of these practices, but also in order morally to transform themselves by fulfilling their potential.

It follows that a post-Marxist New Left should aim neither at the kind of violent overthrow of the political systems of modernity that 'always degenerate[s] into terrorism', nor at the kind of reform 'from within' that leads to collaboration (MacIntyre 1998i, 265). Rather, it should aim at a 'revolution of everydayness', as advocated by Guy Debord, in which local resistance to institutional corruption is galvanised within our communities of practices. A New Left thus understood is, first of all, an intellectual movement that promotes the virtues and values necessary for our individual and collective flourishing. It is based on an intellectual and political activism that speaks out and stands up to power structures which curb and compromise these goals. Furthermore, the political activism of the New Left thus understood is itself a community of practice, where communal learning takes place through seminars and discussions, public lectures, and journalism, thereby advancing the analysis and critique of the social ills of postcommunist capitalism. Eastern Europe, because of its history of failed Marxism, is a good place to advance such a cooperative practice of intellectual and political activism.

15

Where We Were, Where We Are,
Where We Need to Be

ALASDAIR MACINTYRE

It is a mark of the acuteness of my critics in this volume that they have so often raised issues about which I was already uncomfortably aware of having said too little, or of having been too cavalier with objections. In some cases essayists have gone even further and have spelled out more adequately than I have done the content and implications of some of my positions. For this I am particularly indebted to Kelvin Knight and to Sante Maletta. And there are those who by counterposing theses and arguments of mine to either Marxist or Enlightenment theses and arguments have opened up issues with which I had hitherto engaged not at all or only briefly. I begin by pursuing questions about teleology, raised by Anton Leist's essay, and make this a starting-point for an account of social structures, in which I will carry further points made by Knight and Maletta. This will provide a background for responses to other essayists.

I

To understand any living being, an oak tree, say, or a dolphin, or a wolf, or a human being, or any group of living beings, a forest, say, or a school of dolphins, or a pack of wolves, or a human society, we need to know three things: first, what its starting point was, how it originated, the biology of its coming to be; secondly, what by its nature it had and has it in it to become, to flourish *qua* member of that particular species, so that it becomes a perfected member of that species; and thirdly, what in the course of its development from its starting point to its present condition either enabled it to move towards or to achieve that end-state or prevented it from so doing.

Where it is human beings with whom we are concerned, there is a fourth set of questions: What part in enabling them or preventing them from becoming what by their nature they have it in them to become did their own understanding of their flourishing play? Were the goals that they set themselves such as to direct them towards perfecting and completing their lives? Was their practical reasoning sound? Were their evaluations of their activity well grounded? Did they identify the obstacles to their achievement of well-being, both those within themselves and those in their natural and social environment, correctly? Did they have or lack the qualities necessary to overcome those obstacles? Or were they insuperable? Other animal species lack the rational powers that make these questions of crucial importance. Nonetheless in understanding human beings it is important not to lose sight of what we share with members of some other animal species, as well as what distinguishes us. For, if we do not understand this fourth set of questions as a sequel to the first three, as needing to be posed in a context defined by the first three, we will misunderstand ourselves.

This scheme of understanding may seem at first sight complex and cumbrous. It is, however, a scheme of which we all, or almost all, make use—most often unacknowledged use—when we set out to understand not only species other than our own, and societies and cultures other than our own, but also our own society, culture, and institutions, ourselves. It is a scheme presupposed by many of our everyday explanations and it is integral to our self-understanding. Indeed it is an articulation and expression of those types of understanding which we find indispensable in our everyday transactions with others and with ourselves. And the classic version of it, in articulated and expanded form, is of course Aristotle's.

We generally do not learn that we are something close to Aristotelians by reading Aristotle. We learn it instead by engaging—successfully or unsuccessfully—in a variety of practices and then reflecting upon what is involved in so engaging. And our reflections may of course be distorted or deformed by a variety of influences, among them the anti-teleological prejudices of so much post-Enlightenment thought. But insofar as we do learn to think in more or less Aristotelian terms, we find ourselves directed in and through norm-governed social relationships towards the achievement of common and individual goods.

It is because this is so that Leist's discussion and rejection of teleological moral theories, interesting as it is in itself, is largely irrelevant to my position. This is not just because the three versions of teleological ethics that he considers are none of them the type of teleology with which I am concerned.[1] And it is not even because of his well-argued claim that my teleological standpoint is at odds with 'political ideas such as liberty, autonomy, and equality', a claim with which I agree, if those ideas are construed as contemporary liberalism construes them. It is rather because he treats as exclusive alternatives a conception of the virtues in terms of a universal human nature and an historicist conception. But it is my central claim that any adequate historicist account of the virtues, that is, of the virtues as specific to this or that time and place, provides us with grounds for making universal claims both about human nature and about the functioning of the virtues. And the perspective that we need, if we are to understand this aright, is afforded by just that teleological conception of understanding and explanation with which I began this essay. So let me return to it.

II

Why do we need the virtues? Without them we are unable to achieve our common goods or to direct ourselves beyond them to our ultimate good. What it is to pursue common goods varies from social order to

---

1. Consider the differences between Leist's brief remarks on Aristotle's account of the relationship of virtues to goods and to the good and both my exposition of Aristotle in chapters 6–8 of MacIntyre 1988a and my defence of my account of Aristotle in MacIntyre 2006i, to neither of which Leist refers.

social order, and therefore in different historical contexts different aspects and parts of the virtues are needed. But a study of such contexts makes it plain that in very different social orders in different historical settings the activities and structures needed to achieve common goods nonetheless have shared features, features which make it unsurprising that the same virtues are needed. What are those features?

They have to do with the natural law and its varying relationships to the positive laws of different polities and social orders. It is, as Aquinas makes plain, only insofar as these positive laws conform to the natural law, both in letter and in spirit, that the legal institutions of particular societies conduce to the achievement of the common goods of those societies. And in fact positive law as it is enforced is very often at odds with natural law, even if in varying ways and varying degrees. So the scene is set for conflict. Insofar as the rule of law in some particular society accords with the natural law both in letter and in spirit, it opens up possibilities for individuals in that society to achieve their common goods and through that achievement their individual goods. Insofar as the rule of law in some particular society is at odds with the natural law, it will have become instead an expression of the will and interests of those who rule politically and economically. And the conflicts generated by this tension between law as enabling and law as repressing will involve issues both of liberty and of justice.

Maletta in his illuminating account of my views on the natural law emphasises the 'liberating function' of that law. The nature of the liberty afforded by institutions structured by the natural law is of course different both from liberty conceived by liberals as noninterference and liberty conceived by republicans as nondomination, the conceptions of liberty discussed by Knight. It is a liberty that is incompatible with any use of power to interfere with or obstruct deliberation and action aimed at the common good. And such uses of power are characteristic of oppressive and exploitative regimes. So too, with respect to justice, what the natural law enjoins is generally at odds with what is presented as justice by such regimes. But the resulting conflicts are of course always conflicts over particular deprivations of liberty and particular denials of justice in this or that historical setting. Without an historical understanding of the particularities of such conflicts, their significance will be obscured. But it will also be obscured, if we do not interpret such conflicts in terms of the teleological scheme that I sketched, as struggles in which projects that aim at achieving common and individual goods are threatened by and threaten established structures and distributions of political and economic power.

When history is understood in this way, some episodes in the past become salient in ways that they are not on other readings of history. Examples—a few among many—include: Athenian conflicts over the relationship of the goods of the household and of kinship to the good of the political community; the coexistence in medieval Europe of feudal landowning hierarchies with Benedictine communities of prayer and labour; the debates between Las Casas and Sepulveda before the Spanish Royal Council over the justice or injustice of Spanish treatment of the indigenous inhabitants of the Americas; the establishment by the Jesuits of a communist society in Paraguay in the eighteenth century; the defence of their way of life by the hand-loom weavers of Lancashire and Yorkshire in the late eighteenth and early nineteenth centuries against the destructive inroads of what was presented as technological and economic progress. Blackledge is right to insist in his essay on the importance of attending to particular episodes of conflict and struggle. How far he and I would agree about the lessons to be learned from such episodes is another matter.

What the history of such episodes does make clear is not only how, in such tensions and conflicts, what is commonly at stake is not only whether and how this or that particular issue of injustice or deprivation of liberty and of injury to the common good will be resolved, but also what conceptions of justice, liberty, and the common good are to prevail. Knight's account of Hayek makes plain the differences between myself and Hayek over the kind of rules and the kind of order that emerge as societies develop. Where Hayek sees the emergence of cooperative order and rules that enable, I see the emergence of both cooperation *and* conflict, of rules and orders that both enable and oppress. But there is more than this to my quarrel with Hayek. For theories such as Hayek's are not just theories *about* the social order framed from some external standpoint. They are also theories whose defence functions within the social order to strengthen some conceptions of justice, liberty, and common goods at the expense of others. To achieve them is not just to write about, but to engage in social conflict. As Hayek did and I too am doing.

III

In Europe in 1956 two empires confronted one another in the Cold War, each with its own distorting and self-deceiving ideology, each with a moral as well as a political rhetoric well-designed to disguise and to mislead, each with its own internal conflicts. The Soviet Union had unexpectedly become a scene of open unresolved political and ideological conflict. Khruschev's speech to the Twentieth Party Congress was a decisive moment in the movement to acknowledge and expose the monstrous crimes of the Stalin era, a movement that had begun soon after Stalin's death in 1953, with the release from the Gulag of former Communist Party officials, a movement that was to continue with the release and sometimes the rehabilitation of more than four million prisoners before Khruschev's overthrow in 1964.

One large question posed both in the Soviet Union and among Western European Communists by Khruschev's speech was: How are we now to write the history of the Soviet Union from the late 1920s onwards? How do we tell a story that does justice *both* to such achievements as those of mass literacy and industrialisation, and the extraordinary struggle of the Soviet people and the Red Army in defeating Hitler, *and* to the crimes against humanity involved in forced collectivisation, in the great purges, and in the Gulag? Is it possible to write that history so that the crimes of the Stalin era can be understood as a gross and murderous interruption of what can still be a progress towards the realisation of communism? Is it therefore possible for a Communist of integrity to remain loyal to the PCI, or the PCF, or the CPGB?

Yet to answer these questions required moral and philosophical resources of a high order. And for many of those who were trying to think through these questions, reflection was cut short, as Émile Perreau-Saussine reminds us, by the savage Soviet repression of the Hungarian Rising in 1956. What mattered to many Western European Communists was not just the repression, but the fact that the Party leaderships for the most part lied about it. Yet these lies now had a peculiar quality. Such party leaderships seemed to expect of Communist intellectuals that some of them at least would have no problem in recognising the lies that the leadership told as lies, but would be prepared to utter them themselves, just as if they had not recognised them as lies. Communist intellectuals were no longer expected to be among those who had been successfully deceived, but were instead invited to join the conspiracy of the deceivers, of those who knew the worst, but pressed on regardless. So the break with the Party by many Communists was in key part a break in the name of an appeal to truth and truthfulness. But what kind of appeal was this for a Marxist to make?

Perreau-Saussine cites the reflections of Edgar Morin and the reverberations of the earlier debate between Sartre and Camus. And he goes on to discuss the critique of utilitarianism and the rise of a new form of Kantianism in the work of John Rawls. But, as Tony Burns makes clear, I and many others believed, and rightly, that such reflections and discussions led in the wrong direction. For what they presented as 'morality' was in fact an expression of the ideology of the liberal democratic and capitalist West.[2] To identify with morality thus conceived would only be to transfer one's allegiance from one side to the other in the Cold War.

The moral ideology of the West was expressed not so much as a synthesis of—although some moral philosophers aspired to provide just such a synthesis—as an oscillation between versions of utilitarian consequentialism and versions of Kantianism. So in the public moral rhetoric of the West, consequentialist arguments were used to justify the fire bombing of Tokyo and the massacres of Hiroshima and Nagasaki, the overthrow of the government of Iran in 1953 in the interest of the oil companies, and the suppression of democracy in Guatemala in 1956 in the interests of the United Fruit Company. But, when Soviet moral atrocities were condemned, universal quasi-Kantian moral principles were invoked. To what authority was appeal being made when such moral judgments were advanced? The key notion was that of the autonomy of the individual, a notion which played two distinct, if closely related parts in the standard moral arguments of liberal democracy. Moral wrongs, including the wrongs effected by Stalinism, were to be understood as violations of that autonomy. And the standards of rational choice which

---

2. For the critique of that political and economic order in its contemporary form, see my response to another set of critics in MacIntyre 2008q.

were held to inform the choices and actions of autonomous individuals were taken to be the authoritive standards to which appeal was made in acts of moral judgment.

To have accepted this individualist account would of course have been to turn one's back on Marxism—and above all on Marx's insight that it is human beings in their social relationships and not human beings abstracted from those relationships who are moral agents—as those who rejected Stalinism on moral grounds so often did, so that to have become an ex-Stalinist was commonly to have become an ex-Marxist. How then to subject Stalinism to an adequate moral critique but yet remain a Marxist, or how to subject both Stalinism and the capitalist West to such a critique, while still understanding both in Marxist terms? This was the problem that I posed just fifty years ago in 'Notes from the Moral Wilderness' (MacIntyre 1998a).

Perreau-Saussine is right to consider this essay a turning point, but he exaggerates the continuity with my later work. 'The direction taken by MacIntyre's later works was already here in a nutshell'. Tony Burns is closer to the truth in his critique, especially in his emphasis on the absence of any reference to Aristotle throughout the discussion. He is also right in noting incidental resemblences to the thought of the Frankfurt School, although this was a matter of common influences rather than of direct indebtedness. Indeed, the more that I then and subsequently read of the Frankfurt School, the more I was inclined to reject their thought. But what matters about my project is that, although I was able to pose the relevant set of problems and to gesture roughly in the direction that would have to be taken if they were to be resolved, I did not then, and for quite some time later, know how to carry the argument even one stage further.

What I aspired to achieve was to lay bare the connection between right action and desire, not just as a conceptual connection, but as exemplified in social relationships in different historical and social settings. What I did not understand was that to achieve this I needed a conception of those goods at which, in different contexts, desire aims, of the relationships of individual goods to common goods, and of the human good to which these are ordered. Lacking any adequate conception of common goods, I was unable to follow through on my comments on the need to move from 'I want' to 'we want'. Moreover it would only be after I had learned, albeit inadequately, what Aristotle and Aquinas had to teach about these matters that I would be able to discover what it was in Marxism that could be integrated with an adequate ethics and what it was that could not be so integrated. Yet without an adequate ethics there can be no adequate politics, Marxist or otherwise. And in consequence, as I clarified my thought on this in the late 1950s and early 1960s, I gradually recognised that my discussions with even the most insightful of Marxists were becoming barren and that I was going to have to find quite other means for carrying the enquiry forward. Hence there was indeed that time which Burns calls my 'middle period', and his characterisation of it as 'Aristotle without Marx' is partly right. What he misses is the fact that, even then, there were certain sets of truths in Marxism which I took and still take to have withstood every critique, so that any adequate ethics would have to be not just consistent with those truths, but such as to accord them their true importance. What were those truths?

IV

The first set of such truths concerns the nature of capitalism as an immensely productive exploitative system, in which the competition of free markets requires the maximisation of profit, so that surplus value has to be appropriated by the owners of capital, and wages and other labour costs have to be minimised. So a class war is waged against those who have only their labour to sell and who provide the productive manual and mental labour which creates value. A second set of truths concerns the nature of work within that same system. Because of the extent to which labour is made into and valued as a commodity, work often becomes valued only as a means to production and consumption, and workers are correspondingly valued only for their producing and consuming functions. When workers are not or no longer needed, they are discardable. A third set of truths concerns the movement of capital. Capital flows in whatever direction will secure it the highest rate of return, but this is rarely, if ever, the direction in which it would have to flow if it were to be invested to meet human need.

About these three sets of truths we should note that all can be derived from Marx's overall theory of capitalist development and of capitalism as a self-sustaining system. With respect to the second set, Niko Noponen has provided an illuminating account of how Marx's earlier thought on work and alienation can be reinterpreted in terms of my conceptions of a practice and of the ends internal to and external to practices, and the same line of thought is advanced by Andrius Bielskis. Both carrry the discussion significantly further, and both are aware of a fourth set of Marxist truths.

Capitalism inevitably elicits resistance, and that resistance issues in institutions designed to protect workers and the needy from the exploitation and deprivation inflicted on them: trade unions, cooperatives, welfare-legislating political parties. But capitalism, under favorable local conditions, can continue to function well, can indeed enjoy greater stability, insofar as it is able to coopt and domesticate such institutions, so that their reforms and alternative modes of life, while hindering capitalist growth and hegemony in the short run, strengthen it in the longer run. The most important agency of all in this respect is the modern state, which has moved from its earlier nineteenth-century role as the protector of unregulated markets towards a condition of greater and greater integration with the market, so that it has increasingly provided the means for the self-regulation of markets to capitalism's great benefit. When, therefore, further resistance to capitalism is generated, resistance that is informed by an understanding of the dangers of co-option and domestication, those who engage in such a resistance have to recognise the agencies of the state as among those which they should treat with the greatest suspicion and indeed more than suspicion.

What Marx and Marxists provided by formulating these four sets of truths was and is a permanently valuable identification of the most important economic and political obstacles to the achievement of common goods in nineteenth-, twentieth-, and twenty-first century modernity. And, as more than one essayist remarks, it is unsurprising that a certain kind of Aristotelian should find no difficulty in acknowledging these Marxist truths, since Marx was himself so strongly influenced by Aristotle.[3] For an Aristotelian the identification of economic and political

---

3. About which influence, we are all of us in great debt to Scott Meikle; see Meikle 1991 and 1997.

institutions as obstacles to the achievement of common goods entails that a rational agent who had understood how such institutions hindered or frustrated this achievement would have the best of reasons for criticising and reforming or replacing those institutions. So from the standpoint of such a Marx-informed Aristotelianism it is easy to understand the reasoning that issued in nineteenth- and twentieth-century peasant and working-class revolts against capitalism and its political allies.

Such reasoning characteristically involved and involves an appeal against injustice. But what kind of appeal is this? Alex Callinicos gives an admirable summary of some of the difficulties that Marxists have had in thinking about justice, concluding that 'if one accepts Marx's theory of capitalist exploitation, then one needs some kind of non-relativist meta-ethics that will allow us to live comfortably with transhistorical normative principles'. But he then asserts rather than argues that Aristotle's treatment of women and slaves—and, I would have added, his treatment of farmers and craftsmen—shows that Aristotle's overall scheme of thought must be fatally flawed, and Callinicos proceeds to endorse a version of Enlightenment universalism in the form of a claim that through a future socialist revolution the Enlightenment 'promise of liberty and equality', which could not be fulfilled under capitalism, will be fullfilled.

The problem, as Marx understood better than Callinicos, is that both 'liberty' and 'equality' name abstractions and that everything turns on the nature of those social relationships within which and in terms of which liberty and equality are to be realised. Let me consider just one example of what has to be achieved to realise anything worth calling equality and, in so doing, respond to Callinicos's charge that any conception of justice as requiring both a regard for desert in respect of someone's contribution and a regard for a variety of needs 'is quite hopeless'. A basic condition for the realisation of social equality is the realisation of educational equality. Every child has to be given the same opportunity to develop its physical, intellectual, aesthetic, and moral powers. And we know what children need: a stable and comfortable home life, a lead-free environment, hot breakfasts, teachers who begin with each child where she or he is, and who do not let them pass on to the second stage in learning to read, or to do mathematics, or whatever, until they have mastered the first, or to the third until they have mastered the second. A condition for this kind of teacher-child relationship is a very small class size and a massive reallocation of resources, so that there are enough fully trained teachers from pre-school to high school. Such teachers will be among those in the community contributing most to the achievement of equality, and justice will require us to recognise their signal contribution, their merit, and their desert. What teachers give for the sake of equality in meeting the needs of children will have to be matched by what they receive from the rest of us in virtue of what they deserve by reason of their contribution. The standard of need and the standards of merit and desert are complementary. This is of course only one example of the complex relationships that hold between need and desert in any adequate conception of justice. But it may at least explain why I am unmoved by Callinicos's strictures.

No adequate account of justice can be given that does not take account of the relationships between the requirement of justice and both the achievement of common goods, such as those of family, school, neighborhood, and political society, and the achievement of individual goods. And it is because Callincos's account gives no place to the concepts of either common goods or individual goods, let alone to the relationships between them, that his enterprise of supplying Marxism with a trans-historical meta-ethics, characterised as he characterises it, is doomed to failure. His starting point, drawn from James Griffin's *Well-Being*, is, as mine was in 1958, a conception of informed desires, that is, of the 'desires that persons would have if they appreciated the true nature of their object' (Griffin 1986, 11) and, Griffin adds, if they were educated, so that they would be satisfied by attaining the objects of those desires. To be in a state of well-being, so Griffin argues, is to have a certain range of one's desires satisfied. This is what I too believed in 1958, and it was what defeated my attempt to construct a Marxist ethics. For this belief gets things the wrong way round. We need first to know what human well-being, human flourishing, is, if we are to be able to characterise those desires that it is good for us to satisfy. Human flourishing consists in the development of our powers—physical, intellectual, aesthetic, moral—in and through our social relationships, especially our friendships, and the ultimate good towards which we are directed is that in the light of which all lesser goods find their due place. As our desires are disciplined, transformed, and redirected towards the various goods that are at stake in our decision-making and our action, we become the kind of people able to achieve those goods.

What is missing in Griffin's account is any place for certain types of unconditional commitment. Griffin is not in any way a standard utilitarian, and he allows that there are limits to what can be traded off against what. But he fails to acknowledge, indeed his basic positions are incompatible with his acknowledging, the crucial place of unconditional commitments in human life, commitments needed to structure those social relationships through which we can achieve our common and individual goods. Truth telling is a case in point. There are indeed rare and exceptional occasions on which it is right for us to lie (see MacIntyre 2006g). But except on those very rare types of occasion, we owe it to others not to lie, whatever the circumstances, even when not to lie will put us at a serious personal or political disadvantage. And this is one more respect in which a politics of common goods is at odds with the conventional politics of modernity.

V

Callinicos at the close of his essay chides me for thinking of politics primarily and sometimes exclusively in local terms. He argues that such a politics can be no more than a politics of resistance to the contemporary social and economic order, and that from my standpoint one 'cannot even imagine *revolution*', since revolution must involve 'a comprehensive social transformation' and that in turn could only be the work of 'a collective subject that conceives itself as the bearer of some kind of universal interest'. He also emphasises the 'growing body of literature' on how 'a democratically planned economy based on self-management by producers and consumers could replace the market' and suggests that I have ignored that literature.

Let me offer an alternative view of what revolutionary politics is, beginning with the obvious. To imagine a worthwhile revolution is to be able to envisage radically and systematically different types of social institutions and social relationships, institutions and relationships aimed at the achievement of the common good. Revolutions become possible only when enough members of some political society are not only able to imagine such alternatives, but are prepared to participate in realising them in order to achieve their common good. What they also have to recognise, if they are to participate effectively, is that the means for social change afforded by the present economic, social, and political order—the electoral manoeuvres of political parties, the pressures exerted by interest groups, campaigns of protest designed to impact interest groups and parties—are obstacles to this kind of revolutionary change. For any group to satisfy these conditions requires a remarkable shift in social imagination and insight. How might such a shift be achieved?

Only, I believe, by the experience of recurrently trying to make and remake the badly needed institutions of everyday life through grass-roots organisations, trade unions, cooperatives, small businesses that serve neighborhood needs, schools, clinics, transport systems, and the like, so that they serve the common good, and, by doing so, learning that only by breaking with the political norms of the status quo can the relevant common goods be achieved. For those who engage in such making and remaking will encounter that resistance to any breach of those norms which is the characteristic response of the established order. It is that resistance that makes revolutionaries. Of course, as Callinicos rightly points out, local groups and organisations often need to find allies elsewhere, nationally and internationally, and often need to deal with agencies of the state or international agencies, sometimes as obstacles, sometimes as providing resources. But to argue from this, as Callinicos does, and as many others do less eloquently and compellingly, to the conclusion that we need to move not only from shared grievances—'grievances' is, on my view, not the right word—to common programs and strategies, but also from these to a conception of a single collective subject with a universal interest, is to go from good politics to bad metaphysics in remarkably short order.

Consider in this light Paul Blackledge's illuminating discussion of Antonio Gramsci's move from the period of *L'Ordine Nuovo*, with its emphasis on the self-understanding and the self-governance of workers, to his later Leninist conception of the revolutionary party. Blackledge is quite right to lay stress on how much Marxists have been able to learn from Gramcsi about how power and authority must be exercised by workers themselves. Where he is mistaken is in supposing that, once one has distinguished sharply enough between Lenin's party and Stalin's party—as one certainly needs to do—one has done sufficient to show that workers' self-management and self-governance are compatible with the Leninist conception of the revolutionary party and its role before and after taking power.

The problem is that even Lenin's party, however admirable its aspirations, did not and could not have satisfied two conditions that enable genuinely centralised authority to coexist with the self-management and self-governance of those over whom that authority is exercised. The first is that information must flow from center to periphery, from periphery to center, and from different points on the periphery to each other, so that everyone understands what is happening in more or less the same terms. The second is that those at the periphery must be able to put not only the actions of those at the center in question, but even from time to time the theoretical and other beliefs presupposed by those actions. Marxist leaderships have never been able to satisfy these conditions, just because of their view that any just and deep-rooted expression of the convictions and aspirations of the working class will or will soon come to coincide with the party's conception of 'the road to socialism' and of itself as representing a collective subject with a universal interest. Hence in their case centralism has always been at odds with democracy. When the expression of the convictions and aspirations of actual workers does not coincide with Marxist teaching—if workers declare themselves for Fabian socialism or for Chestertonian distributism or for anarcho-syndicalism—then this is explained by Marxists as some form of ideological deformation or false consciousness.

VI

Marxism not only lacks an adequate ethics. It has also lacked an adequate sociology. It is not that the writings of Marx and of a variety of Marxists are not rich in sociological insights. But it is in the writings of some sociologists of non-Marxist standpoints that we find some of the best characterisations of modernity that we possess, and also, as Peter McMylor emphasises in his excellent essay, the best understanding of modernity's mode of self-understanding. Consider briefly three crucial areas: role-playing and compartmentalisation, work, and secularisation.

On role-playing, McMylor has a useful but too charitable account of my treatment of Goffman's intepretive sociology. Tom Burns convinced me quite sometime ago that I had in certain respects parodied Goffman's position—as McMylor does not—by not taking sufficient account of the self that engages in self-presentation, that selects strategies, that puts itself on the line. The self that is never quite liquidated into its role-playing therefore has dimensions of which I did not take account, dimensions brought out very well by Paul Creelan, whom McMylor cites. I was tempted to reply that it is not I but society that parodies Goffman, in those areas in which the self does seem to be effectively liquidated into self-presentation, into role-playing, but this would have been an evasion. For on Goffman's account there are still occasions on which the self stands back from its possibilities and asks: What am I to make of those possibilities? What we do not find in Goffman is any account of those social relationships which might enable us to ask, in the company of others: What are we to make of those possibilities? And this absence is unsurprising, given the structures of modern society, as well as Goffman's perspective. What is it that makes this use of this 'we' so rare, compared with various periods in the past?

It is not only a matter of the compartmentalisation of our lives into a number of different areas, that of the home, the workplace, the arenas of leisure, the school, and so on—so that it is often difficult to envisage one's life as a whole, except in impoverished psychological terms, the terms in which we ask and answer the questions: 'Am I happy or unhappy?' 'Are you happy or unhappy?' It is also that the ways in which we think within each of those areas have been transformed and, in consequence, the ways in which we think of the relationships between them. McMylor aptly cites Bryan Wilson's Durkheimian study of the de-moralisation of social life, in which Wilson contrasts the moralisation 'of nineteenth century social actors—especially, but not only, the working class' (McMylor's words, not Wilson's) with the contemporary conception of what makes a worker a valuable worker, namely, the possession of professional and technical skills to the exercise of which moral character is taken to be irrelevant. Nineteenth-century thinkers—Ruskin especially—preserved and enriched the notion that there is a close connection between being a good human being and doing good work, even while capitalism condemned most workers to a life of alienated labour. But the outcome has been that this connection has been lost sight of altogether in the characteristic contemporary workplace. And we need to restore this connection through joint thought and action with our co-workers in each and every workplace.

Most productive work is and cannot but be tedious, arduous, and fatiguing much of the time. What makes it worthwhile to work and to work well is threefold: that the work that we do has point and purpose, is productive of genuine goods; that the work that we do is and is recognised to be *our* work, *our* contribution, in which we are given and take responsibility for doing it and for doing it well; and that we are rewarded for doing it in a way that enables us to achieve the goods of family and community. This conception of work develops in secular form the core of the Benedictine belief that work is prayer. It stands in the sharpest opposition both to the conception of productive work as something that can best be done by a machine, so that the human worker is, so far as possible, to perform her or his tasks in mechanical routines, and to the closely related conception of productive work as no more than a means to the ends of profitability and of consumption, so that the measure of human work is its cost-effectiveness. Every workplace is a place of potential conflict between these rival conceptions of work, as well as of conflict over the appropriation of surplus value. And the two conflicts are of course closely related.

When productive work was, or when it still is, thought of as a kind of prayer and performed as an act of prayer, this is the strongest possible evidence of a society and a culture not yet compartmentalised as ours increasingly is. So what happens to prayer-informed belief and practice in a compartmentalised social and cultural order such as our own? It is relegated, so far as possible, to the realm of those activities and institutions that fall under the rubric 'religion', religion conceived of as no more than one more compartmentalised area of activity. And by being so relegated it is diminished. The counterpart to such a diminished theism is a diminished atheism, one of the kinds of atheism that I spoke of in the unpublished essay 'Four Kinds of Atheism' which McMylor discusses.

What is missing from these dimished theisms and atheisms is, as McMylor notes 'metaphysical questioning and conflict'. For the dominant social and cultural order of advanced modernity is one from which, so far as possible, metaphysical questioning and conflict are excluded. This exclusion has two aspects. One is a matter of the loss of those social settings and milieus in which fundamental questions about the nature of the human good used to be raised as concerns for everyday life.[4] A second aspect of this exclusion is the attempt to make of metaphysical questioning and conflict nothing more than academic or adolescent enterprises. Metaphysical issues about God and the human good may be suitable matter for university classes, and Plato or Aquinas, Dostoievski or Kierkegaard, may be suitable as prescribed reading for twenty-year-olds, but they are to be left behind when one graduates and enters what the dominant culture thinks of as 'the real world'.

Undiminished theisms do of course survive, and they provide most of those rare voices that address our compartmentalised social and cultural order in terms other than its own, sometimes successfully disquieting those able to hear what they say. Consider in this light the critique of globalisation before the event in Pope Paul VI's 1967 encyclical *Populorum Progressio, On the Development of Peoples,* in the course of which Paul appealed to both philosophical and theological considerations in support of radical political conclusions. By invoking such premises he violated the canons of public debate in the dominant culture. By arriving at such conclusions he violated the norms of that culture's politics. Consider just one such conclusion. 'No one is justified in keeping for his exclusive use what he does not need, when others lack necessities. . . . the right to property must never be exercised to the detriment of the common good. . . . If certain landed estates impede the general good because they are unused or poorly used or . . . bring hardship to peoples', then 'the common good sometimes demands their expropriation'.

Note two things about this passage. The first is that everything in the argument depends on the use of the concept of the common good.

---

4. What kind of settings and milieus do I have in mind? Consider those debates in which Chesterton, Blatchford, Shaw, Wells, and Belloc engaged or those earlier debates in which Mill, Carlisle, and F. D. Maurice took part.

The second is that the theological authority cited immediately before this passage is the fourth-century bishop and saint, Ambrose, who addressed the rich concerning what they took to be their charitable giving: 'You are not making a gift of your possessions to the poor person. You are handing over to him what is his. For what has been given in common for the use of all you have arrogated to yourselves.' The moral dimension of the appropriation of surplus value was a Christian truth quite some time before it become a Marxist truth. Yet to acknowledge the truth spoken by such a prophetic voice—and not to attempt to reduce it to a secular truth—is incompatible with the deepest convictions of the Enlightenment and its later heirs, whether liberals or Marxists. I therefore turn to Sean Sayers's defence of Enlightenment values.

VII

Sayers states the case against my rejection of post-Enlightenment liberalism as well as it can be stated. It is that what I ignore in my account of the emergence of modernity is that it involves not only the 'destruction of the premodern community of shared understandings', but also 'the creation of new forms of social relation and new—liberal—values connected with them: values of liberty, equality, individuality, and tolerance . . . a world of greater individuality and liberty', with its own conception of community. Sayers is of course right, both as to the historical facts and as to my failure to say enough about these values—except perhaps for tolerance (MacIntyre 2006o). He does allow that the hopes of the Enlightenment have not been realised, that 'the enlightenment values of liberty, equality, and community have not been secured by the creation of modern liberal society'. But what he does not seem to recognise is the problematic character of these liberal values.

Belief in liberal values, often passionate belief, was forged in the struggle against the *ancien regime,* and those values themselves were partially defined by the terms of that struggle. So the proclamation of liberty was a denial of the arbitrary coercive power employed by that regime and the assertion of equality was a denial of its unjustified hierarchies. The praise of individuality was a recognition of that in every individual which makes her or him of distinctive value, something to which not only the *ancien regime,* but also often enough its more democratic successors failed to give its due. And, we may add, the rejection of religion as superstition was a denial of an imposed religion, of the principle *ejus regio, cujus religio,* and more generally of the Christian religion, insofar as it had identified itself as the religion of reaction.

About what it was *against,* the Enlightenment was often right in its conclusions, although almost equally often mistaken in the premises to which it appealed in support of those conclusions. And insofar as its values are defined as denials they are generally compelling. But in each case the negative content of liberal values requires a positive counterpart, and it is in its formulations of the relationship between these that the problematic character of liberal values emerges. To be free is not only to be free *from,* but to be free *for.* For what? To be equal is to be equal in some social relationships, but not in others. Which relationships are which? To be educated out of superstition, is to be educated into what? These questions can only be given a compelling answer by identifying those types of social relationship through which we can achieve certain types of common and individual good. But the thinkers of the Enlightenment lacked anything like an adequate conception of those goods, in key part because the earlier sixteenth- and seventeenth-century rejections of Aristotelian modes of thought had prevented them from even entertaining the possibility of the kind of teleological understanding of human action and human relationships that I sketched at the beginning of this essay. The result was that liberal values became in their positive aspects indeterminate, open to rival interpretations, and available to provide, as they have so often done, an underpinning for the ideological justification of those individualist economic, political, and social relationships that have frustrated the realisation of the larger social hopes of the Enlightenment. Sayers takes it that those hopes have not been realised, *in spite of* the nature of the liberal values of liberty, equality, and community. I take it that they have not been realised, *because of* the nature of those values.

Yet I should have been more careful than I have been in giving the negative concept of freedom, freedom as freedom from various kinds of interference and intervention, its due. For there are enterprises that have their own well-defined goods internal to them, where on occasion the

freedom that those engaged in such enterprises need is negative freedom, freedom from oppressive or limiting interventions from outside.
So it was and is with some of the key enterprises of modernity, including post-Galilean natural science and the poetic, visual, and musical arts
in all their diversity. About the importance of this aspect of modernity
Sayers is right.

Let me turn, however, to another part of his critique, his discussion
of the contemporary university. He chides me for having described universities as 'a community of scholars', but that is his phrase for my view,
not mine. In the passage which he cites, what I was emphasising was the
extent to which, in universities nowadays, good work, as I defined it earlier, still goes on, and that networks of teachers and thinkers who cooperate in doing that work do still constitute communities of enquir-
ers. Yet the possibility of doing good work in universities is, just as Sayers
says, 'increasingly threatened by instrumental values, by the external
goods of money and power', a thesis that he spells out in terms of that
monstrous aberration, the United Kingdom's Research Assessment Exercise. With everything negative that Sayers has to say about that exercise
I agree.

The presupposition of that exercise is that universities are to be understood in terms of an input-output model, and its function is to measure one particular kind of output. The notion that it is possible to weigh
in the same scales for any worthwhile purpose whatsoever, say, a seminal
paper on the relationship of archaeological to other historical methods,
a three-volume history of the Byzantine empire, four detailed studies
of the workings of the British Foreign Office between 1923 and 1927, a
number of pieces of fashionable scholarly pedantry, and an imaginative
reconstruction of the thinking of Savonarola is so palpably absurd that
the explanation of how so many highly intelligent university teachers
were prepared to acquiesce in it provides one of the major puzzles of
the age. The bureaucrats who imposed it we can understand; they are
prepared to traffic only in the measurable. Their perverse conception of
work we have already noticed. But that the teachers and researchers on
whom it was successfully imposed accepted it without any widespread
resistance—all honor to those few who did resist—cries out for explanation. And the beginning of an explanation is clear. Those teachers

and researchers were unable to counterpose to the conception of work presupposed by the educational bureaucrats an adequate rival conception of how academic teaching and enquiry should be evaluated, of what good work at teaching and enquiry consists in. For they too lack an effective shared conception of the academic common good.

It is not that there is no common rhetoric concerning these matters, a rhetoric much used by vice-chancellors in the United Kingdom and presidents of universities elsewhere. But that rhetoric—in which the word 'excellence' and its cognates constantly recurs—obfuscates. With respect to the goods external to and incidental to the practices of academic teaching and enquiry—such goods as the provision of skilled manpower, the advancement of research in areas such as medicine and engineering, and a variety of contributions to economic growth—those in authority are admirably clear, as is their intention to provide those goods in the most cost-effective way possible. But with respect to the goods of the mind, the goods of the understanding and the imagination, the goods internal to the practice of academic teaching and enquiry, for the most part they are either silent or they babble.

Unsurprisingly, given this assimilation of the academic to the bureaucratic, academic hierarchies are now bureaucratic hierarchies, in which appointment to and promotion from every level depends on the approval of both one's immediate and one's remote superiors, and that approval depends by and large, if not quite exclusively, upon conformity to the norms to which those superiors have already conformed. Hence the maverick or the radical dissenter or even the highly unusual thinker tends to be marginalised or excluded, and this without any violation of the liberal conception of academic freedom. They are just not at what the dominant figures in their particular academic profession regard as the cutting edge.

Sayers also deplores the narrow conformism, especially in philosophy, of that earlier British university system of the 1950s, in which scarce resources were allocated by the University Grants Committee, on the basis of dubious assumptions about common values. And he points out that the period in which that system came under intolerable strain, as a result of the higgledy-piggledy growth of British universities, was also one that afforded a range of new opportunities for breaking free from the straitjackets of the past, among which the admirable initiatives by Sayers and others that led to the founding and flourishing of *Radical Philosophy* were notable. What I do not understand is why these welcome developments should be thought to provide evidence for Sayers's claim that 'the forces of modernity' created the conditions for this 'diversity of approaches', if by 'modernity' he means liberal individualist modernity. For I take it that in the case of the British university systems those conditions arose at the time that they did by a happy accident.

Yet, as I have already suggested, it would be wrong to ignore the larger issues that Sayers raises concerning the place of diversity and difference in the landscapes of modernity. But these are questions that I cannot pursue here.

VIII

Neil Davidson is a splendid historian. And I admire the narrative that he has constructed from the evidence of my writings during those periods when I was most closely involved with Marxists and Marxism. Moreover I am grateful for the generosity of his interpretations of my motives and my positions. But his is, nonetheless, an odd kind of narrative because of what it omits. It recounts a story of the successive theoretical positions that I occupied, or seem to him to have occupied, with almost no reference to the political events, issues, and causes to which I was responding or to those individuals by whom I was most influenced either positively or negatively. I have said elsewhere that autobiography is a genre that no one should undertake, unless they have the special talents that it requires. I lack those talents and so will not try to replace Davidson's narrative with one of my own.

What I will do is to give some examples of such events, issues, and causes and use these to give a partial explanation of how I came to identify certain problems as crucial for Marxism, Trotskyist or otherwise. Those issues included the Soviet project for a unified, neutralised Germany, resistance to American imperialism in Western Europe and especially to NATO by the French and Italian Communist Parties, problems of working-class housing, the Hungarian rising, independence for Kenya, the Algerian struggle, rank-and-file trade union activity, the Campaign for Nuclear Disarmament, Vietnam, independence for Biafra, and the struggle in the north of Ireland. My attitude to every one of these causes is much the same now as it was then, although I now know the outcomes. What has become clear to me is that each of them was worthwhile because it was worthwhile in itself, and that I would have had sufficient reason for thinking and acting as I did, had I not been a Marxist. But the question would still have arisen: together with whom should I have been and should I be acting in order to act effectively?

I might have become a left-wing social democrat. But, had I done so, I would have failed in two ways. First I would have found myself supporting political organisations—in Britain, the Labour Party—whose leadership for the most part sustained and strengthened the very policies which I took to be wrong and wrong-headed. My activities would have become self-defeating. Secondly, I would have failed to confront the deep malaise of the liberal individualist social order of advanced capitalist modernity and so would have misunderstood the kind of revolutionary transformation that our society needs. But, if I was not to become a social democrat, what should I be?

My first naïve answer was: a sort of communist, a critical, often very critical supporter of the Communist Party of Great Britain (CPGB) and the Soviet Union, although one could not be both critical and a party member, unless a silent critic. The very last public activity that I undertook in this spirit was to participate with comrades from Prague and one of my Manchester contemporaries in an attempt to prevent the National Union of Students from leaving the International Union of Students. But from then on there was no group with which I saw any point in identifying until 1956 and its aftermath. My very different experiences with the New Left, the Socialist Labour League (SLL), and the grouping around the journal *International Socialism* (IS) over time reinforced my belief that one cannot be a Marxist—as against recognising certain key truths in Marxism—unless one is able to identify a class that is potentially revolutionary *and* a form of organisation that is capable of giving leadership to that class *and* a type of relationship between such an organisation and such a class that could issue in a self-governing grassroots participating democracy. I am deeply indebted to the thinkers of the SLL and the IS in a number of ways, among them for having provided what were and are the best possible arguments for holding that such a class can be identified, that such a form of organisation is in being or can be brought into being, and that such a type of relationship can be characterised and realised. By so doing they showed decisively, if inadvertently, that there are no sound arguments for these three assertions, that the best possible arguments are just not good enough.

It would, however, be misleading to end this response to Davidson on so negative a note. I already noted that Davidson's narrative omits the story of my relationships to those by whom I was most influenced in different periods in my thinking about Marxism, whether positively or negatively. And I was and am deeply grateful for what I learned from them: Stefan Lamed, Karl Polanyi, Alick West, C. L. R. James, Raya Dunayevskaya, Edward Thompson, Cliff Slaughter, Peter Fryer, Brian Behan, Michael Kidron, Christopher Pallis, George Lichtheim. Some of these were good friends, one I knew only from reading what he published, some I knew only in political contexts, but their collective influence was to convince me of how much of Marxism has survived its toughest and most insightful critics.

IX

I write this while what may turn out to be the worst crisis in the history of capitalism develops still further. At times of crisis, moral and political platitudes become truths to live or die by. So the relevant maxims are what they always are: protect the most vulnerable, especially children; resist loss of jobs, cutting of school budgets, foreclosures on homes; support organisations that meet immediate urgent human needs—the list could go on. And of course, just as in past crises, every one of these maxims has to be translated into policies that can be effective both within local communities and in obtaining nationally and internationally the resources that local communities need. Yet this particular crisis has a number of distinctive dimensions, all of which deserve discussion in depth. Here let me attend much too briefly to just two of them, as yet insufficiently noticed.

The first is the infliction of the burden of massive debt on an unprecedented number of individuals and societies. Advanced capitalism has functioned by accumulating debt and by so packaging and marketing that debt that the burden of paying it now falls not on those who primarily and mostly benefited from it, but on the worker, the farmer, the small business owner, and the everyday consumer, through increases in taxation, direct and indirect, through deprivation of essential services, through the extortionate rates of interest exacted from credit card owners and on home loans, through mortgage foreclosures, through bankruptcy systems designed to leave debtors in helpless situations. The end result of the flow of credit through the financial system has been such that a remarkable number of individuals, communities, and whole societies find that what has been mortgaged is their future, that they are now imprisoned on a treadmill of debt repayment. And we should note that the measures taken by governments to respond to the crisis often have the effect of adding to the burden of future debt repayment.

A second notable feature of this crisis was the not quite, but almost universal lack of any recognition of its nature and depth until it was too late, whether by those in government concerned with finance, by investment bankers, by academic economists, or—alas!—by those plain persons on whom the burden of debt has now been inflicted. Of the first three we need note only that the members of those morally shameless elites who were the agents of this disaster are now often enough allowed to present themselves as those who will provide a cure for it. But the problem of how to enable the vast mass of ordinary people to learn from and respond constructively to this disruptive experience of exploitation through debt is now our most urgent political problem.

We need to think about it in terms of the teleological scheme that I sketched at the beginning of this essay, in order to press three sets of questions. The first concerns how in concrete and immediate terms we are to characterise the basic common and individual goods that human beings need to flourish: homes, work, schools, medical care, arts, sciences, games. The second concerns how to characterise in similar terms the kind of barriers to achieving those goods represented by the burden of debt that has been so widely inflicted. The third concerns the politics of how, in the particular circumstances of each community and each society, to break through those barriers, of how to achieve the right kind of moratoria on debt repayment, so that homelessness, unemployment, cuts in education and medical care, and cuts in funding for a variety of other activities are not the result of that debt. This now has to be at the core of politics, both within each local community and in that engagement with national and international politics through which local communities defend their interests. And I emphasise that these questions have to be posed in terms that take account of the history and circumstances of each particular time and place, identifying the proximate goods to be achieved, so that imagination, mind, and will are all directed towards them. Yet at the same time, the local and the global have to be understood together, so that Icelanders understand how and why Iceland's crisis is one aspect of a world crisis, or so that autoworkers in Detroit and textile workers in East Asia understand how and why their crisis is also a world crisis.

X

This essay is incomplete in two different ways. First, on each particular topic a good deal more remains to be said. Every one of the essays in this volume deserves much more by way of comment than I have been able to supply, and I am well aware that those essayists with whom I have quarrelled have important responses to make. These are continuing debates in which we are engaged, and on no matter do I have the illusion that I have said anything like the last word.

There is, however, another way in which this essay is incomplete. Human life is sustained by hope, and to rely on hope is always to go beyond what there is sufficiently good reason to expect. Hope is not to be confused with that brisk and cheerful confidence which ignores difficulties and frustrations. Unlike such confidence, hope sustains us in the face of acknowledged difficulties and apparently ineliminable frustrations. Hope allows us to be fully aware of what we would be rationally justified in expecting and yet to hope for far more than that. Hope is a theological virtue. Post-Enlightenment views of the world, whether liberal or Marxist, just because they are anti-theological, leave no room for the exercise of the virtue of hope. (And this is nowhere made clearer than by those post-Enlightenment writers who have tried to find a place for hope in their thought, such as Ernst Bloch.) Yet any account of how human life is to be understood or of how crises in human life are to be confronted, such as the accounts that I have defended or presupposed in this essay, are incomplete unless and until their authors have reckoned with the place of hope in our lives. This I have not done. And so in this respect, too, this essay is an unfinished piece of work.

Bibliography

Abbà, Giuseppe. 1996. *Quale impostazione per la filosofia morale?* Rome: Libreria Ateneo Salesiano.

Ackrill, John L. 1974. 'Aristotle on *Eudaimonia*'. *Proceedings of the British Academy* 60: 339–59.

Albert, Michael. 2003. *Parecon: Life after Capitalism.* London: Norton.

Albert, Michael, and Alex Callinicos. 2004. 'Movement Building 2004: Vision Strategy'. http://www.zmag.org/callinicosalbertdebate.htm.

Allan, David. 1993. *Virtue, Learning and the Scottish Enlightenment.* Edinburgh: Edinburgh University Press.

Altham, James, and Ross Harrison, eds. 1995. *World, Mind and Ethics.* Cambridge: Cambridge University Press.

Althusser, Louis. 2005. *For Marx.* Trans. Ben Brewster. London: Verso.

Anderson, Richard J., John A. Hughes, and Wes W. Sharrock. 1985. *The Sociology Game.* London: Longman Press.

Annas, Julia. 1999. 'Aristotle on Virtue and Happiness'. In Nancy Sherman, ed., *Aristotle's Ethics: Critical Essays.* Lanham MD: Rowman & Littlefield. 35–55.

Anscombe, Elizabeth. 1959. *An Introduction to Wittgenstein's Tractatus.* London: Hutchinson.

Arditi, George. 1987. 'Role as a Cultural Concept'. *Theory and Society* 16: 565–91.

Arendt, Hannah. 1958. *The Human Condition.* Chicago: University of Chicago Press.

335

————. 1968a. 'Tradition and the Modern Age'. In Hannah Arendt, *Between Past and Future: Eight Exercises in Political Thought*, Harmondsworth: Penguin Books. 17–40.

————. 1968b. 'The Concept of History: Ancient and Modern'. In Hannah Arendt, *Between Past and Future: Eight Exercises in Political Thought*. Harmondsworth: Penguin Books. 41–90.

Aristotle [pseudo-]. 1935. 'Oeconomica'. Trans. G. Cyril Armstrong. In Aristotle, *Metaphysics X–XIV, Oeconomica, Magna Moralia*. Cambridge, MA: Harvard University Press. 321–424.

Badiou, Alain. 2003. *Saint Paul: The Foundation of Universalism*. Trans. Ray Brassier. Stanford, CA: Stanford University Press.

Baier, Annette. 1985. *Postures of the Mind*. London: Methuen.

Baker James. 1962. 'The Need to Develop Revolutionary Theory: The Case of Alasdair MacIntyre'. *Labour Review* 7(2): 55–56, 65–73.

Balibar, Etienne. 1990. 'Droits de l'homme' et 'droits du citoyen'. *Actuel Marx* 8: 159–73.

Barker, Colin. 2001. 'Robert Michels and the "Cruel Game"'. In Colin Barker et al., eds., *Leadership and Social Movements*. Manchester: Manchester University Press. 24–43.

Barker, Colin, et al. 2001. 'Leadership Matters: An Introduction'. In Colin Barker et al., eds., *Leadership and Social Movements*. Manchester: Manchester University Press. 1–23.

Baron, Hans. 1966. *The Crisis of the Early Italian Renaissance: Civic Humanism and Republican Liberty in an Age of Classicism and Tyranny*. 2d ed. Princeton: Princeton University Press.

Beadle, Ron. 2001. 'MacIntyre and the Amorality of Management'. Paper presented at the Second International Conference of Critical Management Studies.

————. 2008. 'Why Business Cannot be a Practice'. In Kelvin Knight and Paul Blackledge, eds., *Revolutionary Aristotelianism: Ethics, Resistance and Utopia*. Stuttgart: Lucius and Lucius. 229–41.

Beadle, Ron, and David Könyöt. 2006. 'The Man in the Red Coat: Management in the Circus'. *Culture and Organization* 12(2): 127–37.

Beauvoir, Simone de. 1957. *The Mandarins*. Trans. L. M. Friedman. London: Collins.

Beiner, Ronald. 2003. 'From Community to Citizenship: The Quest for a Post-Liberal Public Philosophy'. In Ronald Beiner, *Liberalism, Nationalism, Citizenship: Essays on the Problem of Political Community*. Vancouver: University of British Columbia Press. 65–82.

Benjamin, Walter. 2003. 'Paralipomena to "On the Concept of History"'. Trans. E. Jephcott et al. In Walter Benjamin, *Selected Works*, vol. 4, *1938–40*, ed. H. Eiland and M. W. Jennings. Cambridge, MA: Harvard University Press. 401–11.

Bensaïd, Daniel. 2002. *Marx for Our Time*. London: Verso.

Berlin, Isaiah. 1962. 'Does Political Theory Still Exist?' In Peter Laslett and W. G. Runciman, eds., *Philosophy, Politics and Society: Second Series*. Oxford: Blackwell. 1–33.

———. 2002. 'Two Concepts of Liberty'. In Isaiah Berlin, *Liberty*, ed. Henry Hardy. Oxford: Oxford University Press. 166–217.

Berry, Christopher J. 1997. *Social Theory of the Scottish Enlightenment*. Edinburgh: Edinburgh University Press.

Bielskis, Andrius. 2007. 'Albert Camus literatūrinė vaizduotė ir pasipriešinimo politika' (Albert Camus's Literary Imagination and the Politics of Resistance). In *Darbai ir dienos*. Kaunas: Vytautas Magnus University Press. 175–84.

Birchall, Ian, and Tony Cliff. 2001. 'France: The Struggle Goes On'. In Tony Cliff, *International Struggle and the Marxist Tradition, Selected Writings*, vol. 1. London: Bookmarks. 159–217.

Blackledge, Paul. 2005. 'Freedom, Desire and Revolution: Alasdair MacIntyre's Marxist Ethics'. *History of Political Thought* 26(4): 695–720.

———. 2006a. 'What Was Done: Lenin Rediscovered'. *International Socialism* 2/111: 111–26.

———. 2006b. 'The New Left's Renewal of Marxism'. *International Socialism* 2/112: 125–53.

———. 2007a. 'Morality and Revolution: Ethical Debates in the British New Left'. *Critique* 35(2): 203–20.

———. 2007b. 'Alasdair MacIntyre: Marxism and Politics'. *Studies in Marxism* 11: 95–116.

———. 2007c. 'Review of Boltanski, L. & Chiapello, E. *The New Spirit of Capitalism*'. *Capital & Class* 92: 198–201.

———. 2008a. 'Alasdair MacIntyre's Contribution to Marxism: A Road not Taken'. In Kelvin Knight and Paul Blackledge, eds., *Revolutionary Aristotelianism: Ethics, Resistance and Utopia*. Stuttgart: Lucius and Lucius. 215–28.

———. 2008b. 'Marxism and Ethics', *International Socialism* 2/120.

———. 2009. 'Alasdair MacIntyre: Social Practices, Marxism and Ethical Anti-Capitalism'. *Political Studies* 57(4): 866–84.

Blackledge, Paul, and Neil Davidson. 2008. 'Introduction: The Unknown Alasdair MacIntyre'. In Paul Blackledge and Neil Davidson, eds., *Alasdair MacIntyre's Engagement with Marxism: Essays and Articles 1953–1974*. Leiden: Brill. xiii–l.

Böckenförde, Ernst-Wolfgang. 1967. 'Die Entstehung des Staates als Vorgang der Säkularisation'. In Ernst-Wolfgang Böckenförde, *Säkularisation und Utopie*. Stuttgart: Kohlhammer. 75–94.

Boggs, Carl. 1976. *Gramsci's Marxism*. London: Pluto.

Boltanski, Luc, and Eve Chiapello. 2006. *The New Spirit of Capitalism*. London: Verso.

Borkenau, Franz. 1962. *World Communism: A History of the Communist International*. Ann Arbor: University of Michigan Press.

Braithwaite, John, and Philip Pettit. 1990. *Not Just Deserts: A Republican Theory of Criminal Justice*. Oxford: Oxford University Press.

Brenkert, George. 1983. *Marx's Ethics of Freedom*. London: Routledge.

Brennan, Geoffrey, and Philip Pettit. 1993. 'Hands Invisible and Intangible'. *Synthese* 94(2): 191–225.

Brennan, Geoffrey, and Philip Pettit. 2004. *The Economy of Esteem: An Essay on Civil and Political Philosophy*. Oxford: Oxford University Press.

Brett, Annabel S. 1997. *Liberty, Right and Nature: Individual Rights in Later Scholastic Thought*. Cambridge: Cambridge University Press.

Brewer, Kathryn Balstad. 1997. 'Management as Practice: A Response to Alasdair MacIntyre'. *Journal of Business Ethics* 16(8): 825–33.

Brinton, Maurice. 2004. 'Socialism Reaffirmed'. *For Worker's Power: The Selected Writings of Maurice Brinton*, ed. D. Goodway. Edinburgh: AK Press. 17–19.

Brubaker, Rogers. 1984. *The Limits of Rationality: An Essay on the Social and Moral Thought of Max Weber*. London: Allen & Unwin.

Burns, James MacGregor. 2003. *Transforming Leadership*. New York: First Grove.

Burns, Tony. 2000. 'Materialism in Ancient Greek Philosophy and in the Writings of the Young Marx'. *Historical Materialism* 7: 3–40.

———. 2005. 'Whose Aristotle? Which Marx? Ethics, Law and Justice in Aristotle and Marx'. *Imprints: Egalitarian Theory and Practice* 8(2): 125–55.

———. 2006. 'Hegel, Identity Politics and the Problem of Slavery'. *Culture, Theory, Critique* 47(1): 81–98.

Caldwell, Bruce. 2004. *Hayek's Challenge: An Intellectual Biography of F. A. Hayek*. Chicago: University of Chicago Press.

Call, Lewis. 2002. *Postmodern Anarchism*. Lanham, MD: Lexington Books.

Callaghan, John. 1984. *British Trotskyism: Theory and Practice*. Oxford: Blackwell.

Callinicos, Alex. 1983. *The Revolutionary Ideas of Karl Marx*. London: Bookmarks.

———. 1990. *Trotskyism*. Milton Keynes: Open University Press.

———. 2000. *Equality*. Cambridge: Polity Press.

———. 2003. *An Anti-Capitalist Manifesto*. Cambridge: Polity Press.

———. 2006. *The Resources of Critique*. Cambridge: Polity Press.

———. 2007. 'Leninism in the 21st Century?' In Sebastian Budgen et al., eds., *Lenin Reloaded*. Durham, NC: Duke University Press. 18–41.

Camus, Albert. 1952. 'Lettre au directeur des *Temps modernes*'. *Les Temps modernes* 82: 317–33.

Cardan, Paul [Cornelius Castoriadis]. 1961. 'Socialism and Capitalism'. *International Socialism* 1/4: 20–27.

———. 1971. *History and Revolution*. London: Solidarity.

'Cardan Debate'. 1965 *Solidarity* 3(10): 22–25.

Castoriadis, Cornelius. 1987. 'Marxism and Revolutionary Thought'. Trans. Kathleen Blamey. In Cornelius Castoriadis, *The Imaginary Institution of Society.* Cambridge: Polity Press. 7–70.

———. 1988. 'Modern Capitalism and Revolution'. In Cornelius Castoriadis, trans. David Ames Curtis, *Political and Social Writings,* vol. 2, *1955–1960: From the Worker's Struggle Against Bureaucracy to Revolution in the Age of Modern Capitalism.* Minneapolis: University of Minnesota Press. 226–315.

———. 1996. *La montée de l'insignifiance.* Paris: Seuil.

Chen, Jeng-Guo S. 2008. 'Providence and Progress: The Religious Dimension in Ferguson's Discussion of Civil Society'. In Eugene Heath and Vincenzo Merolle, eds., *Adam Ferguson: History, Progress and Human Nature.* Pickering & Chatto. 171–86, 222–26.

Christman, John. 2004. 'Narrative Unity as a Condition of Personhood'. *Metaphilosophy* 35(5): 695–713.

Cicero. 1991. *On Duties.* Trans. Margaret Atkins. Cambridge: Cambridge University Press.

Cliff, Tony. 2000. *A World to Win: Life of a Revolutionary.* London: Bookmarks.

———. 2001a [1959]. 'Rosa Luxemburg'. In Tony Cliff, *International Struggle and the Marxist Tradition, Selected Writings,* vol. 1. London: Bookmarks. 59–116.

———. 2001b [1960]. 'Trotsky on Substitutionism'. In Tony Cliff, *International Struggle and the Marxist Tradition, Selected Writings,* vol. 1. London: Bookmarks. 117–32.

———. 2003 [1948]. 'The Nature of Stalinist Russia'. In Tony Cliff, *Marxist Theory after Trotsky.* London: Bookmarks. 1–138.

Cohen, G. A. 1995. *Self-Ownership, Freedom, and Equality.* Cambridge: Cambridge University Press.

Colletti, Lucio. 1975. 'Introduction'. In Quintin Hoare, ed., *Karl Marx: Early Writings.* Harmondsworth: Penguin Books. 7–56.

Collingwood, R. G. 1939. *An Autobiography.* Oxford: Oxford University Press.

———. 1946. *The Idea of History.* Oxford: Oxford University Press.

Collins, Henry, and Chimon Abramsky. 1965. *Karl Marx and the British Labour Movement.* London: Macmillan.

Connolly, James. 1987. 'The Re-conquest of Ireland'. In *Collected Works,* vol. 1. Dublin: New Books. 185–280.

Creelan, Paul. 1984. 'Vicissitudes of the Sacred: Erving Goffman and the Book of Job'. *Theory and Society* 13(5): 663–95.

Daly, James. 1996. *Marx, Justice and Dialectic.* London: Greenwich Exchange.

Darlington, Ralph. 2008. *Syndicalism and the Transition to Communism.* Aldershot: Ashgate.

Davidson, Donald. 2001. 'On the Very Idea of a Conceptual Scheme'. In Donald Davidson, *Inquiries into Truth and Interpretation,* 2d ed. Oxford: Oxford University Press. 183–98.

Davidson, Neil. 2004. 'The Prophet, His Biographer and the Watchtower'. *International Socialism* 2/104: 95–118.

Dawson, D., and C. Bartholomew. 2003. 'Virtues, Managers and Business People: Finding a Place for MacIntyre in a Business Context'. *Journal of Business Ethics* 48(2): 127–38.

Depew, David. 1981–82. 'Aristotle's *De Anima* and Marx's Theory of Man'. New School of Social Research, *Graduate Faculty Philosophy Journal* 8(1–2): 133–87.

Derrida, Jacques. 1994. *Specters of Marx: The State of the Debt, the Work of Mourning, and the New International*. Trans. Peggy Kamuf. London: Routledge.

Devine, Pat. 1988. *Democracy and Economy Planning*. Cambridge: Cambridge University Press.

———. 2007. 'Review of Parecon'. *Historical Materialism* 15(2): 210–17.

Diski, Jenny. 2004. 'Think of Mrs. Darling'. Review of *Goffman's Legacy*, ed. A. Javier Treviño. *London Review of Books* 26(5): 5–6.

Domhoff, George William. 2005. *Who Rules America? Power, Politics, and Social Change*. New York: McGraw-Hill Humanities.

Draper, Hal. 1977–90. *Karl Marx's Theory of Revolution*. 4 vols. New York: Monthly Review.

Driver, Julia. 2001. *Uneasy Virtue*. Cambridge: Cambridge University Press.

Dunn, John. 1969. *The Political Thought of John Locke: An Historical Account of the Argument of the 'Two Treatises of Government'*. Cambridge: Cambridge University Press.

———. 1985. 'Identity, Modernity and the Claim to Know Better'. In John Dunn, *Rethinking Modern Political Theory: Essays 1979–83*. Cambridge: Cambridge University Press. 139–53.

———. 1990. 'The Economic Limits to Modern Politics'. In John Dunn, ed., *The Economic Limits to Modern Politics*. Cambridge: Cambridge University Press. 15–40.

———. 1994. 'The Identity of the Bourgeois Liberal Republic'. In Biancamaria Fontana, ed., *The Invention of the Modern Republic*. Cambridge: Cambridge University Press. 206–25.

Eagleton, Terry. 2003. *After Theory*. Harmondsworth: Penguin Books.

———. 2007. *The Meaning of Life*. Oxford: Oxford University Press.

Elgie, Robert. 1995. *Political Leadership in Liberal Democracies*. London: Palgrave.

Elster, John. 1985. *Making Sense of Marx*. Cambridge: Cambridge University Press.

Engels, Frederick. 1947. *Anti-Dühring*. Moscow: Progress Publishers.

Eriksonas, Linas. 2007. 'About NK95'. www.nk95.org/english.

Euben, J. Peter. 1989. 'Corruption'. In Terence Ball, James Farr, and Russell L. Hanson, eds., *Political Innovation and Conceptual Change*. Cambridge: Cambridge University Press. 220–46.

Ferguson, Adam. 1792. *Principles of Moral and Political Science*. 2 vols. Edinburgh: A. Strathen & T. Cadell (reprinted Hildesheim: Georg Olms, 1995).

————. 1995. *An Essay on the History of Civil Society*. Ed. Fania Oz-Salzberger. Cambridge: Cambridge University Press.

Fish, Stanley. 2007. 'Should Our Lives Be Unified?' In *New York Times*, 18 February.

Fives, Allyn. 2008. *Political and Philosophical Debates in Welfare*. Basingstoke: Palgrave Macmillan.

Fletcher, Andrew. 1997. 'Two Discourses Concerning the Affairs of Scotland: Written in the Month of July, 1698'. In Andrew Fletcher, *Political Works*, ed. John Robertson. Cambridge: Cambridge University Press. 33–81.

Foot, Philippa. 1978.'Virtues and Vices'. In Philippa Foot, *Virtues and Vices*. Oxford: Oxford University Press. 1–18.

————. 1990. 'Nietzsche's Immoralism'. *New York Review of Books* 38(11): 18–22.

————. 2001. *Natural Goodness*. Oxford: Oxford University Press.

Foote, Geoffrey. 2006. *The Republican Transformation of Modern British Politics*. Basingstoke: Palgrave.

Foucault, Michael. 1994. 'The Ethics of the Concern for the Self as a Practice of Freedom'. In *Michel Foucault, Essential Works of Michel Foucault 1955–1984*, vol. 1: *Ethics, Subjectivity and Truth*, ed. Paul Rabinow. New York: The New Press. 281–302.

Francis, Hywel, and David Smith. 1980. *The Fed*. London: Lawrence & Wishart.

Frazer, Elizabeth, and Nicola Lacey. 1993. *The Politics of Community: A Feminist Critique of the Liberal-Communitarian Debate*. Hemel Hempstead: Harvester Wheatsheaf.

Frazer, Elizabeth, and Nicola Lacey. 1994. 'MacIntyre, Feminism and the Concept of Practice'. In John Horton and Susan Mendus, eds., *After MacIntyre: Critical Perspectives on the Work of Alasdair MacIntyre*. Cambridge: Polity Press. 265–82.

Friedman, Marilyn 2008. 'Pettit's Civic Republicanism and Male Domination'. In Cécile Laborde and John Maynor, eds., *Republicanism and Political Theory*. Oxford: Blackwell. 246–68.

Furet, François. 1999. *The Passing of an Illusion: The Idea of Communism in the Twentieth Century*. Trans. Deborah Furet. Chicago: University of Chicago Press.

Gailienė, Danutė. 2005. 'Užburtame rate: savižudybių paplitimas Lietuvoje po Nepriklausomybės atkūrimo'. *Psichologija* 31: 1–9.

Geary, Dick. 2003. 'The Second International: Socialism and Social Democracy'. In Terence Ball and Richard Bellamy, eds., *The Cambridge History of Twentieth-Century Political Thought*. Cambridge: Cambridge University Press. 219–238.

Geras, Norman. 1985. 'The Controversy about Marx and Justice'. *New Left Review* I/150: 47–85.

Geuss, Raymond. 2008. *Philosophy and Real Politics*. Princeton: Princeton University Press.

Gilbert, Alan. 1981a. 'Historical Theory and the Structure of Moral Argument in Marx'. *Political Theory* 9: 173–205.

———. 1981b. *Marx's Politics*. Oxford: Martin Robertson.

Gluckstein, Donny. 1985. *The Western Soviets*. London: Bookmarks.

Goldmann, Lucien. 1964. *The Hidden God: A Study of the Tragic Vision in the Pensées of Pascal and the Tragedies of Racine*. London: Macmillan.

———. 1968. 'Is There a Marxist Sociology?' *International Socialism* 1/34: 13–21.

Gould, Carol. 1978. *Marx's Social Ontology: Individuality and Community in Marx's Theory of Social Reality*. Cambridge, MA: MIT Press.

Graham, Gordon. 1994. 'MacIntyre's Fusion of History and Philosophy'. In John Horton and Susan Mendus, eds., *After MacIntyre*. Cambridge: Polity Press. 161–75.

Gramsci, Antonio. 1971. *Selections from the Prison Notebooks of Antonio Gramsci*. Ed. Quintin Hoare and G. Nowell Smith. London: Lawrence & Wishart.

———. 1977. *Selections from Political Writings 1910–1920*. London: Lawrence & Wishart.

———. 1978. *Selections from Political Writings 1921–1926*. London: Lawrence & Wishart.

———. 1995. *Further Selections from the Prison Notebooks*. Minneapolis: University of Minnesota Press.

Grasselli, Antonia, and Sante Maletta, eds. 2006. *I Giusti e la memoria del bene: Chi salva una vita, salva il mondo intero*. Milan: CUSL.

Grene, Marjorie. 1986. 'In and On Friendship'. In Alan Donagan, Anthony N. Perovich Jr., and Michael V. Wedin, eds., *Human Nature and Natural Knowledge: Essays Presented to Marjorie Grene on the Occasion of Her Seventy-fifth Birthday*. Dordrecht: D. Reidel. 355–68.

Griffin, James. 1986. *Well-Being: Its Meaning, Measurement, and Moral Importance*. Oxford: Oxford University Press.

Haakonssen, Knud. 1981. *The Science of a Legislator: The Natural Jurisprudence of David Hume and Adam Smith*. Cambridge: Cambridge University Press.

Haberkern, Ernest E., and Arthur Lipow, eds. 1996. *Neither Capitalism nor Socialism*. Atlantic Highlands: Humanities.

Hallas, Duncan. 1969. 'Building the Leadership'. *International Socialism* 1/40: 25–32.

Hardt, Michael. 2003. 'An Interview with Michael Hardt'. *Historical Materialism* 11(3): 121–52.

Hardt, Michael, and Tony Negri. 2000. *Empire*. Cambridge, MA: Harvard University Press.

Hardt, Michael, and Tony Negri. 2005. *Multitude.* London: Hamish Hamilton.

Harman, Chris. 1968–69. 'Party and Class'. *International Socialism* 1/35: 24–32.

Harrington, James. 1992. 'The Commonwealth of Oceana'. In James Harrington, *The Commonwealth of Oceana and A System of Politics,* ed. J. G. A. Pocock. Cambridge: Cambridge University Press. 1–266.

Harris, Nigel. 1990. *National Liberation.* Harmondsworth: Penguin Books.

Hayek, F. A. 1952. *The Sensory Order: An Inquiry into the Foundations of Theoretical Psychology.* London: Routledge & Kegan Paul.

———. 1960. *The Constitution of Liberty.* London: Routledge & Kegan Paul.

———. 1967. *Studies in Philosophy, Politics and Economics.* London: Routledge & Kegan Paul.

———. 1973. *Law, Legislation and Liberty,* vol. 1: *Rules and Order.* London: Routledge & Kegan Paul.

———. 1976. *Law, Legislation and Liberty,* vol. 2: *The Mirage of Social Justice.* London: Routledge & Kegan Paul.

———. 1978. 'Liberalism'. In F. A. Hayek, *New Studies in Philosophy, Politics, Economics and the History of Ideas.* London: Routledge & Kegan Paul. 119–51.

———. 1979. *Law, Legislation and Liberty,* vol. 3: *The Political Order of a Free People.* London: Routledge & Kegan Paul.

———. 1988. *The Collected Works of Friedrich August Hayek,* vol. 1: *The Fatal Conceit: The Errors of Socialism,* ed. W. W. Bartley III. London: Routledge.

———. 1992. 'Remembering My Cousin Ludwig Wittgenstein (1889–1951)'. In *The Collected Works of Friedrich August Hayek,* vol. 4: *The Fortunes of Liberalism: Essays on Austrian Economics and the Ideal of Freedom,* ed. Peter G. Klein. London: Routledge. 176–81.

Hegel, G. W. F. 1991. *Elements of the Philosophy of Right.* Trans. H. B. Nisbet. Cambridge: Cambridge University Press.

Hill, Lisa. 2006. *The Passionate Society: The Social, Political and Moral Thought of Adam Ferguson.* Dordrecht: Springer.

Hinds, Dan. 2007. *The Threat to Reason: How the Enlightenment Was Hijacked and How We Can Reclaim It.* London: Verso.

Hochschild, Arlie R. 2003. *The Managed Heart: Commercialization of Human Feeling.* Berkeley: University of California Press.

Hoogland, J., and H. Jochemsen. 2000. 'Professional Autonomy and the Normative Structure of Medical Practice'. *Theoretical Medicine* 21: 457–75.

Horton, John, and Susan Mendus, eds. 1994. *After MacIntyre.* Cambridge: Polity Press.

Hume, David. 1969. *A Treatise of Human Nature.* Ed. Ernest C. Mossner. Harmondsworth: Penguin Books.

Hursthouse, Rosalind. 1999. *On Virtue Ethics.* Oxford: Oxford University Press.

Hyman, Richard. 1984. *Strikes*. London: Fontana.

Imber, Jonathan R., ed. 2004. *Therapeutic Culture: Triumph and Defeat*. New York: Transaction Press.

Jameson, Fredric. 2009. *Valences of the Dialectic*. London: Verso.

Jefferson, Thomas. 1999. 'To Henry Lee'. In Thomas Jefferson, *Political Writings*, ed. Joyce Appleby and Terence Ball. Cambridge: Cambridge University Press. 147–48.

Keat, Russell. 2008. 'Ethics, Markets, and MacIntyre'. In Kelvin Knight and Paul Blackledge, eds., *Revolutionary Aristotelianism: Ethics, Resistance and Utopia*. Stuttgart: Lucius and Lucius. 243–57.

Kelly, John. 1988a. *Trade Unions and Socialist Politics*. London: Verso.

———. 1988b. 'Reply to Jack Robertson'. *International Socialism* 2/42: 137–41.

Keyt, David. 1983. 'Intellectualism in Aristotle'. In J. P. Anton and A. Preuce, eds., *Essays in Ancient Greek Philosophy*, vol. 2. Albany: State University of New York Press. 364–87.

Kidron, Michael. 1970. *Western Capitalism since the War*. 2d ed. Harmondsworth: Penguin Books.

Knight, Kelvin. 1996. 'Revolutionary Aristotelianism'. In Iain Hampsher-Monk and Jeffrey Stanyer, eds., *Contemporary Political Studies 1996*, vol. 2. Belfast: Political Studies Association of the United Kingdom, 1996. 885–96 (reprinted in this volume).

———. 1998. 'Introduction'. In *The MacIntyre Reader*, ed. Kelvin Knight. Cambridge: Polity Press. 1–27.

———. 2000. 'The Ethical Post-Marxism of Alasdair MacIntyre'. In Mark Cowling and Paul Reynolds, eds., *Marxism, the Millennium and Beyond*. Basingstoke: Palgrave. 74–96.

———. 2005. 'Aristotelianism versus Communitarianism'. *Analyse & Kritik* 27(2): 259–73.

———. 2007. *Aristotelian Philosophy: Ethics and Politics from Aristotle to MacIntyre*. Cambridge: Polity Press.

———. 2008a. 'Goods'. *Philosophy of Management* 7(1): 107–22.

———. 2008b. 'Hannah Arendt's Heideggerian Aristotelianism'. *Topos* 19: 5–30.

———. 2008c. 'After Tradition? Heidegger *or* MacIntyre, Aristotle *and* Marx'. In Kelvin Knight and Paul Blackledge, eds., *Revolutionary Aristotelianism: Ethics, Resistance and Utopia*. Stuttgart: Lucius and Lucius. 33–52.

———. 2011. 'Ethics and Agency, Past and Present'. *Historical Materialism*, forthcoming.

Koestler, Arthur. 1946. *Darkness at Noon*. Harmondsworth: Penguin Books.

Kolakowski, Leszek. 1978. *Main Currents in Marxism*. 3 vols. Trans. P. S. Falla. Oxford: Oxford University Press.

———. 1990. *Modernity on Endless Trial*. Chicago: University of Chicago Press.

Korsgaard, Christine. 1996. 'Aristotle and Kant on the Source of Value'. In Christine Korsgaard, *Creating the Kingdom of Ends*. Cambridge: Cambridge University Press. 225–48.

Kouvelakis, Stathis. 2003. *Philosophy and Revolution*. London: Verso.

Kymlicka, Will. 2002. *Contemporary Political Philosophy*. Oxford: Oxford University Press.

Lakatos, Imre. 1978. *Philosophical Papers*. 2 vols. Cambridge: Cambridge University Press.

Lasch, Christopher. 1979. *The Culture of Narcissism: American Life in an Age of Diminishing Expectations*. New York: Warner Books.

———. 1985. *The Minimal Self: Psychic Survival in Troubled Times*. New York: Norton.

Lear, Gabriel Richardson. 2004. *Happy Lives and the Highest Good: An Essay on Aristotle's Nicomachean Ethics*. Princeton: Princeton University Press.

Lih, Lars. 2006. *Lenin Rediscovered*. Leiden: Brill.

Löwy, Michael. 2003. *The Theory of Revolution in the Young Marx*. Leiden: Brill.

———. 2005. *Fire Alarm: Reading Walter Benjamin's 'On the Concept of History'*. London: Verso.

Luhmann, Niklas. 1984. *The Differentiation of Society*. New York: Columbia University Press.

———. 1985. *A Sociological Theory of Law*. London: Routledge & Kegan Paul.

Lukács, Georg. 1971. *History and Class Consciousness*. London: Merlin.

Lukes, Steven. 1985. *Marxism and Morality*. Oxford: Oxford University Press.

———. 2003. 'Epilogue: The Grand Dichotomy of the Twentieth Century'. In Terence Ball and Richard Bellamy, eds., *The Cambridge History of Twentieth-Century Political Thought*. Cambridge: Cambridge University Press. 602–25.

———. 2004. *Power*. 2d ed. London: Palgrave.

Luxemburg, Rosa. 1970. 'Organisational Questions of Social Democracy'. In *Rosa Luxemburg Speaks*, ed. Mary-Alice Waters. New York: Pathfinder Press. 114–30.

Lyotard, Jean-François. 1957. 'Note sur le marxisme'. In A. Weber and D. Huisman, eds., *Tableau de la philosophie Contemporaine*. Paris: Fischbacher.

———. 1963. 'Algeria'. *International Socialism* 1/13: 21–26.

———. 1984. *The Postmodern Condition: A Report on Knowledge*. Trans. Geoffrey Bennington and Brian Massumi. Manchester: Manchester University Press.

———. 1988. *The Differend: Phrases in Dispute*. Trans. Georges Van Den Abbeele. Minneapolis: University of Minnesota Press.

———. 1989. *La Guerre des Algériens: Ecrits (1956–1963)*. Paris: Galilée.

MacGilvray, Eric. 2003. *Reconstructing Public Reason*. Cambridge MA: Harvard University Press.

MacIntyre, Alasdair. 1953. *Marxism: An Interpretation*. London: SCM Press.

————. 1956. 'Review of T. B. Bottomore and M. Rubel eds., *Karl Marx: Selected Works on Sociology and Social Philosophy* and Laslett ed., *Philosophy, Politics and Society*'. *Sociological Review*, n.s. 4(2): 266–67.

————. 1960. 'Letter'. *The Listener*, 17 March. 500.

————. 1962a. 'A Mistake About Causality in Social Science'. In Peter Laslett and W. G. Runciman, eds., *Philosophy, Politics and Society: Second Series*. Oxford: Blackwell: 48–70.

————. 1962b. 'Trotsky'. *International Socialism* 1/8: 33.

————. 1967. *A Short History of Ethics: A History of Moral Philosophy from the Homeric Age to the Twentieth Century*. London: Routledge & Kegan Paul.

————. 1968. *Marxism and Christianity*. London: Duckworth.

————. 1970. *Marcuse*. London: Routledge.

————. 1971a. 'The Socialism of R. H. Tawney'. In Alasdair MacIntyre, *Against the Self-Images of the Age*. London: Duckworth. 38–42.

————. 1971b. 'Introduction'. In Alasdair MacIntyre, *Against the Self-Images of the Age: Essays on Ideology and Philosophy*. London: Duckworth. vii–x.

————. 1971c. 'How Not to Write about Stalin'. In Alasdair MacIntyre, *Against the Self-Images of the Age: Essays on Ideology and Philosophy*. London: Duckworth. 48–51.

————. 1971d. 'Trotsky in Exile'. In Alasdair MacIntyre, *Against the Self-Images of the Age: Essays on Ideology and Philosophy*. London: Duckworth. 52–59.

————. 1971e. 'Marxism of the Will'. In Alasdair MacIntyre, *Against the Self-Images of the Age: Essays on Ideology and Philosophy*. London: Duckworth. 70–75.

————. 1971f. 'Pascal and Marx: On Lucien Goldmann's *Hidden God*'. In Alasdair MacIntyre, *Against the Self-Images of the Age: Essays on Ideology and Philosophy*. London: Duckworth. 76–87.

————. 1971g. 'Marxist Mask and Romantic Face: Lukács on Thomas Mann'. In Alasdair MacIntyre, *Against the Self-Images of the Age: Essays on Ideology and Philosophy*. London: Duckworth. 60–69.

————. 1971h. 'Is a Science of Comparative Politics Possible?' In Alasdair MacIntyre, *Against the Self-Images of the Age*. London: Duckworth. 260–79.

————. 1971i. 'Political and Philosophical Epilogue: A View of *The Poverty of Liberalism* by Robert Paul Wolff'. In Alasdair MacIntyre, *Against the Self-Images of the Age*. London: Duckworth. 280–84.

————. 1971j. 'The End of Ideology and the End of the End of Ideology'. In Alasdair MacIntyre, *Against the Self-Images of the Age*. London: Duckworth. 3–11.

————. 1971k. 'Philosophy and Ideology: Introduction to Part Two'. In Alasdair MacIntyre, *Against the Self-Images of the Age*. London: Duckworth. 91–95.

————. 1971l. 'What Morality Is Not'. In Alasdair MacIntyre, *Against the Self-Images of the Age*. London: Duckworth. 96–108.

————. 1971m. 'Hume on "Is" and "Ought"'. In Alasdair MacIntyre, *Against the Self-Images of the Age*. London: Duckworth. 109–24.

————. 1971n. 'Imperatives, Reasons for Action, and Morals'. In Alasdair Mac-Intyre, *Against the Self-Images of the Age*. London: Duckworth. 125–35.

————. 1971o. '"Ought"'. In Alasdair MacIntyre, *Against the Self-Images of the Age*. London: Duckworth. 136–56.

————. 1971p. 'Some More about "Ought"'. In Alasdair MacIntyre, *Against the Self-Images of the Age*. London: Duckworth. 157–72.

————. 1972. 'Modern German Thought'. In Malcolm Pasley, ed., *Germany: A Companion to German Studies*. London: Methuen. 427–51.

————. 1973a. 'Ideology, Social Science and Revolution'. *Comparative Politics* 5(2): 321–42.

————. 1973b. 'World-Spirit in the BM'. *The Observer Review,* 7 October.

————. 1976. 'On Democratic Theory: Essays in Retrieval by C. B. Macpherson'. *Canadian Journal of Philosophy* 6(2): 177–81.

————. 1979. 'The Poverty of Political Theory'. Review of John Dunn, *Western Political Thought in the Face of the Future. London Review of Books,* 20 December. 4–6.

————. 1980a. 'The Idea of America'. Review of Garry Wills, *Inventing America: Jefferson's Declaration of Independence. London Review of Books,* 6 November. 14.

————. 1980b. 'The American Idea'. In David Noel Doyle and Owen Dudley Edwards, eds., *America and Ireland, 1776–1976: The American Identity and the Irish Connection*. Westport, CT: Greenwood Press. 57–68.

————. 1982. 'Public Virtue'. Review of Garry Wills, *Explaining America: The 'Federalist' and David Hoeveler, James McCosh and the Scottish Intellectual Tradition. London Review of Books,* 18 February. 14.

————. 1984a. '*After Virtue* and Marxism: A Response to Wartofsky'. *Inquiry* 27(3): 251–54.

————. 1984b. 'The Relationship of Philosophy to Its Past'. In Richard Rorty, J. B. Schneewind, and Quentin Skinner, eds., *Philosophy in History: Essays on the Historiography of Philosophy*. Cambridge: Cambridge University Press. 31–48.

————. 1984c. 'Philosophy and Politics'. In J. L. Capps, ed., *Philosophy and Human Enterprise*. West Point, NY: United States Military Academy. 130–61.

————. 1985a. *After Virtue*. 2d ed. London: Duckworth.

————. 1985b. 'How Psychology Makes Itself True – or False'. In Sigmund Koch and David E. Leary, eds., *A Century of Psychology As Science*. New York: McGraw-Hill. 897–903.

————. 1987. 'The Idea of an Educated Public'. In Graham Haydon, ed., *Education and Values: The Richard Peters Lectures*. London: Institute of Education. 15–36.

————. 1988a. *Whose Justice? Which Rationality?* London: Duckworth.

————. 1988b. 'Sophrosyne: How a Virtue Can Become Socially Disruptive'. *Midwest Studies in Philosophy* 13: 1–11.

————. 1990a. *Three Rival Versions of Moral Enquiry: Encyclopaedia, Genealogy, and Tradition.* London: Duckworth.

————. 1990b. 'Individual and Social Morality in Japan and the United States: Rival Conceptions of the Self'. *Philosophy East and West* 40: 489–97.

————. 1990c. 'The Privatization of Good: An Inaugural Lecture'. *The Review of Politics* 52(2): 344–61.

————. 1991a. 'Community, Law, and the Idiom and Rhetoric of Rights'. *Listening: Journal of Religion and Culture* 26: 96–110.

————. 1991b. 'Reply to Roque'. *Philosophy and Phenomenological Research* 51(3): 619–20.

————. 1992. 'Virtue Ethics'. In Lawrence C. Becker, ed., *Encyclopedia of Ethics*, vol. 2. London: Garland. 1276–82.

————. 1993. *The Objectivity of Good.* Canton, NY: St. Lawrence University.

————. 1994a. 'How Can We Learn What Veritatis Splendor Has to Teach?' *The Thomist* 2: 171–95.

————. 1994b. 'A Partial Response to My Critics'. In John Horton and Susan Mendus, eds., *After MacIntyre: Critical Perspectives on the Work of Alasdair MacIntyre.* Cambridge: Polity Press. 283–304.

————. 1994c. 'Interview with Professor Alasdair MacIntyre'. *Kinesis* 20: 34–47.

————. 1995a. 'Is Patriotism a Virtue?' In Ronald Beiner, ed., *Theorizing Citizenship.* New York: State University of New York Press. 209–28.

————. 1995b. 'The Spectre of Communitarianism'. *Radical Philosophy* 70: 34–35.

————. 1995c. *Marxism and Christianity.* 2d ed. London: Duckworth.

————. 1995d. 'Three Perspectives on Marxism: 1953, 1968, 1995'. In Alasdair MacIntyre, *Marxism and Christianity,* 2d ed. London: Duckworth. v–xxxi. Also published as MacIntyre 2006l.

————. 1998a. 'Notes from the Moral Wilderness'. In *The MacIntyre Reader,* ed. Kelvin Knight. Notre Dame, IN: University of Notre Dame Press. 31–52.

————. 1998b. 'Social Science Methodology as the Ideology of Bureaucratic Authority'. In *The MacIntyre Reader,* ed. Kelvin Knight. Notre Dame, IN: University of Notre Dame Press. 53–68.

————. 1998c. 'The Claims of *After Virtue*'. In *The MacIntyre Reader,* ed. Kelvin Knight. Notre Dame IN: University of Notre Dame Press. 69–72.

————. 1998d. 'Practical Rationalities as Forms of Social Structure'. In *The MacIntyre Reader,* ed. Kelvin Knight. Notre Dame IN: University of Notre Dame Press. 120–35.

————. 1998e. '*First Principles, Final Ends and Contemporary Philosophical Issues*'. In *The MacIntyre Reader,* ed. Kelvin Knight. Notre Dame, IN: University of Notre Dame Press. 171–201.

———. 1998f. 'The *Theses on Feuerbach*: A Road Not Taken'. In *The MacIntyre Reader*, ed. Kelvin Knight. Notre Dame, IN: University of Notre Dame Press. 223–34.

———. 1998g. 'Politics, Philosophy and the Common Good'. In *The MacIntyre Reader*, ed. Kelvin Knight. Notre Dame, IN: University of Notre Dame Press. 235–52.

———. 1998h. 'Plain Persons and Moral Philosophy: Rules, Virtues and Goods'. In *The MacIntyre Reader*, ed. Kelvin Knight. Notre Dame, IN: University of Notre Dame Press. 136–52.

———. 1998i. 'An Interview with Giovanna Borradori'. In *The MacIntyre Reader*, ed. Kelvin Knight. Notre Dame, IN: University of Notre Dame Press. 255–66.

———. 1999a. *Dependent Rational Animals: Why Human Beings Need the Virtues*. London: Duckworth.

———. 1999b. 'John Case: An Example of Aristotelianism's Self-Subversion?' In Thomas Hibbs and John O'Callaghan, eds., *Recovering Nature: Essays in Natural Philosophy, Ethics, and Metaphysics in Honor of Ralph McInerny*. Notre Dame, IN: University of Notre Dame Press. 71–82.

———. 2000a. 'Theories of Natural Law in the Culture of Advanced Modernity'. In E. B. McLean, ed., *Common Truths: New Perspectives on Natural Law*. Wilmington, OH: ISI Books. 91–118.

———. 2000b. 'A Culture of Choices and Compartmentalization'. Talk delivered at the Center for Ethics and Culture, University of Notre Dame. http://ethicscenter.nd.edu.

———. 2000c. 'The Recovery of Moral Agency?' In John Wilson, ed., *The Best Christian Writing 2000*. New York: HarperCollins. 111–36.

———. 2001. 'Four Kinds of Atheism'. Public lecture at the University of Manchester.

———. 2006a. *Edith Stein: A Philosophical Prologue*. London: Continuum.

———. 2006b. 'The Ends of Life, the Ends of Philosophical Writing'. In Alasdair MacIntyre, *Selected Essays*, vol. 1: *The Tasks of Philosophy*. Cambridge: Cambridge University Press. 125–42.

———. 2006c. 'Colors, Cultures and Practices'. In Alasdair MacIntyre, *Selected Essays*, vol. 1: *The Tasks of Philosophy*. Cambridge: Cambridge University Press. 24–51.

———. 2006d. 'Moral Philosophy and Contemporary Social Practice: What Holds Them Apart?' In Alasdair MacIntyre, *Selected Essays*, vol. 1: *The Tasks of Philosophy*, Cambridge: Cambridge University Press. 104–22.

———. 2006e. 'Rival Aristotles: Aristotle Against Some Renaissance Aristotelians'. In Alasdair MacIntyre, *Selected Essays*, vol. 2: *Ethics and Politics*. Cambridge: Cambridge University Press. 3–21.

———. 2006f. 'Poetry as Political Philosophy: Notes on Burke and Yeats'. In Alasdair MacIntyre, *Selected Essays*, vol. 2: *Ethics and Politics*. Cambridge: Cambridge University Press. 159–71.

————. 2006g. 'Truthfulness and Lies: What Can We Learn from Kant?' In Alasdair MacIntyre, *Selected Essays*, vol. 2: *Ethics and Politics*. Cambridge: Cambridge University Press. 122–42.

————. 2006h. 'Truth as a Good'. In Alasdair MacIntyre, *Selected Essays*, vol. 1: *The Tasks of Philosophy*, Cambridge: Cambridge University Press. 197–215.

————. 2006i. 'Rival Aristotles: Aristotle Against Some Modern Aristotelians'. In Alasdair MacIntyre, *Selected Essays*, vol. 2: *Ethics and Politics*. Cambridge: Cambridge University Press. 22–40.

————. 2006j. 'Natural Law as Subversive: The Case of Aquinas'. In Alasdair MacIntyre, *Selected Essays*, vol. 2: *Ethics and Politics*. Cambridge: Cambridge University Press. 41–63.

————. 2006k. 'Aquinas and the Extent of Moral Disagreement'. In Alasdair MacIntyre, *Selected Essays*, vol. 2: *Ethics and Politics*. Cambridge: Cambridge University Press. 64–82.

————. 2006l. 'Three Perspectives on Marxism: 1953, 1968, 1995'. In Alasdair MacIntyre, *Selected Essays*, vol. 2: *Ethics and Politics*. Cambridge: Cambridge University Press. 145–58. Previously published as MacIntyre 1995d and republished as MacIntyre 2008q.

————. 2006m. 'Some Enlightenment Projects Reconsidered'. In Alasdair MacIntyre, *Selected Essays*, vol. 2: *Ethics and Politics*. Cambridge: Cambridge University Press. 172–85.

————. 2006n. 'Social Structures and Their Threats to Moral Agency'. In Alasdair MacIntyre, *Selected Essays*, vol. 2: *Ethics and Politics*. Cambridge: Cambridge University Press. 186–204.

————. 2006o. 'Toleration and the Goods of Conflict'. In Alasdair MacIntyre, *Selected Essays*, vol. 2: *Ethics and Politics*. Cambridge: Cambridge University Press. 205–23.

————. 2006p. 'Outside Ethics'. Review of Raymond Geuss, *Outside Ethics*. http://ndpr.nd.edu/review.cfm?id=5922.

————. 2006q. 'Epistemological Crises, Dramatic Narrative, and the Philosophy of Science'. In Alasdair MacIntyre, *Selected Essays*, vol. 1: *The Tasks of Philosophy*. Cambridge: Cambridge University Press. 3–23.

————. 2006r. 'Moral Relativism, Truth and Justification'. In Alasdair MacIntyre, *Selected Essays*, vol. 1: *The Tasks of Philosophy*. Cambridge: Cambridge University Press. 52–73.

————. 2007. 'Prologue'. In Alasdair MacIntyre, *After Virtue: A Study in Moral Theory*, 3d ed. Notre Dame, IN: University of Notre Dame Press. ix–xvi.

————. 2008a. 'Marxist Tracts'. In *Alasdair MacIntyre's Engagement with Marxism: Essays and Articles 1953–1974*, ed. Paul Blackledge and Neil Davidson. Leiden: Brill. 25–32.

————. 2008b. 'The Algebra of the Revolution'. In *Alasdair MacIntyre's Engagement with Marxism: Essays and Articles 1953–1974*, ed. Paul Blackledge and Neil Davidson. Leiden: Brill. 41–44.

———. 2008c. 'Marcuse, Marxism and the Monolith'. In *Alasdair MacIntyre's Engagement with Marxism: Essays and Articles 1953–1974*, ed. Paul Blackledge and Neil Davidson. Leiden: Brill. 77–80.

———. 2008d. 'What Is Marxist Theory For?' In *Alasdair MacIntyre's Engagement with Marxism: Essays and Articles 1953–1974*, ed. Paul Blackledge and Neil Davidson. Leiden: Brill. 95–104.

———. 2008e. 'The "New Left"'. In *Alasdair MacIntyre's Engagement with Marxism: Essays and Articles 1953–1974*, ed. Paul Blackledge and Neil Davidson. Leiden: Brill. 87–94.

———. 2008f. 'Communism and British Intellectuals'. In *Alasdair MacIntyre's Engagement with Marxism: Essays and Articles 1953–1974*, ed. Paul Blackledge and Neil Davidson. Leiden: Brill. 115–22.

———. 2008g. 'Freedom and Revolution'. In *Alasdair MacIntyre's Engagement with Marxism: Essays and Articles 1953–1974*, ed. Paul Blackledge and Neil Davidson. Leiden: Brill. 123–34.

———. 2008h. 'Breaking the Chains of Reason'. In *Alasdair MacIntyre's Engagement with Marxism: Essays and Articles 1953–1974*, ed. Paul Blackledge and Neil Davidson. Leiden: Brill. 135–66.

———. 2008i. 'The Man Who Answered the Irish Question'. In *Alasdair MacIntyre's Engagement with Marxism: Essays and Articles 1953–1974*, ed. Paul Blackledge and Neil Davidson. Leiden: Brill. 171–74.

———. 2008j. 'Rejoinder to Left Reformism'. In *Alasdair MacIntyre's Engagement with Marxism: Essays and Articles 1953–1974*, ed. Paul Blackledge and Neil Davidson. Leiden: Brill. 187–96.

———. 2008k. 'Marxists and Christians'. In *Alasdair MacIntyre's Engagement with Marxism: Essays and Articles 1953–1974*, ed. Paul Blackledge and Neil Davidson. Leiden: Brill. 179–86.

———. 2008l. 'Sartre as a Social Critic'. In *Alasdair MacIntyre's Engagement with Marxism: Essays and Articles 1953–1974*, ed. Paul Blackledge and Neil Davidson. Leiden: Brill. 201–8.

———. 2008m. 'Open Letter to a Right-Wing Young Socialist'. In *Alasdair MacIntyre's Engagement with Marxism: Essays and Articles 1953–1974*, ed. Paul Blackledge and Neil Davidson. Leiden: Brill. 215–20.

———. 2008n. 'C. Wright Mills'. In *Alasdair MacIntyre's Engagement with Marxism: Essays and Articles 1953–1974*, ed. Paul Blackledge and Neil Davidson. Leiden: Brill. 241–46.

———. 2008o. 'Prediction and Politics'. In *Alasdair MacIntyre's Engagement with Marxism: Essays and Articles 1953–1974*, ed. Paul Blackledge and Neil Davidson. Leiden: Brill. 249–62.

———. 2008p. '[The New Capitalism and the British Working Class]' (original essay untitled). In *Alasdair MacIntyre's Engagement with Marxism: Essays and Articles 1953–1974*, ed. Paul Blackledge and Neil Davidson. Leiden: Brill. 221–41.

————. 2008q. 'Three Perspectives on Marxism: 1953, 1968, 1995'. In *Alasdair MacIntyre's Engagement with Marxism: Essays and Articles 1953–1974*, ed. Paul Blackledge and Neil Davidson. Leiden: Brill. 411–25. Previously published as MacIntyre 1995d and 2006l.

————. 2008r. 'What More Needs to Be Said? A Beginning, Although Only a Beginning, at Saying It'. In Kelvin Knight and Paul Blackledge, eds., *Revolutionary Aristotelianism: Ethics, Resistance and Utopia*. Stuttgart: Lucius and Lucius. 261–81.

————. 2010. 'How Aristotelianism Can Become Revolutionary: Ethics, Resistance, and Utopia'. In this volume.

MacIntyre, Alasdair, and Joseph Dunne. 2002. 'Alasdair MacIntyre on Education: In Dialogue with Joseph Dunne'. *Journal of Philosophy of Education* 36(1): 1–19.

Maletta, Sante. 2007. *Biografia della ragione: Saggio sulla filosofia politica di MacIntyre*. Soveria Mannelli (Cantanzaro): Rubbettino.

Marx, Karl. 1969. *Theories of Surplus Value, Part I*. Trans. Emile Burns. London: Lawrence & Wishart.

————. 1973a. *Grundrisse*. Harmondsworth: Penguin Books.

————. 1973b. 'Address of the Central Committee to the Communist League (March 1850)'. In Karl Marx, *The Revolutions of 1848*. Harmondsworth: Penguin Books. 319–30.

————. 1974. 'Documents of the First International: 1864–70: Provisional Rules of the International Working Men's Association'. In *The First International and After*, ed. David Fernbach. Harmondsworth: Penguin Books. 82–84.

————. 1975a. 'Economic and Philosophical Manuscripts'. In *Karl Marx: Early Writings*, ed. Quintin Hoare. Harmondsworth: Penguin Books. 279–400.

————. 1975b. 'Theses on Feuerbach'. In *Karl Marx: Early Writings*, ed. Quintin Hoare. Harmondsworth: Penguin Books. 421–23.

————. 1975c. 'Letters from the *Deutsch-Franzosische Jarbucher*'. In Karl Marx and Frederick Engels, *Collected Works*, vol. 3. London: Lawrence & Wishart. 133–45.

————. 1976. *Capital: A Critique of Political Economy*. Vol. 1. Trans. Ben Fowkes. Harmondsworth: Penguin Books.

————. 1987a. 'The Value of Strikes'. In *Marx and Engels on the Trade Unions*, ed. Kenneth Lapides. New York: International Publishers. 42–44.

————. 1987b. 'Excerpts from the 'The Poverty of Philosophy'. In *Marx and Engels on the Trade Unions*, ed. Kenneth Lapides. New York: International Publishers. 30–35.

————. 1987c. 'Wages'. In *Marx and Engels on the Trade Unions*, ed. Kenneth Lapides. New York: International Publishers. 35–36.

————. 1987d. 'Letter to Schweitzer'. In *Marx and Engels on the Trade Unions*, ed. Kenneth Lapides. New York: International Publishers. 111–12.

———. 1989. 'Critique of the Gotha Programme'. In Karl Marx and Frederick Engels, *Collected Works*, vol. 24. London: Lawrence & Wishart. 75–99.

May, Todd. 1989. 'Is Poststructuralist Political Theory Anarchist?' *Philosophy and Social Criticism* 15(2): 275–84.

———. 1994. *The Political Philosophy of Poststructuralist Anarchism*. Pennsylvania: Pennsylvania State University Press.

Mažeikis, Gintautas. 2005. *Filosofinės antropologijos pragmatika ir analitika*. Šiauliai: Saulės delta.

McCarthy, George E. 2003. 'Karl Marx, Athenian Democracy and the Critique of Political Economy'. In George E. McCarthy, *Classical Horizons: The Origins of Sociology in Ancient Greece*. Albany NY: State University of New York Press. 15–63.

McLaughlin, Terence. 2003. 'Teaching as a Practice and a Community of Practice: The Limits of Commonality and the Demands of Diversity'. *Journal of Philosophy of Education* 37(2): 339–52.

McMylor, Peter. 1994. *Alasdair MacIntyre: Critic of Modernity*. London: Routledge.

Meikle, Scott. 1985. *Essentialism in the Thought of Karl Marx*. London: Duckworth.

———. 1991. 'History of Philosophy: The Metaphysics of Substance in Marx'. In Terrell Carver, ed., *The Cambridge Companion to Marx*. Cambridge: Cambridge University Press. 296–319.

1997. *Aristotle's Economic Thought*. Oxford: Clarendon Press. Merleau-Ponty, Maurice. 1969. *Humanism and Terror: An Essay on the Communist Problem*. Boston: Beacon Press.

Michels, Robert. 1962. *Political Parties*. New York: Collier.

Mill, John Stuart. 1962. 'On Liberty'. In John Stuart Mill, *Utilitarianism and Other Writings*, ed. Mary Warnock. London: Fontana.

Miller, David. 1984. 'Virtues and Practices'. *Analyse & Kritik* 6: 49–60.

———. 1999. *Principles of Social Justice*. Cambridge, MA: Harvard University Press.

———. 2008. 'Hear "Reason", I See Lies'. *New Scientist*, 23 July. 46.

Miller, David, and W. Dinan. 2000. 'The Rise of the PR Industry in Britain, 1979–98'. *European Journal of Communication* 15(5): 5–35.

Miller, David, and W. Dinan, eds. 2007. *Thinker, Faker, Spinner, Spy: Corporate PR and the Assault on Democracy*. London: Pluto Press.

Miller, Richard W. 1989. 'Marx and Aristotle: A Kind of Consequentialism'. In Alex Callinicos, ed., *Marxist Theory*. Oxford: Oxford University Press. 175–210.

Molyneux, John. 1986. *Marxism and the Party*. London: Bookmarks.

Morin, Edgar. 1959. *Autocritique*. Paris: Julliard.

Mouffe, Chantal. 1993. *The Return of the Political*. London: Verso.

Mulhall, Stephen, and Adam Swift. 1996. 2d ed. *Liberals and Communitarians.* Oxford: Blackwell.

Murphy, Mark C. 2003. 'MacIntyre's Political Philosophy'. In Mark C. Murphy, ed., *Alasdair MacIntyre.* Cambridge: Cambridge University Press. 152–75.

Nagle, D. Brendan. 2006. *The Household as the Foundation of Aristotle's* Polis. Cambridge: Cambridge University Press.

Nederman, Cary J. 2008. 'Men at Work: Politics and Labour in Aristotle and Some Aristotelians'. In Kelvin Knight and Paul Blackledge, eds., *Revolutionary Aristotelianism: Ethics, Resistance and Utopia.* Stuttgart: Lucius and Lucius. 17–31.

Nehamas, A. 1983. 'How One Becomes What One Is'. *Philosophical Review* 92: 385–417.

Nelson, Eric. 2004. *The Greek Tradition in Republican Thought.* Cambridge: Cambridge University Press.

Newman, Saul. 2001. *From Bakunin to Lacan: Anti-Authoritarianism and the Dislocation of Power.* Lanham: Lexington Books.

Nussbaum, Martha. 1989. 'Recoiling from Reason'. *New York Review of Books* 36(19): 36–41.

———. 1992. 'Human Functioning and Social Justice: In Defence of Aristotelian Essentialism'. *Political Theory* 20(2): 202–46.

———. 1993. 'Non-relative Virtues: An Aristotelian Approach'. In Martha Nussbaum and Amartya Sen, eds., *The Quality of Life.* Oxford: Oxford University Press. 240–61.

———. 1995. 'Aristotle on Human Nature and Foundation of Ethics'. In J. E. J. Altham and R. Harrison, eds., *World, Mind and Ethics.* Cambridge: Cambridge University Press. 86–131.

———. 1999. 'Virtue Ethics: A Misleading Category?' *The Journal of Ethics* 3: 163–201.

Oakeshott, Michael. 1991. *On Human Conduct.* Oxford: Oxford University Press.

O'Connor, James 1973. *The Fiscal Crisis of the State.* New York: St. Martin's Press.

Pagden, Anthony. 1987. 'Introduction'. In Anthony Pagden, ed., *The Languages of Political Theory in Early-Modern Europe.* Cambridge: Cambridge University Press. 1–17.

Perreau-Saussine, Émile. 2005. *Alasdair MacIntyre: Une biographie intellectuelle. Introduction aux critiques contemporaines du libéralisme.* Paris: Presses Universitaires de France.

Pettit, Philip. 1989. 'The Freedom of the City: A Republican Ideal'. In Alan Hamlin and Philip Pettit, eds., *The Good Polity: Normative Analysis of the State.* Oxford: Blackwell. 141–68.

———. 1994. 'Liberal/Communitarian: MacIntyre's Mesmeric Dichotomy'. In John Horton and Susan Mendus, eds., *After MacIntyre: Critical Perspectives on the Work of Alasdair MacIntyre.* Cambridge: Polity Press. 176–204.

———. 1996. *The Common Mind: An Essay on Psychology, Society, and Politics.* 2d ed. Oxford: Oxford University Press.

———. 1997. *Republicanism: A Theory of Freedom and Government.* Oxford: Oxford University Press.

———. 2001. *A Theory of Freedom: From the Psychology to the Politics of Agency.* Cambridge: Polity Press.

———. 2002. *Rules, Reasons, and Norms.* Oxford: Oxford University Press.

———. 2007. 'Joining the Dots'. In Geoffrey Brennan, Robert Goodin, Frank Jackson, and Michael Smith, eds., *Common Minds: Themes from the Philosophy of Philip Pettit.* Oxford: Oxford University Press. 215–344.

———. 2008a. *Made with Words: Hobbes on Language, Mind, and Politics.* Princeton: Princeton University Press.

———. 2008b. 'Republican Freedom: Three Axioms, Four Theorems'. In Cécile Laborde and John Maynor, eds., *Republicanism and Political Theory.* Oxford: Blackwell. 102–30.

Plato. 1987. *The Republic.* Trans. H. D. P. Lee. Harmondsworth: Penguin Books.

Pocock, J. G. A. 1962. 'The History of Political Thought: A Methodological Enquiry'. In Peter Laslett and W. G. Runciman, eds., *Philosophy, Politics and Society: Second Series.* Oxford: Blackwell, 183–202.

———. 1973. *Politics, Language and Time: Essays on Political Thought and History.* London: Methuen.

———. 1975. 'Early Modern Capitalism: The Augustan Perception'. In Eugene Kamenka and R. S. Neale, eds., *Feudalism, Capitalism and Beyond.* London: Edward Arnold. 62–83.

———. 1979. 'Reconstructing the Traditions: Quentin Skinner's Historians' History of Political Thought'. Review of Quentin Skinner, *The Foundations of Modern Political Thought. Canadian Journal of Political and Social Theory* 3(3): 95–113.

———. 1983. 'Cambridge Paradigms and Scotch Philosophers: A Study of the Relations between the Civic Humanist and the Civil Jurisprudential Interpretation of Eighteenth-Century Social Thought'. In Istvan Hont and Michael Ignatieff, eds., *Wealth and Virtue: The Shaping of Political Economy in the Scottish Enlightenment.* Cambridge: Cambridge University Press. 235–52.

———. 1985. *Virtue, Commerce, and History: Essays on Political Thought and History, Chiefly in the Eighteenth Century.* Cambridge: Cambridge University Press.

———. 1987a. 'Between Gog and Magog: The Republican Thesis and the *Ideologia Americana'. Journal of the History of Ideas* 48(2): 325–46.

———. 1987b. *The Ancient Constitution and the Feudal Law: A Study of English Historical Thought in the Seventeenth Century.* 2d ed. Cambridge: Cambridge University Press.

———. 1988. 'States, Republics, and Empires: The American Founding in Early Modern Perspective'. In Terence Ball and J. G. A. Pocock, eds., *Conceptual Change and the Constitution*. Lawrence: University Press of Kansas. 55–77.

———. 1990. 'The Political Limits to Premodern Economics'. In John Dunn, ed., *The Economic Limits to Modern Politics*. Cambridge: Cambridge University Press. 121–41.

———. 1993. 'Political Thought in the English-Speaking Atlantic, 1760–1790: (ii) Empire, Revolution and an End of Early Modernity'. In J. G. A. Pocock, ed., *The Varieties of British Political Thought, 1500–1800*. Cambridge: Cambridge University Press. 283–317.

———. 1996. 'The Historian as Political Actor in Polity, Society and Academy'. *The Journal of Pacific Studies* 20: 89–112.

———. 1998. 'The Politics of History: The Subaltern and the Subversive'. *The Journal of Political Philosophy* 6(3): 219–34.

———. 1999. *Barbarism and Religion*, vol. 2: *Narratives of Civil Government*. Cambridge: Cambridge University Press.

———. 2003. *The Machiavellian Moment: Florentine Political Thought and the Atlantic Republican Tradition*. 2d ed. Princeton: Princeton University Press.

———. 2004. 'The History of Politics and the Politics of History' (review article). *Common Knowledge* 10(3): 532–50.

———. 2005a. *Barbarism and Religion*, vol. 4: *Barbarians, Savages and Empires*. Cambridge: Cambridge University Press.

———. 2005b. 'America's Foundations, Foundationalisms, and Fundamentalisms'. *Orbis* 49(1): 53–60.

———. 2006a. 'Foundations and Moments'. In Annabel Brett and James Tully, eds., *Rethinking the Foundations of Modern Political Thought*. Cambridge: Cambridge University Press. 37–49.

———. 2006b. 'Adam Smith and History'. In Knud Haakonssen, ed., *The Cambridge Companion to Adam Smith*. Cambridge: Cambridge University Press. 270–87.

———. 2008. 'Cambridge Beyond Cambridge: Political Thought and History'. Paper presented at King's College, Cambridge, 12 May.

Ramberg, Bjorn T. 1989. *Donald Davidson's Philosophy of Language: An Introduction*. Oxford: Blackwell.

Ratner, Harry. 1994. *Reluctant Revolutionary: Memoirs of a Trotskyist, 1936–1960*. London: Porcupine Books.

Rawls, John. 1999. *Collected Papers*. Harvard: Harvard University Press.

Raynaud, Philippe. 1989. 'Société bureaucratique et totalitarisme: Remarques sur l'évolution du groupe Socialisme ou Barbarie'. *Revue européenne des sciences sociales, Cahiers Vilfredo Pareto* 86: 255–68.

Rhonheimer, Martin. 2000. *Natural Law and Practical Reason: A Thomist View of Moral Autonomy*. New York: Fordham University Press.

Rieff, Philip. 1987. *The Triumph of the Therapeutic: Uses of Faith after Freud.* Chicago: University of Chicago Press.

Robertson, Jack. 1988. 'Socialists and the Unions'. *International Socialism* 2/41: 97–112.

Roemer, John. 1996. *Theories of Distributive Justice.* Cambridge, MA: Harvard University Press.

Rorty, Richard. 1989. *Contingency, Irony, and Solidarity.* Cambridge: Cambridge University Press.

Rust, Joshua. 2006. *John Searle and* The Construction of Social Reality. London: Continuum.

Sandel, Michael. 1998. *Democracy's Discontent: America in Search of a Public Philosophy.* Cambridge, MA: Harvard University Press.

Sartre, Jean-Paul. 1952. 'Pour tout vous dire . . .' *Les Temps modernes* 82: 354–83.

Saville, John. 1987. *1848: The British State and the Chartist Movement.* Cambridge: Cambridge University Press.

Sayers, Sean. 1997. 'Who Are My Peers? The Research Assessment Exercise in Philosophy'. *Radical Philosophy* 83: 2–5.

———. 1998. *Marxism and Human Nature.* London: Routledge.

———. 2007. 'Individual and Society in Marx and Hegel'. *Science & Society* 71(1): 84–102.

Schacht, Richard. 1971. *Alienation.* London: Allen & Unwin.

Schnaedelbach, Herbert. 1987. 'What is Neo-Aristotelianism?' *Praxis International* 7(3–4): 226–37.

Schneewind, Jerome B. 1984. 'The Divine Corporation and the History of Ethics Perspectives'. In Richard Rorty, J. B. Schneewind, and Quentin Skinner, eds., *Philosophy in History: Essays on the Historiography of Philosophy.* Cambridge: Cambridge University Press. 173–91.

Sedgwick, Peter. 1982. 'The Ethical Dance'. In M. Eve and D. Musson, eds., *The Socialist Register 1982.* London: Merlin. 259–67.

Shapiro, Ian. 1990. *Political Criticism.* Berkeley: University of California Press.

Skinner, Quentin. 1974. 'Some Problems in the Analysis of Political Thought and Action'. *Political Theory* 2(3): 277–303.

———. 1978a. *The Foundations of Modern Political Thought,* vol. 1: *The Renaissance.* Cambridge: Cambridge University Press.

———. 1978b. *The Foundations of Modern Political Thought,* vol. 2: *The Age of Reformation.* Cambridge: Cambridge University Press.

———. 1984. 'The Idea of Negative Liberty: Philosophical and Historical Perspectives'. In Richard Rorty, J. B. Schneewind, and Quentin Skinner, eds., *Philosophy in History: Essays on the Historiography of Philosophy.* Cambridge: Cambridge University Press. 193–221.

———. 1986. 'The Paradoxes of Political Liberty'. In Sterling McMurrin, ed., *The Tanner Lectures on Human Values.* Vol. 8. Salt Lake City: University of Utah Press. 225–50.

————. 1988a. 'A Reply to My Critics'. In James Tully, ed., *Meaning and Context: Quentin Skinner and His Critics.* Cambridge: Polity Press. 231–88, 326–41.

————. 1988b. 'Meaning and Understanding in the History of Ideas'. In James Tully, ed., *Meaning and Context: Quentin Skinner and His Critics.* Cambridge: Polity Press. 29–67, 291–304.

————. 1989. 'The State'. In Terence Ball, James Farr, and Russell L. Hanson, eds., *Political Innovation and Conceptual Change.* Cambridge: Cambridge University Press. 90–131.

————. 1990. 'The Republican Ideal of Political Liberty'. In Gisela Bock, Quentin Skinner, and Maurizio Viroli, eds., *Machiavelli and Republicanism.* Cambridge: Cambridge University Press. 293–309.

————. 1992. 'On Justice, the Common Good and the Priority of Liberty'. In Chantal Mouffe, ed., *Dimensions of Radical Democracy: Pluralism, Citizenship, Community.* London: Verso. 211–24.

————. 1998. *Liberty Before Liberalism.* Cambridge: Cambridge University Press.

————. 2001. 'The Rise of, Challenge to and Prospects for a Collingwoodian Approach to the History of Political Thought'. In Dario Castiglione and Iain Hampsher-Monk, eds., *The History of Political Thought in National Context.* Cambridge: Cambridge University Press. 175–88.

————. 2002a. *Visions of Politics,* vol. 1: *Regarding Method,* Cambridge: Cambridge University Press.

————. 2002b. *Visions of Politics,* vol. 2: *Renaissance Virtues.* Cambridge: Cambridge University Press.

————. 2002c. 'A Third Concept of Liberty'. *Proceedings of the British Academy* 117: 237–68.

————. 2003. 'States and the Freedom of Citizens'. In Quentin Skinner and Bo Stråth, eds., *States and Citizens: History, Theory, Prospects.* Cambridge: Cambridge University Press. 11–27.

————. 2006. 'Surveying the *Foundations*: A Retrospect and Reassessment'. In Annabel Brett and James Tully, eds., *Rethinking the Foundations of Modern Political Thought.* Cambridge: Cambridge University Press. 236–61.

————. 2008a. *Hobbes and Republican Liberty.* Cambridge: Cambridge University Press.

————. 2008b. 'Freedom as the Absence of Arbitrary Power'. In Cécile Laborde and John Maynor, eds., *Republicanism and Political Theory.* Oxford: Blackwell. 83–101.

————. 2008c. 'What Is the State?' Presentation to the British Academy. 13 May.

Slaughter, Cliff. 1960. 'What Is Revolutionary Leadership?' *Labour Review* 5(3): 93–96, 105–11.

Smith, Adam. 1976. *An Inquiry into the Nature and Causes of the Wealth of Nations.* Ed. R. H. Campbell, A. S. Skinner, and W. B. Todd. Oxford: Oxford University Press.

Smith, Carole. 2002. 'The Sequestration of Experience: Rights Talk and Moral Thinking in "Late Modernity"'. *Sociology* 36(1): 43–66.

Stedman Jones, Gareth. 1983. *Languages of Class*. Cambridge: Cambridge University Press.

Steinberg, Ronnie J., and Deborah M. Figart. 1999. 'Emotional Labour Since The Managed Heart'. *Annals of the American Academy of Political and Social Science* 561: 8–26.

Swanton, Christine. 2003. *Virtue Ethics: A Pluralistic View*. Oxford: Oxford University Press.

———. 2005. 'Nietzschean Virtue Ethics'. In S. M. Gardiner, ed., *Virtue Ethics Old and New*. Ithaca: Cornell University Press. 179–92.

———. 2006. 'Can Nietzsche Be Both an Existentialist and a Virtue Ethicist?' In Timothy Chappell, ed., *Values and Virtues: Aristotelianism in Contemporary Ethics*. Oxford: Oxford University Press. 171–88.

Tawney, R. H. 1921. *The Acquisitive Society*. London: G. Bell & Sons.

Tester, Keith. 1999. 'Weber's Alleged Emotivism'. *British Journal of Sociology* 5(4): 563–74.

Thayer, George. 1965. *The British Political Fringe*. London.

Thompson, Duncan. 2007. *Pessimism of the Intellect: A History of the New Left Review*. London: Merlin Press.

Thompson, E. P. 1974. 'An Open Letter to Leszek Kolakowski'. In Ralph Miliband and John Saville, eds., *The Socialist Register 1973*. London: Merlin Press.

Trotsky, Leon. 1947. *Stalin*. London, Hollis & Carter.

———. 1973. *In Defence of Marxism*. New York: Pathfinder.

———. 1975. 'The Lessons of October'. In Leon Trotsky, *The Challenge of the Left Opposition (1923–25)*, ed, Naomi Allen. New York: Pathfinder Press. 199–258.

———. 1977. *The History of the Russian Revolution*. London, Pluto.

———. 1978. 'Stalinism and Bolshevism: Concerning the Historical and Theoretical Roots of the Fourth International'. In *Writings of Leon Trotsky [1936–37]*, ed, Naomi Allen and George Brietman. 2d ed. New York: Pathfinder Press. 416–31.

———. 1986. *Trotsky's Notebooks, 1933–1935: Writings on Lenin, Dialectics, and Evolutionism*. Trans. Philip Pomper. New York: Columbia University Press.

———. n.d. *Our Political Tasks*. London: New Park.

Turner, Stephen. 1994. *The Social Theory of Practices: Tradition, Tacit Knowledge and Presuppositions*. Cambridge: Polity Press.

Van Maurik, John. 2001. *Writers on Leadership*. Harmondsworth: Penguin Books.

Vannier, J. 1948. 'A Century's Balance Sheet'. *Partisan Review* 15(3): 288–96.

Vasiliauskaitė, Nida. 2006. '"Riba" kaip aporetinė: Jeano Francois Lyotard'o filosofijos prielaida'. *Athena* 1: 82–96.

Viroli, Maurizio. 1995. *For Love of Country: An Essay on Patriotism and Nationalism.* Oxford: Oxford University Press.

Wald, Alan M. 1987. *The New York Intellectuals: The Rise and Decline of the Anti-Stalinist Left from the 1930s to the 1980s.* Chapel Hill and London: University of North Carolina Press.

Walzer, Michael. 1983. *Spheres of Justice: A Defence of Pluralism and Equality.* New York: Basic Books.

———. 1990. 'The Communitarian Critique of Liberalism'. *Political Theory* 18(1): 6–23.

Wartofsky, Marx. 1984. 'Virtue Lost or Understanding Macintyre'. *Inquiry* 27: 235–50.

Wickham, Chris. 2005. *Framing the Early Middle Ages: Europe and the Mediterranean, 400–800.* Cambridge: Cambridge University Press.

Williams, Bernard. 1973. 'Morality and Emotions'. In Bernard Williams, *Problems of the Self.* Cambridge: Cambridge University Press.

———. 1981. 'Internal and External Reasons'. In Bernard Williams, *Moral Luck: Philosophical Papers 1973–1980.* Cambridge: Cambridge University Press. 101–13.

———. 1985. *Ethics and the Limits of Philosophy.* London: Fontana.

———. 1995. 'Reply'. In J. E. J. Altham and R. Harrison. eds., *World, Mind and Ethics.* Cambridge: Cambridge University Press. 185–223.

———. 1997. 'What Does Intuitionism Imply?' In Bernard Williams, *Making Sense of Humanity.* Cambridge: Cambridge University Press. 182–91.

Williams, Chris. 1998. *Capitalism, Community and Conflict: The South Wales Coalfields 1898–1947.* Cardiff: University of Wales Press.

Williams, Gwyn. 1975. *Proletarian Order.* London: Pluto.

Wilson, Bryan. 1985. 'Morality in the Evolution of the Modern Social System'. *The British Journal of Sociology* 36(3): 315–32.

———. 2001. 'Salvation, Secularization and De-moralization'. In Richard K. Fenn, ed., *The Blackwell Companion to the Sociology of Religion.* Oxford: Blackwell. 39–51.

Winch, Donald. 1978. *Adam Smith's Politics: An Essay in Historiographical Revision.* Cambridge: Cambridge University Press.

Winch, Donald. 1996. *Riches and Poverty: An Intellectual History of Political Economy in Britain, 1750–1834.* Cambridge: Cambridge University Press.

Yack, Bernard. 1993. *The Problem of a Political Animal: Community, Justice, and Conflict in Aristotelian Political Thought.* Berkeley: University of California Press.

Žižek, Slavoj. 2007. 'Resistance is Surrender'. *London Review of Books,* 15 November. 7–8.

Žukauskaitė, Audron. 2007. 'Tell Me Who Is Your Other and I Will Tell Who You Are'. *Athena* 3: 112–22.

Index

www.ingramcontent.com/pod-product-compliance
Lightning Source LLC
Chambersburg PA
CBHW060959280326
41935CB00009B/768